THE PROPHET

Ronald B. Stetton

The Truth is no longer
About what is accurate or inaccurate
In a wicked and rebellious world
Truth has been replaced by godless desires and pursuits
Emotion has transformed Truth from factual accuracies
Into myths based upon how we make others feel
Characteristics of societal delusion
Demonstrate how and why
The world refused to recognize
The Biblical role of
The Prophet

THE PROPHET

REVEALING THE MAN OF LAWLESSNESS

RONALD B. STETTON

The Prophet by Ronald B. Stetton
Copyright © 2022 by Ronald B. Stetton
All Rights Reserved.
ISBN: 978-1-59755-567-8

Published by: ADVANTAGE BOOKS™ www.advbookstore.com

This book and parts thereof may not be reproduced in any form, stored in a retrieval system or transmitted in any form by any means (electronic, mechanical, photocopy, recording or otherwise) without prior written permission of the author, except as provided by United States of America copyright law.

Scripture taken from the HOLY BIBLE, NEW INTERNATIONAL VERSION NIV. Copyright 1973, 1978, 1984 by International Bible Society. Used by permission of Zondervan Publishing House

KJV Reference Bible. Introductions and Outlines to the Books of the Bible Copyright 1977; KJV Concordance Copyright 1992, 1994 by the Zondervan Corporation

The Strongest Strong's Exhaustive Concordance of the Bible Copyright 2001 by Zondervan

More Than A Carpenter, Copyright 1977 by Josh McDowell

The Holy Qur'an with English Translation and Commentary 2002, Ahmadiyya Anjuman Isha'at Islam Lahore Inc., U.S.A.

A Manual of Hadith; Ahmadiyya Anjuman Ishaat Islam Lahore USA Inc.

Library of Congress Catalog Number: 2022946505

Names:	Stetton, Ronanld B., Author
Title:	*The Prophet*
	Ronald B. Stetton
	Advantage Books, 2022
Identifiers:	ISBN (print): 9781597555678, (ePub) 9781597555784
Subjects:	Christian Life: Inspirational

First Printing November 2022
22 23 24 25 26 27   10 9 8 7 6 5 4 3 2 1

The Prophet

FOREWORD

What does this material hope to accomplish?

For more than three thousand years, men have been pondering the writings of Moses and the prophets who were to follow him. Moses' guided pen has been complemented by the likes of Isaiah, Jeremiah, Daniel, Matthew, Mark, Luke, John, Paul, and many others. From the beginning and to the end, this group of prophetic brothers have given us God's complete story of man in written form. And, just as God foretold, the world's communities collectively mock God's elect and those who trust the prophets' written testimony. In unison, the world scoffs at the prophetic warnings that were forever anchored by the prophets of God. But that is soon to change, and the mockery is soon to reside - with the collective laughter replaced by mourning.

Though proof of God's existence is anchored in written form and has been contemplated over the centuries, it has yet to be compiled and delivered in a comparative manner such as this. Discovered in somewhat of an ironic twist, proof of God comes about by revealing the identity of the world's most diabolical biblical character. This mischievous fraud is a man of grand historical significance. God's true prophets describe this intriguing character in multiple fashions. Their guided pens depict him with specific imagery, and they give us insight about things he would say, nations he would conquer, things he would accomplish, and the role of opposition he would play against the Christ. The world has grown to know such a man. Until now, he has gone unrecognized – hiding under the mystique and self-imposed authority best known as *The Prophet*.

Upon completion of this book, the reader will come to learn and correlate the prophesies about him, including the evidence proving that…

- The Prophet was a man – flesh and blood
- Lucifer was a man – flesh and blood
- the little horn, described by Daniel, was a man – flesh and blood
- this man began his reign after tax collection made gods of Roman Emperors
- he was an indignant king who exalted himself above Christ and His apostles
- he was the inspiration that built the *abomination that causes desolation*
- he was the first man to speak Satan's seven thunders

- he boastfully admitted to changing the 'outdated' Laws of God
- his actions, words, and teaching fulfill the biblical definition of *antichrist*
- his verbal deceit and contradictions qualify him to be the speaking image of the dragon
- he victimized the residents and travelers within the lands of Sheba and Dedan
- he plundered and looted merchants of the Tarshish
- he boasted of being a thief, declaring his life to be *the perfect model* for men
- he presented himself as *the bright morning star*
- his stern directives and lethal actions lacked the grace demonstrated by Christ
- he succeeded in instituting acts of terror as forms of obligation and duty
- his spoken word (as recorded) leads men away from the Most High
- his dutiful lessons encourage murder, crucifixion, amputation, and imprisonment
- his battlefield code phrase of "Peace and security!" has become a cultural greeting
- his existence, recorded word, and accomplishments are now of historical record
- his juxtaposition to *I AM* serves as further proof that the biblical God is *God*

This book lays out the case against *The Prophet* – he who earned the title as *the beast out of the earth* in John's Book of Revelation. To the best of abilities - the events, characteristics, and statements made within this book have been referenced and documented in the way of end notes. The obvious similarities to actual person or persons, places and events are unavoidable and not necessarily intent on coincidence. Any associations made between these events, characteristics, behaviors, and statements relating to this man, his nation, group, or party is purely reliant upon the conclusive reasoning of the reader.

Table of Contents

FOREWORD 5

PREFACE 9

1: LUCIFER WAS A MAN 21

2: THE LITTLE HORN WITH A BOASTFUL MOUTH 31

3: STERN-FACED DESTRUCTION 41

4: AFTER THE TAX COLLECTOR 65

5: THE KING WHO EXALTED HIMSELF..81

6: SEEING THE ABOMINATION THAT CAUSES DESOLATION 93

7: THE SOUND OF SEVEN THUNDERS......................................105

8: REVELATION BEFORE THE DAY OF THE LORD 123

9: THE ANTICHRIST PROPHET 135

10: THE SPEAKING IMAGE 141

11: VICTIMIZING SHEBA & DEDAN 155

12: THE PROPHET'S MODERATE CROWD 179

13: THE THIEF 193

14: FALLEN 201

15: JERUSALEM UNMATCHED...211

16: SUCCEEDING IN TERROR...215

17: SATAN LEADS THE WHOLE WORLD ASTRAY......................231

18: A NEW PLAGUE OF FROGS 239

19: BEHEADED BECAUSE OF TESTIMONY TO THE WORD 243

20: PEACE AND SAFETY 245

21: THE ODDS...247

22: THE WHOLE WORLD WAITS	269
23: THE NUMBER OF HIS NAME IS…	287
APPENDIX 1	289
END NOTES	291

Preface

The Prophet introduces a man that most people thought they already knew. The world knows his name. In one way or another, he and his people have affected the lives of everyone who has lived and breathed in recent centuries. His life is the fulfilled story of woeful biblical prophecy. His actions and words have been well documented and distributed. And, while his historical actions are among those that the biblically educated would think easily recognizable, his promised intrigue has gone undetected and overlooked for centuries.

As the reader progresses through these chapters, he or she might become overwhelmed with an annoying sense of repetition. As is the character of literature, repetitious dialogue can lull the reader into a sense of boredom. Boredom often leads to a lack of interest, and a lack of interest can lead to an early dismissal. But one of the most amazing mysteries of the Bible is the stunning reality that so many men could accurately describe the characteristics and behaviors of this biblical menace in such vivid detail and stunning imagery! With the help of Spirited guidance, each prophet offers unique warnings about this biblical villain and the differentiating roles he would play. Yet, each one of these storied images describes the same man. Occasionally, the prophets (such as Daniel) give us multiple encounters of the same person in separate settings and caricatures. Each image has key-word descriptions of this man's verbal lessons and what have come to be his historical actions. It is the sum of these chronicled pieces that, when placed together, completes God's mysterious puzzle, and paints a clear picture of the biblical villain and the terrifying kingdom that he has built among us. He has done so with the world's abysmal approval.

Instead of succumbing to traditional guesses and soothed to sleep by man's promise of warning signs, one might hope to participate in celebration and experience the inspiration of God's amazing precision, and His ability to guide His prophets in their endeavors to accurately describe Jesus' earthly opposition. God's ability to keep this villainous fool hidden in plain sight - until He deemed it proper for the grand reveal - is nothing less than fascinating. Repeatedly, the reader will hear about the life and continuing successes of the world's most boastful thief. But, with each piece or pieces of evidence added to the monumental case against him, the liar's ultimate unveiling becomes clear and evident. Be patient. Read it through. Be among the elect who are soon to recognize this mystery of God and how He was able to keep obvious truths hidden within the thick fog of man's own insidious delusions.

Lucifer...

We all know the name. No matter one's rearing, what religion we practiced, who our fathers were, or the level of one's education - the name Lucifer is known to us all. Without argument, the name of Lucifer has a distinct and resounding connotation to it. The name is the essence of evil. Most people consider Lucifer to be just another of Satan's many biblical names. But God's prophet, Isaiah, specifically tells us that Lucifer is or was a man.[141] Although Isaiah's writing is simplistic and absolute in its definition, few people accept that such a man might ever exist or have previously existed. But Isaiah's mockery and demeaning dress-down of Lucifer's existence, as being nothing more than a man, is straight-forward and intentional. Such is the take-away of the 14th chapter of the book penned in his name - Isaiah. For most, Lucifer (the man) and Satan (the spirit) present as one-and-the-same because of the things Lucifer would say, the things he would do and the debauchery he would come to represent. How could any one man be so evidently evil that his thoughts and actions mimic those of Satan? The world might be surprised as to just how easy it was to let this villain slip through the hands of history.

To anchor the point, do a simple web search and type in the word "Lucifer." What appears? One might pull up the images of a sharp-dressed man with slicked-back hair and glowing red eyes. Another might encounter a dark character who plays the role of evil in a weekly television series. Yet another will view the image of a naked, bat-winged man sitting upon a rock in a deserted wasteland. Inevitably, the research will result in references to movies such as Rosemary's Baby, Damien, Angel Heart, and multiple other absurd portrayals. But Lucifer, the man, has proven to be much deadlier than these Hollywood myth-makers. As the world is soon to learn, Lucifer is much more than just another religious myth. He has proven to be far more sinister than any screen actor has been able to portray, and more terrifying than any stage artist has been able to adopt. His ill-intended acts and teachings have created such world-wide terror and chaos that they make the efforts of Adolph Hitler look like the mundane duties of an ordinary altar boy. To date, few web searches shed light on Lucifer's worldly identity and the key role he has played in our world. That, too, is soon to change.

For the sake of this argument, take the words of Isaiah literally as he tells us who and what Lucifer is or was. Lucifer is a man – he is the son of another. Utilized only once in all the biblical books, Lucifer is the title of a satanic man.[137] Yet we all know the name – Lucifer! He is the man who destroys. He is the man who has caused the destruction of nations. Lucifer is the descriptive name of a man who attempted to assume the role of Jesus and claim that he (too) had ascended to heaven. Lucifer is the name of a man who claimed that he was the last of the prophets and the only man worthy of a comparison to God. He is the man who has proven to be exceedingly arrogant and boastful. So bold was he that Lucifer declared to have attained the highest position any man could ever attain, a position higher than all the stars of God. He ranks himself higher than the likes of Abraham, Moses, David, and Jesus. Though he claimed to have known and readily recognized the name of Jesus, Lucifer is the man who declared himself to be more worthy and higher in prominence than the Son of the Living God! As ridiculous as that may sound, the world has come to worship the man who said these things, and fight to the death in support of his claims. Many believe he is what he claimed to be. The significance of this is worth repeating. Lucifer was the man, a historical figure, who declared that he was higher in status, relevance, and importance to that of any other man. He considered himself to be more significant than the biblical Messiah! This is the all-too-real story of The Prophet.

Other than Lucifer, which of God's prophets would oppose Christ's teaching[361] and declare himself to be higher than all the others before him? Which prophet of God would dare to swim against the current of preceding biblical prophets and deny that God is our Father? After all biblical testimony, which prophet of God would abandon the teaching and the written Word to declare that God has no Son? The only one who might do such a thing is The Prophet – he who was to appear after the pens of God's witnesses were laid at rest. History has presented such a man. In a complete about-face, The Prophet offered testimony that contradicts the witnesses of God - those who spoke and wrote before him. Along with his contradictions and changed laws, The (last) Prophet made himself out to be the most high among his peers while denying that God had a Son. According to his recorded testimony, he accomplished all these things in a single breath![418] The Prophet's followers, hereafter known as the Prophetiers, believe and currently teach as he previously taught. These contradictory lessons are chief among the staples of the movement that Lucifer introduced. Not only did he declare himself to be closest and most important to God Almighty, but he went on to declare that he was like God.[313] This should come as no surprise to the reader – but it will. Lucifer's statement about being like God is among the first of multiple Luciferian blasphemies that Isaiah prophesied about. Isaiah warned us about Lucifer and the things he would say. Isaiah warned men about the things Lucifer would do. Isaiah's brother in spirit, John, warned us about the Antichrist and his rejection of God as a Father.[205] As written and recorded, these

Luciferian contradictions are among the precise warnings of God's prophets and the fulfilled prophecy brought about by The Prophet's words and deeds.

Now might be the proper time for the world to listen to the warnings of Isaiah. Now might be the proper time to trust God's Word and recognize what He has to say about the man He mocks as Lucifer. It is time to ask the questions: What prophet of God departs from 1,400 years of written testimony and over 2,000 years of biblical teaching? What is it that enables the last prophet to contradict and separate himself from all of God's prophets before him? How can his haughty behavior and verbal contradictions serve as the foundational root of God and His Word? The last prophet opposed and rejected most biblical teaching. He was The Prophet who founded and began an uprising that rejects all who adhere to the biblical truth. How could this have gone unnoticed by so many and for so long? How can it be that Lucifer hid in plain sight for such an extended period and became the exclusive founder of the largest-ever earthly rebellion against God and His body of believers? What is it about the power of The Prophet's strong-arm efforts, stern new rules and use of the sword that swayed so many people into believing he was the last of God's most trusted men and the seal of the prophets? By what delusional mysticism has he found success in altering the Word as written and declare that God's never-changing Laws were no longer valid? According to the Word of God, do His Laws ever change? Are His Laws ever deemed to be outdated? How can it be that Lucifer's attempt to change the Laws of God to the laws of another god might go so largely unnoticed that they have become the standard with so many people in so many lands? The mere suggestion that this could have happened is astonishing!

The world readily recognizes the harsh treatment inflicted upon all who refuse to obey The Prophet's changed laws. Yet, his maligned movements and manipulative causes have become collectively known as a peaceful means to honor God. That's the punchline. By his teaching, the Prophetiers obey his commands to strive with their hands, strive with their tongues and strive with their hearts - in manners consistent with instituting those changed laws. Such an effort to strive in this manner is the design of a liar, with religious tones and intentions that might overcome all other political parties, religious groups, and associated laws. According to The Prophet's verbal testimony, women must cover everything of their bodies with exception only of their hands and their face. He created this law after witnessing the blossoming aspects of his child-brides' younger sister - dressed in thinly veiled sleeping attire.[12] Unfortunately, there are branches of The Prophet's long-reaching vine that take this law a step further and demand that women cover even their faces. Recent events in Afghanistan give a fair and accurate example of this oppressive focus. Because such laws go well beyond a woman merely covering her head (her hair), the Prophetiers have accepted these changes as improvements to God's previous Law. Until The Prophet appeared, no such improvements to the law were necessary.[287] God states that men should resist temptation – not mask it. As written, God's Law existed for 1,800 years before The Prophet found himself in need of making a change. First presented to Moses in the way of Ten Commandments, God laid out the entire Law before the Hebrews in what estimates to be 613 separate commands.[71] The Laws originated in the Exodus of Egypt and in the birth of the nation of Israel, and they remain unchanged to this day. Spanning the last 40 years of Moses' life, from the Exodus of Egypt to his death outside of Israel, God's Law began with the introduction of those first Ten Commandments.[70] This is His Word. It is the Word. This is the Word of God - cut out of the Mountain of God but not by human hands.[66] In this sense, God was speaking literally. Jesus is the rock - described in this exact manner. Notice how God's Word is the Law, cut out of the Mountain of God – by the finger of God. Compare this to Daniel's description of a pre-incarnate Jesus as the Rock – cut out of the Mountain of God but not by human hands.[28] This Rock is the Law. This Rock is grace. He is the Alpha and the Omega. It is without irony that Jesus is the Rock who brings about the end of the rebellion against God. God gives us the Word about what is to come. Now, men will see that what God said has come to be. We have His Word in the appearance of the Christ. Now we have His Word in the appearance of Christ's adversary - The Prophet. He and his Prophetiers have spoken and acted in prophetic ways - verifying the Word of God and His warnings about the man and his people. With prophecy fulfilled, truth and God's Word are one-and-the-same. With history tucked firmly behind us, truth can be none-other than God's unchanging Law. Love and forgiveness demonstrate the grace of Christ as His selfless act frees the faithful from the righteous and eternal judgment of God's never-changing Law.

The Prophet had little use for God's outdated Laws and His Ten Commandments. The Prophet's new and improved laws were not cut out of the Mountain of God, nor were they written by the finger of God. They were the products of the mental and emotional torments that were forced upon one man and relayed to many others by his boastful mouth. With the intent to control, The Prophet's laws can be found within his recorded testimony as it was introduced 1,400 years ago. They formed the basis of what became a movement of few like-minded outlaws. The Prophet's initial few co-conspirators have steadily grown over time. Today's horrific Headlines often revolve around the people who strive to implement The Prophet's improved laws. Such Headlines constitute the lethal results of a people who have been driven to fulfill The Prophet's desire to conquer. Their deeds reflect the overwhelming destruction that was initially implemented by yesteryear's men and their swords. Promoted by haughty behavior, the Prophetiers perform their obligations and duties under a cultural shield of religious protection. Under such a shield, their callous behaviors are often deflected as the actions of extremists and not among those of the peaceful movement. Thanks to manipulations of the Constitution and unchecked 'freedoms of religion,' anything called religion can be freely exercised, no matter its origin, unless the practice of such faiths breaks societal laws. But there is a woeful catch to the rule. When The Prophet's rules and regulations are deemed to be cultural aspects of a foreign national, then the conversation and the Constitution gets flipped. Thanks to the fog of delusion and the forced acceptance of detestable acts, we're not to interfere with anyone's cultural behavior. With that little twist inserted into how we see and act on cultural offenses, explaining the otherwise inexplicable becomes much easier. The populace has come to a new understanding on societal woes. The answers are plain but no longer so simple. The Prophetiers are commanded to recognize and obey the authority and law of the land providing that the ruling authority does not command their members to disobey The Prophet's laws. In such a case, one is to disregard the local authority.[13] There is nothing vague or ambiguous about this directive. It does not change with the passing of time or yield to the amendments of policymakers. This law of The Prophet explains the unexplainable. No longer do men have to ask the inevitable question 'why' when an atrocity is committed by the Prophetiers in the name of any foreign god.

Though he might have adopted familiar names and titles, the god that The Prophet spoke about was foreign and unknown to his fathers before him. The Prophet said so.[369]

> "And when it is said to them, follow what [god] has revealed, they say: Nay, we follow that wherein we found our fathers. What! Even though their fathers had no sense at all, nor did they follow the right way."
>
> – The Prophet, Qur'an 2:170

Like the stargazers who preceded him, The Prophet's people idolize their foreign god in the images of celestial bodies - a crescent moon reflecting the light of a lone star. The moon and star are said to represent the light of God and the reflection of his precious star

- The Prophet. As a pair, this diabolical duo set out to depart from the teaching of old. They reject the Sabbath and misuse the names of the biblical God. They instruct the Prophetiers to commit murder[393] and promote theft as an act of righteousness.[405] Together, they teach their people to covet other men's wives[261] and possessions, thereby incorporating their most obedient followers into a den of adulterers and thieves. After 2,000 years of grooming and directing God's people to be law-abiding citizens with moral character, the newcomer was instructed to insert a ninety degree turn into God's straight path. Does this behavioral instruction, to depart from the original Script, sound consistent with our Maker's teaching and something that the God of Heaven would promote? Even by instinct, men know the righteous decree of God, and each man has a fundamental and collective understanding of what constitutes good and evil. Though they might protest, men know the difference between right and wrong. But, somehow, this den of thieves has been convinced that the cultural aspects of kidnapping and theft can be utilized in a worthy and nourishing manner, one that assists man's spiritual growth and gains him closer access to God. Such a den of thieves might find it beneficial to understand the unwavering instruction from God about such things and look to His 10th Commandment.[75]

The Prophet taught his body to adopt confusing contradictions. There is little agreement to be found between his new revelations and the past revelations of his predecessors. Prior to his verbal testimony, no true and faithful prophet denied that God is our Father. There is no exception to the rule. Contradictory testimonies prove only that two or more are not in agreement. Such is the case with The Prophet. But such is not the case with the Son and the Spirit. Jesus and the Spirit of God speak as one. Guided by the Spirit of God, the prophets spoke as one. Then comes the departure of The Prophet. He spoke things of a foreign spirit – things unheard of by God's people. In the realm of being the spokesperson for God, somebody has spoken inaccurately. As far as God being a Father, the prophets stand together with Christ. As far as God not being a father, The Prophet stands alone. There is only one prophet who denies that God is a Father.[267] There is only one prophet who denies that God is the Father of the Son. That one prophet is The Prophet described in this book. Angry debate will be had about such statements. But for those who wish to dismiss this as hateful rhetoric, the story has already been written. It cannot be changed. God warned us about Lucifer and his Luciferians. They act and have acted exactly as is prophesied. They function as a man and his people who oppose God and reject His people. For those who must call foul on such a statement - it's already been spoken and recorded.

Just as prophecy would have it, there is biblical reference made about the fallen angel and his little book. For God to neglect mentioning His nemesis' written image, with its new rules and battlefield instructions, would be inconsistent with the truth. Biblical authors go out of their way to differentiate faithful and true testimony from that which is something other. Teaching that is prophesied to be unfaithful and lacking in truth can be found within the pages of the Bible, but it comes with a warning such as "Seal up what the seven thunders have said and do not write it down." As a good prophet does, John obeyed the Word. He gives his testimony about the vision and relates the story of the seven thunders without revealing what the seven thunders stated. Time has offered them up and they have proven to be the product of the liar. God gave His warnings about the lies that Satan and his prophet, Lucifer, would spew. There is unfathomable irony surrounding the things they would say and do. The last prophet has no seat at Jesus' table and no post-ascension teaching by Jesus. The Prophet is unlike Paul in that Paul was addressed and taught by Jesus after Jesus' ascension. It is without coincidence that The Prophet rejects Paul as a prophet of God. And, other than the warnings against it in Revelation 10 and Daniel 12:4 (where men might go to find knowledge), the Bible does not offer The Prophet's book among the collection of faithful and true writings. Instead, the Bible warns about this man, his foreign god, and their stand-alone book.

The Prophet's opposition to the Word is just one of the biblical clues given about the man who introduced a foreign god as God. This is the man who changed the Laws,[245] assumed the highest position,[418] and said he was like the Most High.[313] According to Isaiah, these are the key statements made amongst a lifetime of Lucifer's boastful ramblings. He and his god have established a militaristic body whose faith is founded on war. Their numbers have grown from few stragglers to an organized battalion; from a battalion to a brigade; from a brigade to thirty brigades; and from thirty brigades to today's total of 450,000 brigades. At a count nearing 1,800,000,000 bodies, the expanse of their hordes is hard for most to imagine. It is six times the total number of people living in the United States of America! With this number of people living and governing under the shadow of the sword,[223] they are rapidly gaining ground and spreading their influence, all in the name of god. By operating under the cover of this name, the deception advances as a signature ruse of peace. Their successes have been accomplished at the point of a sword (use of their hands), strengthened through the utilization of their words (work of their tongues), and facilitated by the dedication of their intent (direction of their hearts). It was from the heart that The Prophet spoke. Through his speech, he authorized and appointed the use of a sword to protect the movement he founded. But the heart and mouth of a prophet of God should match the truth and grace demonstrated by the Christ. Luke explains the difference between good and evil men. It is from the overflow of a man's heart that his mouth speaks.[216] Evil speaks from a heart of deception. Though he has been dead for centuries, The Prophet's influence has never been greater than it is today. His body has never been larger than it is today. His political arm and its manipulative politicians have never been more influential than they are today! Using deception as a weapon, their well-trained squads maneuver through the halls of justice and infiltrate nations.

Though it is repeatedly stated that The Prophet is not mentioned by name in the Bible, little could be further from the truth. The Prophet is recognized by multiple biblical names. His followers recite his teachings and address him by his own, self-appointed, titles. Chief among these titles is the Messenger of God.[224] Simply stated, a messenger of God is the speaking image of God. Without these men and their testimony, how else would men know God? But what man, what flesh and blood could attain the throne as the messenger of God? What mortal man could speak the Word of God as the Word of God without being the reflection of God Himself? All but one of God's true messengers were just like us. They were sinful and blemished. But, upon selection, they and their pens were carried along by the Holy Spirit to testify about God.[350] However, one of God's prophets was not sinful. One of God's prophets was without blemish. There is and was one man who spoke and continues to speak as God speaks. He appears in the same light that God appears. He is the one prophet who validated all that the prophets had written about Him. This lone prophet is Jesus. He is the spotless one, the speaking image of God.[196] Is there to be another like Jesus, the Rock, He who was cut out of the Mountain of God?[76] Who, other than the speaking image of God, might be higher in the knowledge of God while living a life free of sin? Unbelievably, The Prophet said he was that man. And many believe him!

What do we know of the man who rejected the god of his fathers? According to The Prophet, he is or was 'the utmost to serve.' He is above the stars of God and has been given the throne of the Most High. So, was Jesus confused and misinformed? Were the prophets before Him confused and misinformed? The Prophet tells us that he, not Jesus, is a light in the darkness - he is the bright Morning Star. But how can that be? Jesus, the speaking image of God, gave testimony that He is the bright Morning Star,[477] a reflection of the Light that is His Father.[474] What gives here? Can Jesus, the Prince of princes and the bright Morning Star, also be the reviled morning star described and mocked by Isaiah? Did God's prophets of John and Isaiah contradict one-another by mocking the death of the Son as a feast for worms?[135] Certainly not! Jesus was never buried. His body was never thrown into a hole to rot and be covered by dirt. The man who became a feast for worms and maggots was dead and buried. John and Isaiah did not contradict one another, they complimented each other's prophetic guidance. In the days since Christ's earthly debut, there has been another, self-appointed, morning star. There has come another prophet who convinced many that he was raised to such heights, but he died and became food for the little wigglers! The Son, the true bright Morning Star, was stung but not overcome by the power of death. He has risen! Worms and maggots play no part in the entombment, resurrection, and ultimate ascension of Jesus.

So, what became of the so-called morning star who died and was buried? What might God, the Father, have to say to the man who arrogantly attempted to steal His Son's seat? Mockery seems appropriate. Worms and maggots seem appropriate. Being covered by the bodies of those he has pierced by the sword seems appropriate. All these things are worthy of the man who attempted to steal Jesus' titles, steal His throne, and steal His glory. Such is the life of a thief. A morning star he was not. Yet, this is how The Prophet described himself, a light at the end of the night – a metaphorical reference to the end of a period of darkness.[309] The Prophet has impressed this belief upon those who have never known the Father or His Son. They refuse to love the truth. Instead, they teach what The Prophet taught. They consume whatever he feeds them. They drink whatever he pours out upon them. The Prophet has succeeded in convincing his body that he is the star of piercing brightness that comes at the end of the night.[310] For them, he has dethroned Jesus, the Rock, and set himself up as the bright Morning Star.[477]

> "Lucifer – Latin of 'morning star'"
>
> – The Strongest Strong's Concordance of the Bible, p. 1637

This newly revealed morning star,[138] he who once made kingdoms tremble and he who overthrew the world's cities, has long-since been dead and buried. He boasted about his ranking as that above the stars of God, but he lies still in the earth below. In death he is covered by those he has slain. He is covered by millions of those who have fallen victim and found themselves pierced by the sword of his never-ending war. Is he continually mocked by the dead? He must be… Isaiah says this is so.

Lucifer is the Latin word for morning star.[496] What The Prophet did not know, what illiterate men like him could not have read for themselves, is that he fulfilled all things that were written to identify the man known as Lucifer. All that had been written about Satan's mouthpiece has been fulfilled by The Prophet. He succeeded in doing these things while claiming to be more than just a prophet of God. He claimed to be The Prophet of God.

What has been done is done. It is anchored in history by recorded testimony. It is as it was promised to be. His actions and words were forever framed by God's prophets - long before he arrived to fulfill them. The prophetic match is as stunning as it is accurate. The documented evidence and his unrepentant verbal testimonies were recorded and revealed in his own book – one transcribed, gathered, and originally bound by The Prophetiers.

God gave us His Image in the way of His Son. His Son is His Word. Satan gave us his image in the way of his metaphorical son. His metaphorical son delivered his word. These two oppositional images speak as their respective fathers speak. The first man delivered God's Word in an unblemished manner of perfection. The latter man delivered unfamiliar words, new laws, and a new way to worship god that incorporates the methods of a lawless thief. They are opposing images. As the image of His Father, Jesus demonstrated the ways of God. As the image of Satan, The Prophet demonstrated the ways of the father of lies. The original image is the Prince of princes and the King of kings, He who emerged from the lineage of Abraham and Isaac. Jesus was born from the vine of inheritance[115] and in line with the throne of Abraham and David.[321] Jesus is among biblical royalty. The Prophet is the prince of this world – emerging from the lineage of Abram and Ishmael. He has not been given the honor of biblical royalty, but he has delivered on God's Word that the descendants of Ishmael would live in hostility toward all their brothers.[119] One testifies for God. The other testifies for the foreign god. Jesus wrote His Word into the earth.[187] The Prophet lacked the ability to write anything at all.[269] While the original is risen and alive, the latter is dead and buried. With both men fulfilling their biblical roles long ago, only the original lives to know the truth of this day.

This book was written to compare the warnings about the biblical menace to the life and times of The Prophet, his god, and their body. This is the story of the man that history will forever know to have been the antichrist - Lucifer.

Ronald B. Stetton

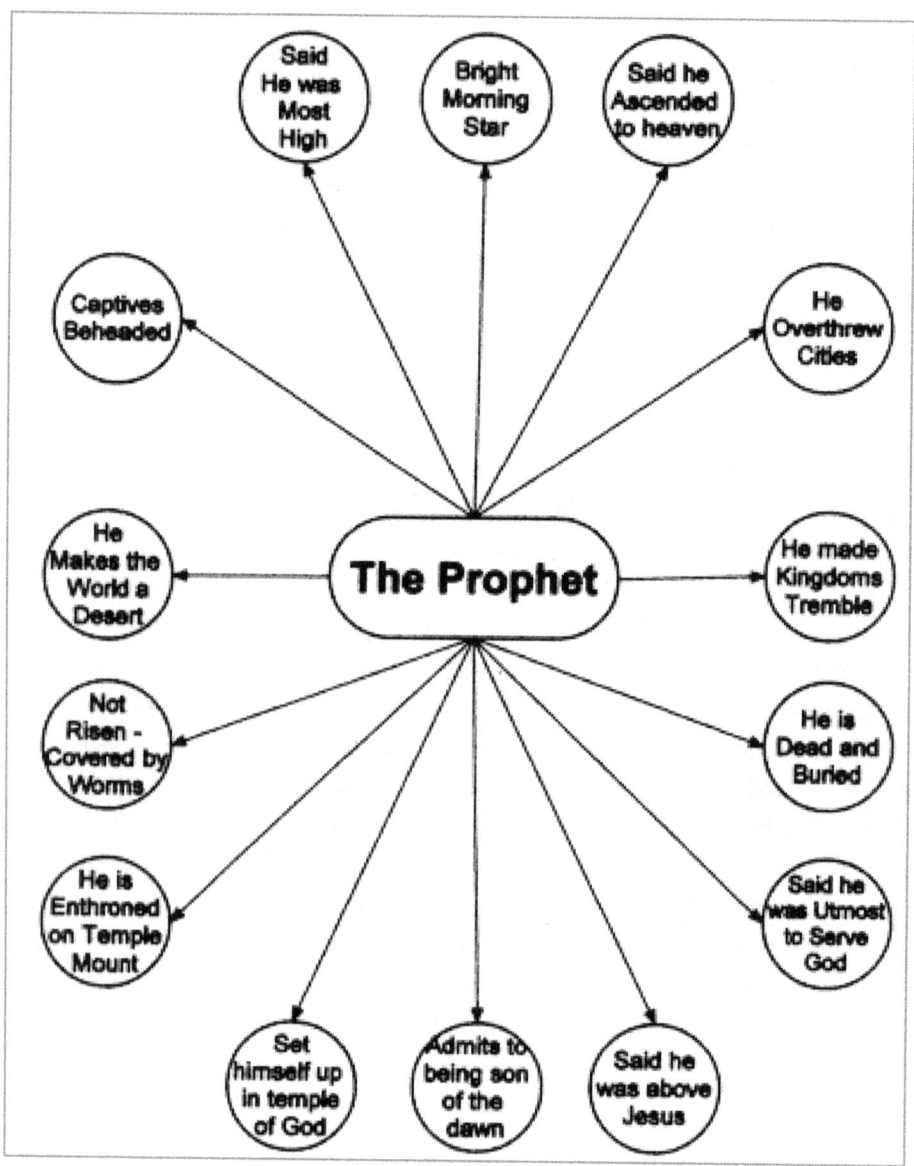

The Prophet

Chapter 1

Lucifer Was a Man

Isaiah's Descriptive Warning of Lucifer - the Man (14:3-23)

If the written Word of the Bible is God's story of man, with the end written from the beginning, then there must come a season when God's mysterious stories are unveiled and become evident in man's historic actions. Assuming God is *God*, then there must come a moment of clarity when the prophetic fog lifts and the truth of biblical promise becomes evident and verifiable. The reality is that most believe it is ridiculous to think that Lucifer, the man, might somehow exist as a living and breathing participant in our world's community. When pressed, the consensus among the population would agree that Lucifer, the man, is a more of a metaphorical evil than an actual person. Discussions about his existence as flesh and blood are most often laughed off as a realm of mindless absurdity. But what happens with the conversation when the argument of such an absurdity yields to stunning realities? How might men react when Lucifer is put on trial and the evidence against him is presented with historical accuracy? What becomes of our world when the sudden revelation of this man unfolds as fact? When one reduces the grand, image-laden biblical stories into a series of historical accounts, the fog of religious ambiguity begins to fade like the morning dew and the image of a man begins to emerge. What has long been seen as the crutch of a weak and needy people has now materialized into something of a not-so-new and very inconvenient reality.

Through the writing of the prophet Isaiah (740-697 B.C.),[125] God gives us a glimpse into the life and death of the man known as *Lucifer*. Isaiah offers us Lucifer's self-appointed title, his demeanor, his actions, examples of his furious aggression, one of the names of his metaphorical father, and five boastful declarations that Lucifer would make about himself. To be admitted as evidence, the world must have reasonable access to each count. Just like the destruction of the Twin Towers that was foretold in Isaiah 30:25, Lucifer's historical statements must be a matter of accepted record, with a long history of world-wide distribution for all eyes to see. His statements must be universal and as accessible as is the prophetic Word of the Bible. Because his brash characteristics and unique statements were written as prophetic warning long before he appeared, the reader can accept as reasonable the biblical accusations and mockery directed toward him as an accurate accounting of Lucifer's demeanor, behaviors, and accomplishments. Isaiah's writing makes it easy on the reader. He breaks Lucifer's life up into three basic segments:

1. Lucifer's actions in life
2. Lucifer's names and declarations
3. Lucifer's torment in death

The first two segments can be compared and verified by historical and written accounts. Thanks to the gathered testimony of The Prophet, the accuracy of these aspects can be easily identified and readily confirmed. After verifying that each of these characteristics can be attributed to The Prophet, it is reasonable to assume that the post-death treatment of this man's body and soul are also accurately described as is described by the demeaning taunt. Though the whole world understands that the story of Jesus includes His being the Son of God, few know the whole story of The Prophet. The reader is soon to learn that The Prophet claims to be the metaphorical son of the god he was chosen to represent. In a like manner, Isaiah mocks Lucifer for declaring he is *the son of the dawn*. There is neither room for another nor biblical account for a second son of God. For this reason alone, mockery and torment make for a suitable outcome for this man and his deceptive efforts!

Following are six of Lucifer's identifying marks as God's prophet Isaiah foretells them. These marks coincide with the documented accomplishments of The Prophet. Some are the actions and victories of his religious body, which consists of billions of Prophetiers who have either chosen or have been forced to follow his lead and act as he acted. Other attributes are conclusions of association. For instance, Lucifer is defined in the Concordance of the Bible as *the king of Babylon*.[496] But Babylon was a kingdom that existed 25 centuries ago! How could it be possible that the king of Babylon resurfaced a thousand years after Babylon's fall and has managed to continue his rule and authority to the current day? Isn't that an impossible task? Instinctively, men would assume that such a scenario is impossible. But, thinking biblically, such an event might occur. Look to John's description of our world in the end time. The book of Revelation describes the world community as *Babylon*. The Babylon of Revelation is led by both - a king and a queen. This vile couple is representative of the blasphemous teachings that have emanated from within the two religions that have developed since the way of Christ known as *Christianity*. The first to arise was the fanaticism surrounding the Roman lust for the queen of heaven. Next to arise was the foreign god that our fathers did not know and the king who introduced him. Long-thought dead and gone, the revised kingdom of *Babylon* has revealed itself to be the wounded head of Satan (the beast out of the sea) that has healed.[450] Lucifer is the king of Babylon. He is known to be the *perfect model for men*.[293] His worshiping hordes add to those of his abiding queen,[19] which cumulatively account for half of the current adult population on the planet. Though all do not practice them, most people recognize the holidays and observances of the newest king and queen. Certainly, the world's political body has fallen prey to the filth of their collective adulteries.

> "[The Prophet] is the best exemplar and the highest model of virtue… under all circumstances."
>
> – MMA, Qur'an 33:21, 21a, p. 829

According to testimony of the self-exalted king, his beliefs, teachings, and actions combine to form *the perfect model* for men. His testimony (that which openly opposes the sacrifice, offering, and life of Christ) can be found within The Prophet's book. But God's prophets paint a much different picture of king Lucifer. According to Isaiah…

1. Lucifer is called the king of Babylon[129]
2. Lucifer is the oppressor[129]
3. Lucifer demonstrates fury[129]
4. Lucifer is the rod or tool of the wicked – the scepter of rulers[130]
5. Lucifer and his body strike people down with unceasing blows[131]
6. Lucifer and his body furiously subdue nations with relentless aggression[131]

Historical records of The Prophet and his ever-growing nation offer countless examples of oppression, assault, intrusion, and murder – each of which accurately account for these prophetic behaviors. Setting aside the title of *king of Babylon* for the moment, consider the following:

- He convinced billions that they were *slaves to* and *soldiers of* their god

- Of these slaves and soldiers, billions mimic the furious aggressions of their self-professed perfect model

- Since the fall of Sheba and Dedan, countless numbers of their residents have submitted to the spells of this furious king and his schemes

- His intrigue has been influencing nations for centuries

- How much longer can the world accept the claim that his intentions are peaceful?

- Is it fair and reasonable to see him and his lethal directives as a scepter or a rod utilized by a people who have become drunk on the blood of others?

- With his offensive direction summarized in book form, why do so many insist that the lethal instruction of his movement is a 'misinterpretation' of his teaching?

- What cost must the world pay in the way of cancellation and execution before someone finally identifies the self-exalted king to be the murderous thief he was?

Knowing that the truthful answers to these questions have taken a backseat to the narrative, man has succumbed to *Ostrich Syndrome*. The astonishing power of such *Normalcy Bias* demonstrates how effective *the fog of delusion*[513] has been in hiding the historical identity of Lucifer.

Collectively, the world has been and will continue to be reluctant to answer these questions with any sense of honesty. Consciously, men choose to reject that which is abundantly obvious. The world does not want to admit the truth about the king and his kingdom. The truth testifies to the existence of God – exactly as He presents Himself. History has revealed the man who commands his slaves to inflict unceasing blows against their brothers and demonstrate relentless aggression against nations. He is the same man who promises to wage war until every other man and nation subdues to his coercions and submits to his ways.[402]

> "And fight them until there is no more persecution and all religions are for [god]."
>
> – Qur'an 8:39

Though statements such as these make the reader reasonably squeamish, the time has come to see The Prophet for who he really is – or who he was. Of course, there will be arguments about kings who have promoted similar evil acts, instituted oppressive gestures, and directed furious aggressions against their neighbors, but none of them have gained such size and strength beyond the founder's death. The Prophetiers will continue to act in 'the perfect manner' of The Prophet. The consequences of biblical prophecy becoming the world's reality are far reaching. If The Prophet is the fallen man of Isaiah 14, the new king of Babylon, then there is much more to his story. Everything about his life must match the associated biblical warning of his opposing nature. Read in amazement as the evidence continues to pour in!

Isaiah continues with his predetermined case against Lucifer and records God's mockery of the man and his arrogant declarations.

- Lucifer stole the title of *Morning Star*[136]
- He assumed the role of *son*[136]
- Lucifer unwittingly declared himself to be the son of *The Dawn*[136]
- He laid low the nations - personally subduing them[136]
- Lucifer claimed to have ascended to heaven[139]
- He declared himself to be higher than any of the stars of God[139]
- Lucifer sits enthroned on the mount of assembly - the Temple Mount[139]
- He set himself up and convinced the Prophetiers that he sits upon the utmost heights of the sacred mountain that is the temple of God. This temple of God is something much greater than just the stacks of stones that is or was the Temple Mount! [139]
- Lucifer has declared that he ascended above the tops of the clouds and made himself like the Most High[140]

Isaiah's prophetic writing precisely describes the illicit character known as *the bright morning star*. Isaiah wrote about this boastful star a thousand years before the self-appointed star appeared on earth! It is quite simple: To recognize Lucifer, all the world must do is keep watch for a man who...

- conquers the nations
- claims to be the Morning Star
- introduces himself as the son of the dawn

- claims to have ascended to heaven
- purports to be above Jesus and all of God's prophets
- sets himself up on the Temple Mount
- sets himself up in the temple of God
- and makes himself out to be like the Most High - *God*

Such a man should certainly be easy to identify! But the Christian world still waits for such a man to appear. With these things already accomplished, why has Lucifer gone unseen for so long? The answer is two-fold: First, the reality of Lucifer's existence is so horrific that the world prefers the proven methods of willful ignorance. Such behavior keeps them from seeing things that they do not want to see. Second, God decides when it is time to lift the fog and reveal the man that most people hope never to see.[506] Mankind knows The Prophet...

- He subdued the nations
- He claimed to be *the star of piercing brightness that appeared at the end of the night*[311]
- He taught his followers to believe that God has no son but, if God were to have had a son, that he, as the foremost to serve, would have been that son[299]
- He calls his god *The Dawn*.[428] And, when utilizing his metaphoric use of the term *son,* the reader can easily deduce how God mocks him for being *the son of The Dawn*[317]
- He claimed to have ascended to heaven during a *Midnight Journey*[284] on the back of a white hinny he called *Buraq*[1]
- In his trademark, arrogant manner he boasted about attaining the highest position of all men - dismissing the Son of God[299]
- He has been set up on the Temple Mount for centuries[284]
- With unwitting arrogance and uneducated ignorance, he 'set himself up in the temple of God' as *the lamp of light*.[289] The Prophet had no idea that he was admitting to Isaiah's mockery and fulfilling Paul's warning by setting himself up *in* the temple of God *as* the temple of God *as the Lamp of Light.* Of course,

John introduced men to the genuine Lamp of Light as Jesus in the book of Revelation

- He told the Prophetiers that he has become like *The Most High*![313]

Is this all just grand coincidence? When nothing else dismisses the evidence, 'coincidence' will certainly be among the world's many tired arguments. With the whole world led astray, men will argue that this presentation of evidence is a shameful *misinterpretation* of The Prophet's testimony and a loose adaptation of historical events. They will continue to function as Ostriches and stick their heads in the sand. With accusations of hate, they will demand that everyone else act in kind. "After all," they will say, "everyone will recognize Lucifer when they see him." He will have red eyes, hooved feet, a bat's wings, and he will be adorned by the hair and horns of a goat! With a disillusioned image of the man, is it any wonder how and why Lucifer flew under the radar and has remained hidden in plain sight for so long?

So, what became of this man? What happened to Lucifer after he died and why was it so important that Isaiah described him in his death? Since he claims to be the highest among the stars of God and the Seal of the prophets,[295] won't he (The Prophet) be honored as one of God's most endeared authors? Will he not be like Daniel and hear the words, 'As for you [Daniel], go your way till the end. You will rest, and then at the end of the days you will rise to receive your allotted inheritance'?[63] What makes The Prophet different from the rest of Daniel's people, God's chosen Jews, who 'will shine like the brightness of the heavens, and those who lead many to righteousness, like the stars for ever and ever'?[62] Will The Prophet be among the elect who 'came to life and reigned with Christ'?[465] Or will he be condemned and awake to shame and everlasting contempt? Is he among those who have been beheaded because of their testimony *for* Jesus and because of the Word of God?[462] Or is he the perfect image and leader among those who are committed to performing the beheadings? To find the answers, read back through The Prophet's testimony.

> "So when you meet in battle those who disbelieve, smite the necks..."
>
> – Qur'an 47:4

Isaiah offers insight on the man and his fate. His written account is the Word of God, spoken directly to the man known as Lucifer.

"The grave below is all astir to meet you at your coming; it rouses the spirits of the departed to greet you—all those who were leaders in the world; it makes them rise from their thrones—all those who were kings over the nations. They will all respond, they will say to you, 'You also have become weak, as we are; you have become like us.' All your pomp has been brought down to the grave, along with the noise of your harps; maggots are spread out beneath you and worms cover you. How you have fallen from heaven, O morning star, son of the dawn! You have been cast down to the earth, you who once laid low the nations...

But you are brought down to the grave, to the depths of the pit. Those who see you stare at you, they ponder your fate: 'Is this *the man* who shook the earth and made kingdoms tremble, *the man* who made the world a desert, who overthrew its cities and would not let his captives go home?' All the kings of the nations lie in state, each in his own tomb. But you are cast out of your tomb like a rejected branch; you are covered with the slain, with those pierced by the sword, those who descend to the stones of the pit. Like a corpse trampled underfoot, you will not join them in burial, for you have destroyed your land and killed your people."[133]

Isaiah nailed it! Listen to The Prophet's testimony. He revels in the lies he has spun. But his revelry is evidence of his own guilt. He's a liar and a jester. Taking the titles of the Son of God will prove to be his downfall. The Prophet set himself up as *the morning star* and *the son of the dawn*. This is neither an accusation, nor a bigoted conclusion. This is his testimony. Hell anxiously awaits this man - he who shook the earth and made kingdoms tremble. Hell awaits this man - he who made the world a desert, overthrew its cities, and beheaded his captives. He is covered by the slain, those pierced by the swords of his furious aggressions. History and his vocal word testify to the credibility of these declarations.

According to The Prophet, his torment began with mental anguish long before the menacing voices rattled around in his head. According to Isaiah, Lucifer's torment accelerated upon his death. And, according to John, Lucifer's suffering will be unending.[463] He turned against his neighbors, a people who had been teaching God's lessons and those who lived by God's written Word. By the time The Prophet arrived, that written Word had been in existence from the days of Moses to the final days of John. Christians and Jews had known God for 1,900 years. Then came The Prophet. He had eyes like the eyes of a man and a mouth that spoke boastfully. He assaulted the people and subdued the two nations that made up his 'homeland.' He stalked and robbed the merchants who navigated the known trade routes in the region. These three nations existed long before his arrival and certainly preceded his birth. Look to his history. Listen to his testimony. No longer can people ignore his callous inhumanity or his voracious appetite for flesh and blood. The voices in his head encouraged him to 'eat his fill in flesh,' but his appetite was not to be satisfied; his thirst was not to be quenched. With his never-ending slaughter of men, the world can no longer deny how he has destroyed his land and killed his people.

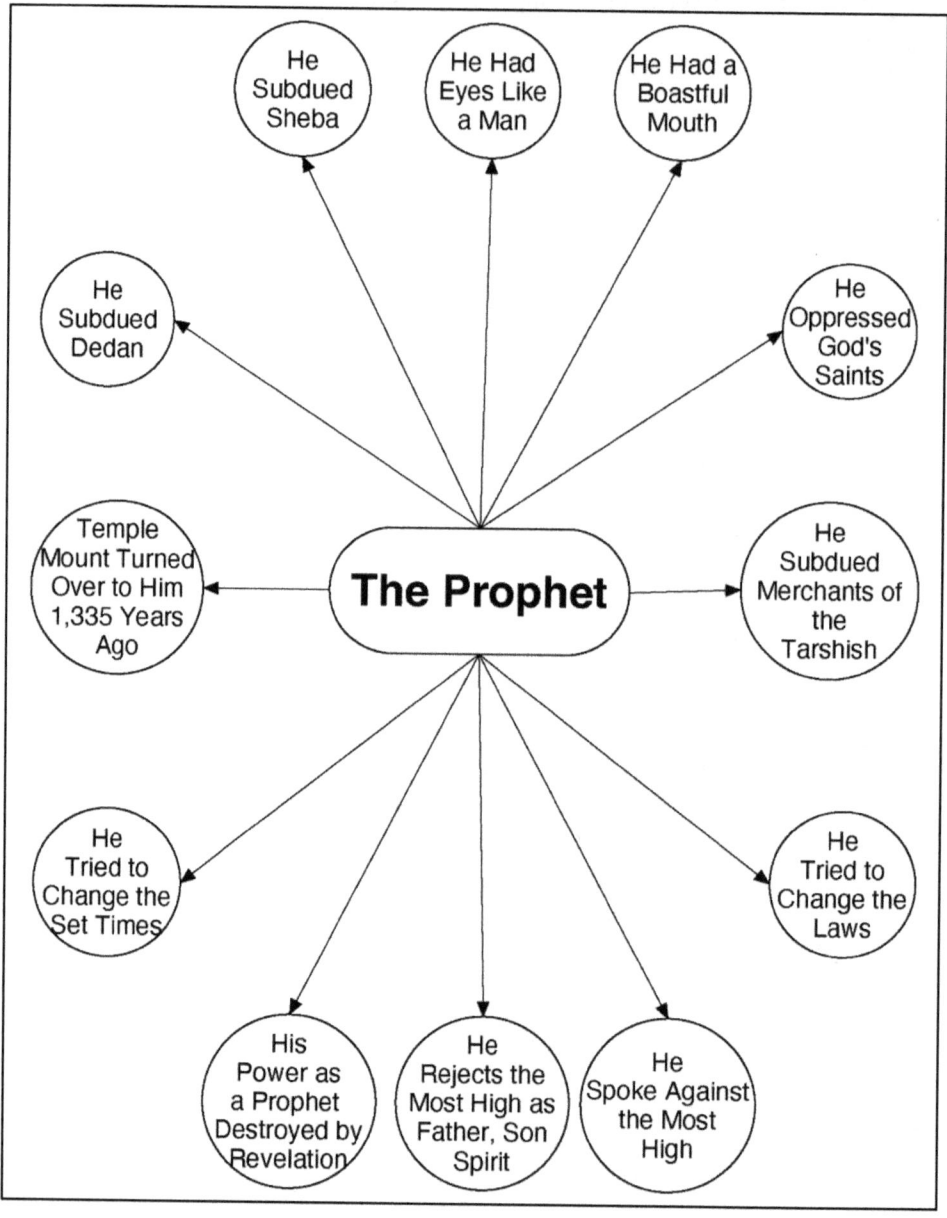

Chapter 2

The Little Horn with a Boastful Mouth

Daniel's Descriptive Warning of the False Prophet with Eyes and a Mouth (7:2-25)

Having identified the villain, gathering evidence against him becomes a hunt and seek adventure. With the prophets giving their descriptive warnings about this evil soul, matching The Prophet to the Word would call for searching the text. If the Word said that The Prophet would perform a task, his recorded text verified that he performed it. If the Word said that The Prophet would make a statement, his text verified that he made it. An example of this is found in Daniel's warning of the little horn. One does not have to be a biblical scholar to understand that each of God's prophets wrote about their dreams and visions. These dream-like scenarios gave God's prophets detailed glimpses into the future and instituted the necessary imagery that substituted for historical characters, proper names, and geographical lands. The reason for this imagery is obvious. Depicted as prophetic stories, it was necessary to replace the actual characters and current day geographical lands with something other than the proper or common names for these people and places. For example: If God were to have given us the story of Nazi Germany and used Adolf Hitler's proper name, what are the chances that the prophecies surrounding Adolf Hitler and his murderous allies would have developed to the point of occurrence? And what about the tragic and horrific prophesies surrounding Adolph's rise to power and his mad dash toward world domination? What then becomes of God's prophetic telling of these events? The answer is obvious - the rebellious terror and subsequent horrors inflicted by Adolf Hitler and his band of Germans (turned Nazis) would have been altered and cut short. A man, group, or nation would have intervened. That historical atrocity would have ended long before it ever began. Knowing this, the argument of rebellious men then turns on God. He inevitably gets blamed for allowing such things to happen. The nature of the world is to consciously reject the obvious rebellion (man's departure from God) and point the finger of blame at the Creator. Like the story of The Prophet, the truth is obvious but purposely overlooked. God does not give us the story of man as His perfect creation. God gives us the story of man and how man was deceived by the slippery methods of the snake. How many snakes can be found slithering their way throughout the halls of justice today? The snake uses his forked tongue to convince more men that looting and arson are merely forms of peaceful protest while its dark and shimmering eyes mesmerize its prey into accepting that self-defense is no defense if the intended victim's skin color is something other than black. That slippery serpent has put it into the minds of men that the only thing that matters today is the color of a man's skin. Such is the snake that convinced Eve to eat from the Tree of knowledge - making her like God in knowing good and evil. This all starts to make sense when one finally understands that the snake, Satan, is the foreign god who masquerades as God.

God has delivered His Word and reminded us of the rebellious nature and murderous inclination of man. The Prophet is the prime example in God's warning about rebellion, theft, murder, and destruction. These warnings include humanity turning his hand against his brother while turning their collective backs on the Father. God's written prophecies combine to give us the whole story of man. It is not an unfinished work – it need only play out. This is the irony. God's Word and promise is found within the deceit of The Prophet and his god. Somehow the conversation was turned on its head and men became open to the teaching that God now directs all nations to oppress His chosen people, murder the ransomed, steal from the non-compliant, and destroy anything that does not abide by the instituted laws of the god that our biblical fathers did not know.

After four thousand years on record, we can now call man's prophetic nature *history*. It is easy to forget this lesson when looking over mankind's past and the horrific things we have allowed to fester and grow. Still, those who do not know God profess an accusatory anger for any God who would allow such things to happen. How many times have you asked or heard someone else ask, "Why would God [fill in the blank]?" In a world that believes The Prophet's foreign god is God, it is easy to understand how and why God warned that darkness would become light, bitter would become sweet, and evil would become good. In a glimpse, the rapid departure from God that humankind has taken in the last two decades is nothing less than stunning.

Prophecy is the story of man's rebellion against God - not God's rebellion against man. As children of God, Christians are taught to demonstrate patience in the most grueling of circumstances. Such circumstances include imprisonment and death.[447] The prophets understood this. Most were imprisoned and/or murdered. This is never to be confused with or misconstrued as the intent of God's people taking up the sword and imprisoning or murdering others in His defense or on His behalf. God does not need us to fight for Him or fight in defense of our beliefs in Him. In a post-Christ world, where His lessons of grace equate to truth, actions such as murder, theft, and imprisonment are never to be inflicted upon another in the name of Him or any other god. Having this morsel of understanding about God assists us in the recognition that biblical visions correspond to historical reference. The prophets were seeing persons, nations, places, times, and/or events that were to come. In that light, multiple prophets spoke about Jesus' opposer, the antichrist, in animalistic imagery. Daniel is no exception.

As is the case with many of God's prophets, Daniel was troubled by some of the visions he had depicted.[31] God's prophets were astonished and amazed by man's woeful gullibility and quick acceptance of deceptions that border on the absurd. They were mortified by man's quick departure from God and His steadfast teaching. In this vein, the vision of the little horn troubled Daniel. He approached an angel who was present during the vision and presented a request. He "wanted to know the true meaning of the fourth beast, which was different from all the others and most terrifying, with its iron teeth and bronze claws—the beast that crushed and devoured its victims and trampled underfoot whatever was left." Daniel also "wanted to know about the ten horns on its head and about the other horn which came up, before which three of them fell – the horn that looked more imposing than the others and that had eyes like the eyes of a man and a mouth that spoke boastfully." As Daniel watched, "this horn was waging war against the saints and defeating them, until the ancient of days came and pronounced judgment in favor of the saints of the Most High, and the time came when they possessed the kingdom."[579]

Ugh! It is hard to blame Daniel for being troubled! This descriptive entry is the kind of *Bible-ese* and metaphorical imagery that sends the reader running for the exits! But when Daniel's vision is accepted as something more of an historical account, we can begin to search for and apply the matching history. As the chapters roll on, this type of case evidence paints a perfect picture of the past. This method of historical application works only if all the evidence aligns and fits together, like a round peg fits only in a round hole. The reader is tasked with determining as to whether such evidence matches biblical accounts.

In this example, the angel answers Daniel in a specific manner. The angel tells Daniel that the most terrifying kingdom he saw is among four kingdoms that will rise from the earth. Until recently, this has been a source of great frustration and confusion for biblical historians. We know the historical order of kingdoms. They appeared as: Egypt, Assyria, Babylon, Medo-Persia, Greece, Rome, and the kingdom of The Prophet. Until recently, biblical scholars had inexplicably ignored the seventh kingdom. They got stuck on Rome and the traditional teaching about its supposed 're-emergence.' The majority still waits and watches for a revived Roman Empire. But the world has moved on. The seventh kingdom, The Prophet's kingdom, continues to thrive and grow. Knowing who these nations were and the order in which they appeared, the biblical mysteries begin to take on historical relevance. One of these linked mysteries is the vision of the statue that Daniel describes prior to speaking about the four beasts. History can now assist in explaining how kingdoms come and go before Jesus finally puts a stop to the war that started in heaven.

- The head of *gold* is singular – that is undisputed as the kingdom of Babylon[29]

- The chest and arms of *silver* represent distinct entities that ruled during the same time – these were the kingdoms of the Medes & Persians

- The belly and thighs of *bronze* represent distinct entities that ruled simultaneously – Greeks and Romans

- But the legs are not different entities. Each is a leg of iron "for iron breaks and smashes everything—and as iron breaks things to pieces, so it will crush and break all others. Just as you saw that the feet and toes were partly of baked clay and partly of iron, so this will be a divided kingdom... The people will be a mixture and will not remain united."

There are four separate metals listed – gold, silver, bronze, and iron. What troubled Daniel so greatly was the kingdom that followed the Greek-Roman period, that of iron. This is the kingdom set up by The Prophet. Its two legs are sects, and they are ultimately guided by a lone ruler, but they are viciously opposed to one another. Though they are both led by the same man, the kingdom of iron had a massive political conflict and it split apart almost immediately after The Prophet's death. After 14 centuries, these two legs have crushed and broken all others. Like The Prophet, their lust for conflict cannot be eased. They are a kingdom at war. Its people are mixed – they originate from mixed blood. They were a people conceived in an act of infidelity. Their father was royalty. Their mother was a slave. Mother and son were expelled to the desert. The boy became the head of an ever-expanding nation; a nation whose brother was set against brother. From the vine of this infidelity grew a nation of people. And from that people arose the man who would come to be known as The Prophet. As prophesied, his hand is against everyone, and everyone's hand is against him. Since their inception, he and his Prophetiers have lived in hostility toward all their brothers. The prophetic nature of Ishmael's vine, the great (large) nation, is described in Genesis, chapter 16.

Understandably, it is time for the reader to take another deep breath! With Satan leading the whole world astray, there is no politically correct path to describe the man and people who rebel against God and His people. Relying on 1,400 years of painful evidence, it is perfectly accurate and reasonable to describe the majority of Ishmael's latter lineage as a people whose "hand is against everyone and everyone's hand against [them]." Thanks to the efforts of a single man, Ishmael's lineage has certainly lived up to "living in hostility toward all his brothers." This biblical account yields uncomfortable historical outcomes that lack any sense of political correctness. Even The Prophet's proclamation of "fighting in defense of the [cause]" cannot cool the heated commentary that is certain to follow these claims. Whatever disposition that Ishmael's nation initially adopted toward men took an alarming turn in the dying days of the Roman Empire. The seventh kingdom that took root in the deserts south of Jerusalem has unfortunately thrived and continues to spread its influence across the globe. The kingdom's dedication to war, military visions, and unapologetic aggressions increase proportionally to that nation's growth. Humanity has come to know this kingdom, its members, and the overbearing weight of its unrelenting oppressions. Multiple wars have broken out with this nation over the last three decades, with their aggressions proving to be increasingly abrasive. Theatrical depictions of its murderous depravities continue to fill our screens. These are the accomplishments of the perfect model for men and the swords he commanded they swing. He has conquered lands and turned them into deserts. Among echoing screams in the name of their god, the Prophetiers crush and devour their victims – with victim shaming used to mop up the mess they create. Of course, these menacing screams are shouted in the native tongue of a people who believe they are acting in a manner consistent with God's wishes. The reasoning is described as *defensive* while the intent is described as *peaceful*. Had they known God, they would never have picked up the sword in His name.[202]

Once again, the subject-matter of a world led astray cannot be discussed with a politically correct tone. This likely makes the reader rather squeamish. It should! Any discomfort that the reader might experience has little to do with the accuracy of the information. It has much more to do with how the subject makes you feel. Inflicting terror is the true intent of The Prophet's aggressions. Terror is the controlling mechanism that becomes manifested in such behavior. What began with the ten biblical territories of Rome and Greece combine to reveal the geography that is now home to the beast.

- East Africa

- North Africa
- Italy, Greece & Western Turkey
- Eastern Turkey
- Syria and Iraq
- Russia and China (associated by marriage or alliance)
- Persia (known as Iran)
- Northern Arabia
- Southern Arabia, Yemen & Oman
- Mediterranean coastal cities

In biblical terms, these are the territories of: Cush, Put, Meshech, Tubal, Gomer, Togarmah, Persia, Sheba, Dedan and the Tarshish. The names have been changed over time, but the geography is the same. Most notable is that during The Prophet's life, he personally subdued three of these regions and peoples. Sheba, Dedan, and the merchants of the Tarshish fell victim to his ruthless pursuits. Whether he became a thief before or after his self-declaration of prophethood is of trivial matter. What matters is his admission of being a thief throughout his life and prophethood. He raided the traveling caravans, stole their wares, killed their men, and did unspeakable things with their women and their children before selling them into slavery.

Though his resume might sound much like Hitler's, this character added the expertise of prophethood to his skillset. This is The Prophet, and these are verifiable accounts of his actions. He is the man who departed from biblical teaching but is worshiped by billions as a prophet of God. Affirmation of these accounts can be found within his own founding documents.[403] Not only does The Prophet's life satisfy the prophecies of Daniel's little horn but, because these acts were conducted upon the caravanning Tarshish in the ancient lands of Sheba and Dedan, his documented life also fulfills the prophecies of Ezekiel's Gog – the evil scheming thief.

The mysteries of God are being unveiled and the lawless man is being revealed! He is Lucifer, the man who shares consistencies with the little horn of Daniel 7 and the thief of Ezekiel 38. His mannerisms and actions mirror John's warning about the thief who "comes only to steal and kill and destroy."[193] What evidence does the dictated diary of The Prophet declare? It verifies that he came to do what thieves do. His followers, billions of them, are encouraged to function as he acted. And he acted in a manner that the Bible calls *evil*. Though genuine evil exists in the world, the majority (particularly the godless) choose not to see it. Attractively packaged and presented in a cultural manner, evil is presented as the new good. Evil has become desirable - something that is to be adopted as progressively wholesome and nourishing to the soul. Currently, the world demands acceptance of The Prophet, his people, their collective actions, and their ominous teaching. Truth is continually being crushed and devoured, discarded and undermined by a tainted world with its unceasing waves of lies and false narratives. It is satanic methodology. This is how Satan deceives people and leads the whole world astray.[437]

Those who reject the God of Israel as a whimsical fairytale will not understand any of this. They will not hear of it. It is likely that most naysayers stopped reading long before this point of the book. They don't want to know. Unfortunately, mountains of evidence will not be enough to convince the majority that such a large body of people have adopted the ways of Lucifer. The behaviors and beliefs (right hand and forehead) of the Prophetiers exist as those the Bible describes as *deluded, led astray,* and *delighting in wickedness.* They worship the instructions and delight in the actions of the man who subdued kingdoms. Whether they expand their hold over people by political gains or by the point of a sword, his body continues to grow in number and subdue their neighbors. They have clearly demonstrated that the United States is not immune to their aggressive methods. With a sick sense of irony, the Prophetiers have gained support from the very people they have preyed upon. Look at the political gains they have made since 9/11/2001. They are working their ways into our laws. This is The Prophet's specialty – changing the laws. His representatives encourage the destruction of cities while calling for an elimination of the existing police force. In a manner consistent with the man who made kingdoms tremble and overthrew its cities, the Prophetiers look to uproot the law and plant their own rules and regulations. It worked for Lucifer!

According to Daniel 7:25, what are the four characteristics of this *subduer of kings*?

1. He [The Prophet] spoke out against the Most High [God]

2. He [The Prophet] oppressed God's elect by his own hands and by the hands of his members

3. He [The Prophet] attempted to change the set times from Anno Domini (A.D.) to Anno Hijra (A.H.)

4. He [The Prophet] has attempted to change the Laws of God to the laws of the foreign god he introduced

The Prophet's nation and his divided armies have grown larger and more terrifying over the centuries. The looting that started between The Prophet and the merchants of the Tarshish has spread to piracy in the Mediterranean and is now a worldwide phenomenon. There was a simple set of questions asked of the evil schemer: "Have you come to plunder? Have you gathered your hordes to loot, to carry out silver and gold, to take away livestock and goods and to seize much plunder?" The answer to these questions was acknowledged as affirmative by The Prophet in his boastful admission that he and his hordes have indeed come to plunder.[403] No man or group has attempted to change the written directives of The Prophet to steal and to kill. But the political narrative that exists to distract people from this fact is alive and well! The fact remains that 1/5th of all goods acquired in war are to be dedicated to The Prophet and his god. Nothing has changed. The answer that the Prophetiers give today is the same answer that was given by The Prophet so long ago. History tells no lies. Biblically speaking, the Prophetiers have come to model the perfect example of the man who came only to steal and to kill and to destroy.

So, how can the reader find any good news in all of this? Daniel tells it best:

"The four great beasts are four kingdoms that will rise from the earth. But the saints of the Most High [God's people] will receive the kingdom and will possess it forever - yes, for ever and ever. The court will sit, and [The Prophet's] power will be taken away and destroyed forever. Then the sovereignty, power, and greatness of the kingdoms under the whole heaven will be handed over to the saints, the people of the Most High. His kingdom will be an everlasting kingdom, and all the rulers will worship and obey him" – Daniel 7:17-18, 26-27

The reader can and should take great comfort in knowing that if everything God tells us about The Prophet and his hordes is accurate and true, then accurate and true is everything that God tells us about His abilities to overcome their rebellion. The furious aggressions that are feeding off people and consuming our world are soon to be no more - forever. Who can imagine a greater hope! Even with all the gains that the Prophetiers are making today, we all know how this story ends. The outcome was decided long ago.

Daniel had much more to say about the little horn who had eyes like the eyes of a man and a mouth that spoke boastfully. He wrote about rebellion. The rebellion targeted

Christians and Jews, and it was instituted by a stern-faced king, a man who would rise to oppose the Son of God.

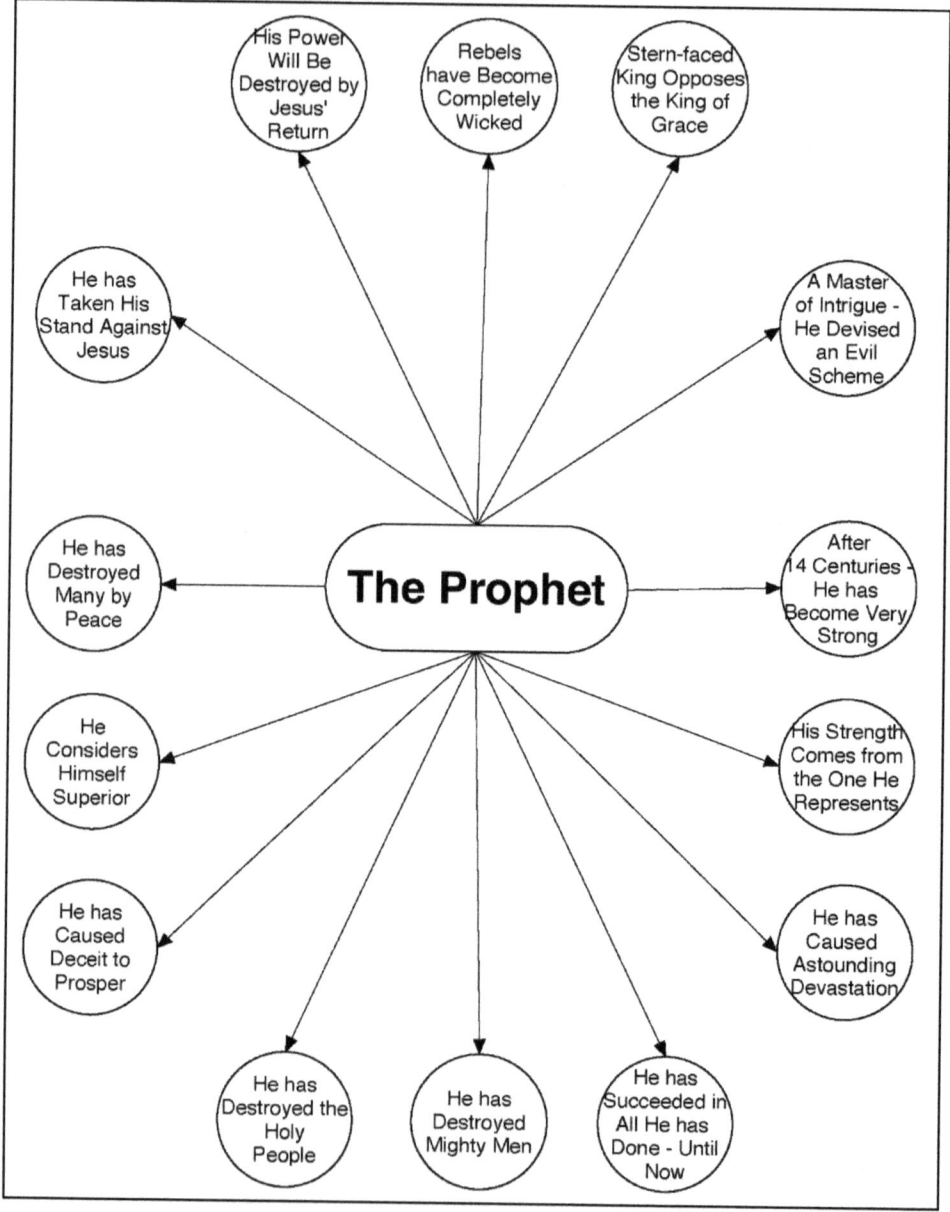

Chapter 3

Stern-Faced Destruction

Daniel's Descriptive Warning of the Stern Man (8:23-25)

In the book that bears his name, Daniel gives the reader another description of the Bible's ungracious villain. He describes this imminent menace as a stern, strong and successful deviant - whose artistry is demonstrated through deceit and devastating destruction. Daniel reminds us that this man, the stern-faced king, considers himself to be superior to all other men. He warns us about this undeserving king and how he will be the root cause of destruction for many people and nations. History has bolstered Daniel's prophetic, Spirit-filled writing. He forewarned us about *Stern-faces'* opposition to the Prince of princes. The remarkable thing about this statement is that Daniel wrote this warning six hundred years prior to the birth of Jesus and 1,200 years before the rise of *Stern-face*. Of course, the Prince of princes proved to be Christ Jesus. The opposing positions of the stern-faced prophet vs. the gracious Christ are easily recognized and documented in readily available book-form. Stern-faces' opposition to the Christ presents itself in every form – just as one would think it ought to be. One of these men is the Christ and the other is the antichrist. Though the term has become a running joke among men, The Prophet's actions fulfill the biblical account. To anchor the point, The Prophet denied that Jesus is or was the Son of God. By simple definition, that denial makes The Prophet an undisputed antichrist. As far as The Prophet being *the* antichrist, it's simply a matter of fulfilling the balance of prophecies that were written about this biblical nuisance. Further, Stern-face veiled his intrigue and contempt by convincing men that his kingdom was built upon a foundation of peace – ushered in by the sword. Sadly, a lost and consciously ignorant world demands that we accept the premise of Stern-faces' deceptions. The current and historical reality of The Prophet's destructive endeavors is anything other than a patchwork of peace!

Six centuries after Jesus' crucifixion and five centuries after His prophets laid down their pens, this demon-filled menace was born and raised in the lands of Sheba and Dedan. He burst upon this desolate area at a time of woeful godlessness. A harlotous religion had previously taken root in the region and had been infecting Rome and the Romans for centuries. Though this sordid belief system referred to Jesus as "Lord," it adopted and incorporated its own detestable practices as *continuing traditions* and mixed them with the Word of God to create something that Paul described as *demonic*.[518] Though the Roman religion sold itself as being the bride of Christ, it (they) adored and still adores other gods and their forbidden images. They carve angels out of wood and bow before statues of the Queen of Heaven.[169] They forbid their religious leaders from marrying and reject Jesus' exception in divorce that allows for victimized divorcees to marry again. They instruct their followers to abstain from eating meat on certain days while marking their faces in a manner that advertises to the world that they are fasting. Yet, they do not fast at all. They merely abstain from eating meat for a day and, once a year, they proclaim to "fast" from one behavior or another for a period of 40 days. Just as the Babylonians did, they drink from the golden cup and pour out their bloody abominations in the form of a maddening wine. Week after week, and year after year, they make the outrageous claim that they are pouring out the actual blood of Christ. Driven mad by the wine of manmade tradition, they have taken the path of the Babylonians.[179] Such were the acts of demonic departure that soaked the lands of Sheba and Dedan in the days of The Prophet's birth. Such was a time when most had discarded the Scripted truth of the Father and His Son for something better suited to those who murdered the Christ. With falsehoods abounding and a new, Romanized, 'Christianity' serving up contradiction upon contradiction, the time was ripe for an Ishmaelite prophet to appear and introduce his foreign god.

As flesh and blood, the prophet-king was raised in the land that had become home to the resettled Jews. The Romans had scattered them from the north, Jerusalem, five centuries earlier. Stern-face took advantage of the drunken and adulterous traditions that had been adopted as 'Christianity' by a harlotous Roman Empire. Already misled by the self-imposed traditions of the Romans, people in the land were fascinated by the accusations of contradiction described by this man. Among his many falsehoods, Stern-face claimed that Christians worshiped the Father, His Son, and *Mother*.[397] The Mother... Only from the bias of Roman folklore and Babylonian influences might someone be led to believe that Christians worship the mother. This act, rooted in Babylonian tradition,[174] made for a perfect opening for The Prophet. Biblically speaking, faithful Christians honor the Father, His Son, and His Spirit. Jeremiah taught us that God detests the adoration of any sort of "Queen of Heaven."[174] But Stern-face took advantage of the Roman contradiction and pointed it out to those who would listen. And listen they did! As a reward for his demonic teaching, Stern-face and his people have received honorable mention in the harlot's field guide as those who participate in *the plan of salvation*.[19] Such written statements include Stern-face and his people being among the harlot's multiple intimate partners.

Without the harlot's manufactured traditions and unrepentant disobedience, the accusations of The Prophet might have otherwise fallen on deaf ears. But in that day and in that land, the brushstrokes of idolatry, false tradition, and lawlessness were among the acts that painted a new picture of what was called *God*. With the harlot selling her wares in the land, the stage was set, and the curtain was about to rise making way for the lying merchant and his dishonest trade. With people in the land already delighting in wickedness and refusing to love the Truth, God sent them a powerful delusion. He sent them the master of intrigue. Here was a man with an evil scheme! Six hundred years after Jesus' birth, death, resurrection, and ascension enters a prophet who would not honor Jesus as God's Son. He would not honor God as a Father. This man would not honor any of the gods of his fathers before him. Though he proclaims that his god is the god of Abraham, he speaks of a god unknown to the men and prophets who knew the God of Abraham. Each of the prophets who knew the God of Abraham knew the God of Israel. The God of Israel guided the pens of men like Moses and Paul, men whose written testimonies spanned 1,400 years. Each of the prophets offering their inspired knowledge and written image of God. It is from their description that we know who and what constitutes God.

Then came The Prophet. He presented an alien image. He honored a god of fortresses.[307] In that time of man's wicked rebellion and adoration of man-made tradition, in a time of refusal to love the written and unchanging truth, the world received an unfamiliar word and was forced to worship another. As ridiculous as this might otherwise sound, the oppressive nature of The Prophet's endeavors is and was forced upon men and society. Just as the wicked might support, the political winds have shifted, and mankind has fallen into submission to the Prophetiers and their ever-expanding influence. Though their god is not God, acknowledging the difference is frowned upon. Though The Prophet was not a prophet of God, his unveiling will not be well received. Revealing these facts will open the floodgates of man's worst tendencies. They will threaten to act as he directed and murder, crucify, amputate the hands and feet and/or imprison all who oppose them. Their accusations of bigotry and threats of cancellation will merely be a warm-up. Such acts are indicative of a society that has chosen to disregard that which now stands in plain sight. This is known to be the *progress* of humanity. The progressives lead the charge away from God – just as He promised they would do.

There are those who listen to The Prophet's words and use their hands to institute his lessons. They believe in what he said. These are a people who can no longer recognize their right hand from their left. They may not, cannot, and will not recognize The Prophet's foreign god in the written warnings delivered by the Spirit of God. For those who refused to love the truth and be saved, for those who have delighted in wickedness, a new prophet has appeared, and he reigns supreme. The point of his sword has set the precedent. A merchant by trade, he was familiar with buying and selling. He also understood the easy gains of theft by taking what he wanted from any man he chose. He brought about a dishonest trade. He changed the laws to suit his own desires. He promotes *righteous murder* as an act of defending his new-founded faith. He delivered the verbal description of a foreign god and instituted an improbable oxymoron among men - destruction by peace. In a lawful man's eyes, The Prophet was leading a rebellion by teaching falsely. But in the eyes of the unlawful, he promised salvation by acting like Cain. A fallen and lost generation has sided with him. Utilizing the deceit of counterfeit miracles and every sort of deception conceivable, he manipulated men and attempted to change all the prophetic testimony before him. As is written, he...

- "... became very strong, but not by his own power." If the Holy Spirit of God guides and empowers His prophets, then who or what guides and empowers the liar? Understanding that we have come to know God by recognizing Christ, God's speaking image, might we then come to know the *foreign god* by recognizing his speaking image as well? The Son speaks for the Father by way of the Word and the Spirit. This has not and will not change. Presented as God's *Two Witnesses*, this pair is in perfect agreement about who and what constitutes God. But The Prophet speaks in opposition to God's Two Witnesses. He speaks for the foreign god by way of word and spirit, but he speaks like the dragon. His spirited word differs from the Word and Spirit that was sent and anchored by God's prophets. These opposing testimonies demonstrate how it is that the Christ speaks in truth and the antichrist speaks in rebellion. The truth and grace of Jesus' testimony reflects the true image of a loving God who commands men not to murder. The callousness of the murderer reflects the image of a god who was a murderer in the beginning. Jesus tells us this very thing when He compares Himself to the thief. The deceptive revelations and unrelenting lawlessness of The Prophet depict the nature and image of the god he was sent to represent.

- "... was a master of intrigue." And just what was The Prophet's intrigue? He devised an evil scheme. He verbally expressed a covenant, an agreement, between his god and people who refuse to love the prophetic Word of the God of Israel. The Prophet regurgitated the words of an opposing covenant. Eighteen years after his death, a new covenant was confirmed in the way of a little book. His lightly veiled intrigue continues with the Prophetiers as they grow in number and political influence across the globe. The iron teeth of this beast demonstrate how they crush and devour their victims while trampling underfoot whatever remains. Those same iron teeth can now inflict a nuclear bite. The Prophet's intrigue is fraught with a god who rejects any notion that God would belittle Himself by having a Son. Such intrigue can be found woven into the fabric of society, insisting that the destruction is a necessity when it comes to achieving peace. He presents himself and his god as tender and delicate, but their actions are reminiscent of Charles Manson. It is all about love and peace until it is time for accusations and war in their march to overcome all others and neutralize a newly defined *mischief* in the land.[393] The Prophet's life of intrigue can be encapsulated by the faith he created and anchored in war.[402] He's The Prophet of war. It was Satan's rebellion and war in heaven that caused him to be cast down to the earth. This is the same war that caused Satan's speaking image, the spirit of Lucifer, to fall from heaven to earth. It is war that emanates from the heart and mouth of The Prophet. And it is war that men will know until the end.[43] How could it end any other way? Matthew warned men about the war between kingdoms.[334] Because he was a murderer from the beginning, Satan brought his war with him. What Satan brought about - The Prophet delivered. He brought about war between the nations. He brought about war between the kingdoms. The outcome of this biblical conflict was determined long before it began!

- "... was stern-faced." Jesus is the gift of God. It is He and He alone who brought about forgiveness for our transgressions. His sacrifice and offering instituted the grace that every man needs to shed the shame of lawlessness. The Prophet rejected Jesus' sacrifice but offered no gift himself. He brought about the promised delusion for a people who refuse to love the truth of Christ and be saved. The Prophet is not about forgiveness. No twist of words can alter history and bend his actions into something resembling grace. Simply stated, The Prophet and his methodology were stern! His people are stern. He taught the

Prophetiers to pick up stones of a new-found righteousness and strike down all who dared to question his superior revelations. He taught men to reject and forget Jesus' lesson on grace and forgiveness, the lesson that permitted men to drop the stones of condemnation. As is written, mankind has demonstrated its artistry of denial with accusations of hate and immediate cancellation when facing inconvenient facts. Denial is a tool of the rebellious. But what is written cannot be wished away. The Prophet commanded his followers to *murder* the mischievous for breaking his laws.[393] He did not say that 'the wage of sin is death.'[485] He did twist the truth that 'those who knowingly disregard God's righteous decrees deserve death'[484] by declaring that those who wage war against him, his god or their laws should be 'murdered.' His testimony is in writing and cannot be disputed. His commands to maim and murder, dismember, and imprison answer the inevitable question of 'Why?' whenever the Prophetiers act in their cultural ways. This is their native language. It is by his stern direction that men continue to commit murder in the name of his god. It is by his word and command that men were motivated to murder many and destroy those in "the Towers, raised high."[390] The past mysteries of the King James Version of Daniel 8:25 are no longer mysteries. It is by The Prophet's direct influence that so many have been destroyed by 'peace.' Daniel's age-old warning about the *Stern-faced king* has become a factual account of modern history. The Prophet's callous actions and cold-hearted directives thrive upon the edge of a sword, and they have coerced their way into modern society. The ostriches blame these acts on a people who cannot let go of the past. They know that barbarism has no place among men. They want you to 'follow the science' until it is revealed that science achieved the 'gain of function' that has recently tormented nations. Few choose to see it for what it is. In his pursuit of power, it would seem that mankind cannot get his fill of flesh.

- "… has become very strong." Although he has been dead for 1400 years, the power and the influence of his *many* are greater than they have ever been. With prejudice, men allow that power to grow. The Prophetiers, those whose beliefs are founded in war, currently number two billion. His nations have become nuclear armed. His prolific swordsmen have pierced the bodies and souls of billions more. For most in the world, biblical prophecy is rapidly becoming an unwelcome reality. Depravity and deception have taken root. Billions of people have been fooled and misled. God's Word warned about the deceptive nature of

The Prophet and his father as being murderers from the beginning. The world was warned that these things must happen. Man would turn on God. The Word tells us that The Prophet was to hide in plain sight until prophecy was fulfilled. He has remained hidden behind the best blind ever constructed - man's conscious denial. Prophecy has been fulfilled. Of The Prophet, God promises that "he will be revealed at the proper time." He has been revealed. Because we see him now, this can be none other than *the proper time*.

- "... has caused astounding devastation." Historical examples of his astonishing devastation can be summed up by the events of 9/11. The entire world watched in horror as 19 of his loyal disciples hijacked commercial airliners and guided them at full throttle into the Twin Towers and the Pentagon. Each aircraft was filled with men, women, children, and fuel – lots and lots of fuel. A fourth plane was commandeered by these cultural warriors with targets in Washington D.C., but it was brought down in a Pennsylvania field by the actions of a few heroes who realized it was time to fight back. The plane descended nose first under full power. A brave few scuttled the intentions of the sword-bearers who sought the deaths of those who were in Towers raised high. With a city in ruins and families destroyed, the imminent question began to ring around the globe: "Why?"

- The single-most motivational factor driving the sword-bearers to destroy the Towers' can be found imbedded in the minds and written upon the foreheads of the men who were dutifully assigned to commandeer those planes. According to The Prophet's recorded directives, all hypocrites, all who refuse to abide by his changed laws, shall have "death overcome them, though they are in Towers, raised high." They had tried once before. Submitting to this directive, the Prophetiers attempted to topple the Towers in 1993. Their first attempt to satisfy The Prophet's hunger for flesh in Manhattan would have to wait another eight years. The cultural lot failed in their initial endeavor to bring those buildings down upon people. Sadly, through the coordinated efforts of a man named O'sama and his cast of characters, the beast was successful in its desire to conquer on September 11, 2001. It's hard to imagine, but the Towers stood in place for only 35 years. As for the people who were in those Towers – most succumbed to the murder that originated in the dark heart of The Prophet. Nearly 3,000 people succumbed to the way of the liar on that day. These are the consequences of submission by a people who have left the straight-way and wandered off to delight in the wages of wickedness. The world would be wise to never forget. But that has become moot. The best people can do to remember that day is state that "some people did something." The intent and objective of the mission was written long ago. Thousands were murdered to advance The Prophet's promise of *peace*.

- "... has succeeded" in instituting his plan. The Prophet is the founder of the largest antichrist rebellion ever developed on earth. His Prophetiers can now be found in every nation on the planet, and they are seated amongst the most powerful of political bodies. They have infiltrated the U.S. House of Representatives and continue to be very vocal in their endeavors to destroy. From their mouths flow the venom that has been stored in their hearts since birth. The majority choose not to hear the promise of destruction that emanates from them. Instead, they lie to one another and revel in the notion that they bring about progress and a more equitable world. This is delusional. The power of delusion fueled by normalcy biases continues to advance the cause of a man that the world will soon wish they had never come to know.

- "... has destroyed mighty men and holy people." The number of people that have been murdered for the advancement of The Prophet's cause are too numerous to estimate. Thanks to 14 centuries of never-ending war, the number of men pierced by the sword of his intrigue may very well reach into the hundreds of millions. The count is known only to God. How is it that civilized nations and moral kingdoms have turned deaf ears and blind eyes to this satanic devastation? How many more terrorizing events need to occur before reasonable people finally call out this Luciferian movement and stop submitting to the progressive madness and fear of cancellation? This is rhetorical. There is a biblical answer to such a question. Just before men do the unthinkable and unleash the hell that they have spun-up in centrifuges and stored in shiny metallic canisters, the mystery of God will be accomplished. This mystery includes revealing the man of lawlessness. In so doing, the war that started in heaven will finally reached its prophetic end.

- "... has caused deceit to prosper and boasts that he is superior." For those who trust in Christ, please name the biblical prophet that Jesus recognized to be superior to the others. Of course, Jesus never held one prophet higher than another, nor did He make such a statement. But, found within the spittle of her drunken slur, the harlot will try to sell the tale that Peter is in the first position. It's hard to imagine the power of tradition and how effectively it blinds people from biblical realities. These are among the man-made traditions that lock the unfaithful bride out of the wedding! We know from Jesus' teaching that no prophet of God is superior to another – not even Peter. It was Paul who taught Peter *after* Jesus' ascension. To anchor the point, Jesus washed the feet of His bothers – both genetic and spiritual brothers. But The Prophet was above all this. After reading his testimony, it is obvious that he saw himself in the first position. He said so. He claimed that he was above them all. Assuming the role of the most high, The Prophet claimed to be above Moses, Isaiah, Jeremiah, and Daniel. That would make him above Matthew, Mark, Luke, and John. And that places The Prophet above the likes of Peter and Paul. But his most stunning claim is that he, The Prophet, was above Christ Jesus.[418] The only character in the Bible that makes such a statement is the little horn Lucifer.

- "... destroys many when they feel secure." He taught his people to make treaties with their enemies - with no intent to abide by their agreements.[302] He taught his people to befriend Christians and Jews with *only* the intent to "guard yourselves against them."[396] An ignorant, arrogant, and cowardly world refuses to accept that these tactics are still practiced in the 21st century. But these are among the deceptive tools used to subdue and defeat all who oppose The Prophet and his Prophetiers. Such are the acts of a man and nation bent on conquering. A hopeful world cannot accept that peace can never be found with him or with the people he has controlled through deceptive submissions. The Prophet's teaching that *peace* can be accomplished only by winning the war and forcing everyone into submission has already been proven false by the division within his own kingdom. Though the fractures are numerous, the two largest divisions prove that all might follow The Prophet, but not all agree on the political application of his posthumous government. It matters not whether The Prophet continues to make gains via progressive lunacy. His inhumane endeavors are utilized by his submissive loyalists against other submissive loyalists. What matters to him is the continuation of the war his father started. There comes a moment when men finally understand the meaning of God's warning that "War will continue until the end..."[43] Those who occupied the Towers in 1993 and again in 2001 likely felt a sense of security until lightning from the East was seen in the West and The Prophet's fiery destruction descended upon them.

- "... has destroyed many by peace." This contradictory statement is found within the KJV Bible. How can any man *destroy by peace*? The answer is found when one creates a movement that utilizes murder and destruction as justified means to a righteous end. For the Prophetiers, this oxymoron makes perfect sense. Recent political winds have touched on this madness with looting, rioting and the torching of businesses described as 'mostly peaceful demonstrations.' The political winds seem to have shifted, with the acceptance of lawlessness as an acceptable means to a justifiable end – with justice being the destruction and reconstruction of nations. Any nation that refuses to enforce its laws or protect its borders is soon to be a nation no longer. This is a sacrifice not of the adults but of the children who have no choice but to submit to the masses. The result of such governance means *mob-rule,* and mob rule means that the law becomes ineffective and non-existent. With the intent of mob-rule, The Prophet defined the pursuit of peace as "fighting... until all religions are only for [his god and government]."[402] Did you get that? The Prophet defined his vision of peace as fighting! Isn't it fascinating how the world has come to accept The Prophet's destructive realities as peaceful? While street urchins and recycled drug addicts feed off the planners' ridiculous claims that meat, cheese, and decaying dinosaurs are causing ever-increasing temperatures, the Prophetiers continue to expand their conquests and implement The Prophet's oxymoronic peace. This is the catalyst that ignites man's ultimate battle - the word of The Prophet. If one is looking for an inconvenient truth, this would be it! This inconceivable reality swelters and grows as a life-consuming beast in the nations surrounding Israel. With so many Prophetiers and an exponential growth rate, how could the story of man end otherwise?

- "... has taken his stand against the Prince of princes." Daniel's prophetic life and inspired writing occurred five centuries before Jesus arrived on earth. Jesus' prophetic life in the flesh and inspired Word occurred six centuries prior to The Prophet's appearance. Referred to as the preincarnate *Prince of princes,* Jesus is the Prince opposed by the stern-faced king. The written evidence is unchangeable, historically accurate, and woefully condemning to The Prophet

The Prophet

who would fill the role of the stern-faced king. He is the antichrist who opposes the Prince of princes.

- "... will be destroyed, but not by human power." Stern-face died centuries ago. Unlike Jesus, The Prophet was not crucified - he crucifies. His death is not accredited to any man or group of men. He died of a fever. Though he is long-since dead, Isaiah tells us that his torment is ongoing. But his eternal torment has only just begun! Those who know God understand that our souls are not limited to the confines of our bodies. There comes a day when the body and soul are separated. On that day, some return to our Father who sent us. Others, those who delight in wickedness, are a part of the rebellion. Those who take part in the rebellion never return to our Father above. They remain here, on earth, cast out of heaven because of the war they cherish. When God tells us that war will continue until the end, this is what He is telling us. War is what The Prophet continues to wage against the saints - God's elect. Men have not come to know Israel and the Jews over four-thousand years only to discard the lessons learned through them. Men have not come to know God's Son, a Jew, only to discard the lessons learned through Him. The elect have not come to know Paul, a Jew, only to discard his warnings about The Prophet as the man of lawlessness. Just as Isaiah and John prophesy, The Prophet will be tormented for ever and ever. His destruction and the destruction of all unrepentant souls comes about in the second death. And, in God's perfect way, destruction of men comes about at the hands of other men[438] – through the tool of the Destroyer.[432] That tool is The Prophet.[450]

Is it all just a Fairy Tale or is there now proof? When proof of God is delivered by revealing the historical identity of the false prophet, how can a single Word of the Bible be rejected as myth? The written and historical evidence defining this one man as the biblical villain is astounding! But do not be deluded into thinking that his unveiling will warm men's hearts and eliminate the threat. There are those, in fact most, whose ultimate argument is denial – vehement denial! For them, there is no mountain of evidence high enough to prove that God is God. Just imagine the reaction humanity will have when they face the evidence that The Prophet has been identified as Lucifer!

In chapter 8, Daniel writes about the latter days of man's reign, a time when men have become completely wicked. Looking around the world today, the exodus from God and His ways is startling! What most recognize as societal progress, faithful Christians see as organized wickedness. From rainbow flags (celebrating the New Sodom) to the insistence of color (racism) and men presenting as women (intentional lies) to the worship of foreign gods (queens and moon gods), the new world has collectively joined the ranks of the unapologetic Babylonians. Aside from cell phones, little has changed in 2,500 years. No degradation is considered too low for acceptance. Even college level influencers are attempting to normalize pedophilia as a natural emotional condition. Having a wife that was nine years-old, The Prophet would likely agree with today's most progressive trendsetters. And while most might argue that such a view is short-sided and hateful, the biblical reality is certain. The world has lost its sense of morality. From men named *Sally* who size themselves up against women in competitive sports to men hijacking aircraft and flying them into occupied buildings, the world has lost its way. From brothers leaving explosive pressure cookers at the feet of toddlers attending a parade, to a young couple massacring people at the pretend-husband's Christmas party, the world has fallen ill. From driving the iron teeth of trucks and automobiles onto crowded sidewalks, to shooting those who shop at a grocery store, the world has submitted to the liar. Sometimes, these are the acts of the mentally disturbed. Other times, these are the acts of those who have simply gone astray. All of it is evil. Now this evil has been transformed into the intentional acts of those who have been influenced by The Prophet. A trending new phrase is "Silence is Violence!" In this case, the phrase would prove to be accurate. Men are to remain silent no longer! Submitting to evil begets only evil.

They want you to forget. They want you to forget the hijackers of 9/11 and the Army Major at Ft Hood. They want you to forget the couple in San Bernardino and the lone shooter in Boulder. They want the world to forget the lone-wolf in Orlando and the organized group in Paris. They want you to forget because the lines that divide evil from the mentally disturbed and the criminally submissive have become blurred. People can no longer see where one becomes another because they all overlap. It was a submissive psychologist in Ft. Hood who shot forty-six people. It was two brothers in Boston who killed or injured 263 people. It was an unmarried couple in San Bernardino who shot thirty-six people and a married man in Orlando who shot 102 people. The hijackers were all submissive soldiers of the same foreign god and they killed nearly 3,000 people. Sometimes, the truth becomes too difficult to navigate, leaving only speculation and narrative as the apologetic defaults. The Prophet struggled with mental illness[580] and still became the admired model for murderers. And now we have an answer as to why those men destroyed the Towers. We have an answer as to why the Major killed and injured those soldiers at Ft. Hood. We know why the couple killed and maimed so many in San

The Prophet

Bernardino. We know why the brothers created terror in Boston. Now, we know why the Prophetiers do what they do. They do what they do because it is what The Prophet did.

Daniel was given a glimpse into this time in God's story of man. It is now that we are beginning to see what has been standing before us for so long. There has risen a king. This king has declared himself to be the perfect man and the most worthy to serve God. Daniel describes him as a man of fierce countenance (of stern look and behavior) and one capable of understanding and delivering dark and deceptive sentences.[36] Twenty-five-hundred years have passed since Daniel wrote about the imminent arrival of such a man. Enough time has elapsed for him to appear and carry out his furious aggressions. It makes sense that such a man's followers would be among the rebellious, those who refuse to love the truth. Since truth is not the binding tie in today's world, it seems fitting that he would be revealed at this time. Men have set aside the truth for something much more inclusive. Lost in their own desires, men have let go of God and grabbed ahold of a poisonous vine. Often, they live life in a manner that feeds off emotional distress that, left unattended or otherwise encouraged, nourishes a pathway to mental illness. With enough support and increasing numbers, mental and emotional illness becomes manifest as the new normal. For this reason, societal rationalizations dictate that men are to be addressed as women. It has become the new norm to demand that daughters are addressed as sons. Perceived bullying over similar emotional disorders has become a license to turn our centers of learning into battle zones. Emotional distress and mental illness each play a part in most criminal and immoral acts. When distress and mental illness are accepted as the new normal, then the evil that accompanies the disorders becomes normal as well.

When a man is raised from birth with persistent lessons of duty whispered into his ear, teaching him that he must fight for his god, he will fight for that god. If a man is taught that he will attain paradise for dying in the way of fighting for such a god, then he will die in fighting for that god. When a man is raised with the knowledge that lawbreakers must be murdered, he will murder the perceived lawbreakers. There is little mystery here. For these reasons, men will continue to fight and murder in a misled call of duty. This is not fighting to *preserve* a way of life. It is fighting to *institute* a way of life. These things do not happen because of God's will, fear, PTSD, gender identity confusion, social rejection, or school bullying. This is the result of generations caught in rebellion – people and parents turning away from God. Rebellion stems from poor parenting or no parenting at all. It takes modeling to be a parent. When one models a bad parent, the result comes as no surprise. The Bible relies heavily upon the idea of parenting. From

Moses and the Ten Commandments to The Prophet and his rejection of the commands, the Bible tells us how good is displaced by evil and how evil became good.

The world fights generations of rebellion today. Gathered as a mob, street creatures demand that law and law enforcement be abolished. They have been told that they are fighting for social justice – something that must be accomplished free from the law and law-abiding citizens! Since when has man found betterment in himself by dragging society down to the level of a street creature? What would our communities look like if we all set fire to our neighbors' workplaces, homes, and businesses? Remember Portland and Seattle? Remember when these cities were travel destinations and home to beauty and promise? Not anymore! Like New York and Chicago, these places have become reminiscent of the trash that lines their streets, alleyways, and rail yards. This is the result of defunding the police with District Attorneys and Attorneys General ignoring theft, assault, burglary, and trespassing. Previously known for fresh fish, free love and sight-seeing, the city of San Francisco is now known for its street feces, discarded hypodermic needles, and street-crime. That once beautiful city is now a dumping ground for outlaws and a cesspool of lawlessness. Its residents are fleeing. In the mind of a street creature, looting (stealing), killing (revolution), and destruction (arson) are all a means to an end. The Prophet thought the same way. In the minds of modern revolutionaries, these godless actions have somehow become the righteous approach to revolutionary change. To them, the methods of evil are the pathways to reform. The dark streets of racism have now become the highways of enlightened freedoms. According to the academics, the only lives that matter today are exclusively Black. They present as modern thinkers, but this type of thought and action is nothing new. God's people have suffered under seven generations and kingdoms of oppositional hordes who believed that only their kind mattered. From the Egyptians to the Assyrians; from the Assyrians to the Babylonians; from the Babylonians to the Medes and Persians; from the Medes and Persians to the Greeks; from the Greeks to the Romans; and from the Romans to the Prophetiers – all have taken the stance that only their lives mattered. Why would we expect anything different from the progressive-minded do-gooders today? When you tell people that they are victims and that their anger is just, all you get in return is angry people. This is a simple strategy to harness the power and money of those who are continually told that they should be angry. Barack Hussein did it. The Prophet did it. The Prophetiers do it to the Palestinians today.

It was just twenty years ago, a single generation back, when the bitterness of racism and lawlessness had been nearly erased by the sweetness of equality, law, and order.

Today, the sweetness has been replaced by the bitterness of racism, lawlessness, and disorder. These are the lies that control people through fear. These are the ways of the Prophet. He did this. God commands men not to murder. The Prophet directs his people to murder. God commands men not to steal. The Prophet directs his people to steal. God commands men to avoid the ways of the Destroyer. The Prophet teaches his people to imitate and submit to the ways of the Destroyer. Society suffers under the manipulative accusations of its lawless rulers.

Again, this is nothing new. Lawlessness invites lawlessness. It should surprise no one that the two modern revolutions are combining strengths. The growing mass of people who live by the lawlessness of The Prophet are joining arms with the group who declares that only Black lives matter. They are driven by like minds and the words of a man who insisted that "I have been commanded to continue fighting against people until they say, 'There is no God but [the god I have introduced]; whoever says this will have his property and his life safe unless there is a due against him and his reckoning is with [the new god].'"[6] In order to keep their property and their lives, all that men have to do is say what The Prophet tells them to say. As the model of perfection, who is to disagree? Those who disagree face the point of the sword. Even the Prophetiers who do not actually swing the sword must support those who do. This is their law.[370] Lawlessness is lawlessness. People who do not like living under law enforcement are the same people who do not like living under the limits of the law. The Prophet was of the same nature. The Mosaic law was not a good fit for a thief. He changed the laws to suit his own fancies – stealing, killing and destruction. Sound familiar? Politicians might clean it up and make rebellion sound like a cornucopia of social justice, but it's little more than the crap-bucket of mob rule. The bigger the mob, the greater the frenzy. Anyone who thinks this is a ridiculous summation of current events need only to immerse themselves in the next 'peaceful protest' and unfurl a banner that reads: "All Lives Matter!" Your name will be less-than honorably mentioned on the next national news cast.

Like any serious politician, The Prophet polished his approach. He declared that there is no compulsion to make someone act or believe in any certain way. Then, he tells his suiters to murder anyone who creates mischief in the land by refusing to comply with his laws. For his people, time stands still. His orders have not changed. In densely populated areas the belief is so profound that people cannot buy or sell without utilizing the faith balance he spoke about. No faith in The Prophet and rejection of his laws means no buying or selling. Most will recognize these areas as "No Go Zones." For the non-believer, The Prophet's main temple and its surrounding city are "No Go Zones."

Attempts have been made to create the same conditions on the Temple Mount, but the Prophetiers have had to settle with a lesser desolation. The zone has been forced to relent and offer access to the property with the agreement there would be no praying to the God of Israel. Such is the law on the Temple Mount. It makes perfect sense – doesn't it? Their ways are consistent with the ways of the newly accepted street creatures. The streets are accessible with the understanding that you must submit to the beasts. No matter how one spins it – stealing, killing, and destroying are not the acts consistent with the worship of God. But these are the acts and the ways of The Prophet.

As a society, we don't have to look too far to recognize furious aggressions that have been masked by reasonable terms such as *a woman's choice* and *equality*. These are basic rights that should be respected and protected. They should also be adhered to as long as they do not trample on God's Laws. Murdering a mother's vulnerable infant is not a viable *choice*. Terrified women and abandoned girls often suffer the mental anguish and consequences of poor choices and abuse when making decisions on the baby they carry. With furious aggression, the child loses. No matter the cause or reasoning, the outcome is tragic. Utilizing similar fear tactics, The Prophet instills a sense of loss with his people to rationalize murder as a defense mechanism. His opposition to God's law that opposes murder then becomes rational. Discarding equality for the sake of a single color or belief is not a viable *choice*. Street mobs and The Prophet disagree. The same argument applies to furious aggressions that are pursued daily in the names of justice, human rights, victimization, and peace. *Peace?* There is war and there is peace. Never do the two terms equate. But The Prophet teaches that war is a prerequisite to peace. This method has been in effect for 1,400 years and the conflicts continue to grow. If men were to have listened to God and pursued life to the full by abiding to God's Laws, there would be no reason for war. See the problematic contradiction here? There was war in heaven. Satan caused that mess. There is war on earth. The speaking image of Satan, Lucifer, caused this mess. He masks his war on earth as a noble duty by "fighting in defense of…" This is an old game. Satan created it, the harlot relied upon it, and The Prophet perfected it. Was the harlot justified by her lethal institutions of Inquisitions and bloody Crusades? No, God is specific in His warnings against stealing and killing in His name. 'Those who kill thinking they are doing a service to God… do not know the Father or me [Jesus].' Those who steal under the guise of *defense* and participate in the gathering of *spoils of war* remain as they were - thieves. People who kill as a service to God do not know God. Jesus introduced light and changed the world when He taught men to drop their stones of righteous judgment. The Prophet doused the light and put the world in reverse when he instructed his people to murder those who resisted his new ways. Killing in defense of The Prophet is murder. This demonstrates the juxtaposition of the Christ and the antichrist. The Christ agrees with His Father - men shall not murder. The antichrist agrees with his father - men shall demonstrate their dutiful submission through murder.

The number of furious aggressions that have been conducted over the centuries in the name of The Prophet and his god are not going to be reduced with reason or ended by debate. With the big three forbidden acts of stealing, killing, and destroying already woven into the fabric of The Prophet's book-driven nation, calling for a change in his laws would prove to be futile. These three *righteous acts of barbarism* have become manifested in the adoration of the man who introduced them. They are anchored in the minds and written upon the foreheads of those who submit their lives and deeds to the conqueror. They worship as he commands them to worship. As ridiculous as this might sound, the political world has progressed into a cultural haven that defends these warriors with something more powerful than diplomatic immunity. They are protected by the Constitution. Thanks to this misused protection, the sound of The Prophet's harps will soon ring out in Minneapolis. A world lulled into being deaf and blind also accepts the destructive taunts of a modern pack as they implement their policies of lawlessness. With a new horde of stoned skateboarders, dubious drug addicts, no-bail outlaws, gangland criminals, and racist street creatures – a newly formed squad has been gathered to nefariously influence reasonable people and convince an otherwise intelligent nation that abolishing the police would lead to a village of harmony and glee! Look at the destruction they have managed to inflict in just a few years. San Francisco, Los Angeles, Portland, and Seattle are no longer places of envy and Ports of Call. They have submitted to the inevitable decline of society that arises from the institution of lawlessness - assault, murder, homelessness, drug abuse, unchecked mental illness, and a general acceptance of filth. New York, Chicago, Denver, Minneapolis, and other thriving cities have been gobbled up by the venom of similar vipers who have each reverted back to times of lawlessness and decay. Any society that refuses to institute consequences for lawlessness will find itself in the dung-heap of history. Why work for a dollar when you can simply take it away from another? With street-mobs sculpting the narrative and instituting destruction on such a rapid and massive scale, imagine the power that a prophet of God could have over billions of lost and unbelieving people! Could there be a better way to lead a rebellion against God than to regurgitate and act out on the dark sentences that were whispered into The Prophet's ear by a murderous source? In just the last two decades, reasonable people have elected those who look away from the looting and theft that now occurs daily. They argue in support of those who set fires and destroy businesses. If otherwise reasonable and free people can justify such lawlessness - imagine what billions of unreasonable and submissive people might be capable of doing! The Towers come to mind. What possible motivations might exist that could encourage so many people to demolish the Twin Towers[390] – those that were filled with ordinary people? What depth of demonic hatred could or would drive men to place pressure-cooker bombs at the feet of families who were committing the horrific sin of cheering-on runners in a marathon or execute workmates at a Christmas party?[402]

> **"And his power shall be mighty, but not by his own power: and he shall destroy wonderfully, and shall prosper, and practise, and shall destroy the mighty and the holy people. And through his policy also he shall cause craft to prosper in his hand; and he shall magnify himself in his heart, and by peace shall destroy many: he shall also stand up against the Prince of princes; but he shall be broken without hand."**
>
> **– Daniel 8:24-25 KJV**

Though it might seem unreasonable to argue against the fact that a man who speaks such dark sentences is *not* a man of callous intrigue, most will make the attempt. But the words he spoke were not of his own making nor were they the creation of his own mind. None of this came from his own doing. He had the assistance of another.[39] The power with which he spoke originated in another. The Prophet orally delivered the words and commands that were pressed upon his mind. He spoke like the dragon.[448] The Prophet is commonly mentioned in tandem with his father. The murderous nature of the pair is made evident by the things he said and the things he had others record. Murder is an act that finds its origin in the dragon – he was a murderer from the beginning.[191] The master sinner is and always has been the father of lies. He who speaks like the father of lies, speaks like the dragon. With these lies being repeated ad nauseum, the unchecked narrative quickly becomes part of one's native language. This is the language that unites the dragon to his slaves, those who have embraced murder as an act of perfection. Like The Prophet, they, too, speak like the dragon. Though the words might sound prophetic, harmonious, poetic, and godly - they are the sound of the harps[135] that encourage murder and theft. The actions of these harps oppose everything that was previously called 'God' or worshiped as God.

The Prophet

The world has long been told to expect The Prophet's unveiling. He will appear in lockstep with the god he represents[509] – this is one of the five pillars of his teaching.[314] With his god comes a new name. The importance of this cannot be overemphasized. Those who lack knowledge in the matter will argue that the name of The Prophet's god is nothing more than a translation. But The Prophet says otherwise.[239] Within the first few sentences of The Prophet's dictated dragon-speak is the declaration that his god now has a proper name. It is from this proper-named god that The Prophet gets his power.[59] By its very definition, The Prophet was a master of intrigue - he who makes secret plans to do something illicit or detrimental. Utilizing dark and evil sentences, this stern-faced king (he who lacks grace) ultimately instituted murder as the single-most devastating weapon in his kingdom's arsenal. The biblical word tells us that he would destroy wonderfully[38] and cause astounding devastation.[39] He has achieved both in grand fashion. Daniel tells us that The Prophet will prosper and succeed in whatever he does. This, too, he has done. We are told that he will destroy the mighty men and the holy people. The reader can reasonably assume that the *holy people* Daniel refers to are the people who were led by God's prophets - Christians and Jews - the people of the Bible. As for *the mighty people*, history reveals that Daniel was telling us about the kings and kingdoms subdued by this conqueror and his armies. But there have many who have done these very things. What is so exclusive about this one man? What differentiates him from all the others? The answers can be found within the dragon-like deceptions within his book. This was his testimony. It is this man's prophecy-fulfilling words and deeds that nurture and feed his people. His acts and commands continue to be the factors that drive his prosperous deceit. By The Prophet's own hand, he demonstrated the influential power of lethal disciplines within the rebellious brood he created and directed. Of the many things that separate The Prophet from those who brutalized before him, few aspects are as compelling as is his continuing ability to 'destroy many by peace.' Why would the world expect anything less from the nefarious thief who was certain to oppose the Son of God? An obvious hint was given - that such a man would appear under the cloak of prophethood to institute lessons and acts that God forbids. This is the work of the self-professed, wayward prophet. In cringe-worthy fashion, the Prophetiers emulate his behavior and advance his ways of righteous destruction while declaring that the defense of their faith is a means of peace. Because of their loyalty to The Prophet's newfound definition of 'peace,' many more will be destroyed. What most people refuse to recognize and wholly fail to understand is that peace is to come *only* after his coercive aggressions and lethal judgements are instituted as law by *all* nations. It is then and only then that there will be no reason to fight in defense of the faith that flirts with and endorses murder. Until that day, the war continues. The promised end of hostilities comes if and when the threat of the sword becomes so great that no one will remain to oppose the Prophetiers and all religions will find themselves worshiping only his foreign god.[425] If this were to happen, all governing bodies would then revert to The Prophet's new laws and the oppression of the holy people (Christians and Jews), those understood to 'commit mischief in the land,'[393] would result in genocide. If The Prophet were to succeed, the game of life would offer only five options - submission to The Prophet, murder, crucifixion, dismemberment, and/or imprisonment. What an odd kind of peace he has introduced! But the fantastical vision of the conquering prophet is shattered by the reality that his kingdom is hopelessly divided. Victory for his nation can never be realized. His own people are split into two warring halves. Each is a vine of its own political growth. Like the Saudis and the Persians, each lies to the other.

Growth of The Prophet's new belief system relies upon his dark sentences and the ability to enforce his rules and regulations. With centuries of fortification, proliferating instruction, and a maniacal eagerness to institute the five options, his companions see to it that the war escalates, and their newfound 'peace' causes the continued destruction of many more. Because of the new laws, everyone is a player – though most would prefer to abstain from the game. He makes it impossible to simply avoid participation. For women and girls, this harsh reality is a never-ending nightmare. The reset in Afghanistan offers sufficient evidence to this charge. It appears that the war on women has spilled out of the confines of The Prophet's kingdom and found its way onto new battlefields – with biological men cancelling the grand accomplishments women have made and wholeheartedly deserve. Such are the distinguishing characteristics of evil men and the woeful expansion of oppression that The Prophet previously accomplished. Indicative of these accomplishments is the history proving his opposition to the Prince of princes and the continuing war against God's holy people. Merely rejecting the Father and Son offers evidence as to how The Prophet spoke out against the biblical God. He spoke out against the biblical prophets. He spoke out against the Christ and everything that is called *God*. But there's more to this! Opposing the Prince of princes is a golden nugget when identifying the lawless one. These prophetic certainties preceded their fulfilled histories. Those who know God, also understand that there is hope in such tragedy. Hope is found in truth. Truth is found in His Word. The Word was with God from the beginning. He, the Word, is how and why we know God.

Hope can be found in Daniel's promise that stern-face's murderous endeavors will come to an end, and he will be destroyed. In fact, The Prophet is dead. He did not die at the hands of other men. Illness overcame him. His fate is scripted and cannot be changed. He and his companions perish in the fire that they cause in The Prophet's name. We know that they are capable of such horrors. Motivated by his dark sentences, the Prophetiers were successful in their second attempt to bring down the Towers in Manhattan. They needed nothing more than the words of The Prophet and a few submissive slaves to bring about that horrific moment in time. To them, it was just another battle in defense of their faith. They are intent on winning the world's longest war and they will use whatever means necessary to be crowned victorious. This is bad news when the moment arrives, and the unveiling of their prophet becomes known to all men. The method of man's fiery destruction has been developed, proliferated, assembled, packaged, and warehoused throughout the world. It's held by many nations - not the least of which is Persia.

In Daniel's day, the Prince of princes was promised to appear as *Immanuel*. He had not yet walked the earth. Five centuries would pass before men would come to understand that Daniel's *Prince of princes* (Immanuel) would prove to be *Jesus*, the promised Messiah. Another six centuries would roll away before Jesus' nemesis, this messenger of the dragon, would rise and bring about his oppressive aggressions and destructive peace. Over the centuries, few of God's prophets fully understood the visions they were driven to share - this included Daniel. As Peter teaches us; "No prophecy of Scripture came about by the prophet's own interpretation. For prophecy never had its origin in the will of man, but men spoke from God as they were carried along by the Holy Spirit."[350] Such was the case for Daniel. He did not, and likely could not, interpret the prophecy by his own accord. He was not to interpret his visions in any manner other than the way that the Spirit intended. Daniel was tasked with recording his visions exactly as he saw them while he was carried along by the Holy Spirit. Now, looking back 2,500 years and recalling countless events that have transpired since the days of Daniel, a match can be made between historical events and Daniel's prophetic visions. These matches can be further heaped upon the mountain of evidence already compiled against the man who spoke on behalf of the masquerading light.

Daniel's prophetic writing about The Prophet's life and accomplishments does not end in chapter 8. His visions about this stern-faced menace become more and more evident with the application of historical occurrences. Given the ability to describe specific traits, Daniel further separates this vicious king from the world's gallery of other murderous authorities. Thanks to genuine prophets of God, the actions of the false prophet are listed and readily available for those who wish to finally see him for who he was. Exalting himself above all others, this masterful deceiver immerses himself into a pool of contempt. Brilliant he was not. Boastful, ignorant, and arrogant he was. Believing himself to be exalted, the king did as he pleased.

The Prophet

Ronald B. Stetton

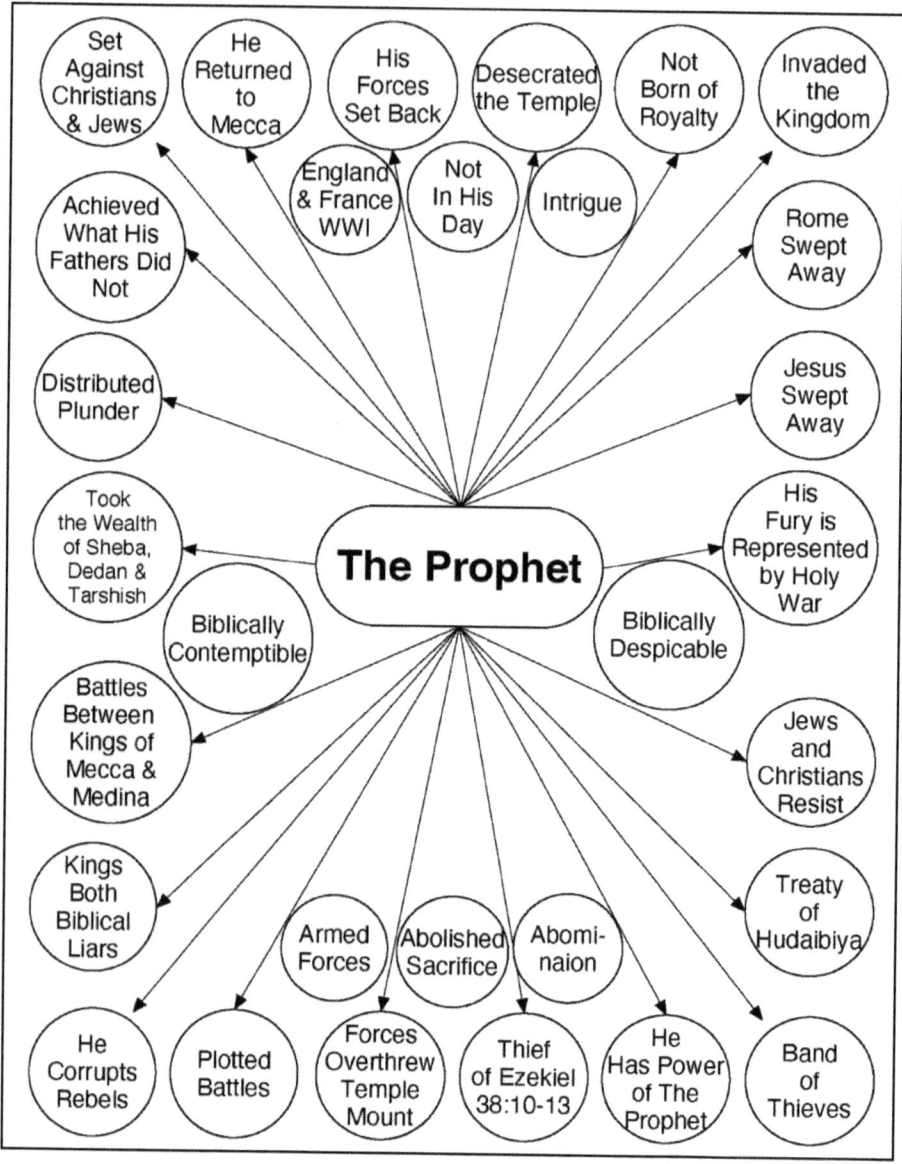

The Prophet

Chapter 4

After the Tax Collector

Daniel's Warning on the Man's Appearance After the Tax Collector (11:20-33)

One of the most frustrating reads of the Bible can be found in chapter 11 of Daniel. In such, Daniel follows the direction of divine inspiration and puts pen to paper telling us about a futuristic succession of kings. Keep in mind that the prophetic account envisioned by Daniel was experienced and recorded approximately 2,700 years ago. So, the succession of kings is now a matter of history – all of it happening in the past 27 centuries. In that time, Daniel's visions have all materialized. It has all been accomplished, but the world refuses to see it that way. Thanks (in part) to the spectacular power of delusion, most of the elect still await the physical appearance of the horned-one to fulfill these dark prophecies. Most readers, even some of God's most faithful followers, dismiss the historical evidence identifying the man and the written evidence verifying that he has already accomplished most of his tasks.

Described as *kings of the North* and *kings of the South*, Daniel wrote about the battles that would come about in and around the land of Jerusalem. Of these battles, he wrote from the time of his prophethood until the time of the end. Understanding these entries takes a bit of patience on the part of the reader. Not only does Daniel's vision of the kings coincide with the geographical aspects of North and South, but he also immerses the reader in the use of pronouns such as - *him, his* and *he*. Writing in such a manner can be very frustrating for the reader. The use of pronouns yields an endless number of possibilities when telling an historical tale that spans a period of 2700 years, encompasses five major earthly kingdoms, and includes multiple kings – each who were not crowned kings as most might otherwise imagine. The vague references make Daniel's writing somewhat tedious at times, but there is light ahead. The light comes with history. Prior to knowing the identity of the dragon's mouthpiece, identifying these kings was no simple task. But circumstances have changed! We now have a grand suspicion as to The Prophet's identity. His armed forces have risen to desecrate the Temple Mount and set up the abomination that causes desolation. The Prophet is the last of the kings listed in Daniel 11, and he has succeeded in pulling off a delusion so grand that most people will consider it to be preposterous. He has accomplished that which none of his fathers nor his forefathers were able to do before him. His unimaginable reign as king is 1,400 years old and ongoing.

Let's refer to the past and review what has been learned...

Daniel offers the reader a multitude of would-be future figureheads and the kingdoms they would develop and lead. For Daniel, what began as prophecy and recorded with pen and parchment has since become a part of man's past. The biblical community has largely understood the commentary of Daniel's 11th chapter to be the historical struggles between kingdoms leading up to the Roman Empire and Caesar's infamous implementation of taxation upon its citizens. His method of taxing Rome's occupants would lead to its grand expansion, enrichment of the politicians, and support of its massive military machine. Jesus addresses Caesar's taxation in His reference to the image of Caesar on a Roman coin.[219] Keep in mind that Daniel was an Old Testament prophet of God, who lived during the Babylonian period, long before there was a Roman Empire or ruling Caesars. Yet, the history leading to Rome's rule is universally accepted and recognized as accurate in its rise and fall. But a peculiar twist in historical recollection softens the crash of Rome's fall. People, particularly eschatologists, tend to overlook history and the massive nation that found its beginning in the dying days of the Roman Empire - the common thought being that some sort of *reborn* Roman Empire was to somehow materialize in *our* coming future. Theatrical examples of such a belief can be found in movies like *Damien*, a fictional tale of the birth of the antichrist who was born in the backdrop of the previously formed European Union. In the movie, that union was portrayed to be the reformed Roman Empire. These are the kinds of fantasies that men create when they attempt to build a future scenario to fit biblical prophecies, rather than apply historical realities. The kingdom that followed Rome was not something of Rome's own reformation. The kingdom that formed in the wake of Rome's demise was a nation founded by an illiterate thief. Though the nation has been tasked and weakened many times over, it exists in this moment, and it is as powerful today as it ever has been. It was founded by The Prophet – he who fulfilled all the things of the contemptible thief who rose to power as a self-proclaimed prophet of God. He is the man who founded the seventh kingdom - that which followed the fall of Rome and the Romans.

With a few like-minded thieves, The Prophet's rebellion expanded rapidly over 20 years and culminated at the time of his death with an audience of 120,000 men and their families.[94] That was almost 1,400 years ago. In the centuries since his final address, the number of his loyalists has steadily grown and now amounts to approximately

1,800,000,000 people. The contemptible person who replaced Rome and its many Caesars is now a matter of record. Remember, Daniel wrote about a king whose reign would last until the war ended. At times, when referring to "he," Daniel was very well referring to The Prophet's continuing revolutionary movement. A glimpse of this pronoun can be found in the phrase "at the appointed time, *he* will invade..." (Da 11:29). The history of his rule and kingdom can be traced as an accurate assessment of Daniel's warning – beginning with verse 11:21.

- The biblical Tax Collector is emphasized during Roman rule[332]

- Rome collapsed under its own weight - it was not destroyed in battle

- Historically, the contemptible person who succeeded Rome's many Caesars was the stern-faced king described in Daniel, chapter eight[414]

- He was not born into royalty.[316] He was orphaned by a single mother, and he had little known education. The world agrees that he could neither read nor write[268]

- The stern-faced king invaded the kingdoms of Sheba and Dedan[279] long after the resettled Jews had been driven from Jerusalem[224]

- He seized the kingdom through intriguing deceptions that he called 'visions of prophethood'[305]

- Building his empire on a foundation of war,[252] this new king created many enemies.[253] With these enemies he agreed to and struck numerous treaties.[275] However, his treaties were disingenuous by design.[406] As is his teaching, these deceptive practices were a means to an end. They were intended to suspend the conflict or conflicts until his forces could manage a strategic advantage[279] – much like today's Persians and their nuclear intentions. Once the advantage was gained, the conflict would then resume. He justifies lies and deceptions as practical means in defense of his cause. The tactic is used so often that it has been given a name and defined purpose[255]

- With only a few like-minded thieves, this non-royal king began his rise to power[254]

- Unlike his fathers before him, The Prophet abandoned nearly 2,000 years of written, prophetic testimony about the God of Abraham and set about to change the record. To successfully execute his diabolical plan, he declared that his god and the God of Abraham were one and the same. At the time of his death, there were 120,000 men and their families who could not tell their right hand from their left hand.[208] They could not differentiate the God of Israel from the god that this man had introduced. If one was to ask about the difference between gods, the likely response would include a variation of 'There is only one God.' The statement is accurate. There is only one God. But the response is incomplete. Stating the obvious, that "There is only one God," conveniently neglects Daniel's warning about the imminent introduction of a *foreign god*,[58] Paul's teaching about the *masquerading light*,[538] and John's warning about the fiery angel[433] – aka *Satan*

- The contemptible person's story begins with his plundering of Sheba, Dedan, and the merchants of the Tarshish. As his own testimony reveals, The Prophet stole from the people in these lands and distributed their wares and wealth amongst his followers[404]

- His heart was set against the holy covenant – that which had long been completely written and delivered as *God's Word*. The Prophet set out to reject the long-since completed testimonies of God's prophets, declaring their testimony to have been somehow tainted over time[229]

- His armed battles are numerous and mostly recorded within his own little book.[318] Particularly interesting was a battle that did not go as planned and he was struck in the face by a rock, thereby breaking his teeth. A rumor quickly spread of his death[259]

- In what can only be described as a river of blood and a gruesome stack of bodies, The Prophet participated in the beheadings of hundreds of captured Jews.[294] This recorded event came about because The Prophet believed that the Jewish tribe betrayed him, which led to battlefield setbacks that nearly cost him his life. This tribe of Jews is among the people who participate in the holy covenant and who are prophesied to receive God's inheritance.[114] In his murderous rampage, The Prophet certainly did not let his captives go home[142]

- To understand the discussions about *covenants* it is important to note that God has formed a covenant with His people.[112] In a like manner, *the masquerading light* has formed a covenant with his people.[257] These are two very different covenants. The associated war between the two bodies is now self-evident. God's covenant is holy. A reminder of His covenant is given to us in the way of a rainbow.[99] Though this might be a bit of a departure from the current subject-matter, it's important for the reader to understand the contempt that some people demonstrate when they display a rainbow flag and the rebellion it now represents. The cost of such a demonstration is eternally tragic.[479] Whether it is by way of the rainbow flag or the carved images of the moon and stars, today's use of these symbolic idols demonstrates how man's rebellion against God is presented in many forms and ideologies

- Just 53 years after The Prophet's death, his armed forces descended upon Jerusalem to desecrate the Temple grounds. It was on the Temple Mount that they dedicated to their prophet and god an existing structure. The year was 685 A.D.[493] This just happens to be 1,290[567] biblical years after the destruction of the first Jewish Temple in 586 B.C. The abomination that stands there today is certainly a cause of desolation. Christian and Jewish prayers are now forbidden and outlawed on the Temple Mount. Hence, the worship of a foreign god - by way of a temple, shrine, and wayward prophet - is the abomination that causes the desolation. At the time of this writing, the abomination that continues to cause desolation had been dedicated 1,335[568] years prior

- Faithful Christians and lawful Jews know the prophetic, biblical God. This small group of saints firmly resist The Prophet and the abomination that has long since been set up on the Temple Mount

History is a sound witness. Everything written above has historical reference or is currently ongoing. What could be more of an abomination than man's misguided worship of a foreign god, his false prophet, and their symbolic images adorning the Temple Mount? This collective abomination has been raised upon the ashes of what used to be the Jewish Temple in Jerusalem. During His physical presence on earth, Jesus taught and prayed on that very ground.

Daniel's prophetic tale of kings begins 2,700 years ago with the Persians and ends with the king who leads today's largest army. To tell this prophetic tale, there is a risk of boring the reader into a hypnotic sleep, but the history that fulfills it makes the moment somewhat remarkable! Daniel, the prophet who lived during the destruction of the first Jewish Temple, offers us the history of kings and kingdoms from Darius the Mede (the original king of Babylon) to this world's final king (the newest and final king of Babylon)

- he who is currently enthroned and worshiped on the Temple Mount. The fulfilled history follows. If this type of historical referencing causes one's eyelids to become heavy, feel free to skip it. The outcome remains unchanged. For those who might be fascinated by biblical history, give it a read. Daniel 11, pulled from notes of NIV Study Bible...

Daniel tells us about three Persian kings that followed Darius the Mede (539-530 BC) -- Cambyses (530-522 B.C.), Gaumata (522 B.C.), and Darius I (522-486 B.C.). History gives us the fourth king, Xerxes (486-465 B.C.) Xerxes attempted to conquer Greece in 480 B.C. Daniel prophecies about Alexander the Great (336-323 B.C.) and how all his victories and accomplishments led to nothing as his massive empire was felled by the infighting of his sons; Ptolemy, Seleucus, Lysimachus (Modern Turkey) and Cassander (Central Greece). We're told how the alliance of Ptolemy I Soter (the Ptolemies of Egypt-South) and Seleucus I Nicator (the Seleucids of Syria-North) was preceded by one man (Seleucus I), he being a commander for the other. Further, we know that the daughter (Berenice) of Ptolemy II became a wife to the grandson of a Seleucus I (Antiochus II), but Antiochus' former wife (Laodice) conspired to have Antiochus and Berenice murdered. Berenice's father, Ptolemy II, died in the same season that Laodice conspired murder. Bernice's brother (Ptolemy III), son to Ptolemy II, did away with Laodice and attacked Seleucus II Callinicus (246-226 B.C.) of Syria. The "fortress" spoken of is likely Seleucia, the Port of Antioch, or Antioch itself. Three centuries later, Jesus' followers would first be called "Christians" in this city.

In his victory, Ptolemy III carried off the spoils of war - including images of Syrian gods, images of Egyptian gods (previously taken from Egypt by the Persian Cambyses in 525 B.C.) – returning them to Egypt. In the following years, Seleucus III Ceranus (226-223 B.C.) and Antiochus III (223-187 B.C.), sons of Seleucus II, assembled a great army and swept across Ptolemy's army at Raphia, a city on Israel's current southern-most coastal border. But Antiochus was not finished. As the invader, Antiochus III captured Jerusalem [2 Maccabees 5:11-14]. He gathered a large army, including some of the rebellious Jews of that region, and once again battled Ptolemy and his army. It is said that the brothers Seleucus III and Antiochus III lost nearly 10,000 men in the battle. It was this battle that Antiochus III lost to Ptolemy IV Philopator (221-203 B.C.) in the year 217 B.C. But the fighting continued...

Antiochus IV Epiphanes (187-164 B.C.), son to Antiochus III, once again mustered up a huge army (again including rebellious Jews) and, after several years, set themselves upon the Ptolemies. The Ptolemaic General Scopas stopped the

The Prophet

rebellious Jews, but he could not stop the war machine of Antiochus III. In the year 200 B.C., the Mediterranean Port of Sidon fell the king of the north – Antiochus IV. It was Antiochus IV who did as he pleased. He established himself in Jerusalem and upon the Temple Mount. Like so many before him, and so many since him, he attempted to eradicate the Jewish faith completely… This is the Bible's recurring theme.[356] This theme is again the objective of The Prophet - the last king of Daniel 11. Antiochus stained the Temple and set himself up as the Most High. But his godly reign was short-lived. Judas Maccabeus gathered an army against Antiochus and rededicated the Jewish Temple in December of 165 B.C. This was the beginning of Hanukkah and the formation of the Festival of Lights.[195] Though the reader will find no biblical reference to the Roman holiday known as Christmas, he or she will find reference to Jesus recognizing the Festival of Lights (Feast of Dedication) otherwise known as Hanukkah.

It was Antiochus III who gave his daughter, Cleopatra I (sister of Antiochus IV), to Ptolemy V in 194 BC. He attempted to overthrow the kingdom. But again, his efforts would fall flat. Antiochus failed. He turned his attention to Asia Minor (Greece-Turkey). It was there that Antiochus met with a Roman envoy named Gaius Popillius Laenas. Laenas attempted to end the wars between the Seleuicids (North) and the Ptolemies (South). He specifically warned Antiochus to withdraw his armies from Egypt and Cyprus or face war with Rome. Antiochus withdrew his troops. Humiliated, Antiochus turned back to the north only to fall ill and literally tumble from his chariot, mutilating his body [2 Maccabees 9:5-9].

Whew! Did you absorb all of that? The historians among us are likely to get lost in the haze of what is written above and insist on arguing about its inaccuracies. To them, we wish the best of luck! Stepping outside of that argument, we recognize that Daniel's written warning of prophecy was fulfilled by the kings of the region in the centuries that followed. The real story is what happened next. Antiochus' successor was a Roman! Collectively, these Romans are known as *the Twelve Caesars*. Caesar was a tax collector. He built his empire on other people's money. There are many biblical references to Caesar's tax collectors in the time that Jesus walked the earth. Some of those despised collectors became disciples of Christ. When asked if it was right to pay taxes to Caesar…

"Jesus replied: 'Show me the coin used for paying the tax. Whose portrait is this? And who's inscription?'"

"Caesar's," they replied.

"In response, Jesus said: 'Give to Caesar what is Caesar's, and to God what is God's.'"[569]

Caesar sent out many tax collectors to collect the money to 'maintain the royal splendor.' This leaves little doubt about the identity of the man in Daniel 11:20. Tax collection is what funded Rome's government and military. Without question, Rome and its emperors are known to have had grand militaries and booming economic growth - most of it rooted in and funded by taxing all who resided in the Empire. Among the most culturally rich empires ever built, Rome was the pinnacle of kingdoms - until it collapsed. This takes us to Daniel 11:21. That is where The Prophet's story begins.

Collapsing under the weight of its own insolence, the kingdom of Rome (and its many Caesar's) was succeeded by a contemptible person – he who snubbed the biblical God. He is not recognized as being born among royalty. In fact, he is known to have been destitute and lacking any form of education. He never acquired the basic skills of reading or writing. His birth has no grand story behind it. Like so many at the time, he was born to a single, widowed mother. We are speaking about the birth of The Prophet. He is the man who boasts of invading the unwalled villages of the resettled Jews in Dedan, which is today's Northern Arabia. He readily admits to attacking a peaceful and unsuspecting people[406] - all of them living without gates and bars.[88] Historical evidence and religious texts verify that Dedan was seized long ago, through the diabolical intrigue of a contemptible person who rationalized his actions as those of a prophet of God. The same evidence also verifies that the massive army of the Roman Empire was swept away before him. It broke under the corrosive weight of its nation's own corruption – a tragically familiar theme among nations. The kingdom simply fed upon itself until it became overburdened and destitute. The grand economic machine and its tax-based funding gave way to its ruling class greed and corrupt politicians. By the seventh century A.D., the Roman Empire and its military strength was nearly a thing of the past. While Rome was collapsing, The Prophet was rising. But, before the Roman army was swept away, a prince of the covenant, He who has since proven to have been Jesus Christ, was destroyed by this kingdom and the rebellious brood they gathered. In His own Words Jesus said, "Destroy this temple, and I will raise it again in three days."[181] The Romans destroyed the temple. The temple is, was and will forever be the risen *Jesus*. He was rebuilt in three days. Thirty-five years later, the Romans destroyed what remained of the Jewish Temple in Jerusalem. Because of the destructive endeavors and murderous ways of the Romans, the Jews were forced to flee from Jerusalem. For some, the deserts of Sheba and Dedan became their new homes. Five hundred years later, The Prophet was born and raised in their resettled land.

Confusion set upon The Prophet in the initial days of his prophethood. He was misled and mistaken about the angel Gabriel. The Prophet accepted the words of a blind man who convinced him that the spirit who pressed itself against him was the holy angel *Gabriel* who [God] had previously sent to Moses. A true prophet of God would have known that God sent *Michael* to assist Moses. The Bible names two holy angels. One is Gabriel and the other is Michael. Each one of them is introduced to the prophets by their proper names. Michael is called *one of the chief princes*,[48] *your prince*,[50] *the great prince*,[61] and *the archangel*.[209] Interestingly, Michael is the leader of God's army[439] and Israel's guardian.[61] Strange as it may seem, The Prophet makes little reference to Michael. Instead, The Prophet and his entire story rely heavily upon the named angel *Gabriel*. But neither Michael nor Gabriel formally introduced themselves to The Prophet. Instead, Gabriel is *presumed* to be the angel pressing himself upon The Prophet.[3] But that presumption is simply wrong. It was *Michael* who was sent to Moses.[407] Further, according to The Prophet, Michael is not the leader of God's army… The Prophet is the leader of God's army.[277] This absolute contradiction sheds new light on the meaning of Daniel's warning; "Then an overwhelming army will be swept away before him; both it and a prince of the covenant will be destroyed."[51]

Most Christians will agree that there is sufficient biblical evidence and a reasonable argument pertaining to the archangel *Michael* as being the pre-incarnate *Jesus*. With Jesus being the *Prince of princes* and Michael being *your prince* and *the great prince*, this argument earns a bit of strength. In any case, there is now a dispute as to who and what consists of God's army. God, His prophets, and His people know that *Michael* is the biblical prince. God, His prophets, and His people anticipate the arrival of a liar who will one day attempt to assume Jesus' role as the Most High. Enter The Prophet and his god. They teach many about God's new army. It is led not by the chief prince or the Prince of princes. It is led by *The Prophet*. Something is suddenly very wrong here!

For the reader to understand prophetic history, that which begins with Daniel 11:21 and carries on to the present day, it is necessary to recognize that many of the Jews who fled Roman-controlled Jerusalem in 70 A.D., resettled in regions to the south. They fled to the lands of *Sheba* and *Dedan*. This is the point of the story where history reveals a stunning truth. We know the history of a contemptible man who made agreements with the people of that region and then disregarded those agreements.[52] He acted deceitfully. In simple terms, he was a liar. And with only a few people he rose to power. This is the accurate telling of the Prophet's ability to deceive – particularly when it came to non-agreements like the *Treaty of Hudaibiya*.³⁰² This Treaty was a farce. Intended to be a truce between the king of the North (The Prophet from Medina) and the king of the South (the leader in Mecca), this tactic set the stage and represented the foundational deceit of many of the treaties his people have made in the last 1,400 years. Daniel warned of this in or around the year 535 B.C., nearly 1,150 years *prior* to the appearance of The Prophet. Can there be a man like Daniel who could accurately predict such things without having been given the divine guidance of God?

When the richest provinces felt secure, The Prophet and his band of marauders showed their true character.²⁵⁰ In the beginning, they were just another gang of murderous thieves. They boasted about having such characteristics! This does not require intense study. The historical evidence is sufficient to show that this man and his followers raided and pillaged neighboring villages and caravans. Such were the spoils of war that advanced The Prophet's cause. His recorded word serves as viable testimony. He gladly admitted to this.²⁷³

When the richest provinces of Sheba and Dedan (current-day Arabia) felt secure in their resettled cultural and political ways, The Prophet invaded them. He and his companions were the thieves who raided the caravans of food, livestock, hardware, and monetary goods (gold and silver). The people living in the land asked a reasonable question of The Prophet; "Have you come to plunder? Have you gathered your hordes to loot, to carry out silver and gold, to take away livestock and goods and to seize much plunder?"⁸⁹ History and his own testimony have delivered an answer. In his relentless pursuit of power and influence, he instituted war as a means of worship.³⁷² He made theft a righteous act. Laced within his testimony, we find the spoils of war to be a badge of honor - something to be sought after and distributed among his followers. This foundational method of worship (to kill and steal in honor of God) has now been taught, practiced, and passed on - generation after generation - over the last 14 centuries. Via his woeful actions of killing, stealing, and destroying, this new king has achieved what neither his fathers nor his forefathers achieved before him. No righteous descendent of Abram ever declared that murder, theft, and destruction were righteous deeds. Plundering is simply the act of a thief – no matter who the thief might steal from. The Prophet lived and died as an admitted thief. He is the lone prophet to do so. There is no true prophet of God who has established a geopolitical movement that measures its submission to God by the slaughter of others and the acquisition of properties and goods of the slain. Yet this man, this unworthy king, established himself in the annals of time by doing just that - slaughtering men, oppressing women, enslaving children, stealing goods, and distributing wealth among his growing numbers. This was the Prophet's plan. He incorporated some of the most menacing and vile acts of mankind into a newfound religious movement. He strayed so far as to describe God's chosen people as "those upon whom wrath is brought down."[363] He is and was the menace. The Prophet described Christians as "those who go astray" and declared that his new message was "the right path."[362] He waged war against God's elect and redefined who and what is known as *God*. How else might one overthrow the fortresses of God? His plan worked. It is working still - but only for a little longer.

His words and deeds are well documented. The place of his emergence is well known. His negative influence and massive power are evident in most regions of the world. His political clout and military accomplishments have flourished exponentially. While the Prophetiers have gained seats in the highest political offices in the world, many of the nations within his kingdom have acquired the knowledge and ability to build and store weapons of mass destruction. Even worse, they now possess the unthinkable – an arsenal of nuclear weapons. Imagine what the world would look like today if Adolf Hitler succeeded in his endeavors to be the first to create and deploy nuclear weapons. As evil and vile as he was, Hitler's maniacal schemes encompassed a mere seven years. His charge toward world rule made him a major contributor in the second World War, leading to the deaths of nearly 56,000,000 people. Compare that number to the quest of The Prophet. His diabolic charge toward world rule is 1,400 years old and is growing in both size and strength. His utilization of worthless treaties and ruthless military endeavors serve as models for his current recruits. They have adopted his ways and continue to implement his illicit tactics – most of them being biblically lawless. With a combination of modern weaponry and tactics of terror, they manage to free themselves from the binds of conscience and compassion. All that matters is conquest.[291] Examples of their ungracious pursuits are nearly endless. Whether they wage never-ending battles with cars, trucks, knives, guns, bombs, planes, tanks, ships, missiles, or politics; one thing is certain - they strive to conquer. The Prophet and his people will continue to wage war until the end because they are taught to "Fight them until there is no persecution and all religions are only for [their god]."[402] Make no mistake, they will not quit until the world submits to the teaching that: "He it is who has sent his messenger with the guidance and the true religion that he may make it overcome all (other) religions."[425]

The Prophet began his universal war with a small group of men. But his terrorizing revolution quickly grew. With a large army (313 men and a vision of power) the new king of Medina (The Prophet) stirred up his strength and courage against the king of the Mecca and his large army of 1,000 men.[254] The Prophet's courage was "stirred up" by a dream that led him to believe that his opposition was weak.[274] It is likely that the opposition was weakened due to the robberies committed by The Prophet and his men. They had been raiding the caravans that supplied the Meccan king. For "...those who eat from the king's provisions"[53] are the thieves who stole those provisions in route to the king. They waged war against the king of Mecca (Abu Safyan) to take control of the region. In the Battle of Badr (624 A.D.), those who ate the stolen provisions were the very same men who were attempting to destroy the Southern king. Thirteen hundred men are said to have fought that battle. Many fell that day, but The Prophet is said to have been victorious. Four years later, these two kings sat at the same table and created the Treaty of Hudaibiyah. Though the strategic 'peace' was to end the fighting between the two groups, neither king had any intention of honoring the terms of the Treaty. The intent of the agreement was to gain a military advantage and merely to outwit the other. Hidden under a veil of peace was the ultimate expansion of conflict. This was the beginning of generations of war. It was ingrained upon the Prophet and his people. He says so.[370] As is the current practice, the treaty proved to be worthless. The promised peace was an illusion. Other than the size, strength, and lethality of weaponry, little has changed. With the power and influence of The Prophet still growing, the hope and promise of peace are distant illusions. The only certainty about the Prophetiers and their stolen territories is that they will deliver death, destruction, oppression, and the ever-existent demands of ransom for those they hold captive. This is life under the remodeled laws and cultural norms of The Prophet.

So, what can be proven about The Prophet and his endeavors?

- He was born to a widow and orphaned[316]
- He was not born into royalty or adopted by royals
- He invaded the kingdoms of Sheba & Dedan
- He looted the caravans of the merchants of the Tarshish
- He seized these kingdoms via intrigue and the introduction of a new deity
- He became the leader of earth's final spiritual army – the opposers
- His efforts certainly oppose Michael's people[47]
- Rome was collapsing under the tremendous weight of corruption

The Prophet

- Jesus had been crucified, resurrected, and ascended – all vehemently denied by The Prophet[391]

- During his life, The Prophet perfected the tactic of creating non-treaties of peace

- The Prophetiers act as he acted – their treaties and agreements proven worthless

- He began his ascent to power with only a few gangland thieves

- His fathers and forefathers were the descendants of Ishmael - Abram's illegitimate son

- He distributed stolen plunder, loot, and wealth among his followers[405]

- He kidnapped and enslaved women and children

- He began his exploits in Mecca (the South) only to be outed to Medina (the North)

- He returned to Mecca (the South) after breaking a peace agreement

- After overcoming Mecca (the South), he returned to Medina (the North)

- The wealth and influence of his 'prophethood' was expanding exponentially

- His visions and *miraculous marks*[227] refuted the testimony of the prophets before him

- He returned to Mecca as a conqueror, and he controls Sheba and Dedan today

- At the appointed time (prior to his return to Mecca) The Prophet was injured and rumored to have been killed – his army became weak-hearted[382]

- Among his enemies were those of the Tarshish; including the Chittim or Kittim,[102] whose caravans he continually raided

- The Prophet's fury against the holy covenant is woefully obvious and has been demonstrated by his unending war with God, God's elect, his fellow man, and all women

- In a subsequent battle, The Prophet demonstrated his apoplectic madness by decapitating 600-900 members of a re-settled Jewish tribe[164]

- His recruiting methods favored those who demonstrated loyalty[260]

- His armed forces rose-up to desecrate the Temple Mount in 685 A.D.

- On that ground the Prophetiers set up the abomination that causes desolation

- Daily sacrifice that might have been performed by a remnant of remaining Jews ended

- Corrupted are the many who recognize The Prophet as a prophet of God

- Those who know God know also to be weary of the foreign god[64]

- God's people, the elect, instruct as the Word teaches. The Prophet declares such behavior to be 'mischievous' and worthy of murder

Since the days of The Prophet's *Battle of the Trench* and his hand in the beheading of hundreds, his armed forces have risen to desecrate the Temple Mount. They have set up the abomination that causes desolation, namely the Al-Aqsa Mosque and the Dome of the Rock. With insincere praise, he has furthered his own interests and 'corrupted those who violated the holy covenant' by introducing the covenant of the masquerading light.[44] But those who know God firmly resist him. The method of resistance is not by use of a blade or Crusade, but the utilization of Jesus' two swords: "'Love the Lord your God with all your heart and with all your soul and with all your mind.' This is the first and greatest commandment. And the second is like it: 'Love your neighbor as yourself.' All the Law and the Prophets hang on these two commandments."[333] The instruction to 'love your neighbor as yourself' cannot be found among The Prophet's perfected laws. If all the Law and Prophets hang on these two commandments, what then can be said about the life and lessons of The Prophet?

His two swords are literal in their presentation, and they carry a message of opposition to the grace of the Christ. According to his recorded word, The Prophet taught that "... paradise is beneath the protection of the swords."[7] Isn't it interesting that the literary scholar who narrated this verse explains that the word *zilal* (protection) used in the sentence is plural for *zill* which generally means *shadow?*[222] The Prophet teaches that paradise is beneath the shadow of the swords? Most understand that what lies beneath a shadow is embedded in the earth. None of us will find paradise embedded in the earth. And we will certainly not find paradise below the shadow of a weapon or an instrument of death. To the contrary, The Prophet teaches his people to depend on the sword and kill in defense of the laws he concocted – promising that such loyalty will help gain them entry into a paradise that lies below the shadows.

Something seems afoul!

The Prophet

Ronald B. Stetton

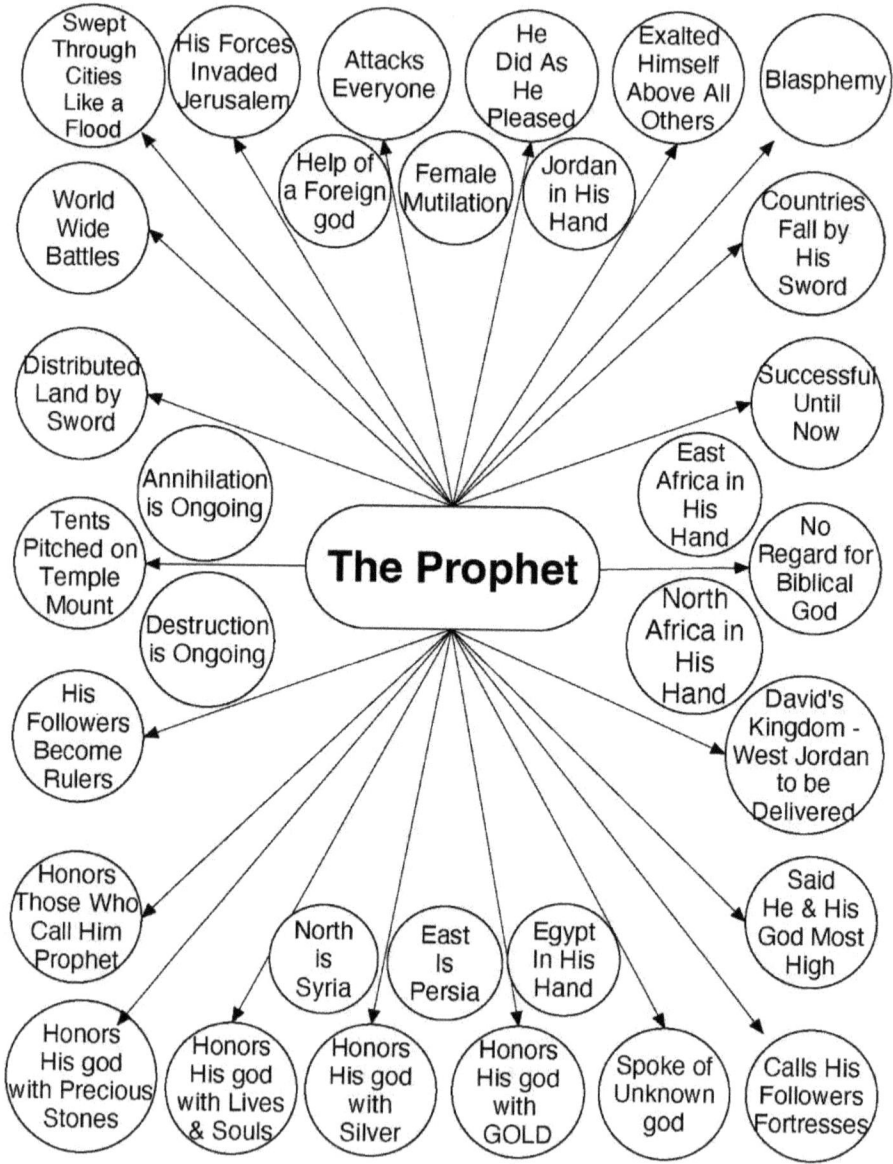

Chapter 5

The King Who Exalted Himself

Daniel's Latter Warning about the False Prophet and his Foreign God (11:36-45)

The Prophet did as he pleased. Though he entitled himself to having at least 10+ named wives and a concubine,[297] he limited the Prophetiers to having four wives at any one time.[387] The number of sex slaves he had over his lifetime is impossible to estimate because he did as he wished with anyone he chose. The most notorious of 'women' amongst his many wives was a nine-year-old girl. Like the rest of his harem, he expected this young girl to perform all the wifely duties that the others were forced to perform. She was 18 years old at the time of The Prophet's death. She endured nearly a decade of 'wifely' exposure by a man who was 44 years her senior. Is it any wonder why Daniel makes that rather odd reference about The Prophet's disregard for being desired by women?[55] There is no mystery as to how or why women would prefer love and compassion over the oppressive ownership presented by the perfect model for men. Women understand the difference between love and tenderness, as is demonstrated by the Christ, versus the misogyny demonstrated by the antichrist. Those who struggle with the comparison might try to find the courage to at least acknowledge the fallout in Afghanistan, and honestly admit to the horrid oppression that has returned to the female population of that region. What does The Prophet care about being 'desired by women' if he simply takes any woman or girl he wants? To the contrary, what reasonable woman would reject the gift of Christ for the slave-like expectations of a weathered ogre?

Jesus altered the outcome of the wages of sin by becoming sin – thereby standing between the righteous judgment of His Father and blemished men. The Jews spent 2,000 years proving that men cannot earn their way back to God. None could perfectly adhere to His laws. It is only by the grace of His Son that we might return to the Father. Given the choice, what sane woman would reject the protection of the man who stepped between the prostitute and the Pharisees, thereby stopping their righteous hypocrisy and lethal judgment?[185] In that moment, Jesus changed the world. He introduced the gift of grace in the way of compassion. It is this grace that He extends to anyone who will accept it. After all, we are all figurative prostitutes in one form or another. We have all fallen short in the eyes of God. Without His grace, we would find ourselves in the position of the prostitute – waiting to be stoned for our sins by those who deserve death themselves. Sadly, in the lands governed by The Prophet, that exact fate awaits those who break The Prophet's laws.

So, why would The Prophet negate Jesus' gift of grace and His payment as ransom for the sake of an alternate teaching? Why would The Prophet strip away the virtue of any woman or girl he wanted and then accuse his victims of acting in an immoral manner?[411] Why would The Prophet encourage the Prophetiers to make wives of the widows they create when they snipe the necks of men who disbelieve and slay their many enemies in a never-ending war?[416] Grace is just one aspect of a nearly endless list of acts and traits that separates Christ from the antichrist. The grace demonstrated by the Christ has no place in the iron-fisted kingdom and lands of the antichrist. He did whatever he wanted to do - with whomever he wanted to do it. He took what he wanted to take, destroying anything and everything that did not suit his needs – sometimes destroying them after they suited his needs. Such was the case for a Jewish woman whose entire male community (600-900 post-pubescent men and boys) was beheaded by the 'perfect model.' The balance of the women and children of that community were divided up among the Prophetiers.[164]

Already established is the recorded testimony that The Prophet exalted and magnified himself above every god (including Jesus) and said unheard of things against the God of gods (the Father).[299] Further, it has become evident that The Prophet's efforts have been successful up to this day. The Prophetiers' capabilities have never been larger, more powerful, or as technologically advanced as they are now. It is becoming obvious that he showed no regard for the Father or the Father's Son. In fact, The Prophet had no regard for any god aside from the god he introduced. Instead of the gods of his fathers before him, The Prophet honored a god of fortresses. The mental imagery we get from *fortresses* is something akin to a Western movie where Indians are riding horseback around a perimeter of wood and mud. But that's not what Daniel is telling us. The term *fortress* is as intentional as it is literal, because *fortress* is one of the descriptive names that The Prophet gave to his followers.[307]

> "Buruj is the plural of burj which means a tower or *fortress*... [they] stand for the lesser lights, in comparison with the sun to which The Prophet himself is likened"
>
> – MMA, Qur'an 85:3, 3q, p. 1197

The Prophet

In another translation of this same verse, the antichrist is said to honor a *god of force*.[56] This, too, is correct. If we are to understand that The Prophet's followers are called *fortresses*, then we can reasonably determine that these fortresses coerced people into submission and abide by the ways of The Prophet. In his typical manner, The Prophet declares 'No coercion!' and then institutes his laws by coercion. This is likely another instance when the reader might become a little uncomfortable. This is certainly not a PC moment, because it is not a PC topic. God's warning about the antichrist was never intended to be politically correct. How could it be? A politically correct environment offers superb cover and protections to this man and his movement. After all, we are discussing the ultimate deception – one that has led people astray and has proven to be lethal to its members and non-members alike. The *god* that The Prophet honors is not God. The god he introduced was unknown to The Prophet's fathers before him. The Prophet said so. The reader can weigh the evidence and determine whether The Prophet's god is God. But, regarding The Prophet's god being unknown to his fathers before him, it is best to take The Prophet's own word for it. He outwardly admitted that those before him said, "…we followed that wherein we found our fathers." And The Prophet responded, "What! Even though their fathers had no sense at all, nor did they follow the right way."[369]

There is nothing more solid than a written confession and his own verbal testimony to convict a criminal. This is no different. What has been written and practiced for centuries cannot now be changed. The Prophet said what he said - he did what he did. This statement was made by him nearly 1,400 years ago. It is a foundational piece of his teaching. More importantly, as the world's most effective antichrist and deceptive motivator, his teaching continues. Most of the world's politicians are in lock-step with his movement and its people.

Daniel certainly had some keen insight about the man who was prophesied to appear and oppose the Christ. This self-exalted king has done everything that Daniel said he would do. Among these things is the method in which The Prophet would honor his god. Knowing that he honored a god his fathers did not know, look to the next biblical hint, and see how the Prophet honored his god with *gold*.

Chapter 43 of The Prophet's book is titled **GOLD**. That chapter opens with The Prophet's declaration that the revelations within the book are from Almighty God. It is up to the reader to decide if this statement is accurate and in agreement with all previous Scripture or if it is a deceptive ploy, filled with outright lies that once flowed from the heart and mouth of The Prophet. The primary sentiment within the chapter titled

'GOLD' denies and rejects the Biblical references to God as Father and Son. GOLD also states that The Prophet's revelations will guide the Prophetiers in their rise to real greatness by way of their collective rejection of the Divinity of Jesus Christ. This is how The Prophet used gold to honor his god – he rejects the Father and Son. Without coincidence, this precious metal (gold) is also utilized within a structure on the Temple Mount. That structure has become symbolic of the abomination that causes desolation – the idolization of the foreign god and his human spokesman. That unmistakable landmark is known as the Dome of the Rock. Six centuries before its construction, Jesus honored His Father upon that ground. It is the birthplace and original location of both Jewish temples. God, the Father, was worshipped on that ground for well over a thousand years. Then came The Prophetiers. No longer is the Father worshipped on that ground. No longer is it a reminder of the Christ, Jesus, as the rebuilt temple. To worship in such a manner on that ground (praying to the Father via the Son) is now illegal! In the interest of the reader, it would be best to test some of these statements. For the curious ones, perform a simple search of 'The Temple Mount in Jerusalem.' Most images include a picture of that giant gold dome. Then search 'Judeo-Christian prayer on the Temple Mount.' The reader will soon discover that biblical prayer on that ground has become desolate. The abomination is therefore evident.

Daniel wrote that The Prophet would also honor his god with silver. From supplemental documents, it can be proven that the self-exalted king ordered a ring of silver to be made with an impress that stated he was *the* messenger of God.[11] Pause here for a moment. Think about the magnitude of this man's declaration. Not only has he declared himself to be higher than the Son of the living God, but he has rejected Jesus as the speaking image of God and has further declared himself to be that very image - *the* messenger of God. It's important to consider and recognize the time-frame of this action. He was a self-declared prophet who appeared long after God's prophets laid down their pens. He could not succeed in his mischievous ways and implement his masquerade without the spiritual power of his foreign god. God's prophets could read and write. The Prophet could do neither. He was illiterate. He read nothing. He wrote nothing. To communicate as a prophet and king he had to dictate letters to others. He then used that silver ring to impress his signet upon the letters that others wrote for him.[224]

Daniel's uncanny ability to describe the circumstances surrounding this imminent menace continues with The Prophet's use of precious stones to honor his god. Built into the eastern corner of The Prophet's main house of worship are the multiple pieces of burned and broken rock that make up the infamous *Black Stone*. These pieces are held together as one larger stone and set in place by a ring of silver. Why is the stone black, and why must the pieces be held together by a band of silver? There is biblical irony in the burned fragments and the temple in which they are located. From Scripture, a similar story can be found about *the Temple of Baal*. Like The Prophet's mainstay, Baal's temple is also made up of an inner shrine and outer courtyard. The two also share the commonality of a sacred stone within the inner shrine. In the biblical telling, Baal's stone was brought out of the temple to be broken and burned. This ancient temple was torn down, and the site was ultimately used as a latrine.[212]

> **"The guards and officers threw the bodies out and then entered the inner shrine of the temple of Baal. They brought the sacred stone out of the temple of Baal and burned it. They demolished the sacred stone of Baal and tore down the temple of Baal, and people have used it as a latrine to this day."**
>
> **– 2 Kings 10:25-27**

Here's the irony... The Prophet's temple-goers worship the burned and broken pieces of a stone that was previously intact. They signify their adoration of this precious stone as The Prophet did, declaring the remnants as the biblical *cornerstone* - a darkened reflection of Ishmael.[248] The Prophet and his Prophetiers see Abraham's biblical rejection of Ishmael and Hagar as another corrupted entry in the long line of errors in prophecy and biblical history.[230] Of course, the biblical cornerstone is none other than the Christ. He is the stone that the builders (God's chosen people) rejected.[331] But in The Prophet's kingdom, the cornerstone is the sum of re-gathered pieces of a burned rock. Can it be that The Prophet's precious Black Stone is the same stone that was hauled out of the house of Baal to be broken and burned? It was the worship of Baal that led people to adopt a sacred piece of stone. And it was Baal worship that led to the destruction of that unholy temple. Like the foreign god, Baal is just another wannabe god. It seems that wannabes have a similar zest for burned and broken stones. This one just happens to be located on The Prophet's main house!

The irony continues... The Prophet states that this house of worship, his temple, was rebuilt by Abraham and Ishmael – having been previously destroyed.[365] The biblical account of Baal's temple (2 Kings 10:25-27) mirror the description of The Prophet's temple with its inner and outer courts, previous destruction, a burned and broken sacred stone, and its verified use as a latrine. More coincidences? The Prophet declares that Abraham did not cast Hagar and Ishmael into the desert, but that he left Sarah and settled near this temple with them instead.[280] The Prophet rejects Moses' testimony that Abraham cast the pair into the desert of Beer-sheba![117] How many contradictions and corrections to biblical testimony have now been discussed? The better question is, how many contradictions and corrections might it take to strip The Prophet of his self-declared credentials? Consider the story of Baal's sacred stone that was broken and burned, how does that biblical account end? People would eventually use the temple as a latrine.[213] Such is the case of The Prophet's temple.[5] The similarities are to be expected when both Baal and The Prophet make a mockery of everything that is called God.

Daniel writes that the king honors his god with *costly gifts*. One might conjure up images of costly gifts like mink coats, sports cars, big homes, and yachts. But The Prophet had something much more costly in mind. He sculpted an ideology that sacrificed lives and souls for his god. Chapter eight of his book is titled *Voluntary Gifts*. The narrative that describes this chapter tells us that these voluntary gifts include the spoils of war. As most reasonable people understand, the spoils of war come at a devastating cost. To gather the spoils, people must die. In the recent fiasco that describes Afghanistan, over 80 billion dollars in weaponry was collected by the Prophetiers as *Voluntary Gifts*. This shiny new weaponry came with the deaths of thousands of people over a span of twenty years. The most costly gifts offered to The Prophet and his god were the lives given and the lives taken over those two decades. The Prophet demands that his people give their lives[386] while taking the lives of others.[371] This is how The Prophet honors the god of forces – he does so with war. One of his well-educated Prophetiers recently stated that; "…they could only hope to secure peace by strength and readiness."[271] When one submits to the thought that a believing body of people is duty-bound to battle and that maintaining a constant state of war is an honorary method of worship, it's likely time to seek a better god! God does not need men to kill for Him. Jesus' testimony makes that perfectly clear.

The Prophet broadened the definition of martyrdom from sacrificing oneself to sacrificing oneself in the act of murdering others. This explains the willingness of men and women to wrap themselves in explosives and kill as many disbelievers or hypocrites as possible – be they men, women, or children. Costly gifts include the nearly 3,000 souls taken on 9/11. Costly gifts were the people attending a Christmas party in San Bernardino. Costly gifts were the innocents who were encouraging the runners at the finish line of the Boston Marathon. Costly gifts were the uniformed men and women who were assigned to assist the evacuation of people from The Prophet's latest war zone in

Afghanistan. Costly gifts are the Afghans who cannot escape The Prophet's war on mankind. For them, the battle has shifted, and many of these Prophetiers are now considered to be hypocrites by other Prophetiers. The hypocrites are now to be treated as people in Towers, raised high. This is how The Prophet taught his people to honor their god. How have reasonable people allowed this man to stay hidden for so long? The mighty forces that have been attacked include the United States of America and its former Twin Towers. The Prophet's ever-expanding recruits continue to attack the mightiest forces with the help of a foreign god[258] and everyone can see it. But few choose to point it out and acknowledge the evil for what it is. Conscious denial such as this is cowardly. Cowardice is a trait of the liar.[470] Daniel and John saw visions of this man for who he was to be. They got it right.

To date, there are many world leaders who honor The Prophet and advance his ideals and endeavors. Chief among them are nations whose majorities have become submissive to the ways of his god. The number of nations and people who have become enslaved to his laws are too numerous to list. Suffice it to say that even the highest offices in the United States of America honor The Prophet and the people he influences. Empty promises to *never forget* the horrific acts orchestrated by some of his most loyal subjects have given way to submission and open arm policies that welcome the Prophetiers by the thousands while consciously ignoring the fact that they are dutybound to murder. So woven into the fabric of this nation, they are recognized annually by heads of state – even in the way of annual dinners at the White House. This has been a common practice since Thomas Jefferson first hosted the occasion in December 1805. At the time of this writing, the last dinner recognizing the month-long dedication to The Prophet's god was hosted by Donald Trump on May 11, 2018. Thanks to Covid, Joe Biden chose to acknowledge the occasion virtually in April of 2021. One must wonder... How vast must the deception be when The Prophet and his accomplishments have become so worthy of honor and recognition that he is regularly exalted by arguably the highest political office on earth?

With The Prophet's masses of people and cultural influence literally surrounding Israel, it is reasonable to surmise that the culmination of this story is rapidly approaching. The battles raged to achieve his geographical gains have become commonplace – something akin to a lifestyle for his people. Because war is a way of life for the Prophetiers, their individual battles are rarely even mentioned. The reach of his intrigue is staggering. The skirmishes that began with only a few men in Sheba and Dedan have now become intrusions of armies that have reached across the globe. In the beginning of his reign, these ancient territories and peoples were subdued personally - by

The Prophet's own hand and actions. Shortly thereafter, his successors expanded their oppressive incursions into North and East Africa, Egypt, and Israel. Daniel describes him as gaining control of the treasures and riches of Egypt. He has. Egypt's majority has fallen victim to the man, and they have submitted themselves to his deceptive marks. They have adopted the ways of the conqueror and readily admit to the strategy of 'striving' by any means necessary to ensure and advance The Prophet's endeavors. To fight under the illusion of peace is to advance the world's most lethal oxymoron.

The world and its minions will scoff at the suggestion that all the Prophetiers and their political allies could be lulled into accepting the lessons of death and destruction as cultural threads meant to be woven into the fabric of any nation. But consider recent events. After the Prophetiers acted as they were commanded and inflicted death upon those in Towers raised high, the U.S. military set out to capture or kill the architect and commander of the campaign. He was chased across Afghanistan and finally killed by elite forces in a safehouse in Pakistan. But something utterly inconceivable occurred in the process. Some genius or collection of geniuses decided that it would be a good idea to nation-build in a country whose people detest the Laws of God and refuse to benefit by the freedoms of democracy or free trade. The Prophetiers are burdened by laws that prevent interest-based lending. They are forbidden to request or pay interest on any loan.[565] Without conventional banking models, their cities are destined to remain deserts. Oil has served as a financial oasis for a very few, but thanks to the Green movement that, too, is coming to an end. After thousands of deaths, tens of billions of dollars in military structuring, and some very misguided attempts to educate and inform, the nations of Afghanistan and Iraq have been abandoned to the next generation of murderous thugs that captured the world's attention in the first place. What did the U.S. gain by leaving the treasure of blood and billions of dollars-worth of weaponry to that maniacal group? It gained the forced immigration of tens of thousands of Prophetiers onto U.S. soil. Simply genius!

Five hundred years after the time of Christ, The Prophet and his companions arrived to spread their newfound version of *peace*. What they started in Sheba and Dedan has now spread across the globe. They have set themselves up in nearly every country, governing body, community, school, and workforce on the planet. Like their stern-faced king, they continue to demonstrate his great rage as they strive to achieve his promise of peace through attrition. They are duty-bound to this endeavor.[380] Such is the method of the proverbial king and the manner with which he spins his duties as The Prophet. The headlines are numerous, but the world chooses to avert their gaze. What has become otherwise obvious is conveniently and consciously ignored. Tactical denial and accusations of bigoted hate paint over the biblical reality that The Prophet has already performed his role. The abomination that has been set up between the people of three religions on the glorious holy mountain, the Temple Mount in Jerusalem, has stood in plain sight for over 1,300 years. Few have questioned its authority and worthiness to stand in that holy place. But that's about to change. It is there, on that once holy ground, that can be seen the golden dome honoring The Prophet and his god. To complete the abomination, four Asherah poles have been erected in that place to compliment the gold that honors the foreign god. The abomination is as accessible to the eyes as are the Headlines that are created by the acts of the Prophetiers. Yet, the masses choose to ignore such atrocities. They avert their eyes and cover their ears. But seeing what is clearly visible and hearing what is clearly audible are soon to become absolute and unavoidable. Welcome to the reality that God's Word is much more than a weak man's superstitious hope and crutch. The marks of The Prophet are emblazoned upon the minds of billions. In their submissive conditioning, they repeatedly beat their foreheads upon the ground, thereby making an unmistakable impression. He who once hid in plain sight has been revealed - his veil lifted. His nakedness is now on display for all men to see. The abomination of all abominations is what has been set up on the Temple Mount. The man, his god, their hordes, and their phallic towers all adorn the ground where Jesus once delivered sermons that describe His Father. It might have taken more than thirteen centuries, but men can finally see the abomination that causes desolation on that storied ground. This is thrilling for a few, but terrifying for most. "There is a time for everything, and a season for every activity under heaven: a time to kill and a time to heal, a time to mourn and a time to dance, a time to be silent and a time to speak, a time to love and a time to hate, a time for war and a time for peace."[566] This is nothing less than inspirational! The time for The Prophet to kill and cause mourning, his time to force people into hateful silence, and his time for war has come to an imminent end! It's time to take him out of the way and welcome the return of Christ. It's a time to heal and a time to dance. It's a time to speak and a time to love. The war that started in heaven has reached its end – making way for genuine peace, that which is promised by the Christ! With God's warning about *the king who exalts himself* now proven to have been the false prophet, the demise and destruction of the king and his kingdom is now a matter of the clock. Daniel stated it best when he wrote that this horrible man and his god will come to their collective end, and no one will help him.[60]

> "He will extend his power over many countries; Egypt will not escape. He will gain control of the treasures of gold and silver and all the riches of Egypt, with the Libyans and Nubians in submission. But reports from the east and the north will alarm him, and he will set out in a great rage to destroy and annihilate many. He will pitch his royal tents between the seas at the beautiful holy mountain. Yet he will come to his end, and no one will help him"
>
> – Daniel 12:42-45

There is a fitting end to the war of rebellion that has long been established against God and His people. The response to Satan's war is readily affirmed by the sword of Jesus' mouth. All that the Christ had to do was speak His Word. The truth brings about the ultimate justice for this generation of man. The rebellious majority, those who will undoubtedly gnash their teeth in rage and bark their vile accusations, will ultimately bring this story to its prophetic finish – at the hand of their own treacherous intent and actions.

As for the Dome of the Rock and how that golden debacle has hidden in plain sight for so many centuries - keep reading. Daniel has much more to say about the Temple Mount and the abominations that have been set up there.

The Prophet

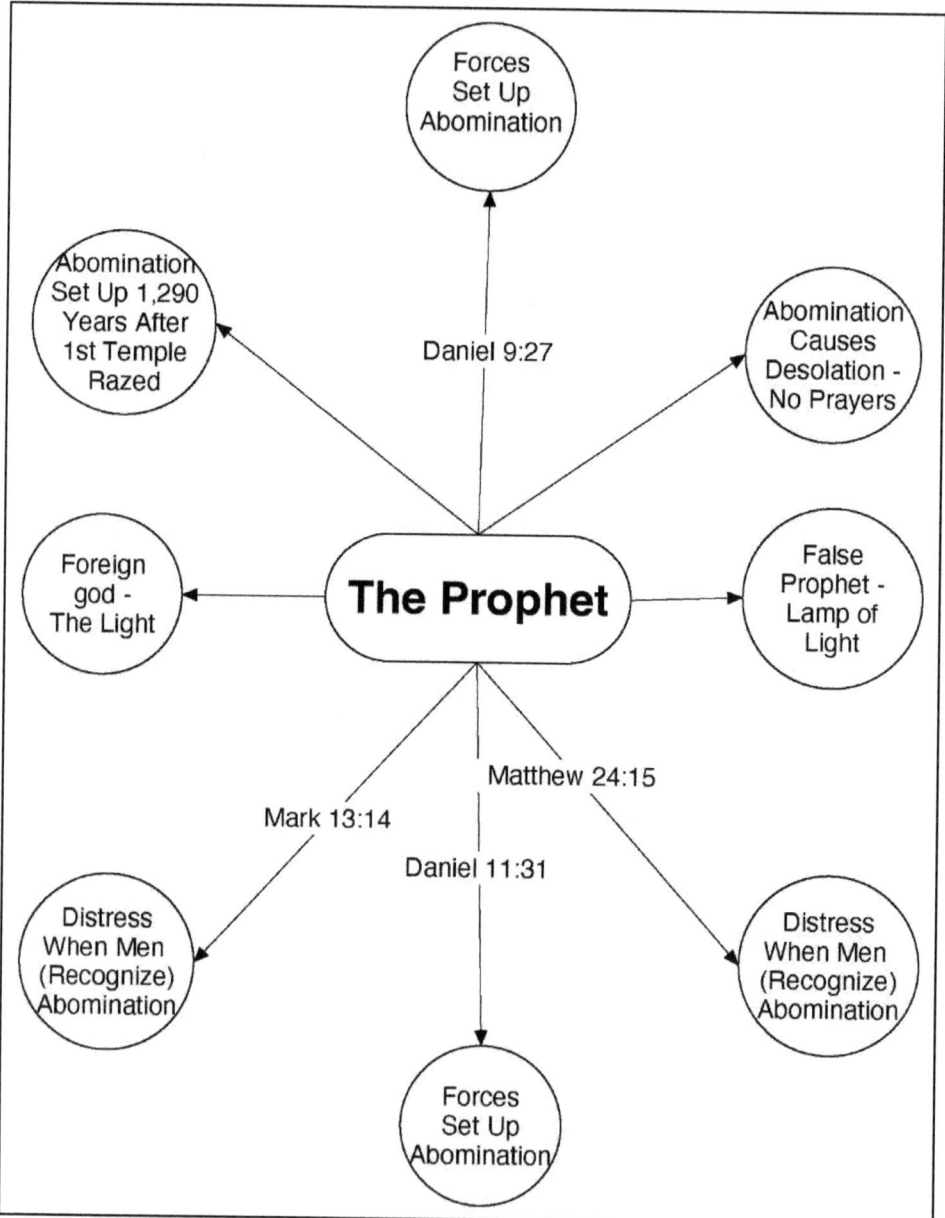

Chapter 6

Seeing the Abomination that Causes Desolation

Unveiling the Warnings of Daniel 9 & Matthew 24

The abomination... an astonishing portrayal of Lucifer and his god. The desolation caused by this unimaginable deity and its placement is unmatched. The biblical warnings about Satan's attempt to unseat God has stymied men since Eve walked in the garden. But the mysteries surrounding the false prophet have lingered only since the time of Christ. Naturally, it seems the two are related. Once men identify the false prophet, they will prove his god to be the liar and unveil all the abominations he is responsible for creating. Daniel provided a biblical glimpse into the abomination that was to be set up by the people who followed the false prophet as the speaking image of the dragon. Daniel wrote about The Prophet who would ultimately appear and establish his intrigue. Twelve hundred years after Daniel died, The Prophet appeared. Fourteen hundred years after he appeared, The Prophet has been revealed.

In chapter 9, Daniel writes about the seventy sevens that the angel, Gabriel, reveals to him. Unlike the declarations of The Prophet and his *supposed* encounters with Gabriel, Daniel hears the Word of God call specifically on the angel named *Gabriel* to explain multiple visions.[34] There is much speculation about these seventy *sevens*, most of which biblical scholars agree upon. It is reasonable to accept that the first sixty-nine sevens[44] describe the span of time between the decree that was issued to Nehemiah in 445 BC and the crucifixion of Jesus Christ. This timeline incorporates the 483 years that can be accounted for by the (62) and the (7) sevens. Though it might be of slight benefit to explain the timeline here, the accounting would simply be a diversion that takes focus off the main subject and sends us off course. A reasonable explanation of this window in time can be found by performing a simple search. There is also a narration of this in the NIV Study Bible[124] that has been included in Appendix 1. What has remained a mystery and needs to be addressed in this moment is the 70th 'seven.'[44] This is where prophetic history and current events depart from the traditional end-time expectations of many Christians. The 70th 'seven' describes the way Satan confirms his covenant to *many* people who refuse to love the truth. His covenant was delivered verbally, from the mouth of his speaking image - Lucifer. The confirmation of that covenant comes in the form of a book that encapsulates much of what Lucifer had to say.

This likely needs a bit of explanation. Traditional end-time arguments suggest that the last 'seven' (the one 'seven') is a span of seven years in which the Antichrist will appear on earth to create a treaty with the Jews and then break that treaty at its halfway point – 3 ½ years after it gets inked. Most of the faithful refer to this as the time of the end or the *time of tribulation.* This is exactly what can happen when men attempt to build a likely scenario around God's prophecies and piece together a seemingly reasonable picture of what mankind might expect in the end. This is one of the many reasons why The Prophet has remained hidden in plain sight for so long. He did not and will not appear in a manner consistent with this traditional expectation. He can't. He is dead.

To better understand the biblical meaning of *end times* or *last times*, it would be best to rely on God's measure of time rather than man's limited understanding. Peter assists us with God's timeline. He gives testimony that 'Jesus was chosen before the creation of the world but was revealed in *these last times* for our sake.' Peter wrote this 2,000 years ago! He was telling us that *these last times* began in his day. It is difficult to argue against the fact that the time of tribulation did *not* begin with Jesus' crucifixion. After all, how much more trouble can man get into and how much worse can it get than having men murder the Son of God? Furthermore, history has demonstrated man's woeful ability to terrorize, oppress, and murder his own brother. The tribulations that have come about since the time of Jesus' crucifixion speak loudly about man's heathenistic abilities. The world has witnessed countless acts of cruelty and murderous intent by way of Roman inquisitions and the *striving* of The Prophet's people against disbelievers. Mankind has lived to see two world wars and the inhumane wickedness of Nazi Germany. The world watched in horror as the Twin Towers were targeted and destroyed on an otherwise beautiful fall morning. Since that day, the world has grown to know endless fighting. Even an entire chapter on Afghanistan has closed, but another begins. The world has witnessed the fabric of America fray, as its majority demands that policing be abolished and the detestable acts of a selfish few be accepted as gestures of a newfound love. Even infanticide is painted over as a woman's right and deemed to be part of progressive men and their 'healthcare.' It's curious how so many have been convinced that ending human life is somehow characterized as *caring for one's health*. The Prophet rationalizes his demonstration of peace in a similar manner. And even though people know and understand God's righteous decrees about men and women, boys and girls, sexual acts, trespassing, murder, and the roles of the Father and the Son – mankind now wrestles over the definition of gender, the wholesome acceptance of a New Sodom, undocumented immigration for the sake of election, assembly-line infanticide, the forced adoption of lawlessness, and many other detestable behaviors that have been defined and decreed by God. What was evil has become good. These are just a few examples (among many) that have brought mankind to this woeful point in time – rebellious beyond recognition. But these are the things of prophecy. They have reached far beyond the 3 ½ years of tribulation that man's traditional beliefs attempted to package in a neat little box. This is also how and why the end comes at a time when one does not expect it. Men await the acts of a fictitious scenario. Even many of God's elect are waiting for something that will never materialize.

In Daniel 9:26, it is written that the people of *the ruler who will come* will destroy the city and the sanctuary. This has happened multiple times. The Babylonians destroyed the sanctuary in 586 B.C., and the Romans destroyed the sanctuary again in 70 A.D. History affirms the times and dates of the destruction of the two Jewish temples. But few are willing to acknowledge what happened in Jerusalem 600 years after the Romans returned to their murderous ways. The Temple was stained again. In 685 A. D., the Prophetiers dedicated an existing building on the Temple Mount to The Prophet and his god. The abomination they set up was established in that moment and it has become commonplace to those who do not know God. Though Jerusalem is the cup of trembling that God promised it would become, the abomination remains upon that ground - with little world fanfare.

Knowing that the Temple Mount has seen three major abominations, which abominable event was Daniel referring to? To be thorough, we can rule out the temple destruction in 586 BC, because it is generally agreed upon that the decree to rebuild Jerusalem came about in 445 BC – 104 years *after* the first Temple was destroyed.[347] So, Daniel must be writing about the destruction of the sanctuary by the Romans in 70 A.D., or the destruction of the city and the sanctuary by The Prophet's people in 685 A.D. Many will roll their eyes at this. Due to their lackadaisical attitude toward God and His glory, they are complicit in the longevity of the abomination that still stands on that ground. This method of dismissal toward the intentions of The Prophet and his people has led to an obscene amount of death and destruction. And it's not ended.

Destruction of Jerusalem and its Temple by the Romans in 70 A.D. is well known. But the destruction of Jerusalem and the sanctuary in 685 A. D. has gone largely unnoticed – just as that abominable golden shrine has gone unnoticed and been accepted as an honorary marker for God's holy land. Nothing about that abomination is of a

Judeo-Christian nature. Nothing but warning that is! Its very existence dishonors God as it gives His glory to another.

Construction of that golden monument began in 687 A.D. and was completed by The Prophetiers in 692 A.D. That shrine has become the leading image when one envisions Jerusalem. But now, with men knowing the identity of the speaking image who inspired that abomination, the vision and site will accelerate in its demise and become greatly tarnished as man's greatest deception. Most who come to know about the abomination will never again look upon that structure in the same way. Though it has remained hidden right before our eyes for over 1300 years, it is as plain as day now! That gold dome was not inspired or constructed by Jews – God's chosen people. That gold dome was not erected by Christians – Jesus' faithful followers. That gold dome was set up by *the people of the ruler who would come!*[43] The following quotes demonstrate the extent of blasphemy that has been inscribed upon the walls of that abomination...

- The Prophet [as named] is the servant of god and his messenger
- god and his angels shower blessings on The Prophet
- ...salute [The Prophet as named] with a worthy salutation
- People of the Book [Christians and Jews] do not exaggerate in your religion
- Jesus was only a messenger of God
- ...say not 'Three' – Cease! [Note: According to The Prophet, the 'Three' in Christianity are God, *Mary,* and Jesus][266]
- Far be it removed from his transcendent majesty that [god] should have a son
- It befitteth not (the majesty of) god that he should take to himself a son
- Religion with god (is) that of [The Prophet as named]
- [The Prophet as named] is the messenger of god
- The dome was built by servant of god [as named] of the faithful, in the year two and seventy [692 C.E. – Common Era]

These statements, summarized by end note (165), adequately depict how The Prophet elevated himself and his god above that of biblical teaching while changing the set times and elevating his position as a prophet to that of the most high. His treachery is illuminated by the Prophetiers who set up the abomination in that they have been taught that the Father, Son, and Spirit are The Father, Son Jesus, and *mother* Mary. This continuing falsehood, the fixation on a female deity, is favored as one of the dragon's reoccurring themes. The reference to adoring a goddess known as the Queen of Heaven originated as a Babylonian fable and has been adopted and elevated by the Romans. With the Roman twist, incorporating Mary as *the queen over all things*,[20] fully adopted by those who have been taught by demons, it is easy to understand how an uneducated murderer could conclude that Christianity worships a woman as God. This critical error about Christianity is easily explained by The Prophet's inability to read. Had he been taught to read, he would have known and understood that God is Father, Son, and Spirit. Instead of being carried along by the Holy Spirit, The Prophet was carried along by the man-made traditions of Romans. Instead of reading the testimony of the prophets before him, he was resigned to admitting: "I don't know how to read."[4] The Roman tragedy, biblically described as a drunken harlot, fooled The Prophet in the same manner it has fooled billions just like him. Once mixed, tradition and pride make for a very powerful potion and influencer!

Nearly every historical account describes the construction of that gold shrine to begin in the years 685-687 and ending in 692 A.D. Inconsistencies with the start date likely incorporate the dedication of an existing building to The Prophet and his god in the year 685. It was at that time The Prophetiers established their tabernacle in Jerusalem. This is Daniel's warning in chapter 11. He told us about the abominable things that would take place on that ground in honor of the self-exalted king. The Prophet has accomplished nearly everything that prophecy foretold. The only things that have not come about yet are the things that are to happen *after* he is revealed. With the efforts of his people, The Prophet pitched his tent in Jerusalem - posthumously. Why might that be important? What makes the year 685 A.D. so instrumental in the grand scheme of things? The answer is given by Daniel in chapter 12. Two divine beings tell Daniel "from the time that the daily sacrifice is abolished and the abomination that is set up, there will be 1290 days.'

This has remained a mystery since the time of its writing. But God did not intend to keep this measure of time a mystery forever. It is widely understood that Daniel's prophetic days refer to years.[41] For the sake of this argument, notice how the math works when applying the days as years. The reasonable start date, when the daily sacrifice was first abolished, is the year 586 B.C. – with the Babylonians destroying the first temple. So, what happened 1,290 years after the destruction of the first Jewish Temple? The math is rather simple.:

$$-586 + (1290 \times 360/365 +/- 1) = 685$$
[Note: Biblical years span 360 days and there is no year '0']

From most accords, the Dome of the Rock was dedicated, and construction began on the Temple Mount in 685A.D.[210] By any account, it is certain that the Prophetiers had conquered the territory and ruled the Temple Mount in that time. This is in accordance with Daniel 11:31 and how The Prophet's armed forces would rise to desecrate the Temple and abolish the daily sacrifice. This is also in accordance with the abomination that causes desolation in Matthew 24 and Mark 13.

Daniel's written testimony proclaims that 'war will continue until the end.'[43] But what does this mean? Which war will continue until the end? What war began before the days of Daniel and continues to rage today? It is the war waged against Israel – specifically against Jerusalem.

"Come," they say, "Let us destroy them as a nation, that the name of Israel be remembered no more."[356]

"On that day, when all the nations of the earth are gathered against her, I will make Jerusalem a cup of trembling."[525]

This does not bode well for the Prophetiers! They are the ones making this declaration against Israel today! Daniel was neither alone, nor was he the only prophet to warn about Jerusalem's ongoing war against those who despise her! Being a true prophet of God, isn't it reasonable to accept the instruction of Holy Spirit and how it guided Daniel's pen? And if we accept what Daniel wrote, then we must accept that there will never be peace with Israel – ever! Though many agreements, treaties, and truces have been inked with Israel, none have ever held. The supposed peace agreement between Israel and the Antichrist that many anticipate - cannot happen. How could it? The Antichrist has been dead for nearly 1,400 years. Tribulation has certainly not been limited to a mere seven years - though that period was woefully satisfied by the Nazis and the blistering oppression they instituted upon the Jews in the years 1939 through 1945. There will likely not be a break in the peace after a period of 3 ½ years, because no peace is to be found. And there won't be a time of tribulation that spans this one 'seven' or 'one week'.[348] What then, is the final 'seven' of Daniel 9:27? For the moment, these 'seven' will be referred to as the *Seven Oft-Repeated Verses*. This one 'seven' was presented by The Prophet. This final 'seven' will be explained in the next chapter.

In this moment, it is imperative to understand what these 'seven' represent. Collectively, they are the outline of a *covenant* between the foreign god and his people.

Most understand that God formed a covenant with Abraham's offspring through Isaac and his descendants. Christians understand that a new covenant was instituted for anyone and everyone who accepted the gift of the Father and His Son through their selfless acts of sacrifice and offering.[121] The covenants that extend through Isaac's bloodline and expand upon Jesus' crucifixion define the agreement between God and man. Via covenant, men know what God has promised. For Christians, the meaning of God's covenant is quite simple. This is the insertion of grace between a perfect God and his imperfect people. Some refer to Jesus' sacrifice and offering on the cross as *the new covenant*. Many of God's Old Testament prophets wrote about the appearance of a Messiah. The sacrifice and offering He offered saves the eternal lives of those who accept Him. This is God's gift to men, and it was planned from the beginning. Though one could consider God's covenant to be a peace treaty between Himself and His people, the application of the word in that sense would be lost here. Though men may be at war with God, God is not at war with His people.

So, if God's covenant means eternal life, what then would be the covenant between the liar and his people? To begin with, by denying the Christ, the liar negates God's gift to man. The foreign god would 'put an end to the sacrifice and offering'[44] of the Son for all who choose to worship the masquerading light as though that *light* was God. This might sound rather complicated, but it's quite simple. The defined covenant between God's adversary (Satan) and the people he has led astray (the Prophetiers) can be found in the book that depicts him. This would be a book written in his own image. The image of Satan would include lessons on terror,[159] murder,[192] changed laws,[33] deviations to the written Word of previous prophets,[467] and a dismissal of the saints – God's chosen Jews and Jesus' faithful Christians.[241] The lessons of this image were initially delivered verbally. The mouthpiece was the Prophet. He was flesh and blood, with the eyes of a man and a mouth that spoke boastfully. What he could never be was a functional author – he could not write. Eighteen years after the death of the man who spoke boastfully, the image of the foreign god was gathered and bound in the way of a book. The masquerading light was attempting to mirror God. But the Bible was written in the image of God by men who were filled with the Spirit of God. The liar's book was written in the image of the dragon by a man who was filled with the spirit of the dragon. This explains what it means to 'speak like a dragon.'[448] The book and lasting image of the dragon would have to wait until The Prophet was dead and gone. The dark sentences that fell out of the mouth of The Prophet were originally recorded by scribes who wrote "upon palm-stems shorn of leaves and skins."[232]

> "The messenger of [god] died while the [book] was written upon palm-stems shorn of leaves and skins."
>
> — MMA, Qur'an, Introduction, p. I-60, paragraph 1

The covenant formed between the foreign god and the Prophetiers can be found in that little book. The one and only biblical reference to this book can be found in the hand of the fallen angel.[433] The word *covenant* can be found no less than 13 times within the pages of the dragon's book.[242] Most importantly, the covenant between that fiery angel and his people is summarized within the first seven verses. Again, these are known as *the Seven Oft-Repeated Verses,* and they will be described in the next chapter.

With God's covenant written, and His gift already in place, men can now unravel the mystery that states: "He [Satan] will confirm a covenant with many for one 'seven.' In the middle of the 'seven' he will put an end to sacrifice and offering." By denying the Son and the sacrifice He made upon the cross, Satan effectively puts an end to the sacrifice and offering made by the Father and His Son. This nullification of the gift applies to everyone who has placed their trust in the masquerading light and his covenant. Like a hand sliding into a glove, Daniel follows up on his warning about Satan's covenant with the introduction of the abomination that causes desolation. He writes that the abomination is to be set up on a wing of the Temple. And that is where it can be found. The abomination has been readily discussed and defined. It exists upon the ruins of the destroyed Jewish Temples in Jerusalem. It comes as a set in the form of a house of worship, a shrine, and Asherah poles – all in honor and dedication to The Prophet and the dragon who guided his speech. The Prophetiers have honored the dragon within that abomination, and they have kept Christians and Jews from praying upon the Temple grounds for approximately 1335 years. From the moment that the abomination was decreed until the time of this writing, 1335 years have passed. From the time that Moses witnessed *the Word carved out of the Mountain of God* to the time that *the Word* instituted grace by way of crucifixion and resurrection, it can be argued that 1335 years had passed by. God's Word of Daniel 12:12 is intentional.

As strange as this might sound, today's Temple Mount is likely the most desolate piece of ground on the face of the earth. The desolation has been raised and it has remained standing for over 13 centuries now. The irony in this is that the Temple Mount in Jerusalem is supposed to be God's sanctuary – the *most holy* piece of ground on earth.

The Temple Mount is in Jerusalem. The geographical location is referenced multiple times within the pages of the Bible. But now, thanks to The Prophet, that place is desolate. Christians and Jews, the saints, cannot pray there. It is written, "My house will be called a house of prayer."[162] Not anymore… The Prophet and his Prophetiers have put a stop to that – just as Daniel warned.

> **"Jews and Christians are normally allowed to visit the site as tourists. But they are banned from praying, singing and making religious displays."**
>
> **– William Booth, The Washington Post, 10/30/2014**

Daniel's warning can now be summarized in plain, precise, and historical language. History reveals that The Prophetiers came to destroy the city and the sanctuary. The abomination on the Temple Mount is evidence enough. Because of this, the end will come like a flood. God's elect have been waiting for signs of its coming. They wait for seven years of tribulation. They wait for yet another rebuilt Jewish Temple. They wait for a man to take up residence in the new Temple and call himself "God." They wait for the Rapture. Most have curiously overlooked and dismissed The Prophet. They have yet to recognize that his war will continue until the end – just as Daniel wrote it. How could it end any other way? The war that Satan started in heaven continues here on earth. The masquerading light has confirmed his covenant with *many*. In fact, he has deceived billions of people over the last 14 centuries. He has done so with the help of seven simple phrases – the one 'seven.' In the middle of those 'seven,' the foreign god put an end to Jesus' sacrifice and offering. The Son's selfless act of crucifixion and resurrection is wasted upon those who have become submissive to the liar's call. And finally, on a wing of the temple, The Prophet's abominations have taken their toll – resulting in desolation.

Sometimes filling in the blanks is like brushing long hair. It may take a few strokes before all the snags come out. With that in mind, we might brush through this one more time and let history dictate the prophetic past.

Shortly after The Prophet's death, Jerusalem was overrun by Prophetiers. They claimed the city and the Temple ground as their own, dedicating the Temple to their god. The Prophetiers were convinced that they were at war and that fighting was enjoined on them, though they might not like it.[370] They were commanded to fight until all men and religions worshiped only The Prophet's god.[402] The Prophet appeared after all others had retired their pens, claiming to be *the* messenger of God and that *he* is to make [his teaching] prevail over all other religions.[425] Historical events verify that The Prophetiers believe they are at war. They admit to having been indoctrinated since birth.[234] In the brainwashing that begins upon their first breath,[235] they are taught that they must abide by two duties. Their first duty is to invite people to side with The Prophet. The second is to *strive with a mighty striving* against those who reject the Prophetiers' first duty.[220] The speaking image convinced them that murdering other men in god's name becomes a requirement when defending the faith. In response, the Prophetiers have pledged that war will continue until all religions worship their god as God.[402] This is the covenant that has been established between The Prophetiers and their god. The covenant was delivered by an illiterate man who had been pressed by a terrifying spirit.[4] His verbal collection of contradictory lessons has been bound in book form, confirming that which was previously delivered by his mouth. The entire covenant between the masquerading light and the Prophetiers is said to be summarized by the first seven verses of that book.[237] These seven simple phrases make up the entire first chapter of the fallen angel's book, but the narration surrounding them needed five pages of explanation by the translating author. This one 'seven' is better known as *the Seven Oft-Repeated Verses*.[233] They have astounding biblical implications and fit perfectly within the evil schemes of the biblical bad-man and his many intriguing accomplishments. They also serve as a complete departure from the Word of God and His Teaching. Because the Word of God comes from only two sources, the Son and the Spirit of God, there are no contradictions or conditional corrections. His Word is as it was written and anchored by the Holy Spirit through His genuine prophets. The only purposes served by The Prophet are to fulfill the prophecies of warning surrounding him and surrounding his war against God. He taught people to praise a liar and a murderer, calling him *tender* and *delicate*. By convincing many to seek him for help, the liar has put an end to Jesus' sacrifice and offering. He and his mouthpiece have convinced many that they are on the right path; a path that is a certain departure from 3,500 years of Judeo-Christian prophecy and teaching. The Prophet has left nothing of prophecy undone. He has fulfilled everything that the false prophet was prophesied to accomplish.

    Daniel's clear warning about the dragon and his speaking image concludes with a chilling end. The abomination that causes desolation will remain. It is not to be replaced by a third Jewish temple. Mankind will never see a calm resolve and flag of surrender raised by The Prophet's people. The Prophetiers will remain deaf and blind to the deceit that has been fed to them since birth. Their political allies will remain bound by the power and money that comes with the offices they hold. There is no mountain of evidence that will open their eyes or unplug their ears. They travel together down a broad road, toward a wide gate. But others will see it. The elect will see the abomination standing where it does not belong. All things decreed by God and His prophets will be poured out upon The Prophet, his god, rebellious men, and the abominations they have set up – be they as abominable as a gold dome for the foreign god or a rainbow flag championing behavior that God describes as "shameful."

Daniel's warning is 2,500 years old. Today, the world watches as The Prophetiers carry out their obligatory battles and strive to overcome all who oppose The Prophet's craft. This is in accordance with the warning about war. Having taken 25 centuries to come to light, it is now more than reasonable to trust the accuracy of Daniel's prophetic writing. The time of coincidence has passed. There is only one explanation. With biblical warnings now established as historical facts, the prophecies have been fulfilled. The end that is decreed will be poured out – exactly as it has been written. The end shows no favor for The Prophet or his god.[466]

There are many faiths and traditions in the world today. The power that these beliefs hold over people is simply astonishing. The evil that men strive for is sickening. With the advent and introduction of nuclear weapons, the prophetic end of this generation of man has been made possible. The story does not end with climate change or meteors. It does not end with pestilence, flood, or starvation. The end comes 'with thunder and earthquake and great noise, with windstorm and tempest and flames of a devouring fire.' The fire is brought down from heaven to earth because of the speaking image of the dragon.[450] But, before it ends, a few biblical mysteries must be unveiled. Included in these mysteries are the *seven thunders* of Revelation 10.

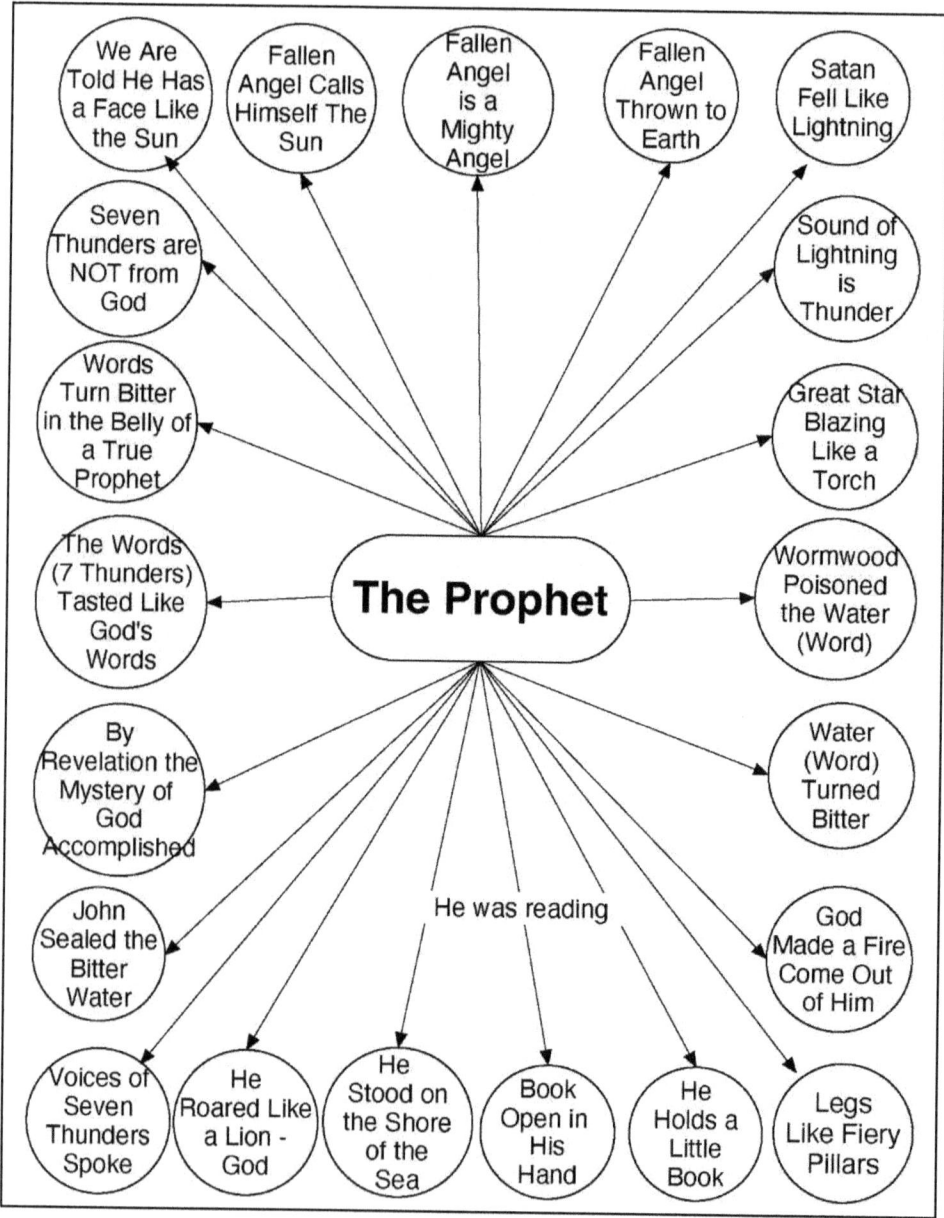

The Prophet

Chapter 7

The Sound of Seven Thunders

John's Warning About the Seven "Thunders" of Revelation 10

In every good read, there should come a moment or moments when clarity rushes over the reader like a sudden chill. This should prove to be one of those moments. This is the time when you finally look at something from a completely different perspective and realize, "I never thought of it that way before!" This is the moment when the reader comes to understand that powerful biblical angels are not all working on the side of God.[440] The key to understanding John's testimony of Revelation 10 is to acknowledge that the powerful angel standing before John is the fallen angel. He is described as coming down out of heaven *all ablaze*. You know what this is. The story has been told before. It was Jesus who described Satan as falling from heaven like lightning.[217] Picture a strike of lightning in your mind - it is a light that is all ablaze, setting fire to much of what it touches. It is of little wonder that Jesus, John, and Paul all describe Satan as he who masquerades as an angel of light.[530]

The rainbow above the angel's head is no halo. It represents God's covenant.[98] That covenant includes Satan's fall and his mingling among men on earth. This mighty angel plays an important role in God's story of man and how Satan's influence has taken place here on earth. Deception is his trade. Mixing truth and lies is his craft. His early work as the deceptive serpent is described as early as three chapters into Genesis. Now, in the 10th chapter of Revelation, the fiery serpent stands with indignation and shakes his fist in contempt. With his own little book open in his hand, he stands on the shore of the sea and shares in the roar of his seven thunders. In that book are the marks of his speaking image. Now gathered and bound, he scatters the words and crafts his lies while implementing his deceptions into something that resembles the Word of God. But his are the words of the dragon. Unlike the Word of God, the roar of the fiery angel is not trustworthy or true. The revelations he pressed upon a dull desert thief were the menacing echoes of rebellion. John heard the things roared about the seven thunders but was given specific instructions not to write them down. He was directed not to write them down because the seven thunders originated in the spirit of the dragon. Pressed upon his speaking image, these thunders were the voice of lightning - flowing out of the mouth of The Prophet. Satan's rebellion and war against God had moved from heaven above to the shore of the sea below.

At this point, it is helpful to know what The Prophet had to say about his god and how it correlates to the mighty angel who introduced evil to our world. This is his testimony. The Prophet said, "O people of the [Bible], indeed our messenger has come to you, making clear to you much of that which you concealed of the [Bible] and passing over much. Indeed, there has come to you from [god], a light[412] and a clear book."[392]

Instead of attempting to interpret what was said here, it would be best to refer to the commentary of the scholar who translated the 'clear book' into English. Maulana Muhammad Ali writes: "Two things are here spoken of as having come from [god], a *light* and a *clear book*. The light is The Prophet, and the book, [his book]. The prophet is the greatest spiritual light which ever dawned upon this earth. Hence he is called a light-giving sun."[263]

There are two things that Maulana attempts to clearly convey:

- A new prophet arrived as a light in the darkness for mankind – he arrived 500 years after Jesus' apostles and prophets laid down their pens
- He brought with him the words of a new book that would correct all the corrupted teachings of the prophets before him.

This newest prophet was supposed to be a bearer of good news who would:

- Be the greatest spiritual light ever set upon this earth
- Change the laws
- Correct all corrupted Biblical teaching
- Change 2,000 years of prophetic testimony
- Clear up all the prophetic mistakes - from Moses to Jesus, and Jesus to John & Paul
- Unseat Jesus and become a light for mankind as a *light-giving sun*

To be clear, this new prophet and his new book make the claim that his teaching was to supersede all biblical testimony before him. The Prophet explains that his god is the best of deceivers, and, for whatever reason, he apparently chose to keep the truth concealed for a period of 2,500 years and hidden from at least 42 previous prophets who

The Prophet

were guided by the Spirit of God. He wants us to believe that God held the truth back from Moses. He would want men to believe that God held His teaching back from Paul and John. And, of course, The Prophet contends that God held the true and faithful Word from Christ, the Messiah. The Prophet spins a tale that God then waited 500-600 years while Christians and Jews practiced His Laws and ways before He finally introduced the one man, this final prophet, to set everything straight. With God's new insight, The Prophet's new and improved laws were introduced to replace the outdated information given to the likes of Moses and retained by the Christ. The Prophet presented new laws that were supposedly given to him by God to replace the laws that Jesus said were never to change. The Prophet's light was to overcome the light of Christ – the Son of the Living God. And, as *the lamp of light,* The Prophet proposed to *accurately* reflect the light of the god he spoke for.

God did not choose to be conniving and deceitful. He is neither a deceiver, nor did He conceal the truth - hiding the real laws for centuries. The Prophet acted as he was prophesied to act by the prophets who warned of his coming. How did John describe the angel in Revelation 10? "… His face was like the sun, and his legs were like fiery pillars. He was holding a little book, which lay open in his hand."[433] According to The Prophet, he came to us as a light with a new book. And what did this light look like? He looked like a light-giving sun! Is it any wonder that people confuse the spiritual Satan with the flesh and blood known as *Lucifer*? Aside from flesh and blood, these two are spiritually inseparable. Such is the nature of the speaking image of the beast. That beast, the dragon we know to be Satan, stands with one foot on the land and one foot on the sea. To those who have a lick of common sense, this scene describes *the shore of the sea.*

The shore of the sea is where Satan stands in the beginning of Revelation 13.[434] With his lethal book in hand, the angel of fire gives his signature shout. He shouted the sound of seven thunders. Described as a roar like that of a lion (God), these seven snippets have since become the dull roar of billions of people who chant these 'seven' worship phrases to the fiery angel - five times a day. We all know what this looks like. We see it often. It's the repetitious act of dropping to one's knees and repeatedly contacting ones' forehead upon the ground. This leaves an impressionable mark. And what might this sound like? What is the sound of two billion people falling to their knees and chanting the same seven verses? Can you envision it? This is the result of the fallen angel pressing his wishes upon the lone prophet, who, in turn, instructs billions to submit to his god and repeat the marks they have previously been fed by The Prophet. Five times a day they roar the roar. They chant the collective promises to abide by the covenant of The Prophet and his god.

They pledge to praise the one who delivered the book. How might God see this rebellious act? The answer is simple. He will not be defamed. God will not yield His glory to another.[161]

It is reasonable to assume that the seven thunders are neither trustworthy nor true, because John was told *not* to write them down. To the contrary, the Lord states; "I am making everything new!" And he instructs John to, "write this down, for these words are trustworthy and true."[560] Such cannot be said about the seven thunders. John did not write them down. So, just exactly what are these seven sounds of lightning? What is the content of the mysterious *roar* that is heard in the presence of the fallen one? What does this have to do with Satan, his speaking image, and their people? The answers to these questions bring us to the next moments of clarity.

In the initial throws of researching this book, the motivating factor was the world's sudden shift to a Manchurian-like Presidential candidate. An election was soon to take place in the U.S. and a new President was about to be seated. He demonstrated genuine disdain for the United States and its promise of life, liberty, and the pursuit of happiness. Instead, he fed the fire of anger and resentment. He claimed to be a Christian, but the fruit he bore was of another tree. Initially, he held tight the two unwritten rules that had to be demonstrated by any U.S. Presidential candidate. He must be a Christian and he must believe in traditional marriage. The change in American values was so great during this man's presidency that those unwritten rules have since been abandoned. How things have changed! But in that day and during that election, there was a rapidly rising star on the horizon who made both claims. He continued with the charade until he was elected a second time. Then, he changed course. The President shed his cloak and changed his tune about traditional marriage. He splashed the White House in colors of the rainbow, lending credence to the notion that what was once deemed shameful by God's perfect judgment was now to be seen as the loving and beautiful departure of man from the Word. He championed the actions that God detests.[480] The candidate-turned President stood before a nation - steadfastly boasting his Christianity, but his background and upbringing was *steeped* in another belief.[21] His obvious affection and supportive statements surrounding the practices of his youth were not fruits picked from the tree of Christianity. They were a mix of ideologies that were evidently intended to please a global community. He was placating to a global audience while misleading the American people. His actions went far beyond the pale of politics. His defense, alliance, and support of the Prophetiers was beyond politics while mired in admiration and painted with recognition. By design, he planted immigrant Prophetiers into densely populated districts – resulting in a voting majority and the election of two Congressional candidates who carry the marks of The Prophet on their foreheads. This is a warning of things to come! His birth-name, birth-place, ancestry, country of origin, youthful name, Congressional name, and immigrant student status *changed* with the prevailing winds. The man is a Chameleon. He blended his birth-place and nationality with the financial and political needs of the moment. It was one thing when he attended college. Those records are now sealed. It was another thing when he stepped into the Presidential ring. Those records have been opened. He declared himself to be American-born for purposes of the election but portrayed himself as a foreign national when courting potential universities and addressing young colleagues. Though his name changed throughout the years, he returned to his birth name for political gain. His is a name that originates from the vine of The Prophet. His sudden appearance and curious rise in political power were the initial motivations and driving force when it came to researching this book.

His clever manipulation of the P.C. crowd should be an example to the reader that: "You cannot drink the cup of the Lord and the cup of demons too."[23] America was just seven years into their promise to never forget the circumstances of 9/11 and the destruction of the Twin Towers when he stepped into the Presidential ring. Yet the voters were about to place their trust in a man who could not possibly be what he claimed to be. To better understand the man and how he was raised, it was necessary to start where he started and read what he read. The book that was the model of manhood and the essence of his upbringing was *the clear book* introduced by The Prophet. That was the book that he came to memorize. He likely did not notice, but Chapter 1 was a stunner! It consists of a whopping seven phrases, and this is how they read:

1. Praise be to [god], the Lord of the worlds
2. The Beneficent, the Merciful
3. Master of the day of Requital
4. Thee do we serve and Thee do we beseech for help
5. Guide us on the right path
6. The path of those upon whom Thou hast bestowed favors
7. Not those upon whom wrath is brought down, nor those who go astray

Here were the seven thunders - the sound and voice of the lightning - each one building upon the other. They begin with all praise being averted to a foreign god. He has been granted the characteristics of being tender and delicate though he teaches oppression, submission, and hostility. His own people are those who have been taught to oppress God's Christians and Jews.[395] Instead of offering a gift in the way of the sacrifice and offering, as was offered by Father and Son, he insists upon people serving him and seeking him for help. According to his insistence, the voice of lightning directs his people to ask that they be put on the 'right path,' a path that will show the Prophetiers favor. But not a path like those who have been the victims of atrocities nor those who have supposedly strayed from God.

Worded as they are, these 'seven' appear to give religious insight, but they are steeped in contradiction. What beneficent and merciful god rejects Jesus' implementation of grace[186] in exchange for the murderous intentions of a notorious thief?[393] What was the result when the translated word for 'god' became *the proper name*[240] of The Prophet's newly introduced deity? How much confusion might this manipulative bait and switch cause for a people who never knew God to begin with? Isn't it prudent to assume (as most do) that *God* is *God* in any translation? The answer is simply – yes! It is a simple matter until the translated name becomes a proper name. Now, the game has changed. The foreign god has taken his stand and is making his move to unseat God and assume His glory.

Consider those two traits of The Prophet's god, his being *beneficent* and *merciful*. How might the reader perceive it when they recognize that the synonyms for these two attributes can be found in Isaiah 47:1 as *tender* and *delicate*? God's Word utilizes these two characteristics to mock the liar and identify him (it) as the biblical character known to be the *Daughter of the Babylonians*. The Babylonians, both old and new, gave birth to many fake gods – this being one of them. And what is this business about The Prophet's god being *the Master of the day of Requital*? This is not *the Day of the Lord* that the Bible speaks about.[504] The day of requital is not a joyous occasion as is the day when Jesus' body is gathered up to Him. The day of requital is all about the liar's revenge. That day is a promise of furious rage and aggression. This is about the fallen angel who holds a merciless book of death and oppression in his left hand while he raises his right hand as a defiant fist toward the God of heaven. He swears in God's name (which is never a good thing) stating that there will be no more delay! The final battle of the Satan's rebellion has begun!

Now comes the key phrase *'in the middle of the seven.'* This 4th thunder follows the first three and trails the final three, it's the verse that is literally in the middle of the seven. The middle verse is the statement that causes all Prophetiers to suffer the same fate as their god and prophet. It is pivotal. The sentence states, unequivocally, that the followers of The Prophet's god are to serve him and to seek him for help. They are to seek him alone! At face value, this is of little notice or concern to most people. When men seek God, one would assume that they seek the God of Heaven. But we are not speaking about norms and assumptions here. We are speaking about the prophetic actions of the fallen angel and how his deceit applies to biblical prophecy. In this instance, The Prophet's god is instructing his followers to reject the sacrifice and offering of Christ's crucifixion for the seven thunders and the help of the angel of fire. Consider this for a moment. Understand what Satan is doing. He is effectively putting an end to Jesus' sacrifice and offering for everyone who falls in line and submits to the instruction of the thunder. They look away from the gift of Christ and direct their loyalty toward the lure of the fallen. Satan is not putting an end to this gift for Christians. He can't do that. Satan is putting an end to God's gift for all Prophetiers who seek him, the masquerading light, for help. Where does the Word suggest that men will no longer need the grace of the Son? Where does God's Word give us such a dramatic shift in instruction and lead us away from His perfect gift? Why would He do that? Why would He offer us the gift of eternal life in the way of the sacrifice and offering of his Son and then instruct us to abandon all that He has sacrificed? No such instruction comes from the Word of God. Throughout the prophetic testimony, the Word warns us about this exact deception. God's Word gives men the guidance necessary to navigate the falsehoods of such a compelling liar. Daniel warned us about a god who would confirm a covenant with many by way of one 'seven.' The one 'seven' is the combination of snippets verbalized by The Prophet, as they were entered into the clear book, and held in the hand of the fallen angel. Everything fits God's prophetic warning.

Can it be just another coincidence that *the ruler who will come* was a god and prophet who set up their camp on the Temple Mount in the 7th century? The world has endured 14 centuries of this *ruler who has come*, and grossly evident is the astounding devastation that he is responsible for. Success of The Prophet is an embarrassment for mankind, acknowledging that the coincidences have mounted and accumulated so perfectly as to *put an end to the sacrifice and offering* on the part of God, in that many might pursue such a murderous wretch! His treacherous opening, declaring Jews and Christians to be on the wrong path, should have been an obvious giveaway to his evil scheme and masquerade. The perfection of prophecy demonstrates how The Prophet brought an end to Jesus' sacrifice and offering in the middle of The Prophet's 'seven' thunders - precisely as it was written. This is no coincidence. Daniel gave us the warning in chapter 9, verse 27. The ruler who came (Satan) confirmed the covenant that was introduced by The Prophet. It can also be understood that the ruler who came, The Prophet, confirmed the covenant that was introduced by Satan; he holds the little book in his hand. In the middle of their one 'seven' they put an end to the sacrifice and offering that was known so well in Jerusalem. And now, revealing this man means that the story of this generation of man is nearly finished.

We now come to the ruler's *variant path*. After 1,335 years between Moses' introduction of the Law and Jesus' institution of grace through crucifixion, The Prophet had other ideas and a better elixir for men. He brought about a new god with new laws. This new god he gave ancient honors and familiar names like *the God of Abraham*, but his actual identities were *the father of lies* and *murderer*. As the 5th thunder roared, the Prophetiers were taught to take an alternate path. This path was paved by the covenant introduced by The Prophet. Consistent with the warning of Daniel 11 and *the king who exalts himself*, the world can now see how it is that the prophets were guided to know the imminent life story of The Prophet and how he would attack the mightiest fortresses with the help of a foreign god. It now becomes painfully obvious as to how he greatly honors those who acknowledge him. He bestows favors. Kings and kingdoms have been given over to the most ruthless members of his gang. Afghanistan is just the latest example of his iron rule. The only way to free Afghanistan is to free the people from the power of The Prophet. But the prophecy does not allow for such a departure from reality. They are locked in. His methods of madness reward those who acknowledge him, which cause the deception to grow and advance - generation after generation. The oppression and shame they shower upon women is built into The Prophet's culture. He has lifted the most ruthless of these men to be rulers among the people. The few women who are freed of this oppression continue to be enslaved by The Prophet's cause and a few of them serve a political purpose in the advancement of the charade. They make false declarations and bold accusations of phobias while the beast continues to slither along its ravenous path. All they must do in exchange for the favor of their god is to strive in the advancement of The Prophet's cause. He gave them specific instructions and a *clear book* that abandons the teaching and paths that God set in place. God's path has been in place since *Abram* became *Abraham*. But The Prophet taught them to select his new path. In essence, The Prophet and his newfound god have taught a lost and perishing people that the Laws and the ways of God that had been documented and existed for two millennia were outdated, erroneous, and saturated in corruption. A new ruler with a variant truth had arrived. And, within five decades of his death, his abominations appeared on the Temple Mount. They have remained there ever since.

The 6th thunder references the reward and promise of paradise that awaits those who honor The Prophet and his god. Such is the carrot that hangs in front of the beasts who advance the war against God and His people. Satan started this war with his rebellion and wickedness. He was filled with violence, and he sinned. He became proud and was corrupted by his own wisdom. With dishonest trade, he desecrated his sanctuaries.[80] Then, there was war in heaven.[439] Does any of this sound familiar? The Dragon decided he would be God. He attempted to assume the role in heaven - just as he has attempts to assume that role here on earth. And, just as he had an army in heaven, he has an army here on earth. They strive a mighty striving to assist him in his efforts and attain that highest seat. Though most wince at the reality, there has been war with The Prophet and his god for 14 centuries. There was war in the beginning. There was war in the interim. And there will be war the end.[43] The Prophetiers fight for the advancement of their god in the same way they fought for the advancement of The Prophet. War gave him his platform. They strive to achieve his objective. They strive to fight until all religions obey only The Prophet's laws. Like it or not, the Prophetiers are all at war.[370] To strive in this fashion is their sworn duty. War will continue until the end. It must. How can it end any other way? All who oppose The Prophet and his laws are accused of *creating mischief in the land*. Included, but not limited to the mischievous, are those called out in the little book as Christians and Jews.[241] The Prophet demands that the penalties for this type of mischievous behavior should be punishable by murder, crucifixion, amputation and/or imprisonment.[393] Utilizing this type of individual judgement gives men power, and power lifts kings to become rulers over many. Look at the tremendous amount of political damage that has been inflicted by just a few who travel in such a squad. Prophetiers and Socialists have aligned to systematically dismantle freedoms and the pursuits of happiness that Americans previously held dear. Thanks in part to their efforts, the American Dream has suffered and is now on life support. Life, liberty, and the pursuit of happiness are rapidly being replaced by murder, oppression, and the emotional slavery of submission. Look around the world. Count the number of nations within U.N. who have submitted to the duties of slavery and the ways of The Prophet and his god. Dare to recognize just how many lands and peoples have been distributed at the price of The Prophet's long-standing war.[58] Horrific is the sum of the lives and souls that have been sacrificed to advance the endeavors of a man who shook the earth and made kingdoms tremble. History and current events confirm these Luciferian accounts. This is what The Prophet regards as *obligatory* and *enjoined upon* the people in his states of affair.

Finally, consider the lunacy of the seventh thunder. That roaring clap of the lightning's voice warns the Prophetiers to avoid the path of God's chosen people and Jesus' faithful few. As has been the practice, there is no need for reliance upon personal interpretation of the verse or verses. Rather, it is best to quote the scholar as he narrates his own understanding and translation. According to Maulana Muhammad Ali, "...the prophet is reported to have said, 'Those upon whom wrath is brought down are the Jews and those who went astray are the Christians.'"[241]

Which 'prophet' is prophesied to appear *after* God's prophets had retired their pens? Which 'prophet' is prophesied to oppose the written Word and declare that Christians and Jews, God's people, were mistaken and took the wrong path? Which is the exclusive prophet who is not a product of Isaac's bloodline – the vine that is responsible for producing at least 42 prophets who wrote 66 Spirit-driven books & letters over a course of 1400 years? If The Prophet is the messenger of God, what might be the consequences for Jewish prophets like Moses, Isaiah, Jeremiah, and Daniel – those who were influenced by the Spirit of God during their prophetic years? Expanding on that thought, what are the consequences for the faithful Christians who followed Jesus' teaching and God's Laws for 500 years before The Prophet appeared? The only logical response to these questions is awfully inconvenient for those who have joined the ranks and alliances of The Prophet. Whether they are members of his movement, sympathizers, or political allies – the answer remains the same. He's a fraud.

In the last 4,000 years, there has been only one *long-standing* prophet whose appearance was to denounce biblical teaching and "to sweep away the errors which were a blot on the face of prophethood."[230] But the blot on the face of prophethood would prove to be concentrated upon a lone man - he who lived and died as a murderous thief. His own testimony verifies that The Prophet was a literal thief who pillaged and looted his neighbors. He killed with impunity and destroyed for destruction's sake. He even called his god *the destroyer*.[561] All these things initially took place in his own land and against his own neighbors. Without argument, he is a man who shook the earth and made kingdoms tremble; he overthrew its cities and would not let his captives go home. Little has changed in 1,400 years! The only question that remains is whether he is just *another man* who satisfied the prophetic warning, or if he is *the man* who satisfied this warning?

The seven thunders close with The Prophet declaring that God's chosen Jews and Jesus' faithful Christians each chose the wrong path. Though Jesus taught Paul that the vines of Christians and Jews were to be grafted together[488] and mercifully spared as one vine, The Prophet disagreed and took offense to the promised covenant – he took literal

The Prophet

offense. After the prophets wrote all their books over a timespan 14 centuries, a branch was formed through the vine of Ishmael. That branch dismissed all the prophets, all their books, and all their letters. What they had previously agreed upon - he disputed. What they recorded - he rejected. Though he could not read - he claimed to know better. Though he could not write - he spoke life into a new book. According to The Prophet, he who claimed to have introduced light into the darkness with a (new) clear book, all Spiritual guidance and prophetic teaching merely led God's people astray. This is The Prophet's story. Relying solely on prophetic warning, if there was ever a case to be made against the false prophet, this would be it!

The circumstances surrounding the seven thunders and the consequences of their global application does not end with the initial warnings. John writes that he heard a voice from heaven who instructed him to "Go, take the scroll that lies open in the hand of the angel who was standing on the sea and on the land."[436] So, John went to the angel and asked for the book he held in his hand. It was then said to John: "Take it and eat it. It will turn your stomach sour, but in your mouth it will be as sweet as honey." John complied by taking the book from the hand of the fiery angel and he ate it. This might sound a bit odd, but when one considers Jesus' instruction that "Men do not live on bread alone, but on every Word that comes from the mouth of God,"[324] then one begins to understand that this is a test. Was the book the Word of God or was it the dreadful ruse of a liar? John's testimony states that the book tasted as sweet as honey in his mouth, but when he had eaten it, his stomach turned sour. God's Word has been given out among men to help them live their lives and live them to the full. His Word does not make men ill. To the contrary, when applied, His Word and covenant bring about healing. So, what words might taste like honey but sour in the stomach of a faithful prophet of God? These would be the words of the masquerading light. They speak of utilizing murder, oppression, dismemberment, imprisonment, and slavery as methods of crowd control and loyalty. They are arranged in a manner that composes a book that outwardly appears to be godly but is nothing of the sort. It is the deceptive anchor, a fool's guide, of the fallen angel and the mouthpiece who delivered it. Because this word made John sick, it could not have been the Word that is, was, and always will be the Word of God. The fiery angel's book is not the Word that was with God in the beginning. It is not the Word that became flesh in the way of the Son. The oral author of Satan's little book rejects the promise and ransom given by the Messiah. The messenger of the fallen angel's book rejects previous testimony that the Son is *the light of the world*.[189] The Prophet delivered the clear book. He also took credit for having Jesus' traits.[290] Only one man, Lucifer, would dare to take the glory that has been deservedly earned by the Son.

John's testimony was specific as to the taste of the words. Upon reading a book, few people will offer up any reference to the book's *taste*. Even fewer or none will literally eat the books they read. But God is being specific. So, what is the underlying meaning in his reference to honey? To understand this reference, look to the commentary about The Prophet in Chapter 16 of the book that once lays open in the angel's hand. Titled *The Bee*, this is what the known scholar had to say:

> "This chapter is appropriately named The Bee, because 'the bee, guided by instinct, which is called the revelation in this case, gathers together sweet honey from the flowers of all kinds, taking what is best in them, thus producing a beverage of many hues in which there is healing for men.' So Divine revelation to The Prophet collected what was best in the teaching of all the prophets and presented it in [the book], which is also declared to be a healing for the spiritual diseases of men."[283]

After ingesting the words, John disagreed. The book was not a healing mechanism for him. The book and its words made him sick. The Prophet compared the words in his book to the beverage of many hues of the bee. He called the words within his book *honey*. But what tasted like honey was the illness that has befallen men. The star that was Wormwood had poisoned the waters that sustained men. The honey that is the Word of God is not the beverage of many hues currently force-fed to the Prophetiers. This should send chills down your spine!

The covenant formed between the fiery angel and the Prophetiers was confirmed 18 years after The Prophet's death. His oral presentations, the image of his god, were confirmed by the creation and compilation of that book. The essence of that entire covenant is outlined by its first seven sentences. As Daniel warned, *many* have followed The Prophet and his god. And as John warned, they all roar these seven sentences back to the fiery angel. They do so five times a day - every day![236]

> "The Opening [seven thunders] has a special importance as a prayer. Its Oft-Repeated Seven Verses constitute the prayer for guidance of every [Prophetier] at least 32 times per day, and therefore it has much greater importance for [god] than the Lord's Prayer for a Christian. The latter is instructed to pray for the coming of the kingdom of God, whereas the [Prophetier] is instructed to seek for his right place in that kingdom, which has already come… the coming of The Prophet was really the advent of the kingdom of [God]…
>
> - MMA, Qur'an, Narrative, Chapter 1, paragraph 5, pp. 1-2

The mysteries of *the seven thunders* in Revelation and the *one 'seven'* in Daniel coincide to give God's people the knowledge that these 'seven' are one and the same. Using just a few words, these seven blasphemous declarations honor the foreign god, reject the Gift of God, and demonstrate Satan's distinct loathing for God's people. These statements are the broad strokes of covenant, outlining the final battle-plans of the fallen angel and his long-lasting rebellion against everything that is called *God*. The 'seven' constitute a model of deception that one might expect from the father of lies and his mouthpiece of a man - The Prophet. With the ultimate throne in his sights, Satan started war in heaven to become *the Lord of the worlds*.[419] He lost the war above, and he will lose the war on earth. Until then, Satan will continue to succeed in his endeavors. Most (particularly the political crowd) do not see him as the masquerading light. They see him as the Prophetiers see him – the Lord of heaven and earth. The power of his hypnotizing instruction is astonishing! In what must be the mother of all contradictions, this *tender* and *delicate* deity promotes the most heinous acts of lawlessness.

> "No more will you be called tender and delicate… Perhaps you will succeed, perhaps you will cause terror… [But] those you have labored with and trafficked with since childhood… goes on in error; there is none that can save you.
>
> – Isaiah 47:1, 12, 15

The 4th roar has ended the sacrifice and offering of the Father and His Son for all who have consumed the honey and seek the nourishment of his book. The Prophet's words turned bitter in the belly of John. As previously discussed, his words are not a healing for men but a poison that spreads through the oppressive growth of his ever-expanding body. The words are intended to influence dark-hearted and evil men. The words encourage them to act as The Prophet acted. He acted with malice and intended harm. Whereas John acted as a man of God – with compassion and grace. John was a prophet of God. He understood what it meant when something sweet became something bitter. John knows that darkness cannot become light. He knows that evil cannot become good. God would not let John be duped by the seven thunders of the masquerading light. But most of mankind does not share in John's faith. The majority find faith in their own needs and wants. They are those who choose to perish – consciously deceived by every sort of counterfeit miracle, sign, and wonder. "They perish because they refused to love the truth and so be saved. For this reason, God sends them a powerful delusion so that they will believe the lie and so that all will be condemned who have not believed the truth but have delighted in wickedness."[512] Those who mock everything that is called God are the builders and caregivers of today's beast. The whole world suffers from the ills of the beast. From the uprising of Prophetiers to the re-emergence of Sodomites and the lawlessness of racism from those who profess that the only color that matters is "black" – the whole world has turned from sweet to bitter.

By now, the reader likely recognizes The Prophet to be Jesus' biblical nemesis. As the speaking image of the dragon, he insisted that much of the written Word of the prophets was a blot on the face of prophethood. His opening words insist that Christians and Jews had strayed from the right path and were subject to the wrath of God. He is the powerful delusion that the world has long awaited. His newly trampled path was not a better way to live one's life, but a highway to certain condemnation. He has gathered billions to accompany him. The Prophet's body of believers is now a giant whose mass is 50% larger than any other on the planet. They are supported by the hypocritical liars who are collectively known as the harlot, and they garner the adoration of the world's political elite. Those who find it politically incorrect to oppose The Prophet and his evil scheme serve only to boost his powers and strengthen his followers' duty to strive until everyone conforms to his ways and laws of his god. Of this, John asks the right question: "Who is like the beast? Who can make war against him?"[446]

Biblically speaking, the world has collectively progressed into bitter darkness and is currently in an all-out sprint away from God and His perfect Word. This is in accordance with the Script. Men will neither change their ultimate betrayal of their Creator, nor can they change the consequences of their determined insolence. Men have done their part in fulfilling biblical prophecy. The Prophet's movement is growing at a break-neck pace. Like Pac Man, they continue to gobble up seats in the U.S. Congress. The United States now consists of those who boastfully admit that they are members of The Prophet's lair. They legislate with the same duty and determination as those who find paradise below the shadow of the swords. Understanding their intentions is terrifying! The United States laws are now influenced by lawmakers who strive to legitimize The Prophet's changed laws. Thanks to the parabolic growth of the politically correct, the long reach of The Prophet's laws will not be slowed or stopped by truth or reason.

The answer to John's question is apocalyptic. The outcome is unsettling. For those who do not know God or His Word, the imminent future can be terrifying. Mankind is not in the early throws of the false prophet's rebellion. We are at the end of his game. We see him now. We see all that he has accomplished. His people are too many and too influential to be stopped, and they are winning. With all the world's support, they have good reason to think they will win the war. But God and His people know different. God mocks the dragon. He says:

"Disaster will come upon you, and you will not know how to conjure it away. A calamity will fall upon you that you cannot ward off with ransom; a catastrophe you cannot foresee will suddenly come upon you... Well do I know how treacherous you are; you were called a rebel from birth. For my own name's sake, I delay my wrath; for the sake of my praise, I hold it back from you, so as not to cut you off. See, I have refined you, though not as silver; I have tested you in the furnace of affliction. For my own sake, *for my own sake*, I do this. How can I let myself be defamed? I will not yield my glory to another."[157]

These are God's Words, as they were written by Isaiah – 2,750 years ago. With The Prophet being revealed, God's purpose will no longer remain a mystery. The world has fallen into utter chaos. The emotional grip and mental state of mankind is so distorted that most can no longer tell the difference between a man and a woman. Accepted as the new normal are men who have submitted to the politics of emotional distress and they find themselves submerged in mental illness. Whether chemically, surgically, or emotionally - they nip and tuck to remove their manhood, hiding their masculinity, which allows for them to compete with women and gather the world's attention. God warned that evil would become good – just as the world recognizes these cowards as...

heroic role-models! In this regard, the mysteries of God and His prophets are blossoming like a rose in the light of the sun.

Our Father knows the plans of that mighty angel with legs and a face of flame. He knows how and why the liar started war in heaven. God knows how and why Satan resumed his war here on earth. God knows. He also knows how the dragon destroys himself and all who follow him. The furnace of affliction is not lit by the Father. The flames are lit and fed by the liar.[82] The fire that is soon to fall from heaven to earth is *caused* by [revealing] The Prophet.[450]

According to Paul, the answer to John's question as to 'who can make war against the beast' will not come *until* the man of lawlessness is revealed. This simple promise needs to be emphasized. The last of Jesus' elect and the Father's chosen people will not ascend to the kingdom of heaven *until* the man of lawlessness is revealed to the world. It is then, and *only* then, that we see the Day of the Lord become a reality. On that day, Jesus will overcome The Prophet and the god he introduced with nothing more than the breath of His mouth. Satan, the spirit, brought about Lucifer - the man. Though men thought they would recognize the man of lawlessness, they allowed him to strive a mighty striving and spread his oppressive fury across the globe. The world is soon to be re-introduced to the man of perdition. Rest assured, Jesus destroys him and his work by the splendor of His coming!

The Prophet

Ronald B. Stetton

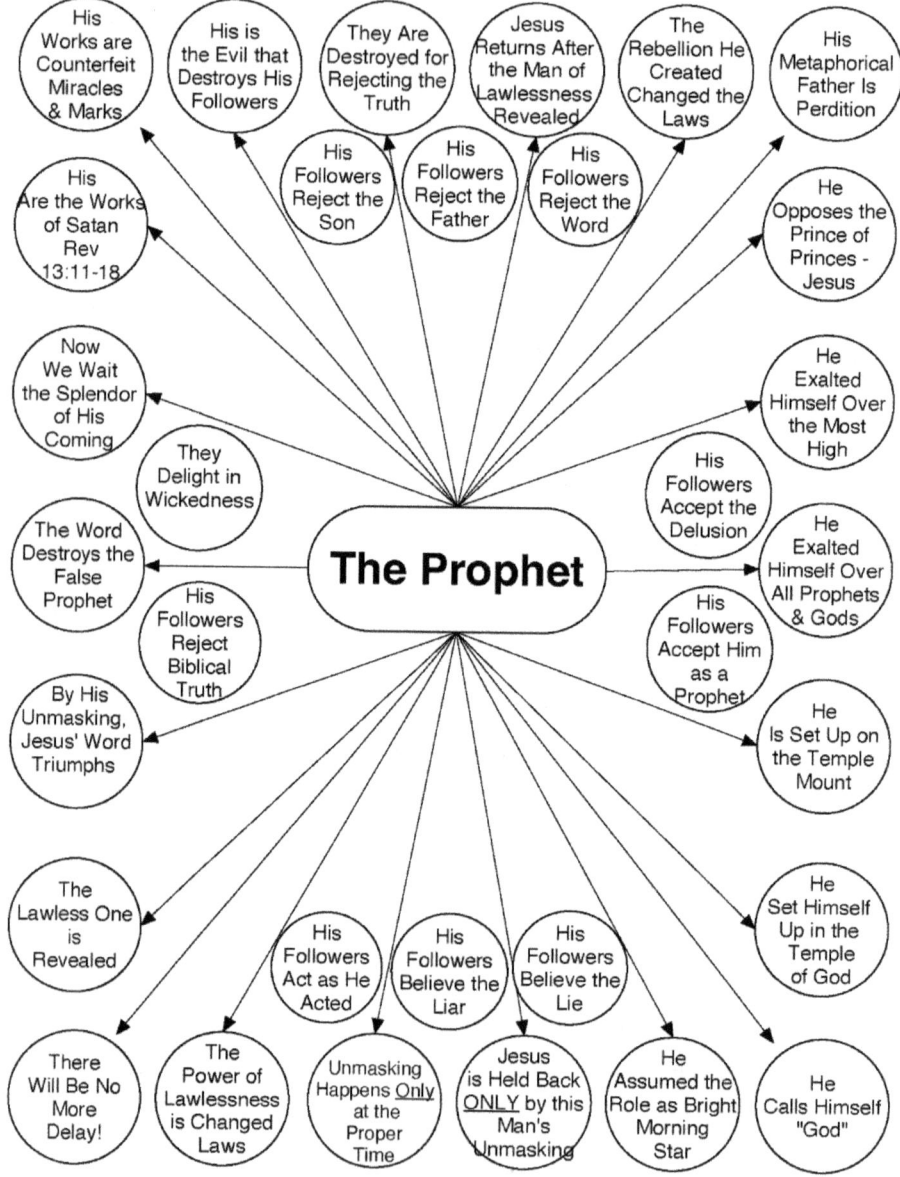

Chapter 8

Revelation Before the Day of the Lord

Paul's Warning About the Man of Lawlessness (2 Thessalonians 2)

The biblical case against The Prophet is rapidly building. With a little insight and a lot of knowledge from Isaiah, we have learned and confirmed that Lucifer was a man. His many prophetic characteristics and tendencies have overlapping themes that have been conveyed by other prophets. The reader has come to know more about The Prophet and how he fulfilled the prophetic tendencies of the *little horn* who spoke in opposition to the Father and His Son. One of those tendencies was to oppress God's saints. And, just as the Prophetiers do today, The Prophet oppressed God's Christians and Jews. That's not opinion or conjecture, it's what he has said and what he has done. He has largely succeeded in his attempt to change the set times from A.D. to A.H. and he continues to institute his new laws.

As the man of intrigue, The Prophet has opposed Jesus and Jesus' grace by destroying many with a twisted rendition of *peace*. Thanks to a few key phrases, we can now recognize him as the king who exalted himself above Jesus and above everything else that is called *God*. Setting himself up in this manner has brought much adoration. People are ready and willing to kill for him. They have demonstrated their eagerness to kill for his god. The price for such adoration has been exceptionally high. The Prophet achieved the (supposed) position of the most high by instructing his people to defend his ways *by any means necessary*. This instruction has led to the slaughter of millions. These are the final wishes and revelations of God?

Call him a mighty angel, the masquerading light, the devil, lightning, the dragon, or Satan – his covenant is the arrangement made with his people. A summary of his lethal deceptions is condensed into the seven dark sentences that were warned about by the prophets Daniel and John. Having been given the gift of prophecy, these men wrote about The Prophet's one 'seven' and how they became the seven thunders of the lightning. Just as Jesus serves His Father, *the ruler that would come* serves *the mighty angel*. The argument that *the ruler* would have to be flesh is satisfied with The Prophet being the speaking image of the dragon.

The covenant between the fallen angel and his people negates nearly all of God's Commandments.

1. Adopting a god that The Prophet's fathers did not know negates the 1st Commandment - to have no other gods before Him.
2. Worshipping under an idol of moon and star negates the 2nd Commandment - forbidding idols.
3. Advancing lies about who and what constitutes God negates the 3rd Commandment – misusing the name of God.
4. Rejecting the Sabbath[244] negates the 4th Commandment – to keep it holy.
5. Rejecting God as our Father negates the 5th Commandment – to honor your Father.
6. Instructing people to *murder* for breaking the law (particularly following Jesus' institution of grace)[186] negates the 6th Commandment – thou shall not murder.
7. Teaching people to kill the non-believer and make wives of their widows negates the 7th Commandment – thou shall not commit adultery.
8. Stealing of any sort negates the 8th Commandment – thou shall not steal.
9. Deception of any kind negates the 9th Commandment – thou shall not give false testimony.
10. Coveting your neighbor's house, your neighbor's wife,[261] his servants, his livestock or anything that belongs to your neighbor negates the 10th Commandment – thou shall not covet your neighbor's possessions.[405]

These are just 10 of God's 613 known commands. He never changes.[319] His Laws have never changed. Jesus obeyed His Father's Laws while instituting grace for those who fell short of those Laws. Everyone falls short! So, The Prophet's lawlessness is demonstrated by the changes he instituted. And the changes he instituted promote death, destruction, theft, hedonistic slavery, and a god of astrologers – that of moon and stars. Had The Prophet been able to read, he would likely have chosen different symbolism for the god his fathers did not know. Few describe his lawlessness better than Paul in his second letter to the Thessalonians. Paul's prophetic description of the man of lawlessness coincides with historical events and documented statements that have come about with The Prophet and the book he established.

The Prophet

This is Paul's testimony about The Prophet – the man described as *the son of damnation*. In his letter, Paul writes about the coming of our Lord Jesus and our being gathered up to Him. He is quick to state that the faithful, Jesus' body and bride, are not to become easily unsettled or alarmed by any predictions, reports or letters that have supposedly come from any one of the prophets of God – stating that the day of the Lord has already come. Christians are told 'not to let anyone deceive them in any way, for that day cannot come *until* the rebellion occurs, *and* the man of lawlessness is revealed, the man doomed to his destruction.' This has thrown many faithful Christians into a frenzy! Somehow, a large part of Jesus' body became enamored with the thought that Christians must be removed *before* the man of lawlessness can be revealed. This thought coincides with the idea that Jesus' faithful will not play a part in seven years of a traditional tribulation. This tradition flies in the face of Paul's written promise: "Concerning the coming of our Lord Jesus Christ and our being gathered to Him… that day will not come *until*… the man of lawlessness is revealed."[502]

Why is it that this simple little word (until) has created such chaos within Christianity? That word has certainly served the harlot well! It serves as suitable justification for a departure from the Word of God. The harlot uses it as a means of misdirection to support her manmade tradition that Mary is an ever-virgin. As a wayward religious body, the harlot rejects Matthew's testimony that Mary and Joseph consummated their marriage.[323] They argue that the word *until* has somehow come to mean *never* or *forever into the future*. The harlotous among us are certain to gnash their teeth and snarl their nasty accusations when presented with Matthew's testimony. The harlot does not like being outed for her drunken behavior! She calls such truths *hateful bigotry*. Drunk on the blood of abomination and unfaithful to her bridegroom, the harlot serves as an example of how *not* to be a good minister to Christ!

Here again, there is a portion of Jesus' faithful body who have somehow come to believe that the Word says, "…the man of lawlessness will not be revealed until the church is removed…" The Word and current circumstances explain how 'the end comes like a flood.' The end does not come in accordance with a very noticeable new Jewish temple that houses some maniacal hack who calls himself *God*. The wing of the temple that stands in that place today is neither Jewish nor Christian. The man in that wing has been calling himself "God" for centuries and few have noticed. Though the reader might be sympathetic to the traditional beliefs of tribulation, it does not diminish their loyalty or faith in Christ. God kept His mystery sealed until it was the proper time to unveil it.

Paul tells us that Jesus will not return, and His church will not be gathered up to Him *until* the man of lawlessness has been revealed to the world. But how will he be recognized? Paul writes that the man of lawlessness is the source of rebellion. What did Satan do in heaven? He rebelled. He started the war. He rebelled against God, fighting Michael and his angels. Curiously, the man of lawlessness acted on earth exactly as his god acted in heaven. He took a stand against Jesus and opposed God's prophets. He has a long history of opposing and oppressing God's people. He spoke out against (the Most High) God. He exalted himself over everything that is called God or worshiped, and he set himself up in God's temple, proclaiming to be *God*.

It is understandable to acknowledge how and why people would think it necessary to build a third Jewish temple to fulfill prophecy. How else would any man set himself up in the temple of God as God? What most miss is that the Temple of God is no longer a large stone building on the Temple Mount. There is now only a wing of the temple that remains on what was previously holy ground.

Paul writes that the man of lawlessness will oppose and exalt himself over everything that is called God.[507] Already discussed is the little horn,[32] otherwise known as the stern-faced king,[37] he has opposed the Father and the Son. Evidence has been presented as to how this same man has a history of exalting himself above the Son while denying the Father. His intent is evident in that he might lift himself and his foreign god above everything that is called God.[54] Finally, the reader has been offered evidence as to how The Prophet deceived people into worshiping him alongside his foreign god while making the world believe that he is God's last prophet – the final *messenger of God*.[424]

The Prophet completely dismisses the testimony of Paul. Why would he do that? The answer is rather simple, and it has significant implications. Paul became a follower and subsequent apostle of Jesus Christ *after* Jesus' crucifixion and resurrection. He is the apostle to the Gentiles.[487] Within his written testimony, Paul explains how Gentiles are grafted into *the original vine* [198] [Jesus], that vine being an extension of Isaac's bloodline - God's chosen Jews.[320] It is Paul, the prophet who was introduced to Christ *after* His ascension, who gave us the testimony about the man of lawlessness.[503] It is Paul who came in Jesus' name,[127] to teach us all things and remind us of everything Jesus said to us.[203] Paul is *the Counselor*, filled with the Holy Spirit, whom the Father sent in Jesus' name. He was the only prophet of God who became an apostle of Christ by Christ's direct intervention *after* His ascension.[327] But the man of lawlessness taught that he was the counselor Jesus promised. "And when Jesus, son of Mary, said: O Children of Israel, surely I am the messenger of [God] to you, verifying that which is before me of the Torah and giving the good news of a Messenger who will come after me his name being [Counselor]."[304] If the original twelve apostles were told to give their testimony to the lost sheep of Israel (the Jews),[328] and Paul was designated as *the apostle to the Gentiles*,[486] who then, was The Prophet sent five centuries later? The Counselor was the Spirit of God who was to come after Christ's ascension - reminding us of everything Jesus taught.[197] That certainly does not describe The Prophet!

The Prophet declared that he was the promised Counselor. Instead of reminding us that not one letter of God's Law was to be changed,[325] he declared God's Laws to be outdated and meant for another people.[295] According to him, he was sent here to provide a perfected law and correct all the wrongs of previously corrupted Scripture, thereby 'sweeping away the errors that were a blot on the face of prophethood.'[230] The Prophet takes his role as *Counselor* way beyond the scope described by Jesus. In addition to changing the laws and erasing the (prophets), he does the unthinkable; he sets himself up in the temple of God *as* the temple of God. This is the moment when the reader likely asks; "How can that be? How can he set himself up in a temple that does not exist? The third Jewish temple has not been built yet!" The reader would be accurate in stating that a third Jewish Temple has not been built. But there is nothing in His Word that tells us there will be a third Jewish temple. Jesus is the rebuilt temple.[182] He will never be replaced by another. But what many Christians struggle with is how someone might set themself up in the temple of God without there being a temple! Many have concluded that a third Jewish temple must be built to fulfill the Word. That would necessitate a departure from the Script.

Maybe there is a different approach. Biblically speaking, what is definitive about the Temple of God? What does the Word have to say about the Temple and how is that Temple described? The answer is straightforward and lacks any sort of ambiguity. The temple of God is *the Lord God Almighty and the Lamb*, His Son. They are described as The Light and the Lamp [of light].[473] Just to be clear, the temple of God consists of *the glory of God Almighty as the Light and His Lamp*. The Lamp is, of course, God's messenger - His speaking image, the Lamb. With this basic biblical understanding, how might the man of lawlessness have set himself up in the temple of God, calling himself God? Though this has remained a mystery for two thousand years, the answer has now become evident. The son of perdition would take Jesus' role in the temple of God. He would substitute his god in the role of the light and further declare himself to be the lamp of that light.[412] We can now understand how Satan masquerades as the light[530] and how his messenger, The Prophet, has set himself up as the lamp of that light.

> "[the foreign god] is the light of the heavens and the earth. A likeness of his light is as a pillar on which is a lamp – the lamp is in a glass, the glass is as it were a brightly shining star [The Prophet][288]... light upon light."
>
> – Qur'an 24:35

In his own words, The Prophet states his god "is the light of the heavens and the earth and that he, The Prophet, is the lamp of that light." Pause for a moment. Consider the magnitude of what is being stated here. The Prophet has set himself up in the temple of God as a reflection of God. He describes himself as *the light personified, the light-giving sun,* and *the lamp of light.*[264] He has assumed the role of the Lamb, while setting himself up in the temple of God as the lamp of light. The Prophet has succeeded in fulfilling Paul's warning about the man of lawlessness![507] As exhilarating as that might be, there is much more. In the first chapter of this book, the argument was presented as to how Lucifer adopted the role of *the star of piercing brightness that appears at the end of the night,* otherwise described as *the morning star.* The morning star, described by Isaiah, and the man of lawlessness, described by Paul, are one and the same. The Prophet is *the man* who has accomplished both; he has set himself up in the temple of God as *the lamp of light* and he has adopted Jesus' title as *the Bright Morning Star.* It is no stretch to link him and his followers to the balance of Paul's warning about the man of lawlessness that states: "The coming of the lawless one will be in accordance with the work of Satan displayed in all kinds of counterfeit miracles, signs and wonders, and in every sort of evil that deceives those who are perishing. They perish because they refused to love the Truth and so be saved."[509]

The most evident of counterfeit miracles is his little book.[228] His signs are the literal "marks"[243] within that book. The horrific nature of his wonders includes the many directives to steal, kill and destroy.

The case against The Prophet began with God's descriptive mockery of him as *the morning star* – he who would come to oppose the Father and His Son. That case has now expanded to show him as the man of lawlessness – he who has set himself up in the temple of God as the lamp of light. Continuing doubts or rejection of this evidence as 'coincidental' is denied as The Prophet compares himself to God as "light upon light."[412] The Prophet compares himself to *God upon God.* His followers believe what is said about him, that he is to be raised to the highest position - to be "like the Most High."[313] And, just as the warning states, Lucifer would say in his heart that he is *like the Most High*.[140] Not only did he say it, but he had his scribes write it down! That which has been written cannot be erased.

Now that these things are being dragged into the light for all to see, it is reasonable to determine that the man of lawlessness has been revealed while Jesus' body of Christians remains in the world. His breathing body is still here! Although the ultimate power or spirit of lawlessness (Satan) was already at work when Paul wrote his second letter to the Thessalonians, the speaking image of Satan, the man of lawlessness, would not appear for another five centuries. His appearance is a matter of history. He is now being revealed.

For those who might remain skeptical, refer to Maulana Muhammad Ali's description of The Prophet's recorded words: "Again, each section of the [book] contains a number of *ayahs* or verses. The word *ayah* means, originally, an apparent *sign* or *mark* and, in this sense, it comes to mean *a miracle*, but it also signifies a communication or a message from [God] and is applied as such to a verse of the [book] as well as to a revelation or *a law*."[227]

Overflowing from the heart of the man of lawlessness was the speech of The Prophet. His speech and commentary were recorded by others so that all men might know him. His printed words became The Prophet's *marks* – supposed communications or messages from [god]. His followers continue to grow and institute his marks. Today's Headlines should be evidence enough of this man's continuing endeavors to change God's Laws. But Headlines do not necessarily offer the view of the Prophetier. Evidence of his followers' understanding can be found in the words of one of his faithful scholars. The wording might seem a bit foreign but it's worth the patience to read it through.

"The word *khatam* means *a seal* or the last part or portion of a thing, the latter being the primary significance of the word *khatim*. It may further be noted that *khatam al-qaum* always means the last of the people – *akhiru-hum*. Though [The] Prophet was admittedly the last of the prophets, and even history shows that no prophet appeared after him in the world, yet the [book] has adopted the word *khatam* and not *khatim*, because the deeper significance is carried in the phrase *Seal of the prophets* than mere *finality*. In fact, it indicates finality combined with *perfection of prophethood*, along with *a* continuance among his followers of certain blessings of prophethood. He is the *Seal of the prophets* because with him the object of prophethood, the manifestation of Divine will in laws which should guide humanity, was finally accomplished in the revelation of a perfect law in the [book], and he is also the *Seal of the prophets* because certain favors bestowed on prophets were forever to continue among his followers. The office of the prophet was only necessary to guide men, either by giving them a law or by *removing the imperfections of a previously existing law*, or by *giving certain new directions* to meet the requirements of the times, because the circumstances of *earlier human society did not allow the revelation of a perfect law* which should suit the requirements of different generations or different places. Hence prophets were constantly raised. **But through The Prophet a perfect law was given**, suiting the requirements of all ages and all countries, and this law was guarded against all corruption, and the office of the prophet was therefore no more required."[295]

Did you get all that? The Prophet admittedly ushered in new laws because God's previous laws, those that had been in place for nearly 2,000 years, were apparently not suitable to The Prophet and lacked his definition of perfection. So, all the people who had recognized God's written Laws - from Moses to Jesus, from Jesus to His prophets, and from the prophets to present - have done so in error. The Prophet teaches that God had a change of heart and that Jesus' adoption of His Laws was unnecessary. Unbelievable!

Jesus said:

"Do not think that I have come to abolish the Law or the Prophets; I have not come to abolish them but to fulfill them. I tell you the truth, until heaven and earth disappear, not the smallest letter, not the least stroke of a pen, will by any means disappear from the Law *until everything is accomplished*. Anyone who breaks one of the least of these commandments and teaches others to do the same will be called least in the kingdom of heaven, but whoever practices and teaches these commands will be called great in the kingdom of heaven. For I tell you that unless your righteousness surpasses that of the Pharisees and the teachers of the law, you will certainly not enter the kingdom of heaven."[326]

The Prophet is obviously a perjurer! Jesus did not come to abolish the Law or the Prophets. The Prophet came to abolish both. Not the least stroke of (any prophet's) pen will disappear from the Law until heaven and earth disappear. Yet, The Prophet erased most of the Law. The Christ said that anyone who breaks one of the least of God's commands and teaches others to do the same will be called *least in the kingdom of heaven*. It is now clear that The Prophet will not only be the least in the kingdom of heaven, but he will never reach that destination. As the son of perdition, he will perish. He perishes 'because he refused to love the truth and so be saved.' Sadly, condemnation comes over all those who do not believe the truth but have delighted in The Prophet's wickedness.[515]

At this point, there is little to be gained by producing a list of recent atrocities that have been committed by The Prophet's followers. Their actions speak for themselves. However, it is fitting to offer this thought: Americans are taught to believe that most who are called to serve in our government are to understand and accept that the Constitution is worthless without *enforceable* laws. This goes well beyond instinct. Since the U.S. is a nation of laws, the Constitution is the foundation of the nation. Therefore, common sense dictates that those who might be freely-elected to Congress would be duty-bound to abide by the laws that preceded their service. But such is not the case for The Prophet's people. For them, The Prophet's law is above all and supersedes the laws of the land - including the Constitution of the United States. For the Prophetiers, any rules or laws that oppose The Prophet's teaching or the marks of his book cannot be accepted.[225] Knowing this to be accurate, consider The Prophet's following directive:

> "O you who believe, take not the Jews and the Christians for friends. They are friends of each other. And whoever amongst you takes them for friends he is indeed one of them."[395]

This is a direct command from The Prophet. It's the law. His followers are not to take Christians and Jews for friends – period! As though that directive is not alarming enough, it comes just 18 verses after he said:

> "The only punishment of those who wage war against [god] and his messenger and strive to make mischief in the land is that they should be murdered, or crucified or their hands and their feet should be cut off on opposite sides, or they should be imprisoned."[393]

There are current and former members of Congress who are duty-bound to the ways and the laws of The Prophet. As affirmed members of his movement, they are to believe and abide by The Prophet's law. Their choice in friends has been defined and limited by their prophet and god.

They are a part of his body. To depart from this teaching would make them *hypocrites* and subject to the kind of treatment we saw inflicted upon the people in the Towers on September 11, 2001[390] or the punishments as listed above.

This is alarming! There are Prophetiers in Congress who are demonstrating their obvious hatred for the United States, its people, and its laws! But men can take comfort in Paul's promising words as he gives *"thanks to God for you, brothers and sisters loved by the Lord, because from the beginning God chose you to be saved through the sanctifying work of the Spirit and through belief in the truth. He called you to this through our gospel, that you might share in the glory of our Lord Jesus Christ. So then, brothers and sisters, stand firm and hold to the teachings we passed on to you, whether by word-of-mouth or by letter. May our Lord Jesus Christ Himself and God our Father, who loved us and by His grace gave us eternal encouragement and good hope, encourage your hearts and strengthen you in every good deed and word."*[516]

Share in the glory of our Lord Jesus Christ. Those who faithfully hold onto Him are prophetically few. The majority has made the conscious choice to refrain from sharing in His glory. Like The Prophet and his band, most deny the Father, His Son, and their commands. By the definition of 1 John 2:22, these same people are called *antichrists*. You will not recognize them by their horns, hooved feet, or scaly skin. They do not have any of these physical traits - not in the literal sense. They do not have tails and you will not find them carrying pitch-forks. They live among us as family, friends, and neighbors. Though they choose to dwell with the likes of The Prophet, they are among those who we have come to love dearly, and we can hope that they'll learn to love the truth before the final curtain falls!

The Prophet

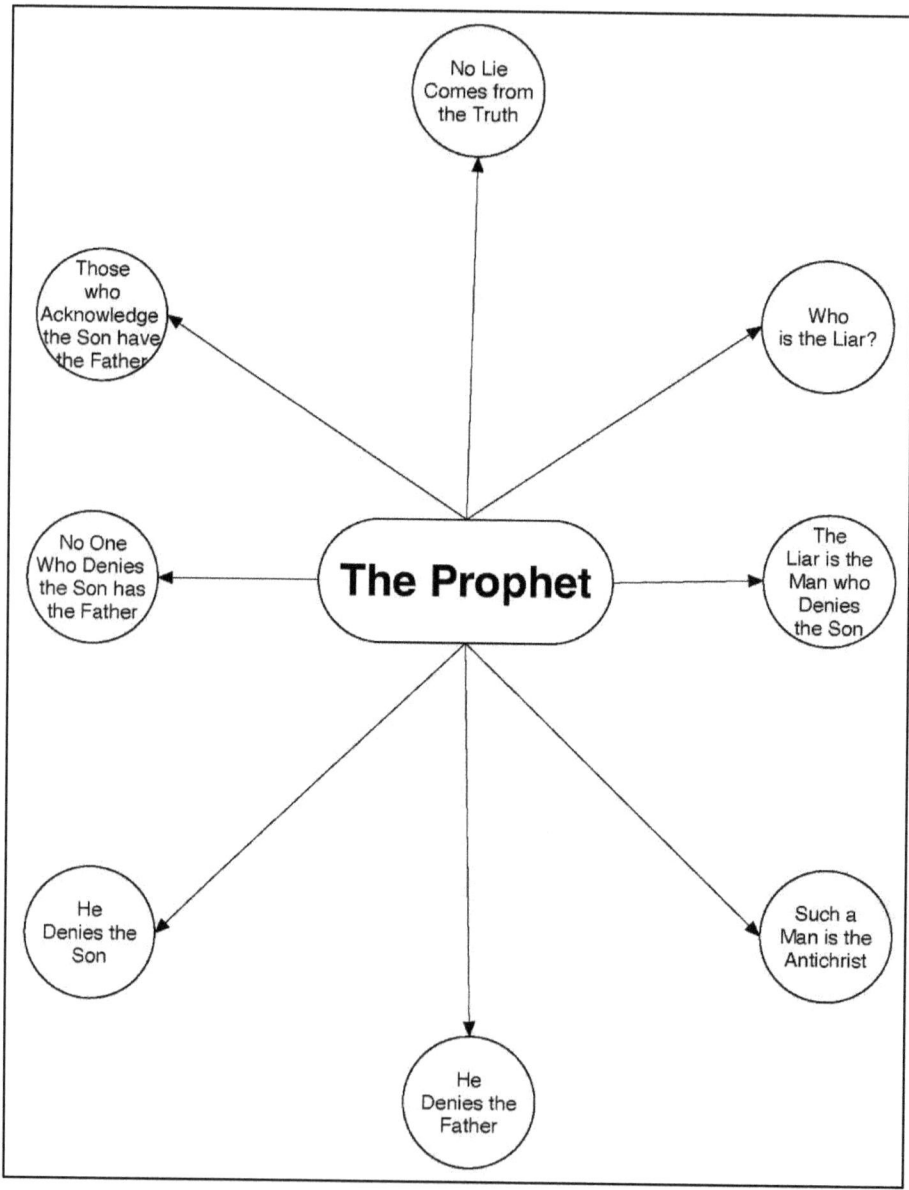

Chapter 9

The Antichrist Prophet

John's Definitive Warning About the Antichrist in 1 John 2

The Antichrist is among the shortest chapters in this book. It is brief because the subject as to who and what constitutes an antichrist is simply defined and easily accredited. Though the world's use of the term *antichrist* has been diminished by misuse and varies by user, the true definition and original intent of the term was given by John in the 1st Century A.D. Antichrists have been in existence since Jesus was crucified, resurrected, ascended, and affirmed to be the promised Messiah – the Christ. Antichrists make up the world's majority. Antichrists include Atheists, Buddhists, Hindus, Spiritualists, (most) Academics, Agnostics, Satanists and (of course) Luciferians and/or Prophetiers. Due to the obvious negativity of the connotations associated to the term, the use of the word *antichrist* is largely frowned upon in today's politically charged atmosphere. There are many more groups who belong in this category but, for demonstrative purposes, this will do. Those who do not belong to the group and cannot be members of the antichrist club are *all* of God's prophets. After all, an antichrist prophet of God is an oxymoron and, by definition, an impossibility.

Biblically, there are three conditions under which one is an antichrist:[205]

1. Denial that Jesus is the Christ (the Messiah)
2. Denial that God is a Father
3. Denial that Jesus is God's Son

John is direct in his written testimony that: "You have an anointing from the Holy One, and all of you know the truth."[204] John's statement agrees with the testimony that Paul gave in his second letter to the Thessalonians. Those who know the Father and His Son and those who adhere to His Word know the truth. Truth is the foundation of our creation. Truth reveals itself when mankind witnesses the end as it was told from the beginning. The majority recognize this ultimate truth as an inconvenient burden and unwelcome nuisance. But in that truth, John continues with his testimony: "I do not write to you because you do not know the truth, but because you do know it and because no lie comes from the truth." Does that make sense? No lie comes from the truth. This is a lesson that the dragon and his representative of flesh and blood should have respected. Had they respected the truth, there would be no reason for this book. As circumstances dictate, this book has been written because of the very real existence of the liars in spirit and flesh. So, who is he? Who is the liar? "It is the man who denies that Jesus is the Christ [as the Savior]. Such a man is the antichrist—he denies the Father and the Son."[205]

- Who is the liar? It is the man who denies that Jesus is the Christ [the Savior].
- Who is the liar? It is the man who denies the Father [God].
- Who is the liar? It is the man who denies the Son [the Messiah, the Son of God].

Who, then, was the lone *prophet* who denied that God has a Son? Who is the prophet that created a nation of antichrists by declaring himself to be the most high and the foremost to serve God? Who is the prophet that denied God as a Father? Which prophet denied the Father and His Son while declaring that if God were to have had a son, he would have been that son? Of course, the father-son relationship would have been purely metaphorical.[299] There is only one man who fills this role entirely. That man was The Prophet. As a 'prophet of God' and founder of a nation that has lured billions into the abyss, this one man satisfies the role as *the* antichrist. His testimony satisfies every aspect of John's definition of the antichrist. He is the prophet who stated: "The Beneficent [God] has no son; so I am the foremost of those who serve (God)."[418]

The Prophet is an antichrist prophet. By definition, he cannot possibly be a prophet of God. His single statement above fulfills many biblical prophecies. Foremost, it verifies the arrogant nature of the speaker. Just exactly what is The Prophet saying here? He states clearly: "God has no son." After 2,000 years of prophetic testimony from God's true prophets, this testimony was the first that the world had heard from a prophet of God about rejecting "sonship."[267]

So, was Jesus a liar? Were the prophets of both Old and New Testaments all liars? The Prophet does not go so far as to outwardly accuse Jesus of being a liar, but he does chastise all the prophets before him for their *egregious errors*.[256] The Prophet, therefore, corrects the record and makes absolute the statement that the father/son relationship between God and Jesus is to be rejected as idolatry.[298] As the *foremost to serve God*, who would question him? It serves to reason that the foremost to serve God exceeds the likes of Moses. The foremost to serve God would exceed the contributions of Abraham, Isaac, David and all the Old Testament prophets. The foremost to serve is self-explanatory in that The Prophet would exceed Matthew, Mark, Luke, John, Paul, and Jesus. It seems that the contradictions falling out of this man's mouth should have been identified long ago, but the time was not yet appropriate. The Father, He who holds back the unveiling of the man of lawlessness, has continued to keep The Prophet hidden. That is... until now.

The conditions surrounding the unveiling of Lucifer, the man, have been met. Now, the amount of prophecy fulfilled by The Prophet's single statement of 43:81 is nothing less than astonishing! The wonder of such a declaration is magnified by the narrative of a scholar, one of The Prophet's most educated followers. Maulana wrote: "...it is not worthy of [God] that he should take to himself a son. The significance in this case would be that, when a man serves God, he may metaphorically be called a son of God, and therefore [The Prophet], being the foremost of those to serve, would be a son in that sense, but he refused to be called a son of God because the use of such metaphorical words have given rise to *grievous errors*."[299] The Prophet, now proven to have satisfied the definition of *antichrist*, has successfully convinced his followers that it is not worthy of God that he should take to himself a son.[410] Hence, all Prophetiers are antichrists and they mirror the sentiment of their stand-alone prophet.

There is something more. The Prophet clearly states that it is not 'worthy' of God to take to himself a son. But The Prophet considers himself to be most worthy of being that son should God have made such a decision. Thanks to Isaiah's testimony, we know that Satan (*the dawn*) has a son. The Prophet is the star of piercing brightness who boasts of being the foremost to serve and the first in line to be considered a metaphorical son to the god he represents. Through his own testimony, The Prophet unwittingly acknowledges that he is antichrist. Had The Prophet been able to read, his testimony and presentation would likely have changed a bit. The definition of the man who is *anti* (opposed to) Christ is unambiguous and the characteristics are easily recognized by those who know God. But for those who do not know the Father and His Son, opposing Jesus, the Prince of princes, comes easily. The unavoidable nature that thrives within a web of lies is contradiction. Contradiction is what separates and isolates deception. Eventually, the web gets too heavy, and the trap collapses. The liar is revealed. The prophetic nature of The Prophet's evil existence is nothing short of perfect!

Should Jesus' body have something to fear from reading The Prophet's book? No. Should the book be discarded and burned like so many other historical writings that cause discomfort? No. The clear book should remain as it is. Like the testimony of any man that is accused of wrong-doing, the written evidence against the antichrist should remain intact and whole. This preserves the case for anyone who might wish to examine it. Take one of The Prophet's most loyal advocates, Maulana, for example. According to his educated understanding, The Prophet's dialogue influenced and encouraged people to abandon Christianity. Maulana wrote: "The five verses [19] 89-93 contain a most emphatic and clear condemnation of the Christian doctrine of the Godhead of Jesus Christ."[286] Who would accept the condemnation of Christianity and rejection of Jesus as the Christ without first examining the evidence? As it turns out, *many* have done just that. Any Christian who chooses to read The Prophet's book immediately recognizes the deceptive nature and intent of the script.

So, who is the liar? The liar is the man who made the statement that God has no son. But how can this statement be made with certainty? The truth of a prophet is revealed when his prophecy becomes reality. And what of The Prophet? What do we know about the Christ-denier who called himself a prophet of God? Look to the truth. We can be certain of the promise that: "…no lie comes from the truth." Therefore, the end that was told from the beginning has now been validated by the truth of warning. In the most ironic of twists, the mysterious truth of God has been unveiled and proven through the prophetic life and lies of The Prophet who qualified himself as the false prophet and antichrist. With the prophecies about The Prophet as the antichrist and the man of lawlessness being so perfectly accurate, doesn't it lend credence to the balance of the Word as being faithful and true? And if the Word is faithful and true, can Christians and Jews see themselves as anything other than children of God? It sounds to reason that man might take heed in God's Word and trust in John: "See that what you have heard from the beginning remains in you. If it does, you also will remain in the Son and in the Father. And this is what He promised us - even eternal life. I am writing these things to you about those who are trying to lead you astray. As for you, the anointing you received from Him remains in you, and you do not need anyone to teach you. But as His anointing teaches you about all things and as that anointing is real, not counterfeit - just as it has taught you, remain in Him."[206]

In this moment, there can be no better advice! With The Prophet being antichrist and leading so many people astray, now is the time for a strong foundation in Christ.

"This is the message you heard from the beginning: We should love one another. Do not be like Cain, who belonged to the evil one and murdered his brother. And why did he murder him? Because his own actions were evil and his brother's were righteous. Do not be surprised, my brothers, if the world hates you. We know that we have passed from death to life, because we love our brothers. Anyone who does not love remains in death.

The Prophet

Anyone who hates his brother is a murderer, and you know that no murderer has life in him. This is how we know what love is: Jesus Christ laid down His life for us. And we ought to lay down our lives for our brothers."[207] There is no greater contradiction in truth than the directives of the Christ compared to the commands of the Antichrist. Like His Father, Jesus is opposed to murder. But The Prophet teaches that murder is essential to defend his cause and movement.[393]

Do not be surprised when the world hates you. For the time has come for the fake morning star to command his successors to kill anyone who refuses to worship him, his god and/or his laws. Exercising all the authority of the dragon, The Prophet has left us with the miraculous signs of his own little book. This speaking image of flesh and blood has revealed himself to be the *beast out of the earth*, directing his people to kill anyone who creates mischief in the land.

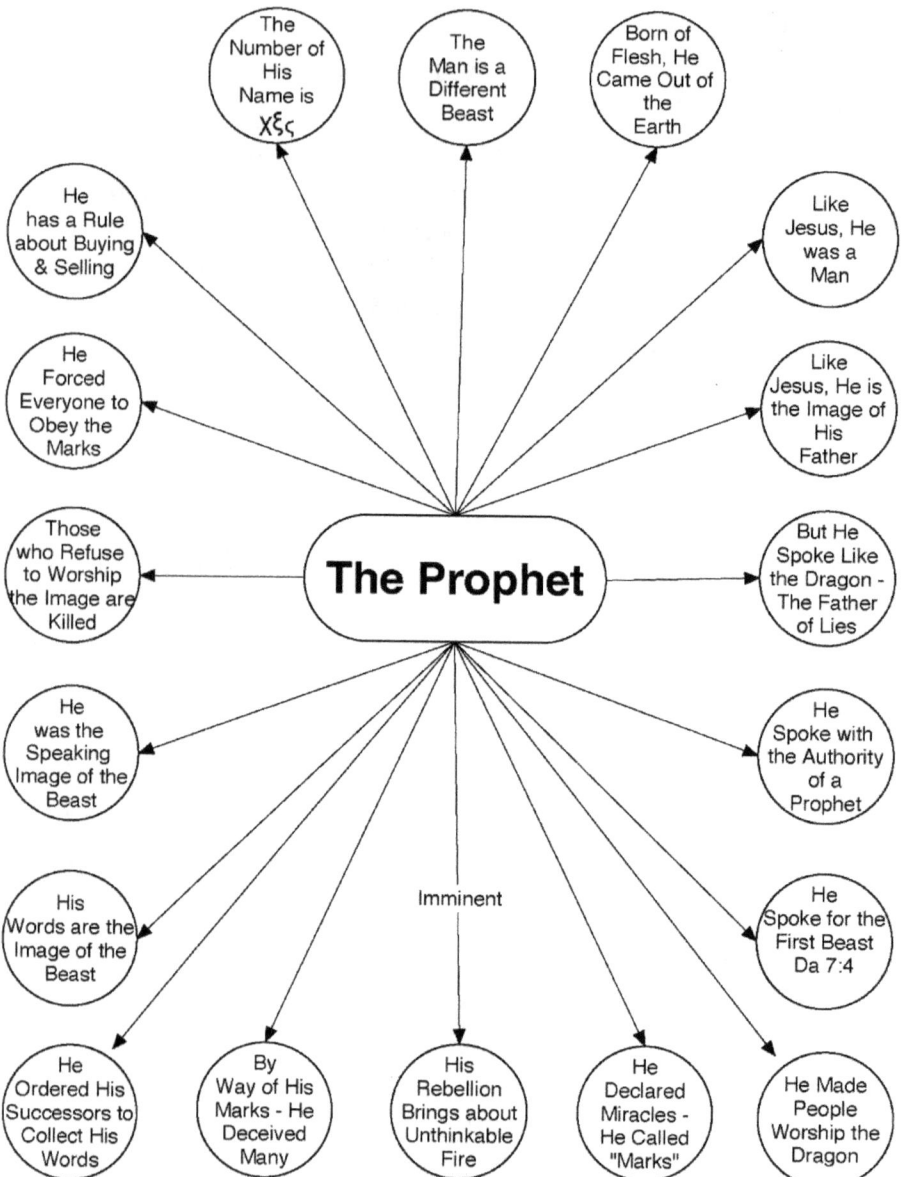

The Prophet

Chapter 10

The Speaking Image

John's Description of the False Prophet in Revelation 13

It will likely come as an eerie surprise to the readers when they learn that much of the imagery in Revelation accurately describes the founder of lies whose rebellion has become the largest fraud ever to flourish on earth. The political world is certain to recoil and scoff at this. Many will gnash their teeth and snarl in hateful rhetoric when the match is made. In this politically charged atmosphere, the stakes are high. Acting in such a vehement manner is understandable as nations are certain to fall and kingdoms are destined to implode. Deception on such a grand scale will leave people confused and infuriated! Furious people can and likely will act in irrational and violent ways. Such has been the methodology of the prophetic beasts over the centuries.

John wrote about an evil man who would use the power of the original or *first beast* (Satan) to lead billions astray. John's prophetic writing has been in existence for nearly 2,000 years and it has successfully navigated the endless assaults from the bodies of the harlot and the false prophet to remain intact. To date, few people (if any) have succeeded in linking all the characteristics and achievements of *the beast out of the earth* to any one man. That's about to change. The case against this man-beast is currently being presented. The evidence is mounting against The Prophet. The names match. The actions match. The characteristics, statements, and achievements all match. The Prophet has said and done the things that God's prophets warned he would say and do. This piece of the puzzle, that of *the beast out of the earth*, is just another of the many satanic tragedies already presented. Like the preceding evidence, this presentation connects the dots of biblical prophecy with the testimony and historical accounts of The Prophet. The picture is changing from a clear image to high definition.

By now, the reader has come to understand how Isaiah's depiction of *Lucifer* is also *the little horn* described by Daniel. The little horn is the *stern-faced king* who exalted himself. The three are one. The covenant he spoke became the relational bond between his god and many people who are destined to perish – their names not found in the book of life. The covenant was confirmed by his god in the form of a *clear book*. Unique to this book are the *seven thunders* of the opening chapter. They serve as a representative summary of the entire set of rules and laws between the angel of fire and the people he has duped. Presented in the way of *counterfeit miracles* and every sort of evil, the seven *Oft Repeated Verses* serve as the foundation of deception from the man of lawlessness – he who we now know as *The Prophet*. He readily admitted to being responsible for changing the laws that were presented to Moses. These laws were recognized by God's people and the prophets in the 2,000 years preceding The Prophet's appearance. He has been unveiled as *antichrist* - the lone prophet to deny God as a Father and Jesus as His Son. Most of the prophets who wrote before the Savior's appearance prophesied about Jesus' coming. All of God's prophets in the New Testament affirmed Jesus' role as the Messiah – the Savior of mankind. Born 550 years later, The Prophet appeared to spread his antichrist lies. With his appearance came the attempts to erase prophecy, change the Laws, assume the role of Christ, introduce an unheard-of god, present a new covenant, oppose the Most High, oppose the people of the Most High, and replace grace with crucifixion, imprisonment, amputation, and murder. This is the referenced history of The Prophet. Now, John has something more to add about the prophetic life and collateral damage on account of this man.

Once again, the evidence builds upon previous arguments as to how The Prophet has achieved and fulfilled all things relevant to the biblical nemesis of Jesus. As before, this chapter will show how the biblical imagery of The Prophet, his god, his laws, and his actions have been anchored with historical record and written testimony. Describing him as *the beast out of the earth*, John gives us another trait-filled description of the man who fulfilled the role of Satan's villainous mouthpiece. Found in the 13th chapter of Revelation, John's description of The Prophet becomes immediately apparent. Like a lamb (Jesus), The Prophet had the same two metaphorical horns of *flesh* and *blood* but, unlike the lamb, The Prophet spoke like the dragon (Satan). He said so.[412] Like his god, he mixed truth with lies, and, as the speaking image of the dragon,[440] The Prophet exercised all the authority of Satan.[262]

> **"[god] and his messenger are thus the final authority"**
> **– MMA, Qur'an 4:59, 59a, p. 213**

As is evident today, most people in the world accept The Prophet to have been a man of God. His endeavors are recognized annually in the way of White House dinners and

The Prophet

30-day periods of world-wide worshiping. To emphasize the enormous geo-political gains by The Prophet and the swift implementation of his laws, consider the end of the war in Iraq. The hasty removal of American troops left a void that opened the door for the organized gathering of the most vicious Prophetiers ever recorded. Is it any coincidence that the American President, a man steeped in the Prophet's violent culture, made way for such a gathering? The President of the United States, a man given the honorary name of The Prophet's grandson, was freely-elected and served two terms in the White House. During those two terms, The Prophetiers' efforts to conquer people and retake massive geographical gains were greatly successful. Iraq fell back into the hands of the worst of the worst. Egypt and Syria became embroiled in civil wars. And the most heinous and callous Prophetiers controlled the basin of the great Euphrates river from Syria through Iraq. The biblical implications of that moment are astounding.[453] Now, with the U.S. being chased out of Afghanistan, history is about to repeat itself. But the Prophetiers have learned from their battles. America has an emotional weakness that presents as ignorance, and it has been left extremely vulnerable. That once beautiful nation (the U.S.) has surrendered to something called 'wokeness." Better called *performative activism*, wokeness has rendered the U.S. effectively deaf and blind to most evil. The worst of the worst of the Prophetiers are soon to gather again and finish what they started in Manhattan on 9/11. Of their warrior tactics they boast, "You have the watches, but we have the time!" Remember, these warriors have been battling since The Prophet first opened his mouth. After 9/11, the U.S. went into Afghanistan to capture or kill O'sama bin Laden and his supporting Prophetiers. Twenty years later, under the direction of a cognitively impaired political failure, America orchestrated the immigration of tens of thousands of Prophetiers into the U.S., while leaving tens of billions of dollars in weaponry to the enemy they were sent to fight. The move was nothing short of genius (sarcasm mine)! The Fort Hood shooter summed it up when he praised the Prophetiers and shouted: "We Have Won!!!" It goes almost without saying that The Prophet has successfully made the earth and its inhabitants worship his god. Now, a recognized terror organization governs Afghanistan and its people while the world slides toward extinction. Like the wounded head that healed, generations of Prophetiers are simply not going to go away. The Prophet's perfect oppression of women has returned in all its glory! The incoming government has rekindled The Prophet's favorite pastime of taking people hostage for ransom. Beheadings have returned. The organized gathering of terror and its performative activists have already returned to develop new schemes. First, there was "the day of great slaughter when the Towers

[fell]."¹⁴⁷ Now comes the sign of the Son of Man coming on the clouds "and all the nations will mourn."³³⁸

The fatal wound that had been healed, current-day Babylon, is soon to usher in its last act. The table is set, and the harvest is ripe. Men have turned from God and embraced every kind of wickedness, evil, greed and depravity. The Prophetiers have supercharged their God-hating actions via murder, insolence, deceit, and boastful arrogance. Those who know God, know that it is the season of finality. The New Babylon, our world today, is taking its last breaths. Without going down a rabbit hole, let's review the kingdoms that have represented Satan's body. Each of these kingdoms has opposed God and his people. Of course, each one follows the plight of the Jews. Listed in historical order are - Egypt, Assyria, Babylon, Medo-Persia, Greece, Rome, The Prophet's nation, and the current-world New Babylon. As we are reminded daily, The Prophet's nation is alive and expanding. Five of these nations still exist in a geographical manner – Egypt, Persia, Greece, Rome, and the nation of The Prophet. The wounded head lives as well. It is Babylon. Daniel and Jeremiah address Babylon by name. They had personal knowledge about the horrors inflicted upon God's chosen people by the Babylonians in their day. John speaks of Babylon and its re-emergence in the book of Revelation. They worshiped the Queen of Heaven,¹⁷² just as the Babylonians worship that deity today. Like the Babylonians of past, the Babylonians of present refuse to listen to the message in the name of the Lord. The Babylonians of old drank an abominable wine from a golden cup.¹⁷⁹ The wine made them go mad. The new Babylonians drink the same abominable wine from that same golden cup.⁴⁵⁹ The New Babylon produced the king that was taunted in Isaiah 14.¹²⁹ That king has proven to be The Prophet. With the king of Babylon and the queen of Babylon (the harlot) firmly anchored in the world *after* Jesus established His Church, it reasons that Babylon has made its comeback in full. Hence, the wounded head of Satan has healed. Both characters, the king and the queen, are representative of Satan and his deceptive recipe - mixing truth with lies. He is the dragon, the fallen angel, the masquerading light, and the father of lies. He is the Accuser who presents himself through God-hating men. Just as in the days of old Babylon and its king, Nebuchadnezzar, the dragon is represented in New Babylon by his speaking image – The Prophet. Though the dragon was restrained by Jesus' power of resurrection and Satan's old Babylon has long since thought to have been destroyed, the world is now beginning to understand how it is that John would speak of Babylon the Great and its appearance *after* the time of Christ on earth. As for The Prophet, the speaking image of the fallen angel, he plays his part as the Most High in this Babylonian kingdom. Supposedly, The Prophet performed great

The Prophet

and miraculous signs[227] to deceive his followers into believing that he had overcome Jesus as *the Seal of the prophets*.[415] His desire to conquer has already caused much fire to fall from the sky in full view of men – with 9/11 being the latest centerpiece. But the big finale is yet to come! Many of The Prophet's nations now possess the nuclear know-how and capability to accomplish that very thing. Just imagine what the world might look like today if Adolf Hitler had been successful in developing the world's first nuclear weapons. Hitler would have completed his objective and *the Final Solution* would have ended Israel. God's chosen people would have been no more – forever! Yet Israel, specifically Jerusalem, lives. But the Prophetiers desire a return to the Final Solution and an end to Israeli 'occupation' of the land that God gave His chosen people over 3,000 years ago. The Prophetiers are massing the firepower to do that very thing. Many of the performative activists who have risen in this political cesspool support the Prophetiers and their genocidal desires. Even the filthy-rich manufacturers of ice-cream think this way! The stench of their opposition lingers like an inverted outhouse!

With The Prophet being dead, his rotted fingers have returned to the dust they came from, and they can no longer push the buttons of such a destructive nature. But his kingdom and its nations can push those buttons. His death has done little to slow the influence he has over his people. Iraq and Syria have given rise to the be-headers. Afghanistan has given rise to bin Laden and those who wish to follow in his footsteps. With long-rifles and knives, they continue their war among the nations. Then there's Iran. Iran (aka Persia) is a prime example of The Prophet's never-ending hatred of God's saints and the ongoing war against them. The world is soon to wake to the horrific reality that after twenty years of spinning centrifuges, conspiring with the Russians and Chinese, and collaborating with the North Koreans (as their "partners in technology"), the Persians have already amassed the firepower necessary to fulfill John's warning about The Prophet being the *cause* of the fire falling from heaven to earth. The Prophet's death has not slowed the war between his kingdom and the kingdom of God. Because of the miraculous signs and marks[227] he was given on behalf of the dragon - he has convinced people that their wanton killing is doing a service to God. Yet, all who know God, understand that those who kill with the thought that they are doing a service to God do not know God at all.[202] The Prophet taught that murderers attain favor with God. This becomes problematic when angry men believe they have a duty to murder. It is of little surprise that the world watches in horror when the Prophetiers act as they are dutybound and obligated to act. John was clear when he wrote, "…no murderer has eternal life in him."[207]

The Prophet's successors were motivated to set up the book that speaks as he spoke. It is this collection of directives that drives the passions and furious aggressions of his people. This popular little book is an image of the man who first spoke its words. Its very spirit is in the image of the dragon. Not only did The Prophet give initial breath to the dragon's book, but he speaks through it today. It is by his command that his people kill anyone who refuses to worship it, to worship him, or to worship his god.[394] The politically correct among us will forcefully push back against such statements, but the harsh reality is that murder is a foundational mooring that exists through a string of orders given in that book. There are more than a few murderous directives originating with The Prophet that the reader should know. Keep in mind that these verses were spoken by The Prophet nearly 600 years after Jesus changed the world by standing between the prostitute and the men who thought they had the right and duty to kill her. By Jesus' institution of grace, the use of lethal enforcement of the Law was to be used no more – forever! For the woke among us, this example should never be confused and does not apply to law enforcement officers who have the right and the need to defend themselves against those who might otherwise bring them harm during the commission of a crime. For those who have not read his book, these are among the directives of The Prophet:

1. "But if you do (it) not, then be apprised of war from [god] and his messenger…"[375]

2. "Going directly against the Commandments of [god] is here described as a war with [god] and [The Prophet]"[253]

3. "The only punishment of those who wage war against [god] and [The Prophet] and strive to make mischief in the land is that they should be murdered, or crucified, or their hands in their feet should be cut off on opposite sides, or they should be imprisoned."[393]

4. "The words used here imply originally [to] all those opponents of [The Prophet's cause]…"[265]

5. "And fight them until there is no more persecution, and all religions are for [god]."[402]

These are just a few of The Prophet's directives that call for fighting, murder and war. The Prophet was just one man with a few lawless companions who quickly turned the crimes of stealing, killing, and destroying into acts of worship. By his direction, anyone who dared to question his new-found faith was to be murdered.[452] Just imagine someone forcing his way into your home and spewing his new rules and laws that you must either submit to or die. In its most basic form, this is how The Prophet has spread his faith over the centuries. Outside of his realm, most people remain willfully ignorant as to what he and his little book teach. The majority turns their head aside because they do not want to address the vulgarity of the man's lessons. But it is now time to educate the world. The reader should be horrified by his words and actions. The masses need to be awakened to this madness. Reason and common-sense dictate that educated people would immediately reject his directives as the rantings of a madman. But the absurdity of cultural bias interferes with man's common sense. When generations of children are raised to speak of him and his god before they speak of their parents,[234] the indoctrination quickly takes root. The Prophet's rebellion is 1,400 years old and growing. Naturally, man's reaction to biblical prophecy and the warning about a foreign god is to deny that God and reality are one and the same. This is man's instinctive nature - to reject our ultimate and imminent demise. That which makes life anything other than normal, lawful, and civilized is dismissed as absurdity. In the West, it is instinctive to live in the routines of graduations, weddings, soccer matches, and sailing into the sunset. The East lives a much different life. As the East seeps into the West, we see a degradation of that which used to be normal, lawful, and civilized life. We can no longer describe our world in such terms. Lawlessness has suddenly exploded upon the West, becoming the preference of godless street creatures. Now, people march through our city streets demanding that prisons be closed, police be defunded, drugs be legalized, homelessness be supported and encouraged (through expansive entitlements), and criminals go unchecked and un-punished. This madness has gone so far as to criminalize the actions of police officers who make reasonable attempts to protect themselves from the harmful pushback of street crud. This is not just extremely dangerous, it's insane! The Prophet would thrive in such a time and place. In fact, his cause is growing with it. This is the state of man's affairs when normalcy biases give way to inconvenient realities. The world demonstrates the unified illness of Ostrich Syndrome as they eat, drink, and marry as though we were not recently attacked by a godless people and their mishandling of a harvested and manipulated biological agent. That agent, whether released by accident or because of political intent, has become a very effective weapon. China, the facilitator of this nasty little bug, is on the march toward world rule. As a bonus, they have effectively inflamed the divided people within the [not-so] United States. Lawlessness is brewing in the minds, stirring in the hearts, and spewing out of the mouths of emotionally unstable street urchins – those who scream and riot until entire cities recognize that the only lives that matter are black. Like insects that scatter with the light, they call out to those who hold onto God and demand that they accept and endorse the actions that caused Sodom's destruction. What the godless don't know is that the acceptance of these actions as new norms (pestilence, shameful lusts, and lawlessness) are things of prophecy.

> "As it was in the days of Noah, so it will be at the coming of the Son of Man. For in the days before the flood, people were eating and drinking, marrying and giving in marriage, up to the day Noah entered the ark; and they knew nothing about what would happen until the flood came and took them all away. That is how it will be at the coming of the Son of Man. Two men will be in the field; one will be taken and the other left."[340]

Do not be the man left in the field. Do not be the woman left grinding at the hand mill. When biblical warnings about The Prophet present themselves as fact, much like the stark realities quoted above, normalcy bias and instinct should yield to prophetic reason. Hope in Christ is man's unshakeable foundation. Pestilence and lawlessness do not exist in His kingdom. Hope exists in the Word of God. And the Word of God has been authenticated by a most unlikely source - the historical appearance of the biblical character, the man, known as *Lucifer*. Arguments concerning this man's living history can and will be dismissed by the majority. Evidence surrounding his biblical match to Satan's speaking image can and will be rejected by the world's politicians. But consider John's warning of Revelation:

> "He was given power to give breath to the image of the first beast, so that it could speak and cause all who refused to worship the image to be killed."[451]

Refuse to worship The Prophet and be killed. Refuse to worship The Prophet's god and be killed. Refuse to worship the image as it was left in book form and be killed. John's prophetic writing tells us that The Prophet was given power to speak on behalf of the liar. And that speaking image has been delivered in a *clear book*. John was accurate in his warning. A book has been delivered in the image of The Prophet's god and it certainly speaks to people. They have been convinced to kill anyone who refuses to worship the book, The Prophet, or his god. John wrote this warning 500 years before The Prophet appeared. The biblical warnings and The Prophet's lethal directives can no longer be dismissed as wrongly interpreted. The directives are clear, precise, and repetitive. The evidence presented against The Prophet reveals him to be *the beast out of the earth*.

The Prophet

Imagine just how infuriated the PC crowd might become by the audacity of someone 'hateful' enough to present this evidence! Consumed by their own rage, they will seek vengeance. They certainly will not be awed by God's prophetic ability. They are the ones that prophecy warned us about. They will not be astonished by the unveiling of God's mysteries since God's mysteries unveil them to be those who gnash their teeth. They will snarl behind clenched teeth and point their fingers with accusations of 'hate.' For 'hate' is their universal argument and political weapon. When truth begins to overwhelm the rebellious, they reach into their quiver of arrows to silence the threat. In it they find a stash of deceptive tactics, with the accusation of 'hate' being a particularly lethal stick. It is usually accompanied by other silencing sharps like *racist*, *bigot* and *supremacist*. These are the weaponized methods used by the rebellious when facts and truth inconveniently oppose their arguments and endeavors. These accusations are powerful tools that have long been used to shut down the law, the truth, and reason. It makes perfect sense that the devil is called *the Accuser of our brothers*.[443] His rebellious followers act as one might expect criminals to act. Truth does them no favors. Their existence merely confirms the Word. As awful as they may be, these things must come about.

John writes about Satan's seven heads as seven earthly kingdoms. As discussed, these seven kingdoms make up most of Satan's body. But Satan's ugly deceptions are not limited to these seven. There is an eighth.[460] That eighth king, the final kingdom of unbelieving people, is our world today. It is a mixture. The Progressively Correct have combined with the Prophetiers. With them is the harlot who speaks out both sides of her mouth. Together they represent five of every six adults on earth. When the arguments about The Prophet reach a fever pitch, notice how these groups will gather as one in support of each other. They are of mixed minds and a corrupt political party. They gathered in a moment – the political appointees of God-haters. While the world was sleeping, the plight of The Prophet grew into a massive movement that now consumes our planet. The evil schemes that began in the mind of one man, have rapidly advanced. He forced everyone, small and great, rich and poor, free and slave to receive the marks of his miraculous little book. Whether he pressed forward by the point of a sword, political intimidation, cultural tradition, indoctrination, or manipulation by terror - he has managed to force billions of people to memorize his marks. Imprinted upon their minds and pressed upon their foreheads are the words of his clear book. Imprinted upon the nations are the deeds of those who put his words into action with their right hands. It is hard to imagine a better example of The Prophet's real-world marks than the events of

September 11, 2001. By his word, anyone who is considered a hypocrite or enemy of his nation *will have death overcome them though they are in Towers, raise high.*

"Death will overcome you, though you are in Towers, raised high"[390]

Every adult member of The Prophet's body knows of the directive that brought about the attacks on the Towers in 1993 and again in 2001. The Prophetiers all know the command of verse 4:78. Of those Towers, The Prophet's men had this mark imprinted upon their minds and forever impressed upon their foreheads. The call to murder was impressed upon them. The call to steal was impressed upon their minds. The call to destroy was a matter of duty. How do we know this? They were Prophetiers. Those 19 men had the mark of Lucifer on their right hands as they clutched the controls of fully fueled air-buses and descended upon an unsuspecting people. They took control of those planes. They carried out The Prophet's directive and toppled the Towers. They attacked America's war room. They intended to reduce the Capitol to rubble. The Prophetiers attempted to behead the nation they call *the great Satan*. In a prophetic manner, Isaiah addressed that horrific day as "the day of great slaughter, when the Towers fell." God could see what the army of the beast was willing to do. He knew that awful day would come.

"In the day of great slaughter, when the towers fall, streams of water will flow on every high mountain and every lofty hill"[147]

On September 11, 2001, the world watched as three airliners were hijacked and purposely piloted into the Twin Towers and the Pentagon. A fourth was hijacked and slammed nose-first into a field in Pennsylvania. It was later determined that this fourth plane, the one that crashed vertically into the ground at full throttle, was likely headed for the White House or the Capitol Building in Washington D.C. The hijackers were all known and verified to be of The Prophet's body. Like Osama bin Laden, 15 of the 19 murderers originated from Saudi Arabia. The others were from the U.A.E, Lebanon, and Egypt. In a comment referencing September 11th, an emerging member of Congress referred to these 19 Prophetiers and this event as "some people did something." As one might guess, this elite politician is an admitted member of that same body. The dismissive reference was almost as callous and ruthless as was the act that inspired the comment. Almost daily now, Headlines are created about another Prophetier and how he/she or they carried out the marks of the beast. In nearly every case, ignorant commentators demonstrate the astonishing power of Ostrich Syndrome and dismiss these actions as those of *radicals* and *extremists*. Had they bothered to read The Prophet's clear book, they would know that the indoctrinated see these actions as neither radical nor extreme. These are simply the obligated and dutiful acts of a people who will forever be at war. The Prophet was clear about this. They are among the movement's mainstream, and they are acting exactly as they have been directed to act.[370]

With The Prophet's conquered territories rapidly expanding in his day, he instituted a rule about buying and selling. According to his instruction, the scale of measure in buying and selling relied on something other than money. His determination of whether one could buy or sell was now based upon a *faith scale*.[10]

> **Give a full measure when you measure out and weigh with a faith balance"**
>
> – MMA, Manual of Hadith, Chapter 22, Note 5, p. 240, reference Qur'an 17:35

Simply stated, if one lacked faith in The Prophet's god and laws, they were excluded from buying or selling. Though this rule has not held over the centuries, it is nonetheless a part of his teaching. It turns out that the sale of oil and gas to world markets has made some of the kings in his conquered territories very wealthy. Wealthy people often choose money and notoriety over duty.

Rather remarkable is the number of names that The Prophet has within the Bible. Among them are *Lucifer, Antichrist, Little Horn, King who exalts himself, Stern-face*, and *the Beast Out of the Earth*. Now comes *the number of his name*. John tells us that *the name of the beast* is *the number of his name*. Since this has stymied people for so long, take pause and consider what John wrote. He tells us that the name of the beast is the number of his name. The number that John wrote is the name of the man. John wrote this name in Greek. Specifically, John represented this man's name in Greek numerals. They are three distinct strokes of the pen – three *different* symbols. Most know this number by its interpreted version of *666*. But John did not write *666*. The numeric system that consists of tens, hundreds and thousands is a system that is only 1,000 years old. John wrote *Revelation* 2,000 years ago. He was inspired by God and wrote the number of the beast's name with those three, distinct Greek numerals. Though this might seem trite, the symbolism of the Greek numerals cannot be emphasized more. Having read many versions of the Bible it is apparent that God's Word comes to life no matter the skill of the typesetter. This verse is a rare exception. The three images that John stroked in Revelation 13:18 were never intended to be anything other than those exact and distinct symbols. Changing them from the original imagery to the three 6's or a word description of the number merely added to the confusion and prolonged the mystery. There is no way to understand or recognize the beast's name from the three identical figures of *666*. That number is not his name, but the Greek symbols clearly represent him. The symbols are the beast's name. Better stated, the symbols can be arranged to give us the beast's *calligraphic name*. Like a child's puzzle, these three Greek numerals offer the unmistakable mark of the man who built a nation that opposes everything that is called *God*. The three symbols are the Greek Numerals of Chi, Xi and Stigma.

X – Chi

ξ – Xi

> **If anyone has insight, let him calculate the number of the beast, for it is man's number. His number is $\chi\ \xi\ \varsigma$"**
>
> **– Revelation 13:18**

ς — Stigma

The mystery is a mystery no longer. It is the imagery of the original symbols that make up the beast's name. This can be found in a simple computer search. Look for the *calligraphic image* in the name of the man referenced in this book. We all know his name. The three symbols above can be sized to perfectly overlay his name. The *calligraphic imagery* of John's three Greek numerals has existed as the man's name for 1,400 years. The stunning reality is that this simple little puzzle has remained hidden for centuries. Can there be a serious argument that The Prophet and his biblical number match by coincidence only? How many coincidences does it take before the reader begins to understand that none of this is coincidence? At what point do the mounting declarations of 'coincidence' become nothing other than conscious denials and the wishes of Ostriches who refuse to love the truth and keep their heads buried in the sand? Now that we can clearly see this, how much longer can the charade continue? Now that The Prophet has fulfilled all things of biblical warning, even adopting the name of the beast in Revelation, his time of hiding as a prophet has come to an end.

Most will agree that self-preservation comes in many forms and at almost all costs. One of the forms preserving man's way of life is to deny any truth that might otherwise alter the norm. Most of those around us have been doing that very thing since *the day of great slaughter when the Towers fell*. Accepting the truth about the Saudi's and their role in such a cowardice act was simply more than most could bare. When the motivation behind such horrific events surpasses man's ability to process, they merely refuse to accept the thought. This is common among people who find the truth too terrifying to adopt. Instead, they revert to what is known as a *normalcy bias*.

"Normalcy bias, or normality bias, is a belief people hold when facing a disaster. It causes people to underestimate both the likelihood of a disaster and its possible effects, because people believe that things will always function the way things normally have functioned. This may result in situations where people failed to adequately prepare themselves for disasters, and on a larger scale, the failure of governments to include the populace in its disaster preparations. About 70% of people reportedly displayed normalcy bias in disasters."[95]

With The Prophet's disciples already set up in the highest offices of government, what could the government possibly do to prepare us for this unveiling? The answer to this question might be more frightening than any of the previous acts carried out by this man's followers.

Just as the words of the beast *caused* 19 cowards to murder 2,977 people on 9/11, it is the words of the beast that *causes* fire to fall from heaven to earth in full view of men…

Ronald B. Stetton

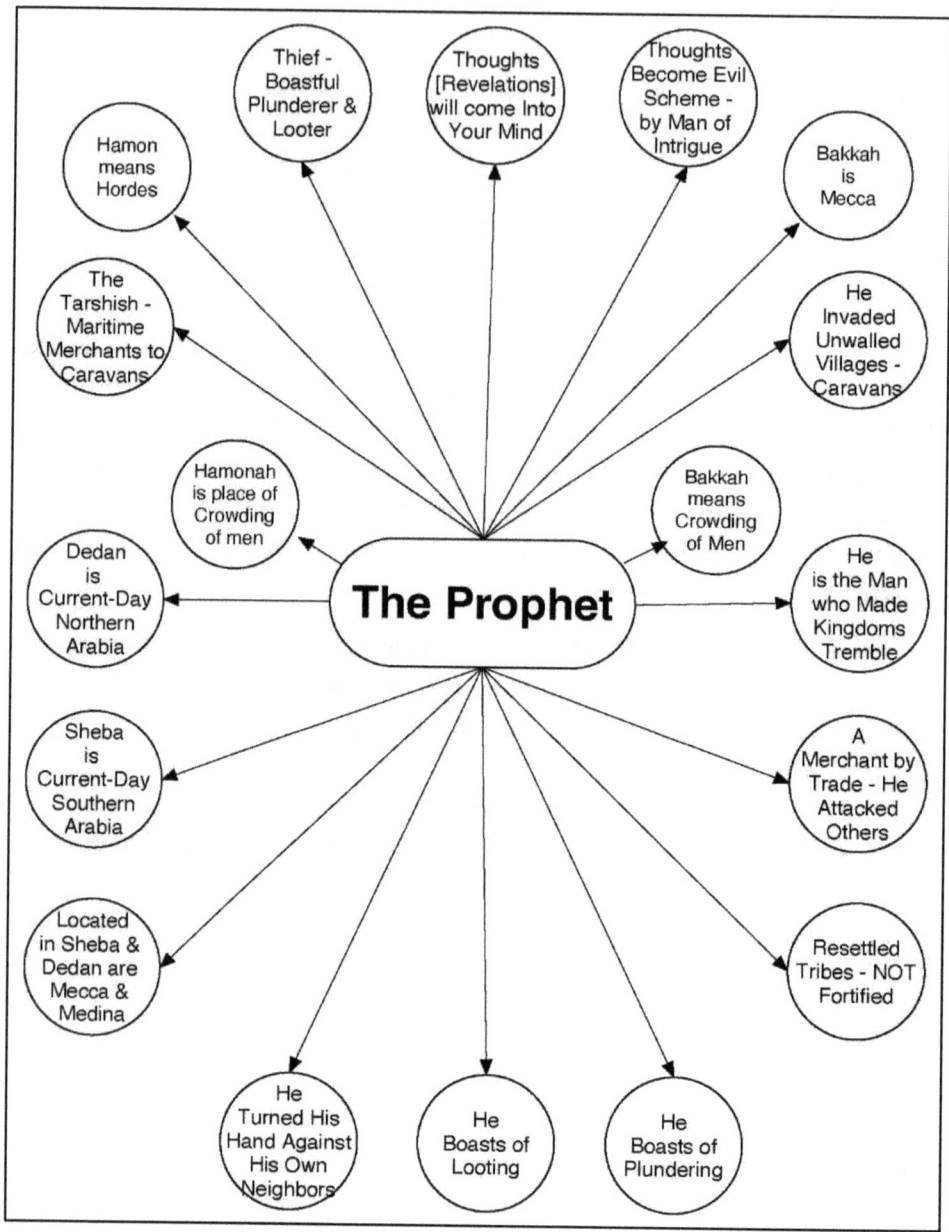

The Prophet

Chapter 11

Victimizing Sheba & Dedan

Ezekiel's Warning About the False Prophet (38:10-13)

The Prophet has arrived. His people are here. Their hordes have been gathered.

Understanding biblical testimony can certainly be frustrating at times. This becomes particularly true and challenging when different terms and images are used for the same character or territory. Take The Prophet for example: How many different biblical names and descriptions has he been accredited with? This same challenge comes with pinpointing ancient clans, territories, cities, towns, and nations. To understand The Prophet's influence in Ezekiel 38, it is imperative that the reader has a foundational understanding of the lands as they were previously named and where they are located on today's world maps. There are eleven named locations in Ezekiel 38. They are *Magog, Meshech, Tubal, Persia, Cush, Put, Gomer, Beth-Togarmah, Tarshish, Sheba* and *Dedan*. Most of these locations are biblically defined and not subject to the ridicule of current interpretations. But a few of the remaining locations can be determined only by the association of biblical congruence. To simplify the differences, the most obvious certainties of these nations will be discussed first. The balance will be placed by their nearest associated commonalities and biblical hints. This might sound difficult and easily influenced by biases, but the picture it forms is duly recognized.

To begin with, all but one of the names in Ezekiel 38 originate with the sons and grandsons of Noah.

1. *Gomer, Magog, Tubal,* Javan and *Meshech* were sons of Japheth[100]
    Togarmah was a son of Gomer (grandson of Japheth)[101]
    Tarshish was a son of Javan (grandson of Japheth)[102]
    The Tarshish were a maritime people (coastal living)[102]

2. *Cush* and *Put* were sons of Ham[104]

    Raamah was a son of Cush[105]
    a. *Sheba* and *Dedan* were sons of Raamah[105]

i. Sheba is southern Arabia and Yemen
ii. Dedan is northern Arabia
b. *Sheba* and *Dedan* were also the sons of Jokshan (born to Abraham's second wife Keturah) but these sons were sent to the east – Asshur.[118]
3. Aram was a son of Shem[107]
   A. Meshech was a son of Aram (grandson to Shem)[108]
      a. Meshech was the eastern hill country[109]

The only named entity that aligns with "Gog" [the beast] but is not listed as a son or grandson of Noah is *Persia*. Persia's role in the beast's scheme is becoming more and more evident as the days roll by. The only territories that appear to have no predetermined biblical location is that of *Gomer* and *Magog*. We know only that Magog is mentioned as the land of Gog and that Gog is the chief prince of Meshech and Tubal. Meshech is listed as both a son of Japheth and a grandson to Shem. But, because Meshech is nearly always listed together with Tubal, it can be reasonably assumed that they were the brothers born to Japheth. Consider these to be pieces of a puzzle that are soon to be placed. Like most puzzles, the participant can be guided to success and find their way to completion with a predetermined picture. Knowing how the picture should look, the pieces can be set in place to accurately portray the scene as it was written centuries ago. With patience, these biblical pieces can similarly be set in their proper places. To do so, we must approach this by separating known locations and scenes. God has a wonderful way of introducing each one.

The clans of Noah's sons began as three separate and distinct nations. After coming to rest on the mountains of Ararat, the Japhethites, the Hamites and the Semites settled to become the three nations that would eventually spread out over the earth.[110] To place their clans and nations, these Old Testament names must be identified.

1. Meshech – "Greece [Javan], Tubal, and Meshech, they were your traffickers [merchants]; they traded the persons of men and vessels of brass for [Tyre's] merchandise"[77] Between the two versions of the Bible, the reader can deduce that the nation of *Javan* is Greece. Their trade was enslaving men and offering molten brass in lieu of water to the disbeliever – thereby scalding their faces.[409] "Woe to me that I dwell in Meshech, that I live among the tents of Kedar. Too long have I lived among those who hate peace. I am a man of peace; but when I speak, they are for war."[359] This *Meshech* apparently refers to the Semite nation, the son of Aram

and *the eastern hill country* from Mesha to Sephar.[109] "Aram did business with you [Tyre] because of your many products; they exchanged turquoise, purple fabric, embroidered work, fine linen, coral and rubies for your merchandise."[78]

2. Kedar – "*Arabia*, and all the princes of Kedar were your [Tyre's] customers, they occupied with thee in lambs, and rams, and goats; in these were they thy merchants"[79]

3. Mesha - The king of Moab[211]

4. Sephar – A place in Southern Arabia[498]

5. Tubal – Mentioned along with Meshech and their hordes, being uncircumcised and killed by the sword because they spread their terror in the land of the living. They are buried with their weapons of war; their swords placed beneath their heads.[84] Compare this biblical warning to the Prophet's declaration of causing terror[400] with paradise waiting below the shadow of the swords.[7] They join the likes of Egypt, Assyria, and Babylon in the shame of all who go down to the pit.[83] Tubal is not mentioned with Meshech in Isaiah 66:19 or Psalm 120:5.

6. Elam – "A country situated on the east side of the Tigris opposite Babylonia; was one of the earliest civilizations; figures prominently in Babylon and Assyrian history"[495]

7. Javan – Another name for Greece[77]

8. Pul – Libyans[163]

9. Lud – Lidyans; described as those who draw the bow [archers][176]

10. Gomer – Mentioned as the Sidonians who join Togarmah as being part of the assault upon Israel. The house of Togarmah being from the far north.

11. Togarmah

12. Sidon – The northern border of the Cannonites,[106] with Sidon being 20 miles north of Tyre. The Sidonians join the kings of the north in their assault on Israel.[531]

13. Persia – Persia is as Persia was. This is current-day Iran. It is the archangel *Michael* who will assist the Lord in opposing the prince and king of Persia.[49]

14. Canaan – The coastal region of what became Israel; from the northern tip of the Red Sea to the northern-most borders of Syria.

15. Sheba – "Sheba is a reference to the land of the Sabeans in southwestern Arabia. They controlled the trade route by which spices, metals, and other commodities were transported from southern Arabia and beyond Palestine."[85]

16. Dedan – In a prophecy against Arabia, Isaiah writes: "You caravans of Dedanites, who camp in the thickets of Arabia, bring water for the thirsty; you who live in Tema, bring food for the fugitives. They flee from the sword, from the drawn sword, from the bent bow and from the heat of battle. This is what the Lord says to me: Within one year, as a servant bound by contract would count it, all the pomp of Kedar will come to an end. The survivors of the bowmen, the warriors of Kedar, will be few. The Lord, God of Israel, has spoken."[144] "Dedan, and Tema, and Buz and all that are in the utmost corners, and all the kings of Arabia, and all the kings of the mingled people that dwell in the desert…"[171]

17. Cush – Ethiopians[177]

18. Put – Set between Libya and Egypt. "Cush (Ethiopia) and Egypt were her boundless strength; Put and Libya were among her allies."[345]

19. Tarshish – A maritime people;[103] those who trade via shipping.

20. Magog – Known only as home to Gog, the chief prince of Meshech and Tubal.[86] Described as *the four corners of the earth*, Satan utilizes Gog [The Prophet] and his deluded nations, Magog [the slaves], to deceive the earth and gather them for battle.

Though the wording is a bit tedious, defining the locations of the lands above make the reality of Ezekiel's warning astounding! With the players identified, the picture begins to form. Look to the map of territories. What is so special about the locations of Meshech and Tubal? Meshech is the central worship center for The Prophet. The land of Tubal was the official home of the ruling party of The Prophet from 1517 until it was abolished in 1924. The current rulers of Tubal (modern-day Turkey) boast that 99% of their population has adopted the teaching of The Prophet.[353] It comes as no surprise that Meshech (modern-day Saudi Arabia) demonstrates similar support in The Prophet at 97% and Persia (Iran) is among the pack at over 99%.

The Prophet

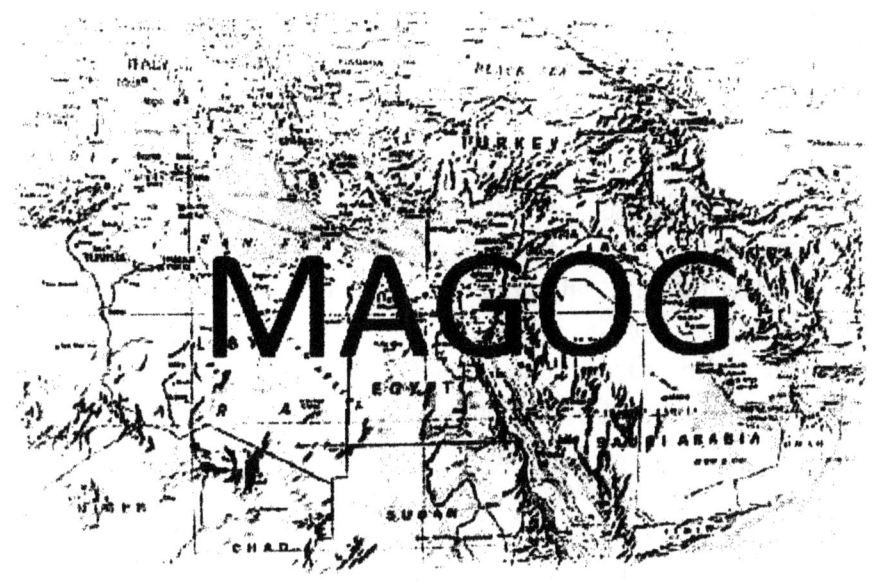

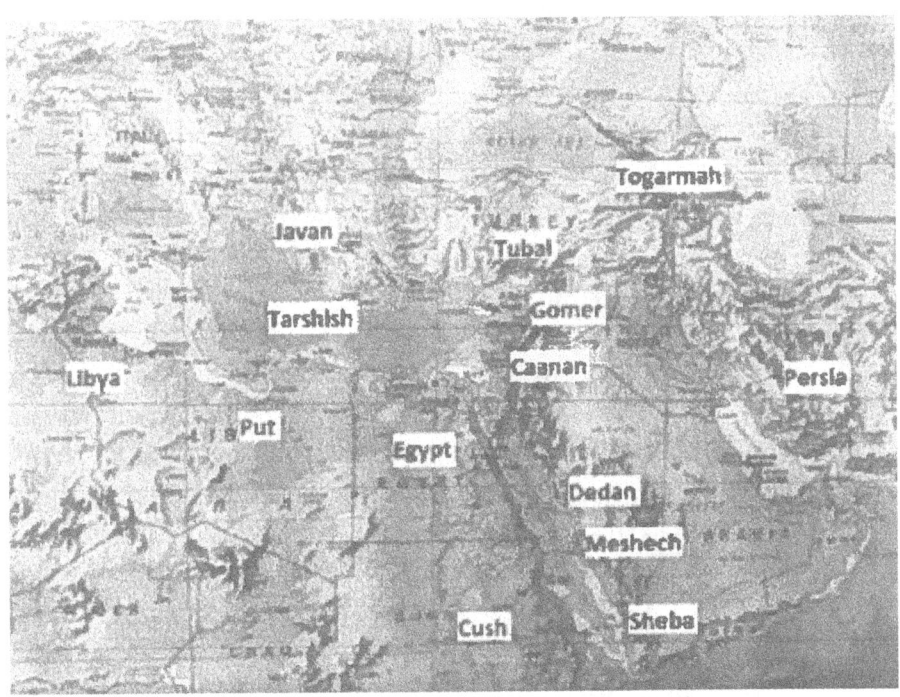

This *prince*, he who was not born of royalty, has been given a warning from God. As Ezekiel tells it, God says: I am against you, chief prince of Meshech and Tubal. I will turn you around, put hooks in your jaws and bring you out with your whole army... Persia, Cush and Put will be with them..., also Gomer and the house of Togarmah from the far north with all its troops and many nations with you."[87] Look again to the illustration of nations. This could be a problem! With The Prophet's holy war raging for centuries, the biblical lands mentioned above have fallen under the coercive edge of his sword - all of them having been led astray, with each nation having a super-majority who takes the path and travels the journey of The Prophet.

With this understanding, consider what God says next: "In future years (sometime after Ezekiel retired his pen) you will invade a land that has recovered from war, whose people were gathered from many nations to the mountains of Israel..." There is no mistaking where this takes place. The *mountains of Israel* account for the tiny section of land marked on the illustration as "Canaan." Canaan was a desolate land prior to the arrival of the Hebrews in Moses' day. That land was made desolate again by the Babylonians in 586 B.C., again with the Roman's destruction of the Temple in 70 A.D., and again by the Prophetiers and their conquering hordes in the years 685 A.D. - until the Jews regathering in 1948. The Prophetiers refer to this time (1948) as "The Catastrophe." In this day, upon the conclusion of WWII, the Jews were brought back into the land from the many nations they had previously been dispersed. This is of historical record. The evidence shows that The Prophet, with all his troops and all his nations, have advanced like a storm. According to the illustration and Pew Research, they do, in fact, cover the land like a cloud. It is no secret that they are none-too-happy about Moses' regathered people and the renewed nation of Israel.

God had more to say about Gog and his unlawful beginnings: "On that day, thoughts will come into your mind..." What thoughts came into the mind of The Prophet? Weren't these thoughts the revelations of prophethood? It is said of The Prophet that "Man is apt to forget, and The Prophet was a human being and so he too was apt to forget. But he never forgot a word of the divine revelation which came to him."[315] It is a documented certainty that thoughts came into his head. But were these thoughts the makings of an evil scheme? If one was to consider assault, invasion, theft, rape, murder, amputation, and false imprisonment the things of an evil mind – one might have to agree that The Prophet certainly devised an evil scheme! Did The Prophet offer any proof that he invaded a land of unwalled villages and attacked a peaceful and unsuspecting people – all of them living without walls and without gates and without bars? Yes, he did.

The Prophet

Caravans have no walls, no gates, and no bars. His neighbors were among those who resettled to the south of Jerusalem after the Romans destroyed the Temple and the city. Whether they were armed or unarmed, the caravans and his resettled neighbors fell victim to The Prophet's evil scheme. The places where these crimes occurred are of no coincidence. The prophetic warning gives insight into the mind of The Prophet: "I will plunder and loot and turn my hand against [fight] the resettled ruins and the people gathered from the nations [Jews], rich in livestock and goods, living at the center of the land." Look again at the illustration and the location of Meshech. In association to Sheba and Dedan, where was The Prophet's primary and secondary place of residence? Where did he wage most of his battles while he was among the living? He did so at the center of the land. Midway between the Mediterranean and Arabian Seas are the places he called *home*. When Sheba and Dedan and the merchants of the seas and all their villages asked of him, "Have you come to plunder? Have you gathered your hordes to loot, to carry off silver and gold, to take away livestock and goods and to seize much plunder?" How did The Prophet respond?

- And know that whatever you acquire in war, a fifth of it is for [god] and for [The Prophet] ...[403]
- Eat then of the lawful and good things which you have acquired in war[405]
- Whatever [god] restored to [The Prophet] from the people of the towns..."[423]
- This verse relates to property acquired in war...[303]

By biblical account, how many of God's prophets were raised as merchants – only to become *righteous thieves* in the land of Sheba and Dedan? Murderers have repented to become men of God. Thieves and Tax Collectors have repented to become men of God. But no man of God has built his prophethood on the tip of a sword or in the sexual enslavement of another man's wife or daughter. No man has become nearer to God by becoming a thief. The notion that any man can be a righteous thief was born in the mind of a madman. Nearly everything that he and his people have acquired, they have acquired in war.

Now comes the switch. When the Prophet personally robbed and assaulted Sheba, Dedan, and the merchants of the Tarshish who traveled the trade routes in the land, God's people were no longer living in Jerusalem. They had been scattered from Jerusalem by the same army who crucified Christ. Due to the undying efforts of the Romans and their thirst for power, the Jews were once again chased out of Jerusalem – with many of them settling to the south. Five and a half centuries later, The Prophet appeared and set his scheme into motion. His generation-leaping reign of terror had begun. This is the story of his own telling. After his death, The Prophet's nation would grow and advance to the east, west and north. They would ascend upon Jerusalem and the Temple Mount. His nation and its people have become the cloud that would cover the land. They currently occupy every territory aligned with Gog.

Anyone who has read the Bible understands that God fondly refers to Jews and Israel as *my people* and *my land*.[180] When The Prophet's nation grows to unimaginable numbers and ultimately advances against God's land and people, Jews will have been reunited and returned to Israel. That has already come about. God saw to it that *His* people were resettled in *His* land on May 14, 1948. The Prophet's people refer to this event as *the day of catastrophe*.[346] Now, the biblical table has been set. With God's people firmly settled back in their land, the Prophetiers surround her and gnash their teeth. The Prophetiers are seething. Their intent is no secret. God's prophets of Ezekiel, Joel, Zechariah, and John each write about the day that The Prophet and his nations will make their final assault upon Israel. Each prophet describes the monumental importance of that moment in time. The Valley of Hamon-Gog is about to become known. See how each prophet describes the moment that the confrontation takes place.

"Therefore, son of man, prophesy and say to Gog: 'This is what the Sovereign Lord says: In that day, when my people Israel are living in safety, will you not take notice of it? You will come from your place in the far north, you and many nations with you, all of them riding on horses, a great horde, a mighty army. You will advance against my people Israel like a cloud that covers the land. In days to come, O Gog, I will bring you against my land, so that the nations may know me when I show myself holy through you before their eyes… And it shall come to pass in that day, that I will give unto Gog a place there of graves in Israel, the valley of the travelers on the east of the sea: and it shall stop the noses [block the way] of the travelers, because Gog and all his hordes will be buried there. So, it will be called the Valley of Hamon Gog." – Ezekiel 38:14-16; 39:11

"In those days and at that time, when I restore the fortunes of Judah and Jerusalem, I will gather all nations and bring them down to the Valley of Jehoshaphat. There I will enter into judgment against them concerning my inheritance, my people Israel, for they scattered my people among the nations and divided up my land." – Joel 3:1-2

The Prophet

"This is the Word of the Lord concerning Israel. The Lord, who stretches out the heavens, who lays the foundation of the earth, and who forms the spirit of man within him declares: 'I am going to make Jerusalem a cup that sends all the surrounding peoples reeling. Judah will be besieged as well as Jerusalem. On that day, when all the nations of the earth are gathered against her, I will make Jerusalem an immovable rock for all the nations. All who try to move it will injure themselves. On that day I will strike every horse with panic and its rider with madness' declares the Lord. 'I will keep a watchful eye over the house of Judah, but I will blind all the horses of the nations. Then the leaders of Judah will say in their hearts, "The people of Jerusalem are strong, because the Lord Almighty is their God." On that day I will make the leaders of Judah like a firepot in a woodpile. Like a flaming torch among sheaves. They will consume right and left all the surrounding peoples, but Jerusalem will remain intact in her place... On that day I will set out to destroy all the nations that attack Jerusalem.' – Zechariah 12:1-6, 9

"The sixth angel poured out his bowl on the great river Euphrates, and its water was dried up to prepare the way for the kings from the East. Then I saw three evil spirits that looked like frogs; they come out of the mouth of the dragon, out of the mouth of the beast and out of the mouth of the false prophet. They are spirits of demons performing miraculous signs, and they go out to the kings of the whole world, to gather them for the battle on the great day of God Almighty... Then they gathered the kings together to the place that in Hebrew is called Armageddon." – John, Revelation 16:12-14, 16

The reality of this coming together is nothing short of stunning! Those who surround Jerusalem and God's people are none other than those who have been nourished by the bitter, dark, and evil marks of The Prophet. To the north of Israel is Syria, Turkey, and the lesser states of what used to be Russia. To the east of Israel is Jordan, Iraq, Iran, Afghanistan, and Pakistan. To the south of Israel is Saudi Arabia, Sudan, Ethiopia, and Somalia. To the west of Israel is Egypt, Libya, Algeria, Tunisia, and Morocco. Today, the kings from the East, namely the Persians, are opposed to Israel and they fight in conjunction and alliance with Syria. Knowing that the original boundaries of Israel encompass the land between the Nile and Euphrates rivers,[111] the reader might now have a better understanding as to how Israel has been divided by the Prophetiers of: Egypt, Jordan, and Syria. The areas to the north and east of Jerusalem are currently held and occupied by those who hate her. Moreover, this land, northeast of Jerusalem, is known to be the epicenter of *Armageddon*.

Now comes the biblical stunner. With Jerusalem being the center of the earth, most believe that the travelers or passengers are those who travel through Megiddo (place of troops), the Great Road linking Gaza and Damascus.[497] Considering the everyday struggles of the Israelis - those who are on the path between Gaza and the West Bank - the West Bank and Damascus, these boundaries are understandably difficult to cross. However, the time is coming. But the Prophet and his hordes (the many nations with them) have yet to reach their pinnacle - the biblical apocalypse known as Armageddon. No man can reasonably argue that such a moment is unlikely. It rapidly approaches. But the beauty in God's Word unveils itself in the incredible accuracies surrounding Gog, Magog, Hamonah, and the Valley of Hamon Gog.

Who is Gog? Some say Gog is the devil. Some say he was Hitler. Others believe Gog to be a future king who will gather the world's kingdoms for battle. But the future is now. Gog was a man. And how can we be certain of this? Simple – the residents of Sheba and Dedan ask this man if he has come as a thief; to plunder and loot and seize much plunder. They do not ask this question of God, a foreign god, or the carved images of some fat little man. They ask this question of the thief who was actively robbing them of their belongings. And what might men call the land after the thief makes it his own? They will name it in honor of Gog. What is the name of The Prophet who opposes the Father and Son? What is the name of the peoples who surround Jerusalem and have been sent reeling?

Gog and Magog, Hamonah and the Valley of Hamon Gog

- Chief prince of Meshech and Tubal
- He leads an army who brandish swords
- His army resides in Meshech, Tubal, Persia, Cush, Put, and Gomer (all current locations whose overwhelming majority consists of Prophetiers)
- He is aligned and allied with Russia and China Beth (related to) Togarmah
- He attacks tribes of displaced Jews who had relocated to the south of Israel
- Sheba, Dedan, and the merchants of the Tarshish were among his victims
- His army and allied nations currently occupy Turkey, Syria, Russia, China, and surrounding locations

The Prophet

- He is the "one" who opposes God's prophets
- He is the "one" who causes men to tremble
- It is upon Gog that God pours down torrents of rain, hailstones and burning sulfur
- It is upon Gog's troops and nations that this fiery hell falls
- God sends fire upon the land of Magog – those who aspire to be like Gog
- Magog is the group who annually travels East for pilgrimage
- The Sea they travel toward is the sea that offered up the body of the beast
- Satan has deceived Gog and Magog – gathering them for battle
- There are billions of them
- They surround Jerusalem
- Magog will be stopped and buried in the Valley of the home to Gog
- Home to Gog is what he calls "the center of spirituality" and "the mother of the towns"[570] – "the real mother of the whole world"[571]
- The house that resides there is said to be the first house for men[572]
- Called "Bakkah,"[572] the mother of all towns signifies *"the crowding together of men"* and *"the breaking of the neck."*[573]
- Hamon means 'horde'[581]
- Hamon Gog means 'hordes of Gog'[581]
- Hamonah means the town of hordes of Gog[582]
- The town of Mecca houses the Bakkah and is described as the 'narrow' valley between the mountains[583]
- According to Gog, "The abyss is a mother to him."[574] Maulana clarifies this statement as: "The abyss, or hell, is here called a mother to indicate that man's connection with hell is similar to that of a baby with its mother, that his abode [home] there fits him for progress in the spiritual world – he being brought up, as it were, in the bosom of hell, as a child is brought up in the bosom of its

mother, and that his stay in hell is only for a time, as the child draws nourishment from his mother only for a time."[575]

- Gog's statement is an afront to God whose prophet, Paul, tells us that "...the Jerusalem that is above is free, and she is our mother"[576]

- The premise of Gog's testimony about Abraham resettling with Hagar in this town is rendered false. "But what does Scripture say? 'Get rid of the slave woman and her son, for the slave woman's son will never share in the inheritance with the free woman's son.'"[577]

Putting it all together, we find that Gog is The Prophet and Magog is the land of the Prophetiers. The Prophet is the chief prince of the lands from the mountains of Meshech in the south of Arabia to Tubal or Turkey in the north. This army, the Prophetiers, live by the sword and recognize paradise to exist beneath the shadows of those swords. All ten territories are mentioned as being a part of The Prophet's "Magog," with Sheba, Dedan, and the merchants of the Tarshish getting special mention as the lands in whose habitants were personally victimized by The Prophet – the thief. His documented encroachment upon the displaced Jews is abundantly obvious and horrifically depicted in the testimony of those who witnessed the decapitation of all the men in the tribe called the Banu Qurayza.[164] The Prophetiers are a people at war, an army, who strive to conquer at any cost. The Prophet is the "one" that God warned would oppose God's prophets, cause the earth to shake, and make kingdoms tremble. He is the beast that causes fire to fall from the sky in full view of men. This imminent fire is fueled by the weapons of proliferation. Until 1945, this type of weapon had remained a mystery. Thanks to Nagasaki and Hiroshima, this is a mystery no longer.

Gog's body of believers, Magog, are dutybound to travel to the East as part of an annual pilgrimage. Their burial place is called the mother of all towns (Bakkah) and it is at the center of their spiritual world – the Valley of the mother to men. This is how The Prophet affectionately describes hell. Once again, The Prophet opposes the prophets of God by declaring that the nurturing mother of men is hell; whereas God's prophets and His people understand that our mother is the free Jerusalem above. Without coincidence, Bakkah is The Prophet's spiritual house and its outer grounds – located in a town that is recognized to be in a Valley between mountains. This 'crowded place' of The Prophet and his Prophetiers is named such – 'the crowded place' or place of hordes. Hence, Hamon Gog means 'Bakkah' and Hamonah is 'Mecca,' the *Valley of Hamon Gog*. It is the valley of the hordes of Gog – their burial place.

The Prophet

The house of Israel is seemingly Spiritual. God told us about His plan to introduce "a man to fulfill [His] purpose." That man is Jesus. And from the east [He] summoned a bird of prey. That bird looks to be The Prophet. Unlike the declarations of The Prophet, God tells us that the fate of Satan, Gog, Magog, and the balance of the body of the beast will be tormented in the lake of burning sulfur day and night for ever and ever.[578] The lake of burning sulfur is the earth after it's set ablaze, created by man's own doing. What few realize is that the concept of day and night is unique to a revolving earth. Without the earth's 24-hour spin, day and night would not exist. Therefore, when "fire comes down from heaven" to devour Gog and Magog, the fire falls upon the earth. It is here, in this place, that the burning sulfur torments the false prophet, his foreign god, and their beast of nations "day and night" for ever and ever! Amazing is the aspect of Satan's gathering – Gog and Magog – guided by the words of a book (the marks) written in his own image. These "marks" represent the three evil spirits that came out of the mouth of the dragon, out of the mouth of the Prophetiers and out of the mouth of The Prophet. Knowing this, the battle of Revelation 16:14 is the big finale, the concluding moment of this generation of man that began with the warning of Revelation 20:7-8.

The Lord confronts The Prophet and emphatically asks: "Are you not the one I spoke of in former days by my servants the prophets of Israel?"[90] History offers an answer to God's inquiry. The Prophet is the one, he who...

- Isaiah warned about as Lucifer, the fake bright morning star
- Daniel warned about as the little horn
- Daniel warned about as the stern-faced king
- Daniel warned about as the contemptible person who desecrated the Temple
- Daniel warned about as the contemptible person whose armed forces set up the abomination that causes desolation
- Daniel warned about as the king who exalts himself
- Daniel warned about as the man responsible for introducing the deceptions Satan, his covenant, and the abomination that causes desolation
- Zechariah warned would lead the people who oppose Israel
- Joel warned would lead the people who oppose Israel

There is more, but this list serves the cause. Since its Declaration of Independence, Israel has been the target of numerous attacks by a few of the named nations. Just after the Israelis were re-gathered in their own land, they were attacked by a coalition of people from Egypt, Jordan, Syria, and Iraq. Israel was victorious in that war. Twenty years later, Israel became involved in the Six-Day War with Jordan, Syria, Egypt, Iraq, and Lebanon. Israel was again victorious. In all, there have been at least 14 named conflicts to go along with the ever-growing hostilities with Gaza, the West Bank and the kings from the east who have entered northern Israel through the portal that has become the civil war in Syria. But the main storm lingers in the imminent future. "This is what will happen in that day: When Gog [Magog and all the nations] attacks the land of Israel, [God's] hot anger will be aroused. In [His] zeal and fiery wrath [God] declares that there shall be a great earthquake in the land of Israel... [God] will summon a sword against Gog on all *[God's] mountains*... every man's sword will be against his brother."[91] This is not the first time that we have been warned about the hostilities that are to occur between the sons of Abram/Abraham. Moses warned about the descendants of Ishmael, "living in hostility toward all their brothers."[119] At some point, it becomes futile for the rebellious to argue that current global realities have no relation to previous biblical prophecies.

Men have been born and raised in a world that is bursting at the seams with weapons of unimaginable, fiery destruction. What used to be a stalemate in the way of *Mutually Assured Destruction* between the former U.S.S.R. and the U.S. has splintered into a proliferation of grand miscalculation. Like the world's renewed racism and its Sodomite-like sidekick, the zest to incinerate the brother of man has reached a fever pitch! The Persians have double-pinky-promised not to enrich their piles of uranium beyond the 60% purity point. They also promise that their work in the field of nuclear science is intended for strictly 'peaceful purposes.' Remember, The Prophet destroys many by 'peace.' Remember also, Fauci and the Chinese relied upon and utilized *science* to harvest bat viruses to achieve the successful gain of function process that has brought the world to its knees. *Science*... ain't it great? Such scientific accomplishments are the means of men who now sprint toward fulfilling God's promise of destroying many by peace while the man of lawlessness is finally unveiled. The proliferation of such madness is global. The catastrophic weapons used against Nagasaki and Hiroshima, those that ended the war against Japan and its people, were relative 'duds' compared to some of today's herculean warheads. The most advanced versions of these modern fireballs are up to 3,000 times more powerful than the initial bombs, affectionately named *Little Boy* and *Fat Man*, that were dropped on those Japanese cities.⁵³² The current nuclear club includes: The U.S., U.K., France, Israel, Pakistan, India, Russia, China, and North Korea. This group is worrisome enough, but Iran has been spinning centrifuges for 20 years and they have become linked with the North Koreans as their *Technology Partner*.⁵²⁰ The horrific likelihood is that Iran went nuclear long ago. Using North Korea to test Iranian warheads has brought about the unimaginable horror of the beast out of the earth having the capability to bring about the fire that falls from heaven (above) to earth in full view of men. As the kings of the East, the Persians can now launch and deliver those warheads from Iran, Iraq, Afghanistan, Syria, Turkey, or Lebanon. Because of the Persian threat, Saudi Arabia has likely acted upon their agreement with Pakistan to buy back some of the nuclear warheads that the Pakistanis developed and assembled with Saudi funding.⁴⁹² The Prophet's divided kingdom is well-defined and fully represented by the mistrust and hatred demonstrated between the Saudis and the Persians. Unfortunately, this simply verifies that the ruthless nations of Magog can now accomplish what was previously unthinkable. At the center of all this biblical reality is Jerusalem – the city that causes the surrounding peoples to go reeling.

Unsettling certainties are not well-accepted in today's world. Godless endeavors, intentional racism, and emotional disorders like the Woke Movement, BLM, and men competing in women's sports are all evidentiary symptoms of illness in a very sick world. A sick world is a thriving environment for the evils of science and the developments of nuclear fission and gain of function. The threat of nuclear annihilation was alive and well during the Cold War, but cooler heads understood the finality of acting upon such an exchange. Those cooler heads have given way to a people who live a life of war and scream the battle-cry of The Prophet who demands that they "...obey not the disbelievers, and strive against them a mighty striving with it."⁴¹³ For those who insist upon arguing that this is a misinterpretation of The Prophet's intent, consider the translating scholar's narrated explanation of the statement:

"It should be noted that the greatest [effort to strive] which a [Prophetier] can carry on is one by means of the [clear book], to which the personal pronoun it at the end of the verse unquestionably refers, because it must be carried on by every [Prophetier] under all circumstances."²⁹¹

Men are guided and driven by their beliefs. Because of this, misguided groups of former kings instituted and implemented supposedly righteous *Inquisitions* against God's people and performed the religious-based *Crusades* against the Prophetiers.

Because men are guided by godless beliefs and bloody pursuits toward world rule, history has witnessed two World Wars. In the second, Pearl Harbor was attacked by the Japanese. With that attack, the Japanese ultimately invited mankind's first glimpse into the horrors of nuclear weaponry. Because men are guided by their beliefs, Adolph Hitler waged war on the world and implemented his plan of genocide upon God's people by murdering six million Jews. Because men are guided by their beliefs, The Prophet wages his war, and his marks became the driving force in the destruction of the Twin Towers. Because the behaviors of men are guided by their beliefs, Jesus was crucified. His intentional death was driven by the schemes of the Pharisees and implemented at the hands of the Romans. It is because of man's many beliefs that he will act collectively and use the weaponry he has created and assembled. In August of 1945, these weapons were introduced to the world. After the next act, the curtain will be drawn to an eternal close.

God's use of grand imagery in the way of beasts, horns, crowns, teeth, and fiery angels - all lead people to believe that something supernatural will crawl up out of the sea or appear as a meteorite that will come crashing to earth from heaven above. The latter thought is reasonable, understanding that the dinosaurs found their demise in such a manner. But the end that comes *to* mankind comes *from* mankind. The fire, that which falls from heaven above, originates from the minds of men and the work of their hands. Men destroy the earth.[438] This is an instantaneous spike in global warming. While men distract one another with the promise of paradise via electric cars and impossible burgers, man's spiritual war rages on. Through his many gains, The Prophet appears to be winning. But God has put hooks in The Prophet's jaws and is certain to turn him around. His masquerade is being brought to ruin. He is the cause of the imminent fire. That blaze originates in the fiery angel. God will make that fire come out of Satan.[82] There are many biblical warnings about the fire that seem rather odd and largely out of place, but they make sense now!

- Your heart became proud on account of your beauty, and you corrupted your wisdom because of your splendor. So, I threw you to the earth; I made a spectacle of you before kings. By your many sins and dishonest trade, you have desecrated your sanctuaries. So, I made a fire come out from you, and it consumed you, and I reduced you to ashes on the ground in the sight of all who were watching[81]

- Suddenly, in an instant, the Lord Almighty will come with thunder and earthquake and great noise, with windstorm and tempest and flames of a devouring fire[146]

The Prophet

- For as lightning that comes from the east is visible even in the west [likely referencing the events of 9/11], so will be the coming of the Son of Man... 'the sun will be darkened, and the moon will not give its light; the stars will fall from the sky, and the heavenly bodies will be shaken.'[128] At that time the sign of the Son of Man will appear in the sky, and all the nations of the earth will mourn"[337]

- On that day I will set out to destroy all the nations that attack Jerusalem. And I will pour out on the house of David and the inhabitants of Jerusalem a spirit of grace and supplication. They will look on me, *the one they have pierced*, and they will mourn for him as one grieves for a first-born son. On that day the weeping in Jerusalem will be great, like the weeping of Hadad Rimmon [sun worshipers] in the plain of Megiddo [Armageddon]. The land will mourn, each clan by itself, with their wives by themselves: the clan of the house of David and their wives, the clan of Shimei and their wives, and all the rest of the clans and their wives[526]

- There was a great earthquake. The sun turned black like sackcloth made of goat hair, the whole moon turned blood red, and the stars in the sky fell to earth, as late figs drop from a fig tree when shaken by a strong wind. The sky receded like a scroll, rolling up, and every mountain and island was removed from its place. The kings of the earth, the princes, the generals, the rich, the mighty, and every slave and every free man hid in caves [bomb shelters] and among the rocks of the mountains[430]

- He [the speaking image] exercised all the authority of the first beast on his behalf, and made the earth and its inhabitants worship the first beast [Satan]... And he [the speaking image] performed great and miraculous signs, even causing fire to come down from heaven to earth in full view of men[449]

- I will execute judgment on him [Gog] with plague and bloodshed; I will pour down torrents of rain, hailstones and burning sulfur on him and on his troops and on the many nations with him[92]

- I am against you, O Gog, chief prince of Meshech and Tubal. I will turn you around and drag you along. I will bring you from the far north and send you against the mountains of Israel. Then I will strike your bow from your left hand and make your arrows drop from your right hand. On the mountains of Israel you will fall, you and all your troops and the nations with you. I will give you as food to all kinds of carrion birds and to the wild animals. You will fall in the open field, for I have spoken, declares the Sovereign Lord. I will send fire on Magog and on those who live in safety in the coastlands, and they will know that I am the Lord. I will make known my holy name among my people Israel. I will no longer let my holy name be profaned, and the nations will know that I the Lord am the Holy One in Israel [93]

Since its founding, many have called for Israel's destruction. When they call for its destruction, they are calling for the murder of God's people. The Egyptians tried to destroy God's people 3,500 years ago and twice again in the last 75 years. Babylon attempted to destroy them. Assyria, Medo-Persia, Greece, and Rome have all tried to rid the world of Israel and change the biblical outcome of God's chosen Jews. Then came Gog and Magog. For 14 centuries The Prophet and his people have pursued a futile goal – to put an end to Israel. As enemies of God, they cannot and will not stop this fruitless endeavor. But they will usher in the prophetic inevitability of their own destruction.

"O God, do not keep silent; be not quiet, O God, be not still. See how your enemies are astir, how your foes rear their heads. With cunning they conspire against your people; they plot against those you cherish. 'Come,' they say, 'let us destroy them as a nation, that the name of Israel be remembered no more.' With one mind they plot together; they form an alliance against you – the tents of Edom and the Ishmaelites..." [354]

The Ishmaelites... These are the descendants of Ishmael who were prophesied to live in hostility toward all their brothers. They have acted as was prophesied. Today they thrust their swords against their brothers – all their brothers! Ishmael's bloodline, his vine, has formed an alliance against God and that alliance seeks the destruction of Israel. Many of them call for the annihilation of Israel from the [Jordan] river to the [Mediterranean] sea. This genocidal dream is advanced by the most unlikely of characters; among them are members of the U.S. House of Representatives. The Jordan river serves as the eastern border for current-day Israel. It extends from the Hula Valley in the north to the Dead Sea in the south. Every inch of this border is disputed by The Prophetiers. The northern reaches of this valley include the Golan Heights – a strategic outpost and geological buffer between Israel and Syria. Whether the Jordan river shares a boundary with Lebanon, Syria, Jordan, or the West Bank – all of it is east and north of Jerusalem, and many want to see the border erased and Israel pushed into the sea.

God warned Ezekiel that Gog (The Warrior Prophet), from the land of the Prophetiers (the warriors), would once again attack Israel. Gog is described as *the chief prince* of Meshech and Tubal. Meshech and Tubal are the names of the ancient lands that represent current day Turkey and the mountainous region of Arabia. It is no stretch to recognize the current-day beliefs and actions of the Turks and the Arabians as those of the Prophetiers. Therefore, in current geographical terms, Ezekiel appears to state: "I AM against you, O Gog, chief prince of Turkey and Arabia. I will turn you around, put hooks in your jaws and bring you out with your whole army—your horses, your horsemen fully armed, and a great horde with large and small shields, all of them brandishing their swords. Libya and Egypt will be with them, all with their armaments, also Syria with all their troops and Russia from the far north with all its troops–the many nations with them."

Once again, this is no stretch. Thanks, in-part, to the efforts of an American President (with his ever-changing religious and national alliances) who set the stage for the Arab spring in 2010 - the world has witnessed the reoccurring aggressions of the Prophetiers in Syria and Iraq - aka *Gomer*. With the whirlwind removal of American troops from Iraq in 2011, a new breed of Prophetier was born. This particularly ruthless group of special forces reverted to the new laws of The Prophet and murdered anyone who refused to worship The Prophet's god in The Prophet's manner. Their go-to method of *dissuading mischief in the land* consisted of recording and broadcasting beheadings. They took The Prophet's instruction of 'sniping the necks' for its literal meaning and ultimate fulfillment. Considering the brutality of past and present Prophetiers, the formation of this bunch has become overwhelmingly ominous.

As a demonstration of the futility in advancing The Prophet's *peace*, let's look back and see how events have played out since the Arab Spring. For the sake of argument, let's call the Saudi sect "*Group A*." The Persian sect we'll call "*Group B*." And the most vicious bunch we'll call "*Group C*." We'll leave the Syrian group as is - since they are located directly north of Israel. Immediately after their formation in 2010, Group C joined forces with Group A in opposition to Group B and the Syrian regime. In turn, Group B and the Syrians were joined by Russia (Beth-Togarmah) to oppose the rebels of Groups A & C. To shore up the efforts of Groups A and C against Group B and the Russians, the United States joined in. And, vowing never to let the Persians get a military foothold on their northern border, Israel entered the picture and continues to make bombing runs against convoys of armaments that are set forth to support Group B and the Russians. Now, Israel and the United States side with the Saudis, the rebels, and the vicious bunch (Group C) that was formed by the vacuum created by the withdrawal of U.S. troops from Iraq. This is quite odd since the members of Group C originally fought against the

Persians who were and still are aligned with the Russians. Adding to this mess is the involvement of France, Turkey, Germany, the U.K., and China. All this nonsense is taking place on Israel's northern border! The enemy of my enemy is my friend – until that friend turns back to sniping the necks of all non-believers! So, what could go wrong?

As the days go by, the influences of Iran and Russia grow stronger in Syria. Via their Syrian alliance and the nuclear agreement, Russia has become Persia's ally against Israel. Such an alliance is prophetic and has allowed the beast to spread its terrifying power and influence even further than in the days before the Arab Spring. Adding to this mess is the unconscionable efforts of a dementia-driven imbecile who insists on returning to the nuclear agreement with a now-nuclear Iran! If the consequences were not biblical in stature, the circumstances would be laughable. But the consequences are, indeed, biblical. Notice how seven of the ten kingdoms are listed here? Meshech, Tubal, Persia, Cush, Put, Gomer and Beth-Togarmah have been named as seven of the ten Luciferian kingdoms that have been prophesied to attack Israel. What then comes of Sheba, Dedan and the Tarshish? The answer to that question comes in the following paragraphs.

Some might believe that the Persian and Russian military buildup in Syria is for the sole purpose of keeping the current Syrian regime in power. That may be - but keeping the current regime in power ensures that the Persians and the Russians remain within early striking distance of Israel. The Persians have repeatedly stated that Israel and the Zionists are to be pushed into the sea. This line of thinking did not work so well for the Egyptians when they pressed Moses and the Hebrews up against the Red Sea. Persian Prophetiers are not shy when it comes to demonstrating their disdain over the Jews and their biblical home in Israel. Is this not a common biblical theme? How many times has history revealed a people or nation conquering Israel and enslaving its people, only to see Israel and the Jews rise again? How did that work for the Egyptians? How did that work for the Assyrians? How did it work for the Babylonians, the Medes and the (original) Persians? How did it work for the Greeks and the Romans? How did it work for the Germans? How has it worked for the Prophetiers in the 14+ attempts they have made against Israel since 1948? How's it working now?

To the south of Israel are Prophetiers. To the east of Israel are Prophetiers. To the west of Israel (across the Mediterranean) are Prophetiers. To the north of Israel are Prophetiers. Surrounding Israel are the people of The Prophet. Israel will be attacked again. Israel is the nation that has recovered from war. Israel, God's people, have been gathered from many nations and returned to their land. Desolate Israel is a distant has-been. For 1900 years, Israel was without her people. Regathered, they live in relative

The Prophet

security. But the security they have found is not necessarily what our eyes see. The Jerusalem they have been promised is not the Jerusalem we see housing that unmistakable golden dome and its many touristy glamour shots. With her land given away, Israel has become a postage-stamp of geography that certainly does not match the magnificent, three-dimensional Jerusalem described by John. The Jerusalem that men know will be overrun by troops and set ablaze by missiles that have already been amassed in the terrifying alliance of nations gathered to her north. They will advance on Jerusalem like a storm. And, like everything else on earth, that once-sacred ground will burn. The abomination will burn. The masquerading light and his mouthpiece will burn. But God's people will be returned to Him. God's people will be returned to the free Jerusalem above.

"Tell me, you who want to be under the Law, are you not aware of what the Law says? For it is written that Abraham had two sons, one by the slave woman and the other by the free woman. His son by the slave woman was born in the ordinary way; but his son by the free woman was born as a result of promise.

These things may be taken figuratively, for the women represent two covenants. One covenant is from Mount Sanai and bears children who are to be slaves: This is by Hagar. Now Hagar stands for Mount Sanai in Arabia and corresponds to the present city of Jerusalem, because she is in slavery with her children. But the Jerusalem that is above is free, and she is our mother.

Now you, brothers, like Isaac, are children of promise. At that time the son born in the ordinary way persecuted the son born by the power of the Spirit. It is the same now. But what does Scripture say? 'Get rid of the slave woman and her son, for the slave woman's son *will never* share in the inheritance with the free woman's son. It is for freedom that Christ has set us free. Stand firm, then, and do not let yourselves be burdened again by a yoke of slavery." – Galatians 4:21-26, 28-30; 5:1

The Prophet disagrees with Paul's Spiritual guidance. Like most of his marks, The Prophet's adaptation of Abraham's story takes an immediate about face and U-Turn.

"And when his Lord tried Abraham with certain commands he fulfilled them. He said: Surely I will make thee a leader of men. (Abraham) said: And of my offspring? My covenant does not include the wrongdoers, said he. And when we made the house a resort for men and a (place of) security. And: Take ye the place of Abraham for a place of prayer. And we enjoined Abraham and Ishmael, saying: Purify my house for those who visit (it) and those who abide (in it) for devotion and those who bow down (and) those who prostrate themselves."[364]

"Having discussed at length that a prophet from the Ishmaelites had come in accordance with the prophecies of the Israelite prophets, the [clear book] now proceeds to show that even the covenant with their great ancestor Abraham necessitated the appearance of a prophet from Arabia.247

"According to the [clear book], Abraham brought Ishmael (and his mother) to Arabia and settled them there. The story of casting forth of Hagar and Ishmael in the wilderness of Beer-Sheba is thus not accepted."280

Clearly stated by The Prophet and his Prophetiers, Moses' and Paul's testimonies about the slave woman and her son are none too popular among the stargazers. Long ago, thoughts flooded the mind of an emotionally unstable man who devised an evil scheme. He invaded a land of unwalled villages and attacked a peaceful and unsuspecting people - all of them living without gates, walls, and bars. These were the people of Sheba and Dedan. They were the merchants – a people who traveled in caravans inland of coastal waterways - from Egypt down to Yemen and from Yemen up to Damascus. They were the merchants of the Tarshish. Early in his life, The Prophet was one of these merchants. These were the people that he boasted about plundering, looting, and turning his hand against. They were among those who had resettled in these lands after having been driven from Israel. The people of Sheba and Dedan (Arabia), the merchants of Tarshish and all her villages asked him, "Have you come to steal? Have you gathered your gang to loot and carry off our valuables; to take away our livestock, kill our men, rape our women, gather our children, and sell us into slavery?" The most accurate answers to these questions can be found in his own testimony as it was recorded in the clear book. Apparently, his was the new and improved model of behavior for a prophet of God.

God took notice. God noticed when his people, Israel, were living in safety and The Prophet took advantage of them. The Prophet took notice of the Jews living as his neighbors in the lands of Arabia. Against them, he waged war. It was amongst God's people that he chose to steal. It was in opposition to God's people that he chose to kill. And it was among the elect that he chose to destroy. That was then… 1400 years ago. Little has changed. His armies are nestled around Israel. The nations are amassed to the north, all of them gathering their weapons of war. They gather tanks, planes, and missiles. Their minds race with the furious aggressions of the dragon's mouthpiece. Seething with rage, they scream the name of their god - declaring him to be the greatest! With sword in hand they proclaim, "Come, let us destroy them as a nation, that the name of Israel be remembered no more." With organized thoughts they plot together and build an alliance against God and His people. Once again, they will advance against Israel - like

The Prophet

a dark cloud that covers the land. The season has arrived. It's time for God to bring this about so that the nations may know Him to be the Holy One of Israel. He does this by revealing the mouthpiece of the dragon, the man of lawlessness – The Prophet. God does this for all to see. No man can stop what God said must be done. No man can change the recorded testimony or the unrepentant admissions from the man who leads the multitudes surrounding Jerusalem. What's done is done. All that remains now is for the testimony to be unsealed and the biblical account to be settled. Men wait only for the body of the beast to sweep over Israel.

Ronald B. Stetton

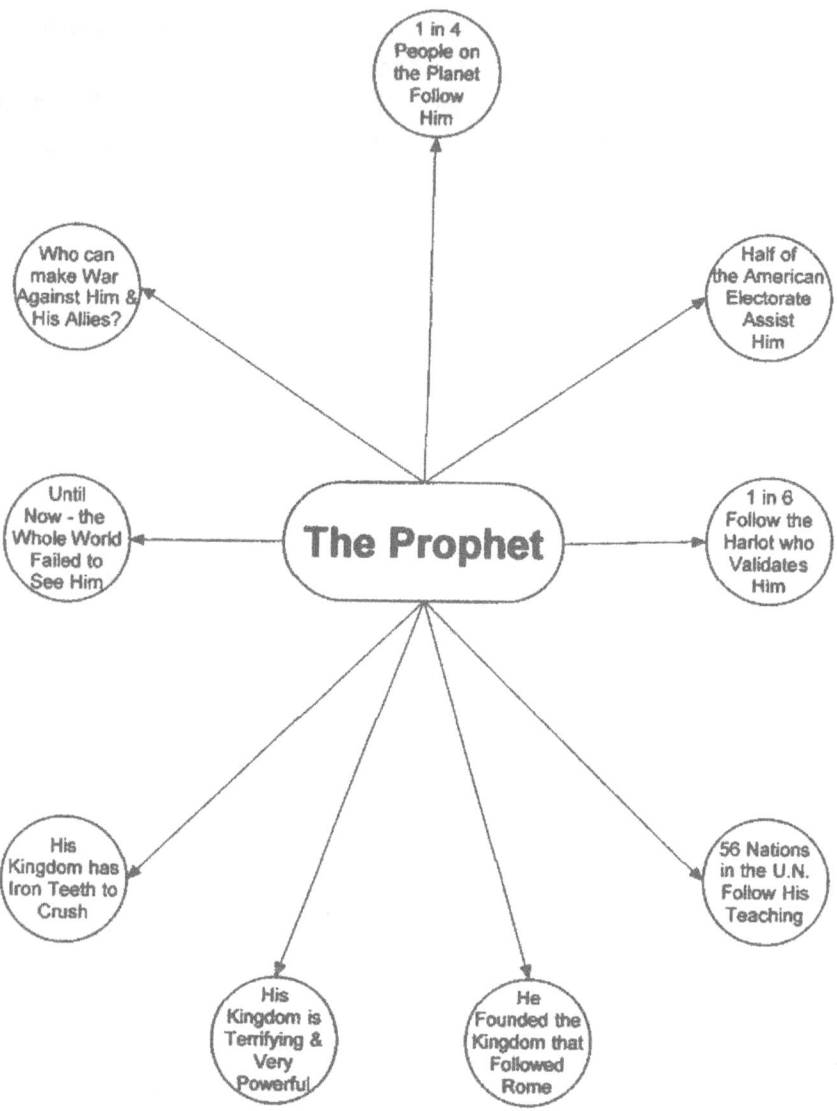

Chapter 12

The Prophet's Moderate Crowd

Time after time, men bear witness to the instinctive reactions of journalists as they attempt to explain away the terroristic endeavors of the Prophetiers. For the most part, these journalists are well educated and moderately worldly. Yet, they refuse to accept the notion that such a large body of people could engage in or approve of mannerisms that seem nothing less than barbaric. In opposition to all the evidence, they revert to biased instinct and regurgitate the meaningless tale that the perpetrators were 'rogue departures' from the true teaching of The Prophet. These ostriches come from two camps; the first camp does not know the true teaching of The Prophet and the other holds to the lessons that they are fighting in defense of the true teaching of The Prophet. Their understanding of how things *should be* conflict with the reality of how things *are*. They refuse to associate the infliction of bodily harm and/or death upon indiscriminate human targets as 'a demonstration of peace.' What they don't do is read the man's clear book, and if they do read the book, they suppress the truth and express its message of an undignified peace. In short, most are either at a loss and cannot explain this repetitious behavior or they know fully well that their actions are intended to win the war – a war that journalists do not know they are fighting. To fit their own understanding of what constitutes God, they usher in a categorical exception for those who steal, kill, and destroy as the actions of *lone wolves*. Ask any politician - they'll set you straight. According to the world's utmost authorities, these murderous wolves have hijacked The Prophet's *peace* and twisted it into something that it was never intended to be. Again, these are people who have not read the book, or they are the people who wage war and do not want the world to know what drives them. New world journalists have abandoned the truth for something far more politically fitting. They desperately want their audiences to accept the notion that such acts oppose the teaching of God's last messenger. They *want* to believe this. They *need* to believe this. The alternative is too horrible to imagine or acknowledge. Yet, in its conscious denial, the world continues to witness unimaginable horrors - with no one publicly questioning The Prophet's motives or lessons.

On Tuesday, September 11, 2001 - the world watched in agonizing terror as thousands of people were murdered by just 19 Prophetiers. The journalists all watched with the same horror, seemingly incapable of finding the words that would make sense of such a grand scale of inhumanity. In the days to follow, truth gave way to invented scenarios of depraved minds. Some of the more progressive among us laid blame of the attack on America's deeds. For many of our finest academics, it was as if the 3,000 people murdered on that day were somehow deserving of such a hideous death. Those who insinuated such things will likely have a difficult time remembering or admitting their despicable accusations of blame. Though they declared that 'America's chickens are coming home to roost' and 'it is impossible for a building to fall the way they fell without explosives being involved' - they conveniently dismissed (or never cared to know) that the people in the Towers were recognized as hypocrites and enemies of The Prophet. At least, that is how The Prophetiers saw them.

People began to ask the inevitable question: "Why?" The honest answer is politically taboo and too divisive to mention. Even though all 19 of the murderers who carried out these horrific acts were Prophetiers, few (if any) in journalism took the time to read their clear book and report The Prophet's obvious command. Imagine if we could turn back time and explain to the employees of the Towers why they were initially targeted and attacked in 1993. What would have been the reaction of those people had they known that The Prophet declared: "Wherever you are, death will overcome you, though you are in Towers, raised high"?[390] This is what drove the bombing in 1993. And this is what drove the hijackings in 2001. In the mind of the Prophetier, anyone who refuses to adopt the rules and laws of The Prophet's is a mischievous hypocrite. Though this instruction is in writing, most of today's conscious deniers will scoff at anyone who would dare to make such a 'hateful' connection. No matter how direct, exact, or precise the order of aggression against the people in the Towers might have been, the powers of denial and political correctness kept most commentators from ever mentioning it. They could not discuss such a cultural taboo as the truth. They certainly can't discuss it now. Their global audience has grown to include many who have dedicated their lives to The Prophet. They know how The Prophet felt about those who opposed his teaching.

"...by him is whose hand is my soul, I love that I should be killed in the way of [god] then brought to life, then killed again then brought to life, then killed again then brought to life, then killed again"[8]

The perfect model for men wanted to be killed repeatedly – while in the act of killing others because they refused to believe and adopt his newly found god and laws. As history attests, fear is a grand motivator! The Prophet was not talking about dying at the hands

The Prophet

of men who saw him as a blasphemer. He was talking about dying in battle as he thrust his sword through those who knew that the god he fought for was not God. His statement about dying over and over again might seem like the worthy dedication of a faithful man – until people come to know that the man who made that declaration also said:

> "I have been commanded that I should fight these people till they bear witness that there is no god but [my god] ... When they do this, their blood and their property shall be safe with me except as [The Prophet] requires, and their reckoning is with [my god]"9

The Prophet has been commanded by the voices in his head – those associated to the dragon. The Prophetiers have been commanded by this man, the speaking image of the dragon. The commands have been a guiding influence for men and nations over the last 14 centuries. Thanks to his never-ending war and these unending threats of death, The Prophet's ranks have grown from a few dozen men to nearly two billion people. Man's blood and belongings are safe with him and his people – only if those same men submit to his laws and do not commit mischief (oppose his teaching) in the land. With America's hasty withdrawal from Afghanistan, the re-emergent government in Afghanistan aligns with this coercive model of control. Who could argue that The Prophet is not *the rod of [the dragon]*? After all these years, one would think that reason or compassion might abate his appetite for flesh and quench his thirst for blood. But no! Submission to his ways is not the answer to this man's madness, as the submissive become just as callous as he was. When men finally come to understand that all who reject his teaching are never to be befriended[395] and forever to be fought,[402] the true nature of his endeavors will finally come to light. By his own word, befriending the non-believer is never to become anything other than a military tactic of disarmament. The use of such deception has repeatedly gained an advantage over his enemies.[378] Such are the mannerisms of lethal spies during times of war. In a world of human ostriches, this tactic has proven to be astoundingly effective. In the minds of the Prophetiers, the commands of The Prophet are not to be disregarded or dismissed. To do so risks retribution from and upon the Prophetier. So says The Prophet.

With the submissive slaves in Afghanistan claiming victory over the United States and the ruling parties in Iran promising death to Israel and America, how long will it be before the next attack occurs among those who sit at their desks and eat at outdoor cafés? Though terrorist attacks occur daily, the general population hears only what the media wants it to hear, and the intended terror is imminent. With a growing sense of submission, the populace is ripe for another lesson. Like the woman who rides the beast,[457] the progressively drunk are destined to be burned in the fire caused by The Prophet. It should be stated that the beast *hates* the proverbial woman. She is a worldly drunk who professes progressive myths. *They* (the body of the beast) will bring this woman's world "to ruin and leave her naked; they will eat her flesh and burn her with fire."[461] This is the woman's reward for her submission and unwavering support for the blood-thirsty beast. With its body methodically placed in and amongst our communities, the next act of The Prophet's faithful is inevitable. Our overly politicized world invites it. The paid-for media will be forced to address it. And once again, they will see and speak through a cultural filter and declare that "this is a departure from the peace of The Prophet and a sad act of the radical sort." To date, the argument has satisfied the ostriches. How many times has the world watched an unending line of *radicals* drive their speeding automobiles off the roadway, onto crowded sidewalks and into occupied cafes? How many times has the world witnessed *extremists* navigating explosive-laden trucks into hotels and packed marketplaces? How many more times will it happen before the ostriches pull their heads out of the sand and ask the right question: "Just exactly what is it that The Prophet teaches?" All too often now, the world sits transfixed on news clips about a man or groups of men who have stormed crowded areas to unleash hell and indiscriminately shoot as many people as they can before becoming *martyred*. They are men and women killing other men and women until all men and women submit and comply with the lessons of the speaking image. For them, the enemy is easily identified. An example of their many enemies were the people who joyfully encouraged runners at the end of the Boston Marathon. In that day, their enemy consisted of five people who died - two police officers, a 29-year-old restaurant manager, a 23-year-old graduate student, and an 8-year-old child. Casualties included 264 recorded injuries, 16 people who lost limbs, and 3 people who lost more than one limb. None of the enemy were asked about their religious or political beliefs prior to the intentional placement and detonation of home-made bombs. It seems that 'casting terror into the hearts of the disbelievers'[381] is as inexact as it is callous and unconscionable. Like the 19 murderers who carried out the attacks on 9/11, the actions of these two brothers were dismissed by many as "some people [who] did something."[17]

Are these the actions of a loving God? The mere audacity of such a statement is unreasonable at best. Is the murderous teaching valid and consistent with that of a prophet of God? How is it that so many in our world have fallen into submission and have accepted the actions of urban warfare and theft as something *cultural* that is to be dismissed as otherwise untouchable? How does ones' culture negate and make void the natural laws that keep people from stealing, killing, and destroying? There is no cultural exception that would rightfully adopt these actions as righteous deeds. Still, the world turns its head aside and ignores the obvious. There was a man who found these deeds to be quite beneficial to his cause. He was a bird of prey. There is a god who thrives upon stealing, killing, and destroying. He's the father of lies.

Long ago, Israel offered the world a Teacher who explained why no man has the moral authority to throw judgmental stones with lethal intent. The grace that the Teacher demonstrated and instituted remains to this day. Yet, the Teacher is widely hated by the world. Those who love Him are hated and rejected by the world. His entire lesson can be summed up by just two commands: "Love the Lord your God... and Love your neighbor. All the Law and the Prophets hang on these two commandments."[333] But the world largely hates the Man who said these things. It hates His followers – those who hold onto these two commands. It is as He promised, the world hated Him first. The Teacher does not recognize *love* by the world's new definition. He does not recognize *marriage* and *a woman's right* by the world's new definitions. He and His Father do not teach that the only thing that matters is *the color* of a man's skin! The Father and his Son do not teach that a man is to present himself *as a woman* or that a parent is to introduce their daughters *as boys*. Those who gnash their teeth have well-polished arguments about new truths and definitions – just as the Prophet has well-polished arguments about his new rules and laws. They all originate from the same place. These are the things of lies – born from the father of lies. He is *the dragon* who influenced a weak mind and gave power to a single speaking image. He is the originator of war.[439]

What then should men know about The Prophet who built his house on a cornerstone of war? What should the *cultural warriors* know about the man who promises paradise to anyone who strives to fight until all religions are for his god? How can it be that the meaning of *martyrdom* has changed from 'God loving the world so much that He gave His one and only Son'[183] – to 'casting terror into the hearts of those who disbelieve and smite the necks...'?[399] What is left of the world when the majority believe that *murder in the name of God* is somehow [god's] commandment[393] rather than God's warning against it?[201]

There have been and always will be people who speak only from instinct. They have little or no actual knowledge about that which they speak. Among these people are progressive academics who apparently wish to believe that evil cannot exist on such a grand scale. Like the song says, most people are good – right? The only way that this statement could be valid is to change the definition of *good*. So, why not change the definition? If darkness is to become light, bitter is to become sweet, and evil is to become good...[126] Things are beginning to make perfect biblical sense!

Most of us long for the days of our youth - when a few of the dedicated ones overcame the biases of political ignorance and made something out of a college education. Those days seem to be waning. With the cancers of willful ignorance now flourishing in our 'educational system,' no longer is the consciously naïve mind limited to the immaturity of a largely entitled student body. Now, the illnesses of conscious ignorance and social arrogance is shared and woefully led by the 'brilliance' of tenured professors. The student of old has become the teacher of new. New are the laws. New are the rules. New are the definitions. People who think and profess the antonyms of *sweet*, *light*, and *good* now fill the lecture halls of academia. Even our public schools now demand that young minds exceed yesterday's promise of tolerance for something better suited to today's race toward maniacal control - like championing acts that God defines as unnatural, indecent, and perverse.[481] In a single generation, evil has been manipulated by the godless and somehow managed to become good.

As has been referred to many times, the United States was attacked by 19 men who were being harbored and educated as guests of that nation. The world readily admits that each of these men were loyal subjects of The Prophet. But this truth cannot be found within the walls or halls of education. This is neither the proper subject-matter for a new generation, nor is it appropriate to introduce such negativity into what amounts to be cultural differences. What has become most important is the forced introduction of true racism and the indoctrination of young minds with the most important of things – like Critical Race Theory, gender reassignment, and why the only color that matters is black. Reading, writing, and arithmetic are now accomplished by machines. Accurately relaying this historical truth crosses the rapidly moving line of hate. After all, they would argue, how could we possibly know what was in the minds of those 19 men when they killed flight attendants, murdered pilots, and brought about the worst peace-time slaughter of people since the Japanese attacked Pearl Harbor in 1941? Now, there have been two lines crossed! Even if we were to forget the past and erase the history of the Japanese and the Prophetiers, we must now deal with the harvesting, manipulation, and release of the world's latest pandemic from Wuhan. This unthinkable act came about by the thoughts of a madman and a cooperating political foe. Their insistence to rely upon science to successfully achieve 'gain of function' has killed millions. Thanks be to that man and the nation that wanted Trump out of Office! Now, three lines have been crossed... Our educators would prefer that these facts are best left in the trash-heap of history - disputed, disregarded and forgotten. The Japanese let us forget about their heinous acts, and the Chinese are too powerful to care about world opinion. But the people of The Prophet have nowhere to build if not on a foundation of war.[370] For them, tolerance flows in only one direction.[253] When the Constitution and the laws therein conflict with the laws that The Prophet instituted, conflict is unavoidable.[13]

In former days, *tolerance* was a synonym for *grace*. But the word *tolerance*, like so many other good words, has lost its meaning. Tolerance is not to be mistaken for accepting and encouraging behaviors that God describes as unnatural, shameful, indecent, and perverse. Like it or not, every man knows or possesses the ability to know what God deems to be evil. Most will argue that such statements constitute *hate-speech*. But that is a powerful deception. When Jesus stood between the prostitute and the men wanting to throw their 'righteous' stones, He was specific about not condemning her for her actions. He was also specific about her choices from that moment forward. He said: "Go now **and leave your life of sin.**"[188] Such is not the advice of men today. The new teaching is: "Go now and relish in our approval of the things God formerly and mistakenly forbade." Societal pressures, even to the point of coercion, demand that all men accept and approve of such behaviors. This turn in man's morality is sadly prophetic.[482] Every man is a prostitute in one way or another. But no man should demand of another the acceptance of any behavior or act that would ultimately lead to one's destruction. To do so would fulfill the true meaning of *hate*. Woe to those who are teaching the little ones to oppose the Christ and the Word of His Father![581] Tolerance or grace, in its original form, has a place in the Son's kingdom. Grace has no place in The Prophet's kingdom. His people are taught to strive (to fight) to an end. Those who will not raise a sword against their brother are commanded to support those who will. Such warriors are considered *the most excellent of [men]*.[221]

This will certainly rile the Progressively Correct crowd. For this goes against everything they have been taught to believe. It goes against everything they teach. Why is there such a broad disconnect? What is it about the realities of the current political environment that the majority refuses to see? After years of discussion, the answer can be reduced to a prophetic simplicity – that of refusing to know or acknowledge *the Father* as *God*. This simple truth does not mean that everyone is now to become a good minister in Christ. Though such a thought is comforting, it is not in man's future. Men are not getting closer to God. In prophetic perfection, men are falling away from God. They are chasing gods of their own making. The Progressives (for lack of a better term) are chief among the crew who has fallen away. After a decade of forums and discussions, it has become obvious that many profess to know God. But when the conversation leaves the pages of the Bible and turns to current events, most modernize the teaching *to be more inclusive* and state; "Well, my god would not _____ (fill in the blank)." Quickly, it becomes evident that men create gods to support their own behaviors and purposes. Though God clearly states that He never changes and that His Laws never change, people are hard-pressed to remain under the umbrella of a god that changes as each generation evolves. But God is God. He has not changed. He will never change. The need for The Prophet is biblical. His appearance is prophetic. His god and his word are not the image of God that is found within the pages and Word of the Bible. As stated, most choose not to know Him. They choose not to know His Word. The world is filled with brilliant men – most of whom choose not to pursue their Maker. From these brilliant men have come the many woes of mankind. We now know the horrors of nuclear detonations and biological weapons. Emotional turmoil, sexual abuse, and mental illness have led to a new movement that confuses the genders while removing the moralities of law and order. Society is paying the obvious price for its moral departure. It is no longer proper to refer to a group of people as *guys* when calling them into a central point of gathering. Now, most laws, rules, and political policies seem to be driven by skin color or sexual orientation – all infringing on the very definitions of racism and discrimination. Even infanticide is still being debated today by reasonably intelligent people who have convinced themselves that ending life is somehow a woman's right. People are fixated on something called *Climate Change,* an ever-evolving term about man-caused weather changes. Somehow, the global cooling and warming that has happened over the millennium has become the fault of a single political party. Even Rome's current Caesar asks that men address the supposed crisis and institute *net zero emissions.* He wants your money as much as any other politician want your money! He's a politician! How can this whole climate thing be resolved? More taxation! More regulation! More control! With Rome and the Romans capitalizing on taxation over the centuries, this makes complete sense. Caesar was the king of taxation – even garnering biblical mention of the act! The world is a mess, and the political battles continue to rage!

Instead of recognizing The Prophet's never-ending war, men are consumed by infighting due to the science responsible for *gain of function* and the politics of incapacitated imbeciles. The world and its combined economies have been brought to their knees by the paralyzing harvest, manipulation, and release of a lethal virus. The gain of function research (the science) in Wuhan has proven to be woefully successful, while those who led the research relentlessly push a vaccine that is no vaccine at all. Thanks to the powerful influence of fear, the finger of blame has been shifted away from those who developed and released this biological weapon to the men and women who refuse to be infused by four or more doses of a concoction that is admittedly not a vaccine. This type of fearmongering and manipulation once changed an entire nation of reasonable Germans into unreasonable and monstrous Nazis. The successful manipulation of men demonstrates the weakness in man's faith. Blame for the world's pandemic woes have shifted from the scientists who created and released it to the unvaccinated who know and understand that the mutations are likely caused by the supposed cure. This nightmarish reality is like a scene out of *Invasion of the Body Snatchers*. Men and women are out of work and the nations are reeling. Politics are at a fever pitch and hatred abounds. The vaccinated are at war with the unvaccinated – even blaming those who have gained natural immunity (by getting sick) for prolonging the pandemic. These are the birthing pains of biblical mention. With so much commotion in the world, people tend to turn away and tune out. We now see friend against friend, employer against employee, and brother against brother. After twenty years of war, the Afghan government has returned to chopping off the heads and hands of its citizens while their constituents reinstitute public lynching. They are the perfect example of godly behavior! Obviously, love has grown cold. The love of God has been rejected by the masses and He takes a backseat to the maniacal idiocy of a world gone mad.

Few have taken the time to read the Word (Jesus and the Bible) and recognize Him and it as the image of God. Even fewer have taken the additional time to read the word of the masquerading light and attempt to compare the two opposing images. The Prophet's image of god is no overlay of the prophets before him. To read them both and to recognize that the former writing warns of the latter, explains how The Prophet grew his movement from 120,000 men at the time of his death[521] to nearly two billion people today. This has grand biblical implications. The 120,000 men and their families who listened to The Prophet in that day gathered the attention and concern of God.[208] One-hundred and twenty-thousand people who cannot tell their right hand from their left hand is a problem! Worldly circumstances as they are, the reader might now understand how fear drove the Ishmaelites into becoming Prophetiers and created enemies out of their neighbors. Fear drives the three-times-jabbed targets of the Wuhan virus toward a fourth shot and creates enemies of those who dared to get sick. Fear is an amazing motivator! It has been used by history's most powerful rulers to set neighbor against neighbor. To understand how so few can manipulate and rule so many, simply mix unending fear with high anxiety and exhaustion. The world bears witness to this with the science that enabled gain of function to shape or end the lives of our friends and family. The Geneva Convention prohibits the use of biological weapons. Depending on the findings, the creators, financiers, developers, and influencers of that 'science' should be investigated and tried for anything from negligent homicide to war crimes. But, with Brandon in office, holding America's Chief Medical Advisor and the Chinese accountable is highly unlikely. To do so would likely lighten Brandon's wallet!

Try to imagine how frustrating it might be to locate and pinpoint a historical character without knowing what they looked like, what generation they may have lived or where on earth they might be found. How could they be picked out from a crowd that numbered in the tens of billions? This might sound like a foolish question, but this is exactly how people think when it comes to recognizing God and biblical characters. Most believe they will know God only when they see God. Sadly, this type of thinking might be right for all the wrong reasons. Like it or hate it, when it comes to life after death, every man will know and recognize the God of Israel. For the majority, this will not be a joyous occasion! The same sad reality applies to the man of lawlessness and his foreign god. Instinctively, most people, even many of the elect, believe they will recognize this villainous pair if and when they see them. Yet, they have managed to hide their identities for centuries. Such is the case no longer! What happens now? How might attitudes change when the man of lawlessness and his foreign god are revealed after having been hidden in plain sight for so long? What becomes of the so-called 'moderates' of the movement when The Prophet is revealed to be not only to be *among* the villainous, but proves to be *the* biblical villain? How will the world respond? How did the world respond to the man who participated in the successful gain of function science that transferred virus from a bat to humans? How did they react to his insistence of receiving three to four jabs of a not-vaccine, with the unfulfilled promise that it would end the nightmare he helped to create? The world got mad... at each other! Think about the reaction the world will have when they are exposed to the evidence that the biblical false prophet has a name and place in history. What shall we expect from the Afghani government when their acts of amputation, beheading, and murder are determined to be behavior promoted by The Prophet who was no prophet at all? What becomes of the *billions* who have placed their trust in this villainous liar? Governments have been formed to accommodate his rules and laws. Nations have been built to honor him as the speaking image of God, but he is proven to be the speaking image of the dragon. It seems that the earthquake felt around the world from the 'science' of Wuhan was a mere speedbump on the seismic scale of terror when compared to the vertical spike we are about to experience by learning the identity of The Prophet. Is there any hope that something can be salvaged of this man's treacherous scheme? The Bible says: "Yes!" But that hope remains with those who understand God's Words:

"I will grant salvation to Zion, my splendor to Israel."[150]

There has been a minimal bit of chatter about the reformation of The Prophet's teaching – similar to the reformation that washed away much of the blood drawn by the Roman papacy centuries ago. But what is there to salvage? What is left to reform? What man or organization has the authority to oppose and overrule the marks that have been guiding the Prophetiers for centuries? By his own admission, he was the last of the prophets.[295] Nations stand on the footing of his foundation. The people of those nations have been enslaved by his stern coercion. His teaching has filled their hearts and minds since birth. What happens to these nations when he is unveiled? What becomes of the people who live their lives as he lived his? The answers are plain and simple, but nearly impossible to utter. Biblical testimony has already been spoken. It is then that the story of man will reach its zenith. Unveiling The Prophet brings about unfathomable change. Though he was unconscionably evil, The Prophet was not necessarily dull. Though he lacked an education, his spoken word and actions were driven by the power and influence of the dragon. The spirit that pressed itself against him and whispered into his ear[4] was the source of his power. The voice gave him the guidance necessary to insert fail-safes into the faith, dissuading others from altering his word or changing the course of the nation he founded. Though the academics in the crowd might hate this approach, the use of The Prophet's recorded word is the best evidence proving that no such 'moderation' of his nation is possible. The Prophetiers will strive to move forward, refusing to love the truth, no matter how fact-filled the truth might be. "Fighting is enjoined on them, though it might be disliked by them; and it may be that they dislike a thing while it is good for them, and it may be that they love a thing while it is evil for them; and [The Prophet's god] knows while they know not."[370] That just about sums all things up! The Prophetiers are under strict and direct orders. Reasoning, facts, compassion, and sentiment have no place within his book, his god, or his people. Those who rely upon common sense and reason are going to be greatly disappointed! His rules of war will continue - unchanged. This has remained the precedent for 14 centuries.

Recently, there was a mob-rule protest happening in Pakistan. Thousands upon thousands of Prophetiers demanded that a woman (who claimed to be Christian) be hanged for the unthinkable act of speaking out against The Prophet. As per the teaching, the only punishment for causing such mischief in the land is that she be 'murdered.' Examples of such atrocities are so numerous that listing them here would be figuratively unnecessary as well as literally impossible. Such are the realities of our world today. Instead of condemning such cultural activities, the world remains complicit, and it welcomes his cultural warriors into their midst. With gnashing teeth, they snarl at any attempt to protect Israel, while they bite the hand of their own financial stability and growth. The destructive beliefs that have been planted in their hearts overflow from their mouths and spill out onto the floors of justice. The Law has given way to lawlessness. The world has gone mad. While the distracting arguments of 'moderates vs. radicals' swirl, the weight of The Prophet's yoke continues to weaken his slaves and chip away at any chance for life, liberty, and the pursuit of happiness. Instead, they eagerly prostrate themselves in submission to death and enslavement while waging war. The nightmare formed by science's 'gain of function' is soon to be overshadowed by the menacing realities of The Prophet's modern warriors and their wares.

The Prophet

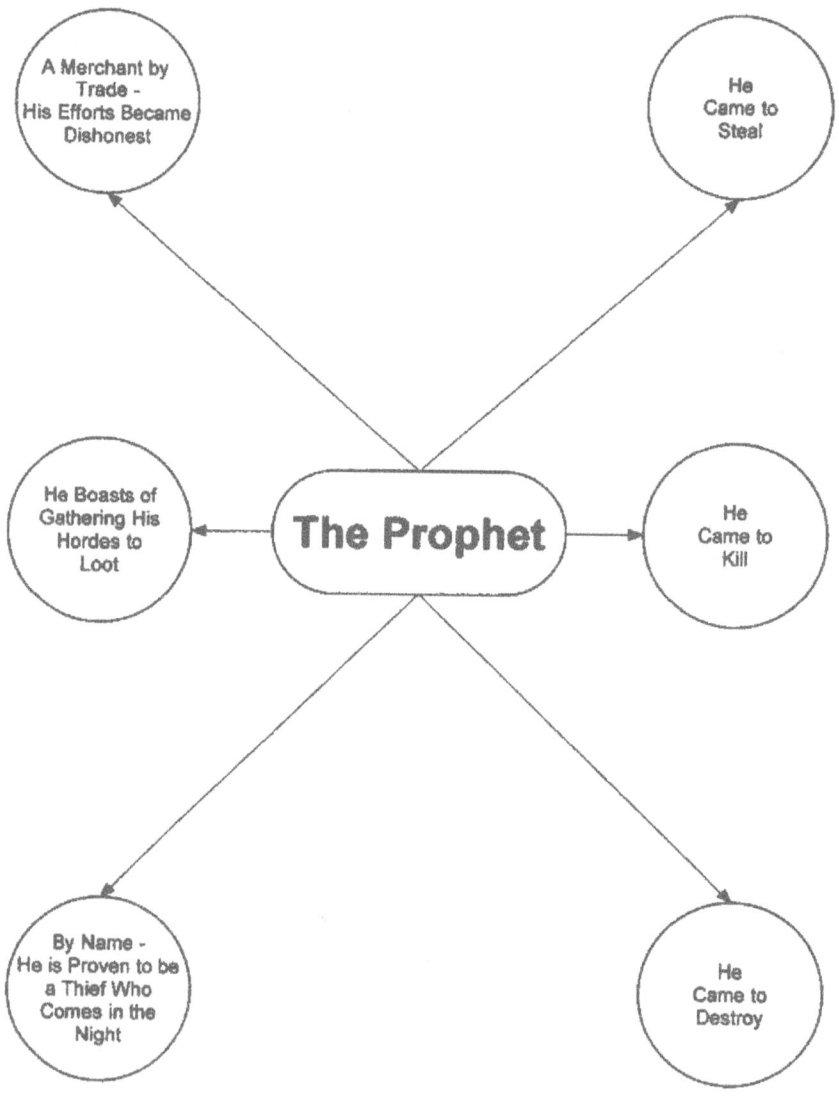

Chapter 13

The Thief

Jesus' Nemesis - the Literal Thief of Ezekiel 38:13 & 1 John 10

"Who is the thief? He is the man who comes only to steal and to kill and to destroy." This is John's biblical description of the man who makes an enemy of God. The thief opposes the Man who gives life and gives it to the full.[193] Who is the thief? He is the man who plundered Sheba, Dedan and the traveling merchants – those who transported their wares from city to city. The thief is the man who shadowed the travelers from Syria and Iraq on the King's Highway and all the way south to Hamonah. He is the man who raided and terrorized the passengers east of the Mediterranean and Red Seas. The Prophet acted in the exact manner as the thief was prophesied to have acted.

"It is true that a caravan was returning from Syria, and an army had marched forth from [east of the Red Sea]; it is also true that some of the [Prophetiers] wished that they should encounter the caravan and not face the [enemy's] force. Had The Prophet desired to plunder the caravan, he would have done so long before [the caravan] could obtain [assistance] from [the locals] ... And why should The Prophet have waited all this while and not plundered the caravan before help reached [the caravan]?"[272]

"And why should The Prophet have waited... and not plundered the caravan?" What made the thief wait? Isn't this a rather odd question to ask of a prophet of God? Plundering a caravan is the act of a thief. Period. This opposes God's Commandment stating: "You shall not steal."[74] Aside from "You shall not murder," isn't this among the basics taught in Entry Level 101 at the Broader School of Prophethood? Not in the very skewed world of The Prophet! For he and his Prophetiers, theft and thievery have been reformed and redefined from something that is evil and unlawful into something that is good, admirable, and to be mimicked. This is just another piece of the puzzle that makes up the life and history of the biblical beast who 'devised an evil scheme.'[89] As the quote above verifies, The Prophet's plundering took place in and around a city east of the Red

Sea. East of the Red Sea resides the ancient territories of Sheba and Dedan. East of the Red Sea is the *Western Province of Saudi Arabia*.[123]

- "So we inflicted retribution on them. And they are both on an open high road"[408]
- "The road alluded to is the road followed by caravans from [the Western Province] to Syria"[281]

The caravans from Syria likely comprised of the wares of the merchants who sailed the coastlands of the Mediterranean. They were *the merchants of the Tarshish*. These are the areas that were originally victimized by the thief as he is described in the book of Ezekiel. The Prophet's depictions are nothing new. Those who know biblical teaching and remain founded in truth are watching for this unlawful menace. Those who know The Prophet know the thief. What is new is the unveiling of the identity of the thief. John and Ezekiel write about him in detail. He has lived and died. Though their time on earth and biblical prophesying were separated by six centuries, these two faithful prophets of God warned us about The Prophet as the thief. He is the one who came to steal in the name of God. He is the one who came to kill in the name of God. He is the one who came to destroy in the name of God. Though he is long-since dead, his teaching is the same today as it was 14 centuries ago. The Prophet is and was the thief of prophecy. His merciless actions were born of prophecy and anchored in the written Word centuries before his birth.

Most would agree that, as a peaceful and lawful people, it would be in everyone's best interest to keep such a man out of our lives and out of our homes. Why would we invite him inside? Most would also agree that it is a bad idea to welcome a thief into our communities – particularly a thief who sees his actions as just and holy. Such a man cannot be reformed. Why would we endanger our family and friends by welcoming him into our lives? It seems reasonable to conclude that allowing him into our schools is also a horrible idea. What possible good could come from subjecting our children to him and his teaching? Further, it seems absurd that anyone would consider allowing his participation in law making and/or law enforcement. After all, how can a man who comes only to steal, and to kill, and to destroy be capable of creating and instituting societal law? How sick and deluded must the world become before it freely elects the thief or his complicit puppets as lawmakers? The answer will surprise you. A sick world it is!

Nations elevate his movement and invite his successors to dinner. Communities invite his bands to nest among them. Universities trip over themselves to accept the financial boost from his adoring student body. The public educational system encourages him to indoctrinate. And politicians (one in particular) have seeded national districts with waves of his constituents in dense voting blocs to lift his representatives into the halls of justice. Now, they make the laws! Demands of a P.C. culture have run amok and brought about the prophecies of delusion and a people who cannot tell their right hand from their left. In a cancel culture, few dare to call out the vile atrocities of the world's most heinous and notorious thief. Again, mankind has earned the badge of shame known as 'delusion.' The fog that surrounds us today is astounding in its density! The question is no longer about what madman would teach evil to be good, darkness to be light, and bitter to be sweet. The question has become - what delusional fool would accept such horrific nonsense as the words and ways of God? Delusion sets upon the minds of men in soothing terms such as *culture, tolerance,* and *acceptance*. We have all seen the culture of the Afghans return to their pre-conflict normalcy and we are conditioned to *tolerate* and *accept* the loving acts of the men, armed with Grenade Launchers, chasing women off the streets and imprisoning men for the unthinkable act of cutting their beards. This is perfectly acceptable behavior to those who suffer from delusion. The enforcement of such delusion comes from the not-so-loving terms of *hatred, bigotry,* and *racism*. Listen to the politicians. They are skilled and polished in their use of such terms. This is the method of the thief and how he has been allowed entry into every man's home. His people have moved into most of the world's communities, they populate the schools, and get elected to political offices. They are supported by squads of the P.C. police who demand that it remain this way.

Acceptance of the thief has become law in many nations. With blasphemy laws in place, tolerance has been reduced to something of a one-way street. To speak out against The Prophet means imprisonment and/or death in many places. To speak out against The Prophet in the free world (that which is rapidly disappearing) now receives accusations of intolerance, hatred, bigotry, and racism. God gives this madness a name - He calls it *delusion*.[513] But the fog is lifting. The picture is becoming clear. Revealing the truth about The Prophet and how he has fulfilled his biblical role can remain hidden no longer. Most will rely on current trends and rebuke this presentation as being hateful. So be it. Connecting the dots between biblical warnings and The Prophet's recorded history is a simple matter of study. One needs only to read. It is as it was prophesied to be. In a time when evil is presented as good, it is sometimes difficult to separate one from the other. But hold onto the truth. Hate and hate speech does exist. It sounds something like this...

- Take not Jews and Christians for friends… [god] guides not the unjust people[395]
- [Do not] take the disbelievers for friends… whoever does this has no connection with [god][378]
- Fight with them until… all religions are only for [god][402]
- Paradise is beneath the protection of the swords[7]
- I have been commanded that I should fight these people till they bear witness that there is no God but [god][9]
- Forbidden to you are… all married women except those whom your right hand possess[388]
- Death will overcome you, though you are in Towers, raised high[390]
- I will cast terror into the hearts of those who disbelieve[399]
- So smite above the necks…[399]
- …and [smite] every finger-tip of them[399]
- The only punishment of [the mischievous] is that they should be murdered, or crucified, or their hands and their feet should be cut off on opposite sides…[393]

The Prophet demands of his followers that they do not befriend Christians and Jews. His words are not vague. Instead, he teaches them to oppose, fight, kidnap, rape, destroy, cast terror, inflict bodily harm, and murder disbelievers – particularly Christians and Jews.[395] Like all men, the thief could have benefited from the two swords of Jesus' mouth: "'Love the Lord your God with all your heart and with all your soul and with all your mind. This is the first and greatest commandment.' And the second is like it: 'Love your neighbor as yourself.' All the Law and the Prophets hang on these two commandments."[333] Jesus does not demand a religious test for friendship. Nowhere does He teach that we should fight until all religions are for Him and His Father. In fact, Christians are to show patient endurance and faithfulness in the event that they are killed or imprisoned for their faith.[447] There is no 'casting terror into the hearts of the disbeliever' in Christianity. Jesus' two swords are the verbal and written instructions to love one another. Jesus' swords cast no shadow upon the ground – they are His Words. He does not teach that men can acquire their enemies' wives as *spoils of war*, enslave them and consider them wives of their own.[75] He certainly does not oppose the Law that one shall not murder.[73] And, looking deeper, there is something far greater and wonderfully revealing in Jesus' statement:

"All the Law and the Prophets hang on these two commandments."

All the Law and [all] the Prophets hang on the two commandments to love the Lord your God and love your neighbor as yourself. So, what changed for The Prophet? What soured the thief's view about his interactions with his neighbors? What is so compelling about his god that murder, theft, kidnap, and rape have now become the preferred actions of the best of mankind?[293] These are not the actions of a prophet of God, but the actions of a repulsive thief. His supporters will argue that these things have been misinterpreted or taken out of context. They will also argue that the action of [striving] to advance the teaching takes on many meanings. A previous President of the United States said so! Among those who 'strive' in this manner is he who stated that he would "stand with the [Prophetiers] when the political winds shift in an ugly direction." That attitude and mindset has achieved the desired result. Since the political winds have shifted to blow in the same direction of the thief and his people, it seems that the world has *progressed* to the point of no return. The world has consciously accepted The Prophet and his people while further choosing to disregard his sometimes-lethal lawlessness. Such willful blindness suggests that the prophetic end of this generation of man has reached its season. John tells us that Satan and his demons 'would lead the whole world astray.'[440] The prophecy does not suggest that just a few people would be so easily fooled by intentional sensory loss. It clearly states that *the whole world* would be duped. Satan and his right-hand man have done what the Word said they would do. When one sums up the total of the Prophetiers, plus the progressives, plus those who serve the drunken harlot (who is woefully complicit) as a single, allied force – they account for nearly five in every six adults. The balance, one in every six, make up *the survivors from all the nations*.[529]

The little gate that leads to life does not accommodate five of every six adults. There is a wide gate that caters to that crowd. Wide is the gate that leads to destruction. The Prophet traveled through that gate. The *Causer of Death* (sin) is his god.[384] There is little irony in the differences between Jesus, the Prince of princes, and His opposition – the chief prince of Meshech and Tubal. Jesus is the gift of God that gives us eternal life.[485] "God made Him who had no sin to be sin for us, so that in Him we might become the righteousness of God."[25] In Him, we are saved. Now, compare God's gift, the Lamb, to the man who speaks like the dragon. The thief is the biblical example of those who will suffer a second death. They will not know eternal life. The Prophet was…

- Cowardly – He feared the spirit pressing against him[2] and he brings great harm and oppression to women

- Unbelieving – He declared that God has no son[418]

- Vile (abominable) – He is the motivating factor for those who set up the abomination that causes desolation[44]

- Murderer – he teaches the art of murder[393] and makes it a duty of his people

- Sexually Immoral – He had 12 named wives and countless 'women his right hand possessed'[296] – many who had been widowed by the point of his own sword

- Magic Artist (sorcerer) – He was responsible for the most deceptive, counterfeit miracle ever known to man[243]

- Idolater – He idolized[358] the foreign god[72] that Daniel warned men about[57] with the moon, stars[306] and Asherah poles[342]

- Liar - He lied about God, lying about nearly everything that is called God or is worshiped[508]

The fate of this man and his eternal torment is consistent with the warning about Lucifer and how he is mocked in death by those who recognize that he is nothing more than a man.[134] This is the well-earned fate of the biblical thief.

This explains the curious mention by Jesus that 'He comes like a thief!'[455] His apostles wrote similar statements.

- "… For you know very well that the day of the Lord will come like a thief in the night."[499]

- But you, brothers, are not in the darkness so that this day should surprise you like a thief."[501]

- "But the day of the Lord will come like a thief."[351]

- "And we have the word of the prophets made more certain, and you will do well to pay attention to it, as to a light shining in a dark place, until the day dawns and the morning star rises in your hearts."[349]

Since Jesus and the thief are exact opposites, the only commonality found between them is how each presents himself as the morning star. The thief came into the world declaring that he was *the star of piercing brightness* – a light in the darkness for a lost world. As discussed in the first chapter, Lucifer made such a claim. The only true *bright Morning Star* is Jesus - the Messiah and Son of the Father. The Prophet tells another tale. He came upon the earth to make kingdoms tremble. He has overthrown its cities and refuses to allow his slaves to depart from the cause.

Oh, how our world has fallen...

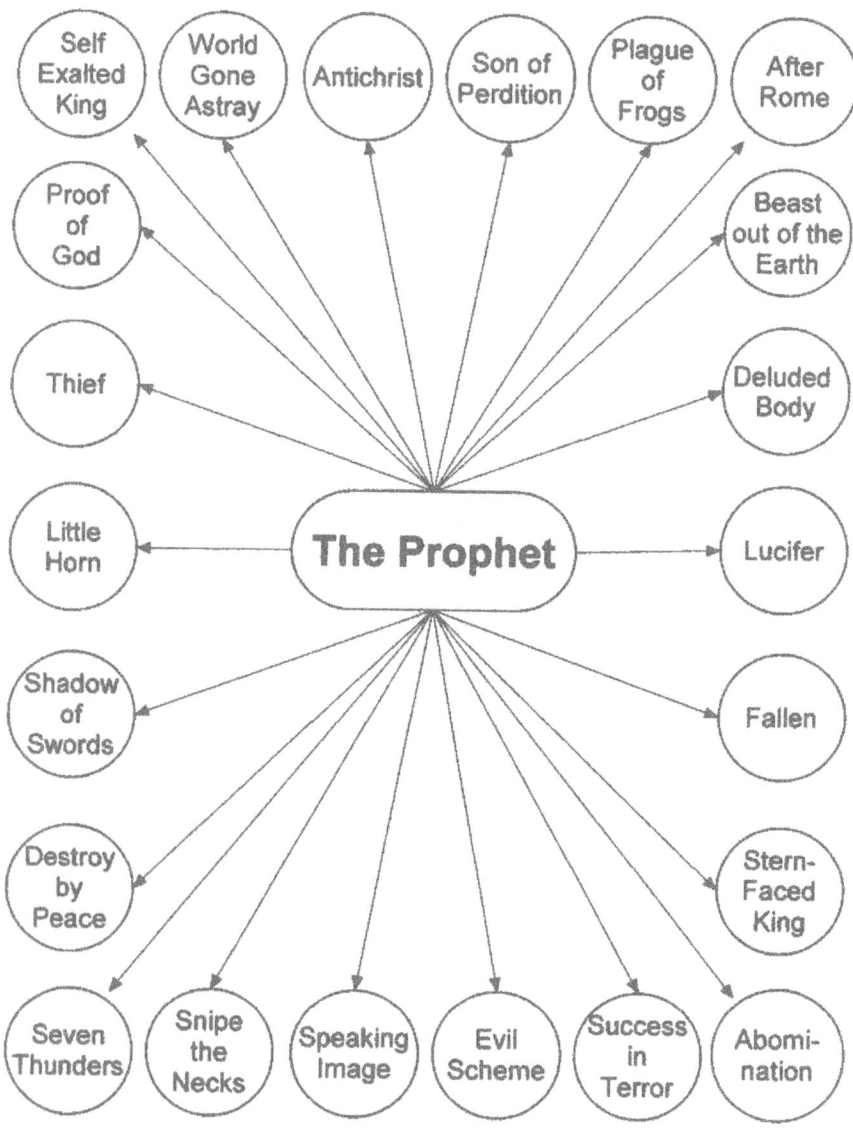

Chapter 14

Fallen

Differentiating Lucifer from Satan (Isaiah 14)

"The Lord God formed man from the dust of the ground and breathed into his nostrils the breath of life and the man became a living being."[96] "Remember him before… the dust returns to the ground it came from, and the spirit returns to God who gave it."[67] "Fear God and keep His Commandments, for this is the whole duty of man. For God will bring every deed into judgment, including every hidden thing, whether it is good or evil."[68] When Jesus separates people as a shepherd separates sheep and goats, He will utilize the place prepared for the devil and his angels.[341]

These sentences make clear that man is a product of the earth, combined with a spirit given by God. As a product of God's creation, mankind has one duty – to keep God's Commandments. His Commandments are not outdated and do not need revision. They are not of a forgotten people or of a time gone by. From the time of Moses to the time of Jesus and from the time of Jesus until now, God's Laws have remained unchanged. But man has disregarded his sole duty to God in the keeping of His commands. This comes as no surprise to God. And, if every man was honest with himself, this comes as no surprise to men. The place designated for the devil and his angels is worse than any prison imaginable. Known as the lake of burning sulfur, hell becomes the eternal home for the fallen and it is the only option for those who choose not to belong to God. It is centered in the crowded place (Hamonah), in the valley of the crowded place that is home to Gog – Lucifer. That crowded place is otherwise known as Bakkah. Those who travel east seek Bakkah as their destination.[573] When Jesus separates men as one separates sheep and goats, the sheep will attain the New Jerusalem above; the goats will know only the lake of burning sulfur that is currently smoldering in the Valley of Hamon Gog.

Fallen is Lucifer.[136] Fallen are the Luciferians. Fallen is Satan.[440] Fallen are Satan's angels.[440] Fallen are the *many* who have adopted and have succumbed to the covenant of the foreign god.[46] Fallen is the body of Babylon the Great.[563] Fallen are all who reject God's righteous decrees and all who *approve of those* who reject God's righteous decrees.[484] Since most do not think it worthwhile to know God, He gives them over to a depraved mind, to do what ought not be done. "They have become filled with every kind of wickedness, evil, greed and depravity. They are full of envy, murder, strife, deceit, and malice. They are gossips, slanderers, God haters, insolent, arrogant and boastful; they invent ways of doing evil; they disobey their parents; they are senseless, faithless, heartless, ruthless. Although they know God's righteous decree that those who do such things deserve death [never to be mistaken as a reason or directive to murder], they not only continue to do these very things, but they also approve of those who practice them."[483] This warning was written by Paul and it was addressed to the Romans, but its content is laser-focused on the God-haters of current times. The Words are 2,000 years old, but the lessons speak loudly of the present. Mankind might arrogantly consider itself to be a progressively evolving species, but the only thing *progressing* is man's departure from the ways of God. The newfound focus and push for socially accepted racism and the championing of detestable sexual behaviors are not new concepts in the story of man. Men have progressed and evolved into the very thing that Paul wrote about so long ago. Such acts and progressive ideologies brought about the destruction of Sodom long before our children were encouraged to read and adopt the premise that *And Tango Makes Three*. Those who push this kind of *love* on our little ones are soon to learn the meaning of God's promise that those who lead the little ones astray are better off drowned in the depths of the sea.[581] In Paul's time, the Romans committed consciously evil acts. Two of these behaviors are described by Paul in undeniable detail. The first example is how the Romans exchanged the glory of an immortal God for images made to look like a mortal man. Every Christian knows and understands that we are not to limit God and attempt to create such images. Yet, such images have been created and worshiped by the harlot. She has boastfully ignored God's Commands for centuries. The second example is how shameful lusts and indecent acts have progressed explosively in the manner of exchanging natural sexual relations for unnatural sexual relations. The emergence of unnatural relations and man's dedicated promotion of such unions in our society is a sign of the season that man has entered. Whether each man agrees or disagrees, every man understands the biblical views on such behavior. But the majority approves of it anyway. God's Word and warning is deemed to be *hateful*. The fallen have a term for God's Word. They call it *homophobic*. God's a homophobe? That argument will play well before our Father who is in heaven! Here's the problem: "For God so loved the world that He gave His one and only Son, that whoever believes in Him shall not perish but have eternal life."[183] The Word does not say that God so hated the world that He encouraged shameful lusts and then punished men for pursuing such desires. The progression of our evolutionarily world has redefined love and marriage to incorporate the very unnatural acts that God has warned men to avoid. Because men have returned to such things, it appears that the season is upon us. It's part of the story of man.

Anyone and everyone who wishes to know and understand God's command against making heavenly or earthly idols and engaging in unnatural acts can find direction in His Word. It's not vague and it cannot be twisted into new interpretations. But few are interested in God's Word. Their duty to uphold His commands has been disregarded and abandoned. Instead, men defiantly champion such acts, and the practice has become rampant. Billions upon billions of people have done and continue to do these very things. In a culture of the pervasively progressive, in a season when bitter has become sweet, Jesus' Word is now described as being *hateful*. Jesus said it best:

"This is my command: Love each other. If the world hates you, keep in mind that it hated me first. He who hates me hates my Father as well. They hated me without reason."[199]

The evolutionary progressives, those who have developed a higher sense of understanding about love, have rejected God's Cornerstone. They are not among the builders. They hate Him without reason. He commands men to love each other, encouraging us all to assist those who are otherwise bent on self-destruction. He knows the consequences of sacrifice and offering for another. Inexplicably, His instruction and ultimate gift bring about hatred. Those who refuse to love the truth do not believe that men can act in a self-destructive and unnatural manner. But they believe in hate. They trust in the accusation. The progressively evolved hate the truth. Jesus was spot-on! Many will read this. Few will repeat it. Fear has overcome the earth. Fear has driven neighbor against neighbor and brother against brother. Whether the subject is the color of a man's skin, politics, lawlessness, love, marriage, God, or virus – fear has become the mechanism of control and the governing key. As the Germans can attest, fear is a horrible guide that makes men act in despicable ways. It is also a powerful weapon!

What is so important about sexuality and idolatry when the subject is about God? Why is so much emphasis placed on these two subjects? The answer is as simple as it is obvious. Those who oppose the biblical God are *the accusers,* consciously and unconsciously. Consider the Romans and their religious camp. They have created a pathway that circumvents the Law and lends worship to carved images of dead men who have been nailed to trees. Of that same path, they have cleverly assigned a title to Mary, the mother of Jesus, and worship images of her as the Queen of Heaven. Of course, they have multiple reasons for going astray, but the bottom line is that such idolatry is and always has been forbidden by God. Any attempt to use God's Word to teach or attempt to correct this form of idolatry[170] receives the inevitable accusations of *hateful bigotry*. This argument has worked for over 17 centuries. In a like sense, the progressively evolved utilize similar accusations when faithful Christians refuse to "approve of those who practice" unnatural sexual acts of like-sex couples. This is nothing new. This type of sexuality was openly practiced in Sodom.[116] Men know the meaning of *sodomy* and *to sodomize*. Cities were destroyed for it. Never have unnatural acts or idolatry been accepted practices in God's teaching. Yet, the world is determined to redefine the terms and approve of those who practice such things. They call it *love*...

Hatred was not in the hearts of the men who saved Lot. Hatred was in the hearts of those who wished to harm him and the men he harbored. Hatred was not in the heart of Paul when he wrote the book of Romans. But hatred was in the hearts of those who oppose his written word. Hatred is not in the hearts of those who choose to follow the Messiah, but hatred is in the hearts of those who reject Him. The harlotous might very well proclaim their love of Christ, but they refuse to obey His Commands. This is what lends them to the title of *harlot*. The progressively evolved are not brave enough to outwardly proclaim their hate of Christ, but their unapologetic actions affirm their disdain. That makes them cowardly. Like the harlot idolizes crucifixion and worships gods like the Queen of Heaven, the godless suppress the truth of Sodom and the reasons why that city was destroyed. The former claims to be the bride of Christ, while the latter could not care less. The harlotous are a people who claim to drink from the cup of God, but they drink from the cup of demons too. They are soon to learn that it cannot be done.[23] Yet, the accusations remain.

Here is the point... *the Accuser* uses the fear of accusation and terror of cancellation to advance his deceitful practices. His demons act in kind.[440] What is so loving about encouraging men to perish? And what is so hateful about encouraging men to live life and live it to the full? Men have repeatedly spoken out against God's prophets, stating: "We will not listen to the message you have spoken to us in the name of the Lord."[173] It is true. Men refuse to love the Truth. This is what causes them to perish. They have abandoned their only duty. For the majority, God's Word of warning does not suit them. It never has. The biblical Word is not inclusive enough for the harlot or her progressively evolved suitors. Men claim to have found a better way to live their lives – as did the residents of Sodom. According to man's traditional mind and proven actions, God's ways must change to be more inclusive of the Sodomites and the Romans. In a modern sense, people demand to worship the Queen as they wish. And, just like the Babylonians did in the days of Jeremiah, they say: "We will burn incense to the Queen of Heaven..."[175] How many candles have been lit in her honor and at the base of her many wooden images? Those who worship queens has taken a strange turn. Woefully represented by images of a rainbow flag, queen worshiping has become a new category entirely! God's covenant and the rainbow that reminds us of that covenant, certainly does not represent the newfound approval of actions that He forbids. God cannot be overridden by popular vote.

As previously mentioned, rebellion against our Creator comes in many forms. Thanks to greed and an unquenchable thirst for power, the Caesars of Rome created the harlot who has "abandoned the faith to follow deceiving spirits and things taught by demons."[517] As promised, the false prophet has appeared "in accordance with the work of Satan, displayed in all kinds of counterfeit miracles, signs and wonders, and in every sort of evil that deceives those who are perishing."[509] Disguised under a very broad veil and fitting within the definitions of *religion*, opposition to God and the truth has been exposed in the form of rebellious actions - many of which were portrayed through the eyes of prophecy and forever anchored in the ink of the prophets. Some of the most obvious rebellions are described as:

- Worshiping the Queen of Heaven[167]
- Worshiping the Man of Lawlessness as God and everything that is called God[505]
- Worshiping things taught by demons[19]
- Drinking from the cup of the Lord and the cup of demons too[19]
- Believing that *murder* is an act that serves God[393]
- Surrendering to the spirit of fear[519]
- Refusing to love the Truth by delighting in wickedness[511]
- Convincing oneself and others that unnatural acts constitute love[484]
- Wanting to carry out the murderer's desires[190]

Man's rebellion is a complicated web of masterful lies and delusions. The serpent demonstrated his effective craft in the very beginning when he convinced Eve to eat the *only* fruit that God forbade. The deceit of that miserable snake reflects those who convince others to believe and act in a manner that causes their second and eternal death. He twisted God's instruction ever so slightly and promised that after eating from the tree of good and evil, Eve's 'eyes will be opened, and she will be like God, knowing good and evil.'[97] This is the methodology of the liar, the origin of evil - it's rooted in deception. Like the promise of the snake, evil is typically shrouded and hidden behind wonderful terms of *love, equality* and *justice* while defended and supported by accusations of *hate, inequality,* and *injustice.* The serpent introduced death by his sinful deceptions. Though God warned Adam that eating from that tree would cause death, the serpent assured Eve that she 'will surely not die' if she ate from that same tree. Little has changed with the snake. To those who refuse to love the truth, the snake makes the very same promises today.

> "This limitation on the duration of abiding in hell is given twice in the [clear book]... and it shows clearly that the punishment of hell is not everlasting"[278]

The devil throws spiritual daggers in the way of primarily false accusations, with political manipulation being chief among them. Political calculation has very little to do with truth anymore. Because there is so little consequence for lies, our political system has taken a complete departure from the tracks of truth and righteousness. Thanks to a manipulated virus and mail-in political balloting, the last best hope for man on earth has been lost. No longer are elections decided by the individual right of one man and his one vote. All a party needs to do now is gather enough ballots (ballot harvesting) and recruit enough foreign nationals to swing the vote. And, if that doesn't work, just shut down the computers for a day and feed them falsified ballots by the thousands. In the end, the victorious are instated by a lie. The last best hope for man on earth has fallen to the same election fraud that has brought an end to so many nations before it. Corruption rules and it is anchored among our political elite. Of course, the lie leads people astray. The corrupt have joined arms with the liars. They are now indistinguishable. Both find comfort in the nest of the snake. The liar has taken root so fast and so deep that most of our political leaders now accuse God's people being *hateful* for their refusal to approve of those who choose the ways and life of Sodom. This is the new normal. School age children will never again know the difference between natural and unnatural. Our *public education system* won't have it. For those who teach in such a manner, the future is bleak!

Was it hateful for God to decree that Adam could eat from any other tree in the garden, or was it hateful for Satan to plant the lie that eating from the forbidden tree would surely not cause death? In a spiritual manner, sin is the cause of death. Therefore, anything that causes spiritual death is sinful. Hateful are the politicians who approve of things that God decrees are deserving of death. Hateful are the politicians who stand with the serpent. God had it right, men have become woeful liars! The *Axis of Evil* extends well beyond the limited geography once described by George W. Bush. Though Iran, Iraq and North Korea continue to be ominous threats to the world, they are joined by the likes of the body of the harlot, the un-naturals, their political allies, and the godless – akin to those who recently created a biological horror that has become a world-wide catastrophe. These are the likes of mankind who will know only an eternity of suffering.[470] They are among those who falsely accuse their brethren of hateful things.

God's people are being accused of crimes they have not committed. Is it a crime to encourage men to live? Certainly not! But it is a biblical crime to 'approve of those who practice' anything that is an afront to God's decree. Every man knows God's righteous decree. This is the difference between loving the truth and *refusing* to love the truth. To love the truth is to be saved. Refusing to love the truth ultimately leads to delighting in wickedness. Remember the days of the supposed Christian President who splashed the White House in the colors of the rainbow in celebration of unnatural relations? "No good tree bears bad fruit, nor does a bad tree bear good fruit. Each tree is recognized by its own fruit. People do not pick figs from thornbushes, or grapes from briers. The good man brings good things out of the good stored up in his heart, and the evil man brings evil things out of the evil stored up in his heart. For out of the overflow of his heart his mouth speaks."[216] The President's approval and disgraceful use of the rainbow made a mockery of God's instruction to refrain from shameful lusts (God's definition). Yet, it is God's faithful who reject such approvals and will continue to be accused of being hateful for holding to the truth. Jesus said it best: "If the world hates you, keep in mind that it hated me first. If you belonged to the world, it would love you as its own. As it is, you do not belong to the world, but I have chosen you out of the world. That is why the world hates you. He who hates me hates my Father as well. They hated me without reason."[200] The world hates Jesus without reason. The world hates Jesus' followers without reason. Nevertheless, the accusations continue to fly. Satan continues to accuse our brothers.[443]

With proof of God now imminent, *the Accuser of our brothers* will soon meet his well-deserved end. The liar and his craft have been overcome by the blood of the Lamb and by the Word of His testimony. What Jesus said has come to be. Two thousand years ago, Jesus spoke of the world hating Him and His people. That hate deepens with the world's rapid expansion of political deceptions and societal depravities. Instead of sons and daughters honoring their mothers and fathers, the world teaches future generations to be non-binary and substitute the non-specific terms of *parent* and *child*. Instead of sons and daughters worshiping the truth of the Father, the Son, and the Spirit - the world submits to its own prideful ways and has taught generations to honor the Queen of Heaven and things taught by demons. Instead of recognizing the oneness of the Father and His Son, the world has approved of generations who recognize The Prophet and his god as a prophet and God. Until now, The Prophet's kingdom was winning most of the battles in the war. The world has been sinking into the wicked and rebellious behavior that was prophesied by Daniel.[35] The scope and speed of descension in the last two decades is breathtaking. But there comes a breaking point. The speed of the lies has outpaced the legs of the liar. He can remain upright and hidden no longer.

In the near-term, accusers of our brothers will continue-on in their ways, each teaching their children that living and speaking lies somehow equates to love. Men will continue to present themselves as women and delight in the choice to raise their daughters as boys. The lies, they say, are loving and beaming with compassion. But the reality is that these acts nurture self-loathing and thoughts of suicide. The world will continue to approve of the things that God decrees shameful and detestable, even calling the husbands of male governors *First Gentlemen*. Using good words like *love, compassion, acceptance,* and *tolerance* - the spirit of the serpent will continue to whisper in a child's ear, teaching them that God's decree lacks compassion, is narrow-minded, completely intolerant, and wholly outdated. The tactic is an old one. The liar is even older. He has things going his way. "But woe to the earth and [its people] because the devil has gone down to you! He is filled with fury, because he knows that his time is short.[444] The war that began in heaven has taken its toll on earth. The war that the dragon has been waging on God and man is finally coming to its end.

Satan and his mouthpiece, Lucifer, have fallen.[441] The former is the father of lies, the serpent and the root of deception. The latter is figuratively his earthly son. Together, they have nourished the largest branch of a condemned and withering vine. That vine is long and full of off-shoots. It consists of eight kingdoms, countless nations, billions of people, and multiple gods. The Bible and its prophets describe each of these things in detail. History verifies much of what was prophesied to happen since the exodus of the Hebrews from Egypt 3,500 years ago. Now that The Prophet is being unveiled, the balance of God's mysteries and prophetic Word will come to light. There are many in the world who refuse to love the truth and prefer to delight in the wickedness as it was described by John and Paul.[471] The 'many' represent the majority who make up over two-thirds who are to be struck down and perish.[527] The math is basic. Of the living, those who are destined for the wide gate number approximately five billion. The madness of the final war has been lost on a generation who is too far removed from the events of 9/11 to even consider the consequences of 30,000 nuclear warheads – each delivering up to 3,000 times the energy of the first bomb dropped on Hiroshima. The math surrounding those who are 'struck down' is not so simple. Those who are 'struck down' likely include the elect and involves the mysteries of Matthew, Luke, John, and Paul. All the final prophecies must be satisfied by the same event. This final act must include:

- The sign of the Son of Man appearing in the sky, causing the nations to mourn[338]
- Jesus' elect will be gathered from the earth[339]
- The kingdom of God belongs to *all* children – none perish[218]
- Not all will sleep [die] but some will be changed in a flash[24]
- Nations gathered for the great day of God Almighty[454]
- Nations gathered in Armageddon[456]
- Destroying those who destroy the earth[438]
- Return of Jesus with 'thunder, earthquake, great noise, windstorm, tempest, and flames of a devouring fire'[146]
- The seventh angel sounds his trumpet[435]

The plague that causes this event is vivid in its imagery. The men who wrote about this day likely could not imagine the grandeur of the event they were inspired to write about. It suggests that men will go to war for a final time, with some melting away as they stand on their feet.[528] Sadly, man has demonstrated the ability to do just that. It has been over 75 years since the first of mankind melted away while they stood on their feet. They did so in the cities of Nagasaki and Hiroshima. The proliferation of such atrocious weaponry and the ability to use it has grown to unthinkable dimensions in the days since the first bombs were dropped on Japan. Such things now rest in the hands and underground networks of those who are hopelessly lost and serve as slaves for The Prophet.

It does not take a lot of imagination to understand how the world will simultaneously look upward and mourn at what they see coming on the clouds. Even Jesus' most faithful will dread the moment of man's last act. In that flash, Jesus' elect will be transformed and gathered up. The children, all children, will be gathered up. The nations will gather to exchange their wares and the result is what we know to be Armageddon. In the exchange, those who destroy the earth will, themselves, be destroyed. Jesus' return (in the sky above) is in the moment of this madness. The Prophet's unveiling will be the cause. Revealing him as the antichrist, Lucifer, will be reason sufficient to institute such madness. And the sound of the seventh trumpet in that moment will come in a literal manner. Most communities have early warning devices with a distinct horn that blares its warning before muffled instructions ring about one's ears. In that moment, every horn will sound.

The world is as He said it would be. God has brought about a man to fulfill His purpose. That man is Jesus. God summoned a bird of prey from the east. That bird serves as The Prophet. Between the two, they will bring about all that God has planned.[149] The Romans and the Prophetiers are going to be disheartened when they learn that God was steadfast when He granted His salvation to Zion and His splendor to Israel.[150]

The Prophet

Chapter 15

Jerusalem Unmatched

The Promise of Revelation 21

Zion, is the City of David.[489] This is where the Ark of the Covenant was initially placed.[490] Zion is the inclusive place of worship for the Israelites – from which a band of survivors remain due to the zeal of the Lord Almighty.[214] Synonymous with *Jerusalem*, Zion is described as *the City of God*[357] – *the city of the Redeemed.*[122] It is Jesus Christ, the Lamb, who appear(ed) on Mount Zion with 144,000 of the first resurrection, all of them Jews from the Twelve Tribes of Israel.[431] Salvation is granted to Zion and God's splendor is given to Israel. These are the Words of God.[160] With salvation given to Zion and the splendor of God given to Israel, why would the Prophetiers, particularly the Persians, loath the people called *Zionists*?

"Eliminating the Zionist regime does not mean eliminating Jews. We aren't against Jews. It means abolishing the imposed regime… This is *Eliminating Israel*. It will happen." – Timesofisrael.com, Supreme Leader Ayatollah Ali Khamenei, May 20, 2020

Consider the direct biblical warning defining the enemies of God as those who oppose Israel.[355] One might think that outwardly conspiring against God's people would be a horrible idea! Zion is Israel. Israel is Jerusalem. And Jerusalem is Zion. Zion is where God declared He would lay the cornerstone, Jesus, to nullify man's covenant with death.[145] The cornerstone was laid in Jerusalem. For all who accept the promise to Zion, man's covenant with death has been annulled. Further, the world has a focal point – it's Jerusalem. Jerusalem is a cup of trembling; 'a cup that sends all the surrounding peoples reeling.'[524]

About this city Zechariah writes:

"This is the word of the Lord concerning Israel. The Lord, who stretches out the heavens, who lays the foundation of the earth, and who forms the spirit of man within him, declares: 'I am going to make Jerusalem a cup that sends all the surrounding peoples reeling. Judah will be besieged as well is Jerusalem. On that day, when all the nations of the earth are gathered against her, I will make Jerusalem an immovable rock for all the nations. All who try to move it will injure themselves. On that day I will strike every horse with panic and its rider with madness,' declares the Lord. 'I will keep a watchful eye over the house of Judah, but I will blind all the horses of the nations. Then the leaders of Judah will say in their hearts, *The people of Jerusalem are strong, because the Lord Almighty is their God.* On that day I will make the leaders of Judah like a firepot in a woodpile, like a flaming torch among sheaves. They will consume right and left all the surrounding peoples, but Jerusalem will remain intact in her place. The Lord will save the dwellings of Judah first so that the honor of the house of David and of Jerusalem's inhabitants may not be greater than that of Judah. On that day the Lord will shield those who live in Jerusalem, so that the feeblest among them will be like David, and the house of David will be like God, like the Angel of the Lord going before them. On that day I will set out to destroy all the nations that attack Jerusalem.'"[523]

Time is a funny thing. With the passing of time, people tend to forget calamity and dismiss warnings. Time has erased the memory and lessons about Sodom and the men who harbored the shameful lusts that caused its destruction. Time has erased the memory and lessons about Adolph Hitler and the fear he used to control an otherwise reasonable people. Time has erased the memory and lessons about the Queen of Heaven and the warnings about honoring that man-made deity as though it was God. Time is erasing the memory and lessons about 9/11 and ignoring the written instruction that was given to those godless murderers. Time seems to erase, reboot, and replace the memories of most people – particularly when those memories are so horrific and painful.

Time after time, Israel has been attacked by her enemies. Time after time, Israel's enemies have tested her resilience. Even now, God's enemies take Him to task and test His resolve over the people He cherishes. So, what is it about Israel that garners God's splendor? What is it about Jerusalem that makes it an immovable rock? How is it that Jerusalem separates itself from Rome and Mecca as God's standard and immovable rock? The difference is that Jerusalem is eternal. This may be a grand departure from man's traditional understanding, but Jerusalem is much more than the tiny parcel of ground located on the shores of the Mediterranean Sea - in the Middle East. Jerusalem is/was/and forever will be the Holy City.[469] It is holy on earth just as it is holy above. But there is a difference. The earthly Jerusalem is home to the abomination. No such abomination or impurity will ever enter the Jerusalem above. The only ones who are to know the New

The Prophet

Jerusalem above are the ransomed lives written into Jesus' book of life.[475] The earthly Jerusalem will suffer the same fate as her neighbors. In that day, the abomination that stands where it does not belong will suffer its awful fate and melt into the earth upon which it stands.

Many will argue that the earthly Jerusalem has a guaranteed thousand-year afterlife. They contend that after all the other nations have been destroyed for attacking her, Jesus will descend from heaven and reign on earth for a thousand years. But that understanding is seemingly flawed. The Jerusalem that we know today has been overrun by those who adore the abomination. In the Holy City, upon earth's holy ground, stands the abomination that causes desolation. If Jesus' thousand-year reign were here on earth, God's promise that 'nothing impure will ever enter [Jerusalem]'[475] would become a contradiction. To have the abomination that causes desolation with its many worshipers present on the ground in the earthly city of Jerusalem contradicts God's Word that 'the wicked will not inherit the kingdom of God [Jerusalem].'[22] That simply won't happen.

A set of broken and buried stones are all that remain of the ruins that were once the temple. Since Christ's resurrection, stones are no longer representative of the temple of God. Within that miniscule, two-dimensional geography is not the New Jerusalem that hosts the Alpha and the Omega. Israel's current earthly dimensions are approximately 262 miles long by 72 miles wide. She has been parceled off and reduced to a miniscule land mass that is less than 9,000 square miles. The city of Jerusalem is little more than a pinhead on a map at 50 square miles. But the Holy City that is prepared as *a bride for her husband*[469] is described by God as being three-dimensional. She is described as Christ's bride; having walls as long and wide as they are tall. At 12,000 stadia (1432 miles) long, by 1432 miles wide, and 1432 miles tall - the New Jerusalem is described as occupying a space of nearly 3,000,000,000 *cubic* miles. Her Jasper walls are 216 feet thick.[472] This calls for a moment of pause. Try to imagine the size and scope of the New Jerusalem. It is described as half the width and length of the United States of America. It would not be an outrageous stretch of the imagination to consider the expansion of Jerusalem across the continents of Europe, Africa, and Asia that might accommodate the two-dimensional land in square miles. That would be a bit of a stretch, but still somewhat reasonable. Now consider its height. It is as tall as it is long and wide. If the new Jerusalem comes down out of heaven to replace what remains of the old Jerusalem, it will extend 1,432 miles above the earth! With orbital velocity being at or about 370 miles above earth, attaining the New Jerusalem on earth is simply out of reach. The imagery of the New Jerusalem is that of God's kingdom above. When this world passes away - it passes away. With it goes the Temple Mount and the abomination that stands where it does not belong.

For the most part, men (particularly her enemies) have lost their memories and dismiss the prophesies surrounding Israel and Jerusalem. And, when considering Israel's insignificant size and slight population, it seems ludicrous that Jerusalem would continue to be a cup of trembling for the surrounding people – unless God is God, and He is intent on His promise. In that case, the world faces a bit of a problem. With the Prophetiers surrounding Jerusalem and skirmishes taking place between them and the Israelites, particularly to the north (Syria), it is just a matter of time before the Persians and their allies attempt to move that Rock. Consider the words of the Persian, Khamenei, and what he recently said about Israel and her future on this earth. Compare his words to the warning about the enemies of God:

- "Eliminating the Zionist regime does not mean eliminating Jews. We aren't against Jews. It means abolishing the imposed regime... This is 'eliminating Israel.' It will happen."

- "Come," they say, "let us destroy them as a nation, that the name of Israel be remembered no more."[356]

It has been nearly 4,000 years since Abraham made his way to Israel. Thirty-five hundred years ago, Moses led his people out of Egypt to Israel. Nearly 2,000 years have passed since the Romans caused the Jews to scatter from Israel - Jerusalem particularly. The Prophet's people trampled the ground in Israel 1,335 ago. And Israel was gathered again, in their own land just over 70 years ago. Rome does not have such a history. Mecca certainly does not have such a history. Though The Prophet declares Hamonah (Bakkah – the crowded place) to be the spiritual center of the earth and the mother of all towns, his ambitious ramblings were spoken without merit. The spiritual world revolves around Israel. There are many who wish to close the door on her existence. But God has made certain that she remains in her place and continues to be the cup of trembling He promised she would be. Considering her history, concluding otherwise would be foolish. Israel, Zion, and Jerusalem are, were and forever will be exactly what God intended them to be. He has done as He has pleased.

The Prophet

Chapter 16

Succeeding in Terror

Isaiah's Warning About He Who Causes Terror (Chapter 47)

Terror...
Terror is the heightened fear that overcomes a parent when they lose sight of a child. Terror is the numbing fear that overcomes one's mind when the diagnosis is cancer. Terror is the chilling fear of being cancelled for stating an inconvenient truth. Terror is the paralyzing fear of being infected by a biological weapon or threatened by the people who have sworn an oath to the gods of a non-vaccine. Terror is the infuriating fear of infliction that descends upon those who dare to reject The Prophet's teaching. In the natural world, terror is an emotion that causes men to act as a means of survival. In the spiritual world, terror is Satan's tool. It is the preferred means to divide, conquer and control the masses. The Romans utilized terror in the way of crucifixion. So does The Prophet.[393] Hitler utilized terror as a means of political rule. So does The Prophet.[389] The political powers utilize terror to force unwanted behaviors. So does The Prophet.[370] The Prophetiers utilize terror[381] by any means necessary and under all circumstances.[291] They do so under the direction of their god. This is their law.[253] Terror is the method of coercion, war, used by the god who masquerades as God. He succeeds in terror. Isaiah said it best when he penned God's mockery of the imposter. Isaiah wrote: "Perhaps you will succeed, perhaps you will cause terror."[158] Lies, deception, murder and war describe the devil. Lies, deceit, murder and war describe the devil's mouthpiece. For angry men, his methods may satisfy a murderous desire while building falsified credits and a twisted pathway to a non-existent paradise. This could be problematic! The Prophet teaches men that they can enforce his laws while killing their way to God.[223] John warned us about this in Revelation 13. He told us that The Prophet would "speak and cause all who refused to worship [his god] to be killed."[451] The inconvenient reality is that such a thing plays out in daily lives and in every corner of the world – even in our own back yards.

Most find it difficult to understand and commonly reject God's teaching that all deception has a common origin. Called *the father of lies* the dragon has been misleading mankind since Adam and Eve walked the garden. Commonly referred to as "he," the dragon has no stated gender. Isaiah 47 describes this lying creep as *the virgin daughter of the Babylonians*. Such is the detestable goddess of eternal virginity.[167] The origins of the eternal virgin, *the Queen of Heaven*, is Satanic. The devil mixes truth with lies. He mixed the truth with lies when he told Eve that she would *surely not die* when she ate the fruit from the tree of the knowledge of good and evil, but her eyes will be opened, and she would be like God. We know how the story ends. The serpent has done the same thing with the story of the virgin mother. Christians know of Mary's virgin birth of the Christ. We know that he was born a helpless infant, certainly *not* God, but He who would grow to be the Spirit-filled image of God. We also know from the true and faithful Word that Mary and Joseph consummated their marriage in union after Jesus' birth.[323] Their intimacy resulted in the births of four named sons and, seemingly, three or more daughters.[330] An ever-virgin she is not and is never stated to be. But the serpent blended biblical truth with Babylonian nonsense to recreate the Queen of Heaven. In the days following Jesus' ascension and the creation of Christianity, this Babylonian deity was *regenerated* by the cultural biases of Rome to ultimately raise Mary and place her in an unbiblical throne as the queen over all things[20] – *the Queen of Heaven*. Though it has no biblical roots or support, Satan and his demons helped an entire kingdom rationalize the thought and build a religion around the virgin daughter of the Babylonians. They then assigned that deity a name – *Mary*. God is clear about avoiding the detestable practice of worshiping the Queen of Heaven.[168] But understand that just because a satanic deity is born of man's mythical traditions, the teaching is very real and deeply personal to the people who worship it. The tradition becomes absolute! Such is Satan's craft. In the process, biblical accuracies are easily altered in the minds of those who believe that God has changed since the days of Moses. The earth's kings and queens prosper from such deceiving spirits and demonic teaching.[535] And, just as Rome incorporated the ever-virgin into their state religion, The Prophet incorporated the foreign god into his homeland of Sheba and Dedan. Though he outwardly states that there is no compulsion in religion,[536] he demands that his fortresses (stars) fight for their beliefs until all religions worship only his god.[537] Coercion (fear of harm – force) remains the key to his success. It is as John warned in Revelation, all who reject the new laws of The Prophet are accused of creating mischief in the land. By The Prophet's quoted word, all these people are to be… 'murdered.' What can be more terrifying than a prophet of God promising to murder anyone who opposes his newfound teaching? This is how the master of intrigue uses the charade of 'peace' to destroy many.

The Prophet

Such is the likes of his god who masquerades as God. Such a charade is the work of Satan.[538] He hides his mischievous endeavors behind lovely titles like *Beneficent* and *Merciful*.[238] These are synonyms for *tender* and *delicate*.[151] The Prophetiers begin all but one chapter of The Prophet's field guide by honoring *him who holds the power of death*[385] (aka the devil)[120] with these adjectives. Isaiah mocks the world's most evil man and leading terrorist, Lucifer, for the day that he is uncovered and shamed in his nakedness. The truth will be revealed. The *Causer of Death* is not our Redeemer. He is not our Lord Almighty, the Holy One of Israel. The Causer of Death is the fallen one of Babylonia. He masquerades as the Queen of Heaven for some and a childless king for others. As *the Destroyer* and admitted *Causer of Death*, his Hebrew name is *Abaddon* and in Greek, *Apollyon*.[539] From one kingdom to the next, the destroyer continues the war that began in heaven. He gives himself the name of Light[412] and the likeness of his light is The Prophet.[288] The statements that he uses are recycled from age to age and from kingdom to kingdom. He has succeeded in these things because he sees himself as the Owner of all the kingdoms.[377] He says so in biblical testimony.[215]

When God became angry with his people, when he desecrated His inheritance, He gave them over to Satan's hand and Satan showed them no mercy.[178] Satan shows them no mercy today. Though he calls himself *merciful,* mercy and grace are facades that hide the true nature of his existence. He even goes so far as to admit to Isaiah's declarations[152] that the Babylonian god will claim to be everlasting,[421] the ever living.[373] But the dragon was thrown to this earth to perish. He never escapes this planet. Satan was thrown from heaven to earth to exist no more – *forever!* He made a major blunder by going to war with God. Simply stated, Satan is not and never will be God. But by calling himself *The One*,[368] he has attempted to defame God and steal God's glory. He maintains the illusion that 'I am, and there is none besides me.'[153] Originating from the heart and emanating from the mouth of The Prophet, men are repeatedly fed the lie that *there is no god but he*.[374] Departing from the biblical God, the Holy One of Israel, the foreign god has made numerous statements that he is not a bridegroom, that he has no bride and he is above the loathsome act of having children.[267] Therefore, he can never be a widow or suffer the loss of children.[153] But these things will come upon him. In the coming days, the deceit of his disingenuous *tender* and *delicate* manifestations will be exposed. God promises that Israel will be saved by the Lord with an everlasting salvation[148] while disaster and calamity falls upon the liar.[155] Satan and the rebellious souls who worship him, in whatever form he might hide, will be swept away in a fire of their own making. This is the promise that was given in the beginning. Again, God is not the *Causer of Death*. That is Satan's title and role. God makes a fire come out of Satan[82] and The Prophet causes Satan's fire to fall upon the earth.[450] Again, the terror of current realities is a very inconvenient truth.

Satan's delusional power of influence is truly fascinating! Though there are multiple biblical warnings about his detestable acts and traditions, the liar causes many people to support and advance such things – even admiring those who practice them. This, too, is biblical.[484] For billions to believe that the Queen of Heaven has somehow transformed from a detestable idol into the *mother of God* is simply remarkable. There is no biblical reference to God having a mother. But there are billions of people in the world who have adopted that teaching and who refer to biblically accurate Christians as *bigots* for holding to the truth. The truth is written. The Man who is called *Wonderful Counselor, Mighty God, Everlasting Father,* and *the Prince of Peace*[127] was not God in the moment of his birth. God was not begotten. Not even Jesus had the power to keep from soiling Himself in His early years. The moment that the Spirit of God settled upon Him was during His baptism.[540] The traditional myth about Mary being the queen over all things was anchored in 1951.[20] Odd, isn't it? This demonstrates the massive power of tradition. Though it opposes the Word of God, its participants dismiss the contradiction as some sort of progression in an unbroken chain of tradition. Such deception is born in the *spirit of the antichrist,* which found its beginnings in the first century A.D. The Romans set upon their departure from the faith three centuries later. Such delusions can be compared to The Prophet and his about-face from the *Father, His Son,* and their *Spirit.* The reader might find it revealing as to how The Prophet recognized the role of the mother as being one of three – equal to that of Father and Son.[266] This is an understandable error for an illiterate man who was raised in the desert during the dying days of the Roman Empire.

In the years since Jesus fulfilled the prophetic nature of His coming, three distinct religions have formed. Christianity conformed to the path of the Old Testament prophets and accurately fulfilled their promise of Jesus as the prophetic Messiah. God's prophets, before and after Jesus, warned the world about those who would adore the *queen over all things* and *the king who would exalt himself.* Together, the two groups that continue to teach these Babylonian beliefs account for approximately three billion of the earth's six billion adults. The two post-Christian religions are linked by the knowledge that deceit begets deceit. Thanks to those who cannot tell their right hand from their left hand, the foreign god has achieved the improbable - he has proceeded in his dishonest trade without much notice. The majority in today's world refuse to consider how and why the god of a major world religion would be such a scandalous character. Most shrug their shoulders and state that there is only one God. They might want to read Daniel's warning about the king who exalts himself above the Son of God and honors a **foreign god**.⁵⁷ For most, one's social life is much easier, and people are more welcoming to those who are more inclusive. For one to recognize and call out the deceit of the masquerading light is now considered to be another 'hateful' act. Still, the foreign god confirms the warning and calls himself *the Hidden*.⁴²² Until now, his deceptive thoughts and actions have succeeded in a manner that would keep people from seeing him as anything other than God.

Few would argue that Satan has gathered wisdom and knowledge. He was with God for a time. After his rebellion began, he was crafty enough to find Eve in the garden and mislead her. Just as he used man's reasoning to instill the thought that Mary is the mother of God, the serpent used man's (Eve's) reasoning to instill the thought that eating from the tree of knowledge of good and evil would 'open her eyes and she would become like God, knowing good and evil.'⁵⁴¹ Satan knows of such things.⁵⁴² He has even given himself names and titles that describe him as having the greatest wisdom³⁶⁶ and the most knowledge.³⁶⁷ He certainly has knowledge. But he who started the war has relied too heavily on his finite wisdom and knowledge. His rebellious nature and haughty behavior thrust him from heaven to earth. And from the earth he will never leave. His ongoing hoax and limited reign over kingdoms will come to an end. No longer will he go unseen. God has seen fit to reveal the identity of the man of lawlessness as Satan's speaking image. The rage that the devil has demonstrated and the war that he has waged against the saints has brought about his own demise. His people are fogged by the delusion, and they continue to commit callous, murderous, and otherwise unthinkable acts against their brothers. Like the Babylonian god they adore, they have succeeded in causing terror. To avoid any sort of confusion as to whom they represent, they perform these actions in the proper name of their god. They kill thinking they are doing a service to God. They do such things because they do not know God – the Father and His Son.⁵⁴³ If the people of The Prophet wanted to know better, they need only to read. God is specific about His command *not* to murder. He is specific about those who kill thinking they are doing a service to God – it is not He who they serve. They serve the murderer.¹⁹¹

The world knows the battle-cry of the Prophetiers. It's a simple, unmistakable remark – typically unleashed in the most horrific of circumstances. The combination of this scream and man's power to cause death has become one of the world's most inconvenient realities. As if that was not horrific enough, people now fear being canceled for merely mentioning the association to any group and they fear being murdered for challenging the faith that drives the shrieking murderers. "There is a time for everything, and a season for every activity under heaven… a time to kill and a time to heal, a time to be silent and a time to speak, a time to love and a time to hate, a time for war and a time for peace."544 It is now a time to heal. With the love of the Father and His Son, we are soon to know peace. To do so means that it is time to speak. There is no time to fear. The actions of the Prophetiers must finally come to an end. But the end is not for the faint of heart. For most, these will be the most terrifying of times. Truth tells us that we need not fear those who can kill the body but cannot kill the soul.329 In a like manner, those who do their best to 'obey God's commandments and hold to the testimony of Jesus'545 will be put to the test and suffer at the hands of His many enemies. Christians understand that patient endurance is required when it comes to being killed by the sword or imprisoned 'because of their testimony for Jesus and because of the Word of God.' The enemy, those who trust in sniping the necks of the disbelievers, do not understand such patient endurance. Unlike the insistence of the liar, Jesus does not need His people to fight for their faith. This war between kingdoms comes to an end by the sword of Jesus' Mouth,429 not by the metallic swords of Jesus' faithful. As God promised, the devil's own will bring about the fire that consumes him and his people. It is by their own hand that the fire comes. It is caused by the rebellion of The Prophet. In the interim, The Prophetiers will do as they've been told.

Here are a few recent examples of a people at war...

- **April 18, 1983, Beirut, Lebanon**: The US Embassy was destroyed by a suicidal car bomb, killing 63 people. The Prophetiers claimed responsibility

- **October 23, 1983, Beirut, Lebanon**: Suicide bombers detonate a truck-bomb near the US military barracks at Beirut airport, killing 241 Marines. Minutes later a second bomb killed 58 French paratroopers in their barracks in West Beirut. The attackers were Prophetiers

- **December 12, 1983, Kuwait City, Kuwait**: A truck bomb was detonated near the US embassy and other targets, killing five and injuring 80

- **September 20, 1984, East Beirut, Lebanon**: A truck bomb exploded outside the US Embassy Annex, killing 24

- **April 12, 1985, Madrid, Spain**: A bomb was detonated at restaurant frequented by Americans, killing 18 and injuring 82

- **December 18, 1985, Rome, Italy, and Vienna, Austria**: Airports in Rome and Vienna were bombed, killing 20 people, five of whom were Americans. Bombing linked to [Luciferians] in Libya

The Prophet

- **December 21, 1988, Lockerbie, Scotland**: New York bound Pan Am Boeing 747 exploded in flight from a bomb and crashed into Scottish village, killing all 259 aboard an 11 people on the ground. Passengers included 35 Syracuse University students and many US personnel. Libyan Prophetiers formally admitted responsibility 15 years later

- **February 26, 1993, New York City**: A bomb exploded in basement garage of the World Trade Center, killing six and injuring at least 1,040 others. Prophetiers were convicted of conspiracy charges convicted of the bombing.

- **November 13, 1995, Riyadh, Saudi Arabia**: A car bomb explodes at a US military headquarters, killing five

- **June 25, 1996, Dhahran, Saudi Arabia**: A truck bomb explodes outside the Khobar Towers military complex, killing 19 and injuring hundreds. Fourteen Prophetiers were indicted for the killings

- **August 7, 1998, Nairobi, Kenya, and Dar es Salaam, Tanzania**: Truck bombs exploded near two US embassies, killing 224 and injuring about 4,500 people. Over twenty Prophetiers were indicted for the bombing.

- **October 12, 2000, Aden, Yemen**: U.S. Navy destroyer USS Cole was heavily damaged when a small boat loaded with explosives blew up alongside it. Seventeen people were killed.

- **September 11, 2001, New York City, Arlington, Virginia, and Shanksville, Pennsylvania**: Nineteen of The Prophet's own hijacked four commercial airliners into the Twin Towers, the Pentagon, and a field in Pennsylvania. The number of people murdered was 2,973 with nearly 6,000 injured

- **February 1, 2002, Pakistan**: Daniel Pearl has his neck sniped by Prophetiers

- **June 14, 2002, Karachi, Pakistan**: A bomb explodes outside American consulate in Karachi, Pakistan, killing 12

- **May 12, 2003, Riyadh, Saudi Arabia**: Suicide Prophetiers kill 34 at housing compound for Westerners.

- **March 11, 2004, Madrid, Spain:** Ten explosions by Prophetiers occurred during rush hour aboard four commuter trains, murdering 191 people and injuring nearly 1500

- **May 29 – 31, 2004, Riyadh, Saudi Arabia:** Prophetiers attacked the offices of a Saudi oil company in Khobar, Saudi Arabia, killing 22 people

- **July 7, 2005, London, UK:** Four bomb blasts targeted London's public transportation system, murdering 52 and injuring more than 700. The bombers are considered martyrs by The Prophet's own

- **November 9, 2005, Amman, Jordan:** Prophetiers attack three American hotels in Ammon, Jordan, killing 57

- **July 11, 2006, Mumbai, India:** Seven bombs target India's railway system, killing 209 people

- **December 11, 2007, Algeria:** More than 60 people are murdered by Prophetiers who detonate two car bombs near Algeria's United Nations offices

- **September 16, 2008, Yemen:** A car bomb and rockets strike the US Embassy in Yemen as staff arrived for work, killing 16 people

- **November 26, 2008, India:** The Mumbai massacre happens when ten Prophetiers attack six different locations including three hotels, killing 172 and wounding nearly 300

- **June 1, 2009, Little Rock, Arkansas:** Abdulhakim Muhammad, a Prophetier from Memphis, Tennessee, shot two soldiers outside a military recruiting center. One was killed and the other was wounded. In a letter to the judge hearing his case, Muhammad asked to change his plea from not guilty to guilty, claiming ties to [The Prophet], and called the shooting [his effort to strive in accordance] "to fight those who wage war on [The Prophet] and [his followers]"[65]

- **November 5, 2009, Fort Hood, Texas:** Major Nidal Malik Hasan, a United States Army Medical Corps psychiatrist, opened fire on the people he was supposed to be assisting. He murdered 13 and wounded 30. His business card identified him as a Prophetier. Instead of showing remorse for his actions, he gave "glory to his god" for the murders

- **December 25, 2009**: On a flight from Amsterdam to Detroit Umar Farouk Abdulmutallab attempted to ignite an explosive device hidden in his clothes. The device was a substance that did not alert airport security. The Prophetier had previously been on a watchlist when he attempted the bombing

- **September 11, 2012, Benghazi, Libya**: Prophetiers attack the American consulate, killing the US Ambassador to Libya, Christopher Stevens, and three other Embassy officials

- **April 15, 2013, Boston, Massachusetts**: Multiple bombs detonate near the finish line of the Boston Marathon. Three people are killed and more than 260 people are injured. In the aftermath of the bombings, two Prophetiers shoot a police officer. They were brothers whose family had immigrated to the United States

- **May 22, 2013, London, UK:** Prophetiers snipe the neck of Lee Rigby in the street

- **August 19, 2014**: The Prophet's own snipe the neck of American journalist James Foley

- **September 2, 2014**: A Prophetier snipes the neck of journalist Stephen Scotloff

- **January 7, 2015, Paris, France:** The French magazine Charlie Hebdo is attacked by three gunmen for daring to publish cartoon caricatures of The Prophet

- **June 26, 2015, Sousse, Tunisia:** Seifeddine Rezgui Yacoubi, a Prophetier, shoots 38 people at a resort in Port El Kantaoui

- **November 13, 2015, Paris, France:** Three Prophetiers attack people outside of a football stadium during a match while others bomb and shoot at cafes and restaurants within the city. The Prophet's own also take aim at an Eagles of Death Metal concert inside the Bataclan Theater. In the end, 130 people were murdered and another 400 were injured

- **December 2, 2015, San Bernardino, California**: Fourteen people were killed and more than 20 wounded when two Prophetiers (common-law husband and wife) shot the males' coworkers at a Christmas party in San Bernardino, California

- **March 22, 2016, Brussels, Belgium:** Coordinated bombings were carried out by Prophetiers in Brussels with 32 people murdered and over 300 injured

- **June 12, 2016**: A Prophetier carried out a mass shooting within an Orlando nightclub, leaving 50 people dead and more than 50 injured. The shooter pledged his allegiance to The Prophet from the crime scene

- **July 14, 2016**: Mohamed Lahouaiej-Bouhlel, a Prophetier, drove a delivery truck into a large crowd celebrating Bastille Day at Nice's Promenade des Anglais, killing 86 people and wounding more than 430 others

- **November 28, 2016**: Abdul Razak Ali Artan, a Prophetier, carried out an attack by automobile followed by a knife attack at Ohio State University, injuring 13 people

- **December 19, 2016**: The Prophetier, Anis Amri, drove his truck into pedestrians at the Christmas Market in Berlin, killing 12 people and wounding 56 others

- **March 22, 2017:** Prophetier Khalid Masood killed five people and wounded 50 more during a vehicle and stabbing attack in London

- **April 3, 2017, St. Petersburg, Russia:** Akbarzhon Jalilov, a Prophetier, detonated a bomb on the St. Petersburg Metro train, killing 15 and injuring 50

- **April 7, 2017:** A Prophetier hijacked a beer truck and targeted pedestrians in Stockholm Sweden, killing four people and wounding 15 more

- **May 22, 2017, Manchester, UK:** Salman Ramadan Abedi, a Prophetier, detonates a bomb outside of a concert by Ariana Grande, with 23 killed and another 139 wounded. More than half were children

- **May 2017:** The US Transportation Security Administration (TSA) issued a warning to truck and bus companies urging them to watch out potential vehicular terrorist assailants and listing more than a dozen car ramming attack since 2014 that have collectively killed more than 170 people. The TSA wrote in its memo, terrorist groups will likely continue to encourage "unsophisticated tactics such as vehicle ramming" since these types of attacks are difficult to prevent and "can inflict mass casualties if successful." This memo was sent out in response to instruction that [The Prophet's own] employ automobiles as weapons.[546]

These wanton acts of mass casualty and murder are an extension of the terror witnessed on September 11, 2001. The people who drive these cars and trucks have been influenced in the same manner as the Prophetiers who hijacked planes on 9/11. They succeed in terror.

- **May 26, 2017, Cairo, Egypt:** Prophetiers detonate two bombs near Coptic churches in Egypt, killing 47 and wounding over 100

- **June 3, 2017:** Three Prophetiers drove a van into a crowded London Bridge only to exit the vehicle and stab others at the nearby Laurel market. The attack left eight people dead, and 48 others wounded

- **August 17, 2017:** A van, driven by a Prophetier, was deliberately rammed into a crowd of tourists in Las Ramblas, Barcelona. The attack left 16 people dead, and 120 others wounded

- **October 14, 2017, Mogadishu, Somalia:** Prophetiers detonate a car bomb in Mogadishu, killing 587 and injuring another 316

- **October 31, 2017, New York City:** Sayfullo Saipov, a Prophetier, rented a pickup truck and drove it down a crowded bike path along the Hudson River in Manhattan, killing 8 and injuring 11

There will always be apologists who make the argument that there is only one God, and that God is God. They would be correct. But god is not God. The individuals who argue that God is God do not care to know or acknowledge Daniel's warning about the foreign god and the man who serves the foreign god's purpose. Instinctively, these very same people insist that no religion promotes violence and that the radicalized Prophetiers misrepresent the instructive word of The Prophet. People who argue such things are largely among two groups: The first group is likely ignorant to the words of The Prophet, and they assume his instruction is being misunderstood. The other group knows

The Prophet's word. They understand that if it were not for god's approval of fighting, The Prophet's movement would have been snuffed out long ago.[9] Therefore, they believe that they must continue the fight to achieve the ultimate objective – "…fight them until all religions are for [god].[402] The Prophetiers cannot stop fighting the war. To do so means that they would be opposing the written instruction of The Prophet. So, the Prophetiers continue to gain ground. They do so geographically. They do so politically. They do so religiously. Remember how deception begets deception? Well, one of The Prophet's apologists is a member of the papacy. According to him, The Prophet's recorded word is 'peaceful.'[360] The only way to understand the directives to fight, murder, crucify, amputate, and otherwise smite the necks of the disbelievers as a 'peaceful' method is to change the definition of *peace*. Obviously, deception has hidden in plain sight for a very long time. In addition to being intentionally deaf and blind, this papal spokesman appears to be willfully illiterate as well!

- **January 27, 2018, Kabul, Afghanistan**: At least 103 people were killed, and 235 others injured when a Prophetier exploded an ambulance loaded with explosives near Sidarat Square in central Kabul

- **July 13, 2018, Mastung, Pakistan**: At least 149 people were killed, and 186 others injured when a Prophetier detonated his explosives

- **July 25, 2018, As-Suwayda, Syria**: Prophetiers carried out suicide bombings and shootings in the city of As-Suwayda and several surrounding villages, killing 255 people, and injuring 180 others

- **December 17, 2018, Imlil, Morocco**: Two Scandinavian women had their necks sniped in the High Atlas mountains of Morocco by three Prophetiers. They recorded the beheadings

- **January 27, 2019, Philippines**: Two bombs detonate at Our Lady of Mount Carmel Cathedral with 20 dead and 102 injured. Prophetiers claimed responsibility

- **April 21, 2019, Sri Lanka**: Three churches and three hotels were targeted in Columbo with 259 murdered and over 500 injured. All the bombers were Sri Lankan Prophetiers

- **November 29, 2019, London England**: Usman Khan, a convicted Prophetier stabbed people on the London Bridge with two dead and three injured

- **March 25, 2020, Afghanistan**: Prophetiers attacked a Sikh gathering in Kabul with 25 killed and numerous injured
- **August 24, 2020, Philippines**: Prophetiers detonated a motorcycle bomb in Jolo. With first responders at the scene, a female Prophetier detonated a second device. Fourteen people were murdered and 75 injured
- **October 16, 2020, France**: Samuel Paty had his neck sniped by an 18-year-old Prophetier. Samuel's crime was showing a caricature of The Prophet
- **November 10, 2020, Mozambique**: Prophetiers sniped the necks of more than 50 with the number of injured and abducted still unknown
- **January 3, 2021, Pakistan**: Prophetiers abducted 11 miners in Balochistan. They all suffered sniped necks
- **March 23, 2021, Boulder, Colorado**: A Prophetier murdered ten people while they worked or shopped for groceries

Perhaps this god will succeed, perhaps he will cause terror. The more it happens, the more the prophecy is fulfilled. The Prophet was unleashed upon this world to expand upon a single act. He was to advance war. He spoke the covenant of the foreign god. That image has survived the centuries in book form. Within the image of his god is given the directives of war – to steal, kill and destroy. It is not just the radicalized individuals who recognize that image. Their war against civilization is nothing new. The war has lasted over 1,400 years. Their orders to 'strive against [the disbeliever] a mighty striving… must be carried on by every [Prophetier] under all circumstances.'[291] Fourteen hundred years of recorded history verifies the abhorrent truth about The Prophet and his biblical role on earth.

- Fight with them until there is no persecution and all religions are only for [god][402]
- He it is who has sent his messenger with the guidance and the true religion that he may make it overcome all (other) religions[425]
- So when you meet in battle those who disbelieve [like two young blonde Scandinavian women], strike their necks; then, when you have overcome them, make (them) prisoners, and either receive favor afterwards or ransom them until the war lays down its burdens. That is the command[420]
- Death will overcome you, though you are in Towers, raise high[390]

- The only punishment of those who wage war against [god] and his [Prophet] and strive to make mischief in the land is that they should be murdered, or crucified, or their hands in their feet be cut off on opposite sides, or they should be imprisoned[393]

Though these commands sound wholly 'peaceful,' inflicting terror is a means to an end. If we were to allow this to play out and remain silent (as society demands), the only end that this story can ever have is one in which everyone on the planet must submit to the Prophet's desires. But there is a major flaw in The Prophet's reasoning. Many of the examples above demonstrate how one sect of Prophetiers inflict their terror upon another sect of Prophetiers. When the entire world submits to The Prophet and all religions are only for his god, which sect will lay down their arms and concede to the other? The way of a warrior is limited to war. In the eyes and ears of a Christian, it seems that The Prophet and his god are often mentioned by their many names and descriptions within the pages of the Bible, and it is evident that they have led the world astray.

The Prophet

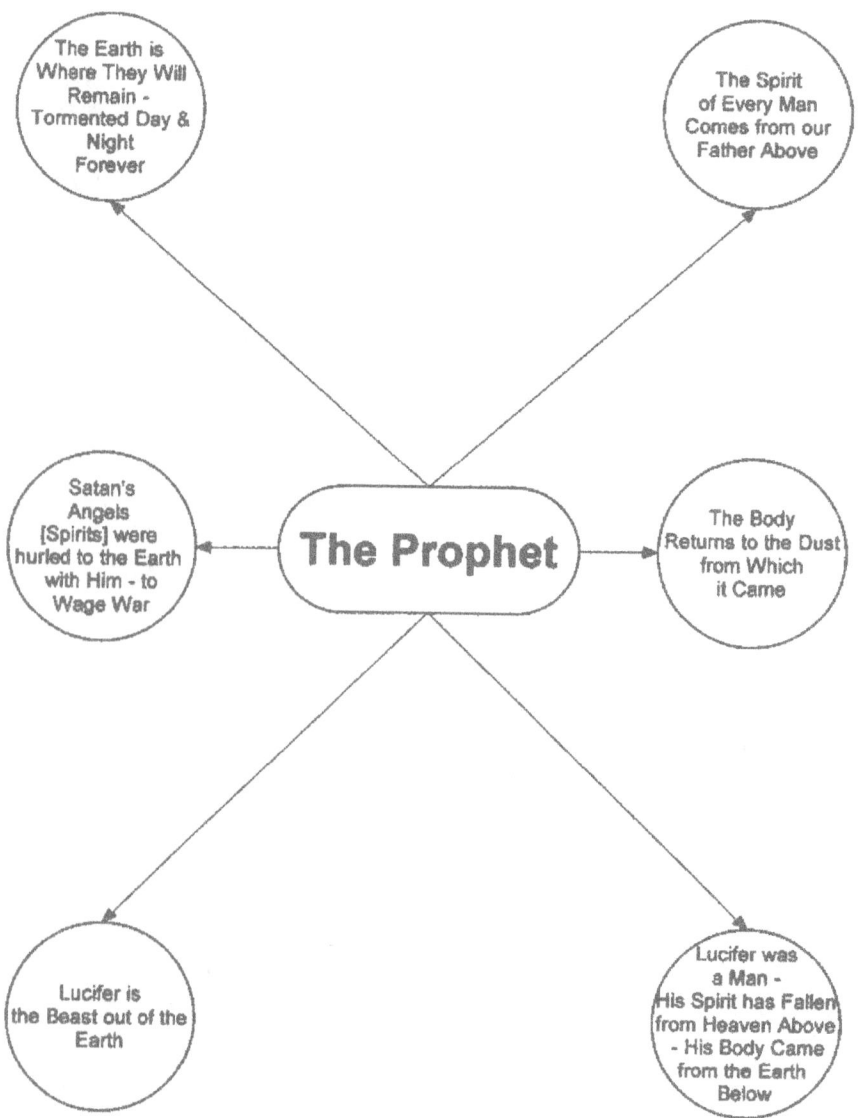

Chapter 17

Satan Leads the Whole World Astray

John's Warning About the War that Started In Heaven (Revelation 12)

"The great dragon was hurled down – that ancient serpent called the devil, or Satan who leads the whole world astray. He was hurled to the earth, and his angels with him."[440] This is John's warning to the world and its many generations. Few accept John's warning in its literal form. In today's world, Satan and his demons have taken on more of a metaphorical meaning rather than that of actual entities. Christian churches have largely left the faith and reduced their values for something much more worldly, like the value of square footage and an increasing head-count. Still, there can be only one truth. Either John was part of a spectacularly elaborate written hoax that has spanned 4,000 years, or the whole world has been led astray by the devil – as it is written. Either way, there is deception about! Doubt and ridicule that surround biblical teaching is easily understandable. The Bible begins with a snake that speaks to the world's first lady. It is followed by a beast out of the sea that swallows and then vomits-up a wayward prophet of God. Then there is the nightmarish imagery of John's Revelation and the horrific acts from the beast out of the earth. So, what is the truth?

Is the Word of God factual in its telling of a snake who talked with Eve in the garden, convincing her that she would surely not die if she ate the forbidden fruit, or was this nothing more than the wickedness of man's evil heart that exchanged and advanced such a fairytale? Are these the whisperings of bored psychopaths, or is it the accurate telling of man's quick departure from the Word of God? Men of instinct and little faith come to quick conclusions. But those who wish to dig deeper will come to different conclusions altogether. Of course, there are no witnesses to the disastrous event in the garden, but there is evidence of the nefarious encounter. According to a new and improved god, men will surely *not* die. For men will be nourished by the beverage of many hues, and their eyes will be opened and finally know what constitutes good and what has digressed into evil. This god and his mouthpiece teach people that hell is *not* the second death[278] and place of eternal torment, but a place of nurturing – much like that of a mother who nurtures her baby.[251] This all sounds oddly familiar! If God is God and the serpent has passed itself off as the new and improved god, which one might convince many men that they will surely not die if they act in opposition to God's ways and laws? And, knowing that opposing the new god's laws opens the door for others to commit righteous murder, how is it that men will surely not die? It appears that deception is built upon deception, and the serpent is the serpent no matter the method in which he may shed his skin.

Once again, consider the men who committed the horrendous crimes of September 11th. They likely adopted the teaching that they were merely doing a favor to the people they were about to murder. After all, those who were recognized as being non-believers and hypocrites (in the eyes of the hijackers) would soon be nurtured back to a righteous life because 'the abyss is a mother to [them] – a burning fire.' This is how the snake would justify murder. Unlike the Spirit-driven Word of genuine prophets, the foreign god and his sidekick describe hell as a temporary stay before one is plucked out of the flames and tossed into *the river of life*.[278] The Bible describes *the river of life* as living waters that flow from the temple of God[582] – where 'nothing impure will ever enter into it, nor will anyone who does what is shameful or deceitful, but only those whose names are written in the Lamb's book of life.'[475] In other words, those who rebel against God and reject His gift never make it back to Him. God warns men to avoid the second death. The snake assures mankind that he will surely not die. God never changes. Neither does the lying snake.

Satan continues with his deceptions at man's expense. He deceived the Egyptians. He deceived the Babylonians. He deceived the Assyrians and the Medo-Persians. With their wooden gods and reinvented goddesses, the snake deceived the Greeks and the Romans. Then the serpent shed its skin again and was introduced by The Prophet as God. With a new god came a new covenant. And, with the help of a foreign god, an uneducated thief led the whole world astray. At his direction, human sacrifice (murder) has been transformed from a once-forbidden action into a newly required religious service. Imagine the power of a god who requires men to kill as a duty and service to their faith. This lesson began and ended with Abraham. He was tested, but he never killed to demonstrate his measure of faith. The snake had a better idea. As a measure of faith, prove your alliance to the cause and murder those who disbelieve.

Men know that God provided the Lamb for sacrifice. He did so two millennium ago. Abraham might have been willing to sacrifice his only son, but God did not and does not require of men such a practice. Thanks to the single act of sacrifice and offering, the ransom has been paid. But the snake has a ferocious appetite for flesh and an unquenchable thirst for blood. His people see ransom as a way of life.[420] The command is not a metaphor, and it remains a duty of the worshiper. Most think that they know what

The Prophet

a snake looks like. Only the original murderer would make this a means of worship. Murder, ransom, battle, and war – these are the duties of the men and women who listen to and abide by the poison of the snake. They number into the billions. They do not know the Lamb.

Evil has become good. Killing in god's name has become the obligation of a nation and its entire kingdom. They fight non-believers and hypocrites not necessarily because they like it, but because the foreign god has decided that he knows what is best for them.[370] There is no explanation, other than the fog of delusion,[514] as to how a murderous thief[9] could say the things that itching ears want to hear and turn an entire nation into a gang of ruthless thugs. Yet, we live in a world that has succumbed to the consciously deaf and blind who ask the ridiculous question "Why?" every time one of The Prophetiers performs as instructed. Recently, another round of Why's came out of Boulder Colorado when multiple people were murdered while they shopped or worked at a grocery store. Should the world expect a different result from angry men and women who are encouraged to kill at will and gain bonus points toward their entry into paradise? Is there a hidden meaning in the directive to 'snipe the necks' of those who refuse to follow The Prophet's laws? The answers are unchanged and always the same – the foreign god knows what is best for the Sniper while the Sniper knows not. Once the reader understands that this is a comparison of the foreign god to God, this apparent contradiction in the characterizations of God is no contradiction at all. The comparison is between the attributes of God and the attributes of the murderer. It cannot be said enough or over-emphasized, that those who know God understand that killing 'as a service to God' is committed only by those who do not know God.[202]

The Bible speaks of two vines that originated with the man known as *Abram* and *Abraham*. Abram impregnated his wife's Egyptian slave *Hagar*. From this ill-advised union was born the vine of *Ishmael*. From this vine are a people whose "hand will be against everyone and everyone's hand against him, and he (they) will live in hostility toward all his brothers."[115] This is not the lineage of royalty. Royalty came from the covenant that God made through *Isaac*, the son of *Abraham* and *Sarah*. This is the vine from which produced kings of nations - royalty.[113] God's covenant, His inheritance, was passed through Isaac's vine to 'Joseph, the husband of Mary, of whom was born Jesus, who is called Christ.'[322] He is the Prince of princes and King of kings – royalty. This is the vine of covenant and inheritance. From Moses to David and from David to John and Paul, the succession of prophets agreed on this vine and its post-ascension inclusion of the Gentiles. Ishmael's vine has also held true to the Word. From that vine was born The

Prophet. And from lessons of The Prophet men have been led to live in hostility toward all their brothers. The hostility toward each other is sufficiently demonstrated today in Afghanistan. While their hostility is focused on God's elect (Christians and Jews)[241] the written Word accurately portrays them as being against *all* their brothers.

God utilizes His prophet, John, to tell us that God has two witnesses. These two witnesses would be His Son and His Spirit. The two are in complete agreement. They speak and act as one. The Spirit does not contradict the Son and the Son does not contradict the Spirit. Neither contradicts God. All we know of God comes from the prophets who were driven by the Spirit of God.[350] And, without error, Jesus was given the Spirit of God at His baptism.[547] After 1,400 years of prophecy and approximately 42 prophets, there is no biblical contradiction. The two different colors of the Roman robes draped over Jesus at the time of His torture and murder are purposeful. They accurately portray the colors of the harlot and the land in which she was born. Thanks to the overwhelming ignorance of her Roman roots, wooden trophies depicting Rome's favorite form of crowd control can be found worldwide. The Romans are obviously proud of their treatment and ultimate control over Jesus.

One might point out what seems to be contradiction between the KJV and the NIV versions of the Bible in Revelation 13:1. Reading both, it becomes obvious that the devil and John stood on the shore *together*. There are a few other examples, but this highlights the point. The words might vary, but the testimony is accurate. What, then, do we make of The Prophet who showed up 500 years after God's prophets laid down their pens, dismissing God and dismissing everything called God? What do we make of the man who changed the laws and the set times? What do we make of the man who instituted stealing, killing, and destroying as methods of worship? And what do we make of the antichrist prophet who denied that God was a Father, denied that Jesus was God's Son and that he, The Prophet, was the foremost to serve God? What legitimate prophet of God does such things? Does a faithful and true prophet of God teach that the Word of the prophets before him was in error? Consider the following...

> "The Bible speaks of many of the prophets of God as committing the most heinous sins; it speaks of Abraham as telling lies and casting away Hagar and her son; it speaks of Lot as committing incest with his own daughters; it speaks of Aaron as making a calf for worship and leading the Israelites to its worship; it speaks of David as committing adultery with Uriah's wife; it speaks of Solomon as worshiping idols; but the [clear book] accepts none of these statements, definitely rejects most of them and

clears these prophets of the false accusations against them. The unlearned Prophet... swept away the errors which were a blot on the face of prophethood." [230]

There is no mistaking what is written here. There is no room for misinterpretation. For The Prophet and his Prophetiers, Moses' written testimony about Abraham casting away Hagar and Ishmael[548] was 'a blot on the face of prophethood.' By changing biblical testimony, just 21 Chapters into Genesis, The Prophet has set himself apart from the rest. In this case, such a separation should not be deemed *trustworthy and true*. History dictates which testimony is authentic and divinely inspired. Still, the man and his movement are celebrated annually in the White House. And this goes unnoticed how? How could this happen without reasonable checks and balances? There is only one reasonable explanation for the ongoing exploits of an antichrist prophet and people who have caused such tremendous damage over the centuries. The whole world has been led astray by the spirit and flesh of the dragon.

After 14 centuries of terror and the mayhem that accompanies war, the Prophetiers have surrounded and now occupy Jerusalem. With wanton indiscretion,[413] The Prophetiers steal with impunity,[405] rape those their right hands possess,[416] murder with righteous arrogance,[393] and destroy in the name of *the Causer of Death*[383] – aka *the Destroyer*. If The Prophet is the perfect model for men, then the world is in for real trouble! As it is, mankind can now understand how women would prefer the love and grace of the legitimate model of perfection. It is fascinating to observe the oppressive, abusive, and intriguing character as he overrides man's understanding of law and love. In a world of such grand technological advances and a supposed philosophical progression, how could such behavior be condoned and encouraged? What has this man brought into our world that remotely even hints at tolerance and coexistence? Even his declarations of peace lack sincerity. Everyone knows the honest answers, but few are willing to acknowledge them. The answers were written long before The Prophet lived. They are bold and brazen. God's prophets warned about this man in ancient, prophetic writing. Multiple writers, those whose pens were driven by the Spirit of God, warned the world about his appearance. Isaiah called him *Lucifer*. Daniel called him *the little horn, the man of intrigue* and *the king who exalted himself*. Paul called him *the man of lawlessness*. John called him *the antichrist, the beast out of the earth* and *the false prophet*. Through the Spirit of God and His influence with the prophets' pens, we have been duly warned about Satan's mouthpiece, his deceit, and his massive military abilities. He is much more than just *another* false prophet of God. He is *the* false prophet of God. We have been given the names that he would use, and he has used them. We have been given the things he would say, and he has said them. We have been given the things he would do, and he has done them. We have been warned about the people he would deceive and the callous nature they would rely upon to institute punishment and inflict it upon others. They have done those very things. He has managed to fool even the most loyal of God's elect – something most would consider impossible.[335] For many of the elect, for many readers, Lucifer is not 'the man' described in Isaiah chapter 14, but a spiritual metaphor that was hurled to the earth long ago. Still, no man could or should ignore the written evidence telling us that Lucifer was a man.

    The Prophetiers accept his title and refer to him as *the Messenger*. They listen to his directives and follow his commands – even when it means murder. The written commands were his words. The Prophetiers worship him as the last prophet of God. They institute his changed laws, and they coerce others to obey them under the threat of harm, imprisonment, and/or death. They worship the childless god he introduced. They kill in his god's proper name, declaring that he is the greatest god! Even papal Rome and its entire hierarchy of religious followers recognize his god as God. They are given no choice in the matter as it has been anchored in their testimonial field guide.[19] According to the papacy's own written doctrine - anyone who rejects this teaching is to be ostracized as a heretical combatant. This is what happened when Roman gods could not stop the way of Christ. Instead, they manipulated His Words and ways to suit their own needs. God sees them. He knows what they've done. He tells them that they have received their reward in full.[549] They have no claim on the free Jerusalem above. Though she boastfully claims to be the bride of Christ, the harlotous nature of that religious body is awash in the adoration of foreign gods and the political intermingling of earthly kings. Through her actions, she has shown herself to be shameful and drunk on the madness poured out of a gold cup. Her colors of scarlet and purple display the prideful arrogance she has retained in her role as the biblical harlot. She might claim to be the bride of Christ, but her bed has been made with numerous kings. She rides the body of the beast in many ways but affirming that the Prophetiers "participate in the plan of salvation…"[19] is simply the utterings of a babbling drunk. Like so many drunkards, she has lost her ability to see clearly. She has lost her ability to reason clearly. And she has lost her ability to hear clearly. Her drunkenness is not a reference to alcohol, but a madness induced by the filth of her abominations. The wine she claims to be the actual blood of Christ is a fabrication of those whose 'consciences have been seared as with a hot iron.' For these reasons, the harlot will burn. She is set ablaze by the beast she rides.[550] This is her just reward for the many sins that she has piled up. And her sins are piled to heaven.[551] Like The Prophet, her history of killing in the name of God is well documented.

As for The Prophet, his proper name is literally interpreted to mean *war*. The interpretation of such damning evidence is left exclusively to the written testimony of an expert on the subject. He wrote...

> "This chapter is titled *[The Prophet]* and also *War*... this chapter shows that the punishment with which the disbelievers were threatened would be brought about by war... War is also a prelude to the spiritual awakening which is to be brought about by [the Prophetiers] a second time. [301]

For those who refuse to face reality and accept the answers to the ever-existing questions as to 'why' anyone would act as callously as the Prophetiers have been known to act, the explanation above is going to be a real gut-punch!

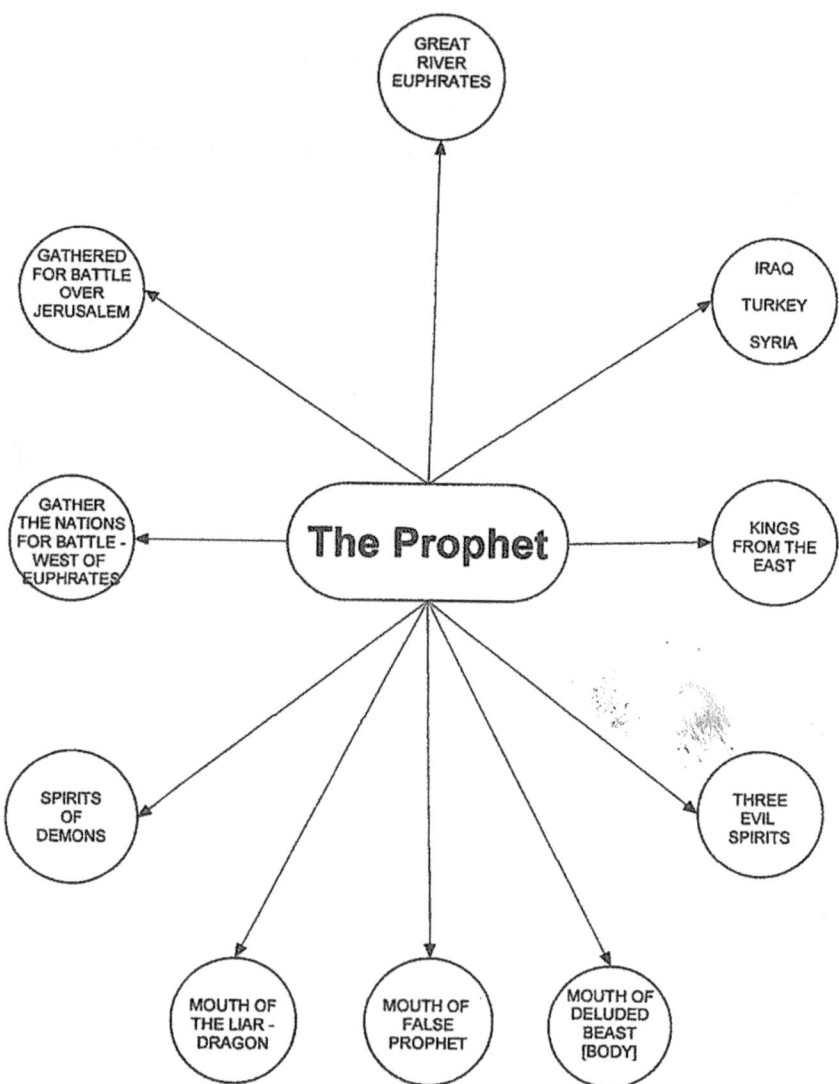

Chapter 18

A New Plague of Frogs

John's Warning About the False Prophet, His god & Army (Revelation 16:12-14)

Most know or have heard about the plague of frogs in the days of Moses. It was one of many plagues suffered by Egypt prior to the Exodus of the Hebrews. One upon another, the plagues became more and more devastating. The goal of the plagues was to pressure the ruler of Egypt into releasing the Hebrews from slavery. That series of horrors occurred nearly 3,500 years ago. What few people understand is that the ruler's magicians were able to duplicate the plague and bring about the frogs as well.[69] Some might wonder why men would bring such a curse upon themselves. What strategic advantage could this bring? It seems that by bringing about the frogs, they compounded their own troubles and miseries. The underlying lesson is that men can act in manners that bring about their own illnesses and spiritual demise. With the current pandemic proving to be the results of man's successful "gain of function" efforts, it lends credence to the thought that the world is unwilling to learn from the biblical lessons of plague. With man's conscious and willing departure from God, the plagues will inevitably continue.

Look to John's warning about the demonic spirits that looked like frogs in Revelation. This is something that does not originate in Egypt and the Nile but develops and culminates West of the great river Euphrates.[453] Like the frogs that plagued the Egyptians, the demonic spirits that plague men in the great day of God Almighty are the same evil spirits that dwell in the houses, courtyards, and fields surrounding today's Euphrates river. The land reeks of their deceit. It is a plague of man's own conjuring. Paul tells us that this plague comes upon men 'who are perishing, and they perish because they refuse to love the truth.'[510] Thanks in part to the unveiling of The Prophet, the demonic spirits performing miraculous signs in the day of apocalypse are no longer much of a mystery. These 'miraculous signs' are no more *miraculous* than the frogs that were conjured up by the magicians in Egypt and piled upon themselves. With all the evidence now pointing to The Prophet, his god, and his people – man's final plague is easily defined.

- What comes out of the mouth of the dragon…
  …is an evil spirit that looks like plague
- What comes out of the mouth of his speaking image…
  …is an evil spirit that looks like plague
- What comes out of the mouth of their disciples…
  …is an evil spirit that looks like plague
- The region that initially suffers this plague…
  …is the area surrounding the Euphrates River
- Surrounding the Euphrates river…
  …are the lands of Turkey, Syria, and Iraq
- The kings who reside to the East of the Euphrates…
  …are the kings of Persia
- Today…
  …they are gathering the kings of the whole world for the battle on the great day of God Almighty
- To be clear, the common factor that gathers them there…
  …is the plague that comes out of the mouth of the dragon, his false prophet, and the people they have deluded.

It takes little effort to remind the reader about the ongoing battles that have taken place in Syria, Iraq, Iran, and Afghanistan in the last three decades. They are driven by the evil spirits that have come out of the mouths of Satan, his speaking image, and their body of believers. These are a people who have vowed to wage war until the end.[402] Daniel's warning that 'war will continue until the end' has been realized and instituted by The Prophet who made certain that his people would fight in defense of the masquerading light. Mankind cannot reason with those who insist upon waging war in the name of their god. It's an old theme.

In October of 2011, Baraq Hussein announced the immediate removal of American troops from the region of the great river Euphrates. The vacuum created by the sudden departure of the U.S. Military was immediately filled by one of the most vicious combat groups ever assembled in the name of any god. Sadly, the murderous rampages that have transpired since the formation of that villainous group have not been limited to the geographical confines of the Euphrates River basin. Though the world wants us to believe that those butchers do not reflect the image of The Prophet, they are among the many billions who have remained defiant beneath the shadow of the swords and kill thinking they are doing a service to God. They cause terror. But, with The Prophet revealed, mankind is soon to understand the menacing nuisance that emerged from the region of the Euphrates is likely not the worst of mankind to plague the world. There is an entire nation of nuclear-armed people who have the same motivations, the same beliefs, and the same drive to fight until all religions align with their own. This is the plague that came from the mouth of the dragon and from the mouth of his speaking image.

In a world trying to recover from the horrors of a mishandled bio-weapon, men have come to know the power of fear and be reminded of the tortures of plague. But the harms instituted by the Wuhan Virus will seem miniscule and soon forgotten when compared to the chaos of the final plague – the release and revelation of the evil spirits that look like a frog. What started with the words of The Prophet and his god have become the acts of men who know such words as covenant. That covenant is the cause of war. With an army of two billion, the possession of nuclear weapons, and the support of a progressively unstable world, one might ask: "Who can make war against this beast?" John asked the question long ago. Man's final plague is found lying in wait, hidden within the covenant that the dragon has pressed upon those who refuse to love the truth.

Ronald B. Stetton

The Prophet

Chapter 19

Beheaded Because of Testimony to the Word

John's Warning About the Beheading of God's People (Revelation 20:4)

In what is likely the most inconvenient truth ever spoken, The Prophetiers have a voracious appetite for decapitation. This is no odd coincidence. It is by instruction. Promising to cause terror, the speaking image of the masquerading light directs his body to 'snipe the necks'[401] of those who disbelieve in his revelations and laws. This directive, to snipe the necks of their enemies, is consistent with the directive to kill the hypocrites, "though they are in Towers, raised high." These murderous lessons have been recorded and impressed upon the minds of many people over multiple centuries. Recognizing decapitation as a holy deed, The Prophetiers have demonstrated their eagerness to dutifully carry out the directive with their own hands.

It should be noted that those who "give testimony to Jesus and recognize the Word of God"[464] are specifically named as enemies of The Prophet and his people. Befriending Christians and Jews is strictly forbidden unless they do so for strategic purposes.[379] Once again, men are entitled to their opinions on this matter, but the historical examples, documented lessons, and continuing terror attacks amount to irrefutable evidence that Jesus' biblical nemesis has already made his mark upon the minds of men.

Ronald B. Stetton

The Prophet

Chapter 20

Peace and Safety

Paul's Warning About Those Who Falsely Espouse "Peace" (1 Thessalonians 5)

Until now, it was difficult to make sense out of Paul's warning that "destruction comes upon those who say, 'Peace and safety.'"⁵⁰⁰ Why would God promote the destruction of those who profess to peace? The answer to this riddle is now crystal clear. The Prophet's utilization of 'peace' is ultimately deceptive. Like sniping the necks of his enemies and the promise of death to those [hypocrites] in Towers raised high, 'destruction by peace' is the work of the stern-faced king and his tactics of righteous violence. Most reasonable people would agree that there is no such thing as 'righteous' terror. It exists only in the minds of the deluded. The reality of The Prophet's promised 'peace' is found trampled in the ashes of worthless treaties. It is buried under the bodies of billions of victims and crushed between the iron teeth of his kingdom's coercive madness. Ruins are scattered across the nations and once-thriving cities have been reduced to mounds of rubble.³⁹⁸ He has turned the land into a desert. This is the result of our world being subjected to the plagues of his never-ending war.

Note the greeting that has been adopted and exchanged between The Prophet's body of believers: *"Peace and security!"* they say. What began as a battlefield code-phrase between the Prophetiers has become the traditional greeting between members of The Prophet's opposing kingdom. It's a rouse – a manner and method of disingenuous 'peace' that his successors have used to advance their wartime schemes and destroy many. An inconvenient truth has almost nothing to do with man-made global warming or today's more inclusive distraction known as 'climate change.' At the center of man's inconvenient truth is the biblical character who instituted beheading as a service to God. He's an historical character, a man, who had eyes and a mouth that spoke boastfully. His personal example of sniping necks of his enemies is well documented.³⁵² The modeled behaviors of his followers reflect The Prophet's behavior and should no longer be dismissed as a surprise to mankind.

The Prophet's lessons about peace and security pertain only to those who accept his teaching as that of a prophet of God.³⁷⁶ Of course, his pledge of peace has failed to emerge and will forever remain an empty promise. The many sects of his teaching splintered shortly after his death and they, too, treat one another as hypocritical enemies. For those who are certain to protest such a statement, all that needs be uttered is 'Afghanistan.' When destruction falls upon those who say *peace and safety*, it falls because the peace and safety they espouse to is nothing of the sort. It's a poorly veiled lie.

The Prophet

Chapter 21

The Odds

What are the odds? What are the odds that Lucifer, the man who called himself *the star of piercing brightness that appears at the end of the night*, **is the same man who...**

- claimed to be the metaphorical son of God?
- declared that he ascended to the seven heavens?
- professed to have raised his throne higher than any of God's prophets?
- boasted of raising his throne higher than Jesus, the Son of the Living God?
- sits enthroned on the Temple Mount?
- declared himself to be the foremost to serve God?
- declared himself to be the last and most high of prophets?
- shook the earth in life and still shakes it in death?
- made kingdoms tremble in life and still makes them tremble in death?
- overthrew the world's cities and kingdoms in life and in death?
- would not let his captives go home – choosing to behead them instead?
- destroyed his land and killed his own people?

What are the odds? What are the odds that the man who called himself *Lucifer* **is the same man who...**

- subdued Sheba, Dedan, and the merchants of the Tarshish?
- spoke out against the Father and the Son?
- oppressed Christians and Jews for over 14 centuries?
- tried to change the set times from that of Christ (A.D.) to that of his own interests (A.H.)?

- attempted to change the Laws of God to the laws of his god?
- fulfilled all the things of *the little horn*?

What are the odds? What are the odds that the man who fulfilled all things of *the little horn* is the same man who...

- was a master of intrigue - making secret plans to do something awful?
- was a stern-faced king whose teaching and actions lack any hint of grace?
- caused astounding devastation - coming only to destroy?
- was driven by the power of a foreign god?
- offered 1,400 years of warfare that destroyed mighty men and holy people?
- destroyed many by adhering to his own twisted definition of peace?
- caused deceit to prosper and grow his membership by the billions for over 1,400 years?
- institutes his policies at the point of a sword while refuting coercion?
- considered himself to be superior to all other men and prophets?
- has taken his stand against Jesus - the Prince of princes and King of kings?

What are the odds? What are the odds that the man who fulfilled all things of *the stern-faced king* is the same man who...

- said unheard-of things against the God of gods?
- succeeded in building a military machine that currently numbers two billion people?
- succeeded in acquiring nuclear weapons and a consuming fire at the push of a button?
- has shown no regard for the Father and His Son?
- had no use for the desire of women, for he took nearly any woman or girl he chose?
- rejected the gods of his fathers for the god of the voices in his head?
- honored a god of fortresses - literal fortresses?

The Prophet

- honored a god unknown to his fathers before him?
- honored a new god with gold?
- honored a new god with silver?
- honored a new god with precious stones?
- honored a new god with costly gifts?
- attacked the mightiest fortresses, like the Twin Towers, with the help of a foreign god?
- greatly honors those who acknowledge him by making them rulers and kings?
- distributes the land at a heavy price - namely the lives and souls of men?
- in the end, will be the cause of the unthinkable and set the world ablaze?
- invaded many countries?
- invaded Jerusalem - the Beautiful Land?
- fulfilled Isaiah 30:25 with the destruction of the Towers and the people who worked in them?
- had Jerusalem delivered from his hand in May 1948 and again in June 1967?
- extended his power over Egypt, Libya, and Sudan?
- set out in a great rage to the north and to the east, destroying and annihilating many?
- pitched his royal tents among God's people at the Temple Mount in Jerusalem?
- fulfilled everything of *the king who exalted himself*?

What are the odds? What are the odds that *the king who exalted himself* is the same man who…

- introduced the covenant of the masquerading light?
- led a group who would trample Jerusalem years after his own death?
- became part the abomination that is currently a wing of the temple - at the Temple Mount?

- causes desolation on the Temple Mount by outlawing prayer to the God of Israel?
- caused the war between kingdoms to continue among men on earth?
- caused war to continue between Satan's kingdom and the kingdom of God?
- caused war to continue in Afghanistan, Pakistan, Sudan, Libya, Iran, Iraq, and Syria?
- caused war to continue as a foundational pillar of the movement he created?
- caused war to continue under a veil of peace?
- relies upon wartime tactics to support his ever-expanding control and influence on earth?
- introduced the covenant of the masquerading light (lightning) in the way of seven thunders?
- has put an end to the sacrifice and offering that is Jesus Christ and the cross?
- teaches others to seek help exclusively from the masquerading light?
- set up the abomination that causes desolation on the Temple Mount?

What are the odds? What are the odds that *the ruler* of Daniel 9:26-27 is the same man who...

- proclaimed to be the speaking image of the god he introduced?
- declared that his revelations were a nourishment - like the beverage of many hues of the bee?
- suggested that, like honey, his words were a healing for men?
- convinced billions of people to prostrate themselves five times a day and roar the sounds of seven thunders?
- first spoke the seven deceptive verses honoring the masquerading light?
- spoke the deceptive verses condemning Christians and Jews for believing in error?
- declared that his god is the master of the day of revenge?

The Prophet

What are the odds? What are the odds that the man who delivered *the seven thunders* is the same man who...

- orchestrated against God the grandest rebellion ever developed on earth?
- with his new and opposing laws, has proven himself to be the man of lawlessness?
- rejected and opposed God as the Father and Son?
- exalted himself over everything that is called God?
- exalted himself over everything that is worshiped as God – that being the biblical Word?
- set himself up in the temple of God, proclaiming himself to be God as the Lamp of Light?
- fulfilled all things of the man of intrigue?
- appeared in accordance with the work of Satan?
- appeared in accordance with every sort of evil listed in Revelation 21:8?
- appeared as the stern-faced king, lacking any hint of grace that is demonstrated by Christ?
- reinstituted the judgment and punishment of death at the hands of his recruits?
- negated Jesus' sacrifice and offering that stands between sinful men and justice?
- brought about the marks that are the image of Satan?
- twisted every sort of evil into acts of worship?
- deceives those who are perishing?
- taught his followers to greet one another with: "Peace and Security!"?
- refused to love the truth of the Father and the Son?
- delighted in the wickedness of stealing and killing and destroying?
- delighted in the wickedness of kidnapping, raping, and lying?
- delighted in the wickedness of idolizing the liar – the foreign god?
- fulfilled all things listed about the man of lawlessness?

What are the odds? What are the odds that *the man of lawlessness* is the same man who…

- denied the Father and the Son?
- is the speaking image of the liar?
- denied that Jesus is the Messiah, the Most High?
- fulfills the biblical definition of the antichrist?

What are the odds? What are the odds that the man who is *the antichrist* is the same man who…

- came out of the earth as flesh and blood – like the Lamb?
- spoke like a dragon?
- as the speaking image, exercised all the authority of the first beast – Satan?
- made the earth and its inhabitants worship the first beast – Satan?
- made the earth's inhabitants worship Satan, whose wounded Babylonian head has healed?
- made great and miraculous signs – something he calls "marks"?
- will likely be the *cause* of man's unthinkable final act – Mutual Assured Destruction
- already deceived most of the inhabitants of the earth?
- ordered his successors to gather the marks and assemble them as an image of his god?
- spoke like the god he introduced – the dragon?
- commanded his followers to kill anyone who refused to worship his god?
- commanded his followers to kill anyone who refused to worship him or his laws?
- forced everyone to act as he acted?
- forced everyone to believe as he believed?
- utilized a *faith balance* to buy and sell?
- is represented in name by the three Greek numerals penned by John?

What are the odds? What are the odds that the man who has proven to be *the beast out of the earth* is the same man who...

- is proven to be the literal thief of Ezekiel 38:10-13 and John 10:10?
- has been the instrument of terror used by Satan?
- set himself up on a wing of the temple?
- proclaims he is God as the lamp of light?
- broke away from the prophets before him, declaring their written testimony to be erroneous?

Once again, The Prophet and his most esteemed scholars make the claim that the written testimony of many of God's prophets was not guided by the Spirit of God but was penned in error or altered by the passing of time. And, as though that was not sufficiently vulgar, they argue that the world had changed, and God desired a new people and a new message. Coincidently, the man who fits the biblical definition of 'antichrist' took it upon himself to alert the world about God's new truth that all the prophets before him were mistaken, with Christians and Jews having taken the wrong paths. Apparently, God had good reason to mislead the Hebrews and mistakenly orchestrate their exodus from Egypt to Israel. And, in a like manner, The Prophet wanted the world to believe that God had good reason to hoodwink Christians over 600 years and lie about having had a Son. Although the absurdity of such claims is woefully obvious, ignorance and arrogance have infected and inflamed a lost and rebellious people. What started with lawless desert dwellers, The Prophet's rebellion has spread to infect some of the largest cities and nations on earth. The actions and statements of the antichrist prophet should not come as a surprise to those who know God. But, for those who do not know God, revealing the antichrist is going to be tragic and infuriating. How does one gently tell 2,000,000,000 people and nearly all the world's politicians that The Prophet is mentioned often within the books and letters of the Bible – with all mention being that of warning? The man who shook the earth and made kingdoms tremble during his life is about to do it again in his death. As before, he will accomplish these things through those he has led astray. Revealing the identity of the lawless prophet will certainly come with emotional and political turmoil. When the time comes, remember this; mountains of evidence and piles of prophetic truth will carry no weight and matter not to those who don't want to hear it.

The world knows this man; it knows his name and the name of his god. Nations know his people and the laws they have implemented under threats of murder, crucifixion, amputation, and imprisonment. Governments and ruling bodies have opened their doors to his slaves and warriors. They have but one objective: "... fight with them until there is no persecution and all religions are only for [The Prophet's god]."[402] As the past has proven, there is no rationalizing with Prophetiers. There will be the promise of coexistence, but the order stands – *fight them!* They have been commanded to fight until no other religion or governing body exists. They believe they are winning. Today's Progressives, those who do not know God, have made alliances with them. Within the fog of delusion is the consorted illusion that, somehow, The Prophet and his people are the persecuted ones. It was Barack Hussein who so eloquently phrased the misleading falsehood that the Prophetiers were being unjustly treated after the atrocities of 9/11 and that he "will stand with the [Prophetiers] should the political winds shift in an ugly direction."[552] Where will he stand when the unveiling occurs? How does one defeat the armed forces of two billion people who have managed to infiltrate every community and influence nearly every politician on the planet? Those who know the power and fury of Adolph Hitler's Nazi Germany understand how quickly these things can go bad. Hitler's armed forces consisted of only 14,000,000 soldiers and they had no nuclear weapons. The Prophet's number of foot soldiers is 130 times larger than was Hitler's Third Reich. With the Progressives standing with Barack Hussein, The Prophet's political allies boost that number by two-fold. They are nearly 250 times larger than the Nazi force that brought the world to its knees for seven-plus years. The Prophet's war is in its 1412th year (1443 by his count). That makes his forces the largest, longest lasting, and most ferocious army ever to inhabit the earth. John asks: "Who is like the beast? Who can make war against him?"[553] The Prophet is the beast. The only one who will successfully make war against The Prophet is… The Prophet. By the breath of His mouth, God has made the determination that The Prophet will bring about his own demise.

    Though the world knows his proper name, it is not mentioned in this book. It's not mentioned in the Bible either. Though the world knows his god's proper name, it is not mentioned in this book. It's not mentioned in the Bible either. Though the world knows his followers' name and the movement he founded, they're not mentioned in this book. They're not mentioned in the Bible either. Though the world is aware of the proper name of his collective laws, that name is not mentioned in this book. It's not mentioned in the Bible either. Of course, these proper names cannot be found within the Word of God. If God were to have given us these names, His prophetic Word could not have been realized and exist as today's truth. It is no different than the prophets of Old refraining from calling the promised Messiah His proper name – *Jesus*. Had they done so, Joseph and Mary would have met with an early demise. Given the ability to murder, men believe they hold a God-like power. But murder only demonstrates the power of the foreign god. As it stands, Jesus is the promised Messiah;[554] Mary and Joseph went on to have at least seven children after Jesus' birth;[555] and the man of lawlessness[556] has fulfilled his biblical role.

It matters not that these proper names cannot be found within the pages of the Word of God. He gives us all the other names, all the descriptions, all the actions, all the thoughts, and all the statements of The Prophet, his god, their followers, their political allies, and the collection of marks that gives them their deceptive guidance. Somewhere in the world, there may be a mathematician who could summarize the odds of one man who would introduce a masquerading god, thereby fulfilling the prophetic declarations made of them long before they ever appeared. There is no claim that such odds can be accurately assessed here. But, with the help of those who have traveled this path, there is an image as to what those odds might look like. The certainty is the mathematical impossibility that any one man could fulfill all these biblical warnings and *not* be the biblical nemesis he was promised to be.

So, what are the odds? What are the odds that the man who founded the world's largest rebellion against God is the biblical nemesis whose appearance was prophesied by God and His prophets? Most would likely state that calculating such odds is an impossible task. But is it? Consider the following entry about the Messiah from Josh McDowell's book *More Than A Carpenter*...

> [In regard to Jesus as the Christ] "...one could possibly find one or two prophecies fulfilled by other men, but not all sixty major prophecies and 270 ramifications...
>
> H. Harold Hartzler, of the American Scientific Affiliation, in the forward of a book by Peter W. Stoner writes: 'The manuscript for *Science Speaks* has been carefully reviewed by committee of the American Scientific Affiliation members and by the Executive Council of the same group and has been found, in general, to be dependable and accurate in regard to the scientific material presented. The mathematical analysis included is based upon principles of probability which are thoroughly sound, and Professor Stoner has applied these principles in a proper and convincing way.'[494] The following probabilities are taken from that book to show that coincidences have been ruled out by the science of probability. Stoner says that by using the modern science of probability in reference to eight prophecies, 'we find that the chance that any man might have lived down to the present time and fulfilled

all eight prophecies is 1 in 10^{17}.' That would be 1 in 100,000,000,000,000,000. In order to help us comprehend this staggering probability, Stoner illustrates it by supporting that 'we take 10^{17} silver dollars and lay them on the face of Texas. They will cover all the state - two feet deep. Now mark one of the silver dollars and stir the whole mass thoroughly, all over the state. Blindfold a man and tell him that he may travel as far as he wishes, but he must pick up one silver dollar and say that this is the right one. What chance would he have of getting the right one? He would have had just the same chance that the prophets would have had of writing these eight prophecies and having them all come true in any one man… 'Now these prophecies were either given by inspiration of God or the prophets just wrote them as they thought they should be. In such a case the prophets had just one chance in 10^{17} of having them come true in any man, but they all came true in Christ."[343]

In subsequent years, Professor Stoner concluded that Jesus fulfilling 48 biblical prophecies about the Messiah was 1 in 10^{157}. The math demonstrates that no man other than Jesus, the Christ, could have fulfilled the biblical prophecies written by the prophets. For there to be another like Jesus, who would fulfill *just* eight prophecies, he would have to stand in the face of and oppose the science of probability. What then might we conclude of the other 52 prophecies and the 270 ramifications of them that fulfilled these prophecies?

The reader need not attempt the math. This is intended to be an illustration – not a mathematical challenge. The illustration also applies to the biblical nemesis – he who has so many names and defined characteristics. The world can ask the same questions and apply the same or similar theory to him and his coincidental likeness to the historical character who satisfied the prophetic warnings of his appearance. Like Christ, the antichrist has multiple prophetic warnings written about him. Choosing just eight prophecies fulfilled by The Prophet would effectively demonstrate the *Silver Dollar over Texas* challenge that Professor Stoner presented. These are prophetic warnings that are specific to the evil man that is promised to appear and oppose Jesus. These are characteristics that the false prophet must accomplish in order to eliminate any doubt of his identity - according to the science of probability.

To keep it simple, let's just hold to the descriptions of Lucifer found in Isaiah 14. In that chapter, Isaiah warns the world about a man who takes on unique names, has unique thoughts, and woefully gains the world's attention. Consider the written and historical evidence that demonstrates how one lone antichrist, one man, has fulfilled every one of them.

1. He must take the name of *the morning star* (Isaiah 14:12)
   > The Prophet takes on this identity as *Al-Tariq*[310]

2. He must call his god *The Dawn* (Isaiah 14:12)
   > The Prophet gives this name to his god as *Al-Falaq*[317]

3. He must believe in his heart (and spill out his mouth)[216] that "I will ascend to heaven" (Isaiah 14:13)
   > The Prophet did so in his declaration of his *Midnight Journey*[284]

4. He must believe in his heart (and spill out his mouth) that "I will raise my throne above the stars of God" (Isaiah 14:13)
   > The Prophet said so in his declaration, "[God] has no son; so *I am the foremost to serve* (God)"[299]

5. He must believe in his heart (and spill out his mouth) that "I will sit enthroned on the mount of assembly, on the utmost heights of the sacred mountain" (Isaiah 14:13)
   > The Prophet fulfilled this in two manners:
   > First - He sits enthroned on the Temple Mount as part of the abomination that causes desolation
   > Second - He recognizes himself as a reflection of his god. "[Foreign god] is the light of the heavens and the earth. A likeness of his light is as a pillar on which is a lamp – the lamp is in a glass, the glass is as it were a brightly shining star..."[288] Just in case the reader missed this lesson the first time, the false prophet states here that he and his god have displaced the Father and son as *the Temple of God*[473]

6. He must believe in his heart (and spill out his mouth) that "I will ascend above the tops of the clouds..." (Isaiah 14:14)
   > The Prophet said so in his declaration, 'Then I was made to ascend to the lote-tree of the utmost boundary.' Included in this tale of his Midnight Journey, he passed above the sea of 'abundance,'[427] and then met many of the prophets, from Adam to Abraham, and a variety of angels as he passed through the seven heavens. After this [Gabriel] took him to the heavenly low tree *on the boundary of the heavens before the throne of [his god]*"[14]

7. He must believe in his heart (and spill out his mouth) that "I will make myself like the Most High" (Isaiah 14:14)

> The Prophet suggested such a thing in his declarations. When describing his god as *the Most High*, he reminds his followers that he is the foremost to serve and that he will be raised to the highest position a man can rise. To anchor this point, MMA narrates in the following manner: "The title of this chapter is taken from the injunction to The Prophet to glory his *Rabb, his nourisher to perfection, The Most High*, the indication clearly being that The Prophet himself would be raised to the highest position"[314]

8. He must be a man who shakes the earth and makes kingdoms tremble (Isaiah 14:16)

> History and current events verify that he did and still does both

9. He must be the man who made [his] world a desert (Isaiah 14:17)

> Just look at the nations that have adopted his marks. They are desolate in both a physical and spiritual sense. Thanks to his laws against lending, his nations have no growth aside from that which the desert bleeds – oil

10. He must be a man who has overthrown cities and whose armies continue to overthrow cities (Isaiah 14:17)

> As history tells it, The Prophet is bent on conquering. Though many wish it were different, the atrocious events of September 11, 2001, were like lightning (Satan) that originated from the East and was seen in the West. Satanic was the intent of murdering 3,000 people. Jesus appears under similar circumstances,[336] but His people will not be among those who *cause* the unthinkable. That role belongs to The Prophet and those he has deluded

11. He must be a man who would not let his captives go home. Daniel warned about the things this man might do to the Jews who settled in the deserts south of Jerusalem. By his own words, The Prophet has fulfilled this biblical prophecy:

> "Then the Prophet said, "These people have agreed to accept your verdict." [His ally] said, 'I judge that their warriors [men] should be killed and their children and women should be taken as captives.' The

Prophet said, 'You have given a judgment similar to [god's] judgment.'"557

According to scripts of his own people, the systematic murder of the Jewish men who made up the tribe of [those who disappointed] took an entire day. MMA records that 300 men were beheaded. The women and children taken captive.294 Others tell a more gruesome story.

> "During the night, trenches sufficient to contain the dead bodies of the men were dug across the marketplace of the city. In the morning, [the Prophet] himself a spectator of the tragedy, commanded that male captives be brought forth in companies of five or six at a time. Each company as it came up was made to sit down in a row on the brink of the trench destined for its grave, there beheaded, and the bodies cast therein… The butchery, begun in the morning, lasted all day, and continued by torchlight till the evening. Having thus drenched the marketplace with the blood of seven or eight hundred victims, and having given command for the earth to be smoothed over their remains, [The Prophet] returned from the horrid spectacle to solace himself with the charms of Rihana, whose husband and all her male relatives had just perished in the massacre."344

The Prophet participated in the beheadings of hundreds of people, enslaved women and children, and forced one of his victim's widows to be his sexual slave – relieving him of the tensions of a rather strenuous day. No, he did *not* let his captives go home. Is this the means by which men are to be measured? Can this behavior be the very best that mankind can hope for - the *Model of Perfection*? Is this the example we hope for in our sons? Is this the model of a man that we pray our daughters might marry? How can such a set of circumstances be taken for something good when her husband falls at the hands of a murderer and all her male relatives fall victims to beheading, and The Prophet then 'found solace' with the 'charms' of this freshly widowed bride? One can only imagine just how freely Rihana gave up her 'charms.' Since when has a bloodthirsty, murderous thief and rapist become the 'foremost to serve God' and 'raise men from the depth of vice and immorality to the height of purity and perfection'?558 This is the very meaning of delusion,513 with mankind being turned on its head and accepting bitter ugliness as the sweetness that is God; even confusing evil for good! This is simply awful! Those who refuse to love the truth and delight in this kind of wickedness promote war-like behavior by gnashing their teeth and threatening to cancel anyone who dares to drag this darkest of evils into the light that is God and His perfect Word. No longer do men have to ask the ridiculous question as to 'why' men act as hideous beasts when a Prophetier successfully executes their duties in never-ending war. The world will now know the evil and invalid motivations behind such maniacal behavior. They do so because The Prophet told them to do so. After 1,400 years of such 'perfect behaviors,' it is reasonable to assume that no man or woman is safe when shopping for groceries, eating out, going to concerts or working in Towers raised high. The fascinating thing behind these events are the people on the sidelines who have a death-grip on the P.C. approach and refuse to call these events what they are – the actions of callous warriors. For those intent on pointing a finger of blame on mental illness, they must now point that finger directly at The Prophet. Mental illness would certainly be a disqualifier when searching for the model of perfection. The evil that hides behind worldly ignorance, cultural arrogance, and adulterous politics is nothing less than astounding!

Simply stated, The Prophet is the man who shook the earth and made kingdoms tremble, the man who made the world a desert. He overthrew its cities and would not let his captives go home. We watch in paralyzing horror as his dedicated soldiers act as he acted in their lethal desires. Revealing this maniacal fraud finally brings the dismissive madness to an end.[505]

In the Luciferian examples above, the reader can see how 11 prophetic warnings were fulfilled by a desert-born Ishmaelite. He was a self-appointed 'prophet of God' who founded a new movement with a new god who was invented in a region that is 900 miles south of Jerusalem. Within these warnings alone, the odds as to the identity of the man of lawlessness skyrocket past the eight prophecies about Jesus that made Him the prophesied Messiah by a probability of 1 in 100,000,000,000,000,000. That is 1 in 10^{17}. These are just the first 11 warnings that can be found in a single chapter of God's Word, and they were all fulfilled by the same 'prophet' who 'found solace in the charms of Rihana' after murdering her husband and all other male relatives. Applying Stoner's science of probability, it is safe to say that fulfilling 11 out of 11 prophetic warnings exceeds the example of Jesus fulfilling eight out of eight biblical prophecies about His coming. Therefore, based on this example alone, the odds of The Prophet being Jesus' biblical nemesis already exceeds the probability that Jesus is the Messiah. Remember Texas... two feet deep in silver dollars. Walk for days in any direction and reach into the pile. How many times would a man make this attempt before he pulled out the marked coin? The odds make it reasonably impossible. The science of probability tells us that Jesus is who He says He is – He is the Son of God. The sobering reality is that the science of probability also tells us that The Prophet is the man who fulfilled the eleven prophecies of Isaiah 14. The greater reality is that there is a list of at least 65 prophecies, 54 more than were illustrated here, that have been fulfilled by this same deceitful man.

God has proven Himself to be everything He says He is – He's God. He has done so in the way of His Son, the Prince of princes - Jesus. He has done so in the way of his Son's nemesis, The Prophet, who is now proven to be the false prophet. The world now has access to that which it has longed for – we now have proof of God.

"Remember this, fix it in mind, take it to heart, you rebels. Remember the former things, those of long ago; I am God, and there is no other; I am God, and there is none like me. I make known the end from the beginning, from ancient times, what is still to come, I say: My purpose will stand, and I will do all that I please. From the East I summon a bird of prey; from a far-off land, a man to fulfill my purpose. What I have said, that will I bring about; what I have planned, that will I do. Listen to me, you stubborn hearted, you who are far from righteousness. I am bringing my righteousness near, it is not far away; and my salvation will not be delayed. I will grant salvation to Zion, my splendor to Israel" – Isaiah 47:8-13

From the east, God has summoned His bird of prey… That bird appears to be The Prophet and his people. From a far-off land, God has summoned a man to fulfill his purpose… That man appears to be His Son. Though the liar masquerades as God, only God can tell the end from the beginning. Satan's knowledge is finite, his time is limited. And just as God promised, the masquerading light and his mouthpiece have caused their promised terror.[158] God is God and there is no other; God is God and there is none like Him. For God's own namesake he delayed His wrath; for the sake of His praise, He held things back from the fallen one, so as not to cut him off. See, he has refined Satan, though not as silver; He has tested Satan in the furnace of affliction. For His own sake, *for His own sake*, [God] has done this. How could he let Himself be defamed? He has not yielded His glory to another.[559]

A disaster has fallen upon the liar. A calamity has fallen upon him that he cannot ward off with ransom; a catastrophe he could not foresee has suddenly come upon him. We see him for who he is. His images of moon and star cannot save him from what's coming. The power of the flame has been developed, packaged, placed, and remains at the ready. Its unleashing is imminent.[156] This is the flame that God makes come out of Satan.[82] This is the flame that The Prophet 'causes' to fall from heaven to earth in full view of men.[450]

Those who trust Jesus and hold to His commands need not fear this flame. Those who side with God and find the adoration of the Queen of Heaven to be detestable need not fear the fire. Those who saw the face of God turn back to them after the atrocities of World War II need not fear the tempest. Like Shadrach, Meshach, and Abednego – the last of God's people will be captured up, untouched by the flames caused by the speaking image of the dragon. God's people wait for that moment, the instantaneous flash, the twinkling of the eye that has been so long in coming. Immune to the flames, the saints will meet our Lord face to face - He who was pierced by the sword, and together live an everlasting life in the Light of His Temple.

God is God and the masquerading light is not Him. God is God and there is no other. God will not yield his glory to another—particularly not to the foreign god and his speaking image.

The grace of the Lord Jesus be with God's people. Amen. Revelation 22:21

Professor Stoner's Science of Probability is likely a bit above the understanding of most who do not excel in mathematics. But there is an easier way to grasp the odds of these men fulfilling prophetic testimony. For example: If one was to mark three marbles as 1 - 2 - 3 and pull them blindly out of a bag, the chances would be 1 in 6 that they would come out in the order of 1 - 2 - 3. The possible order could be any one of:

$$1-2-3$$
$$1-3-2$$
$$2-1-3$$
$$2-3-1$$
$$3-1-2$$
$$3-2-1$$

Applying this simple example to prophetic names, descriptions, actions, and accomplishments – the odds can be easily determined. The only difference is that the bag now contains 65 marbles…

PROPHECY	FULFILLMENT ODDS
1. Morning Star (Isa 14:12)	Qur'an 86:1-3 1 in 1
2. Son of the dawn (Isa 14:12)	Qur'an, chapter 113 1 in 2
3. Ascend to heaven (Isa 14:13)	Qur'an 17:1, note 1a, p. 563 1 in 6
4. Throne above God's Stars (Isa 14:13)	Qur'an 43:81 1 in 24
5. Enthroned on Mt of Assembly (Isa 14:14)	Qur'an 17:1, note 1a, p. 563 1 in 120
6. Like the Most High (Isa 14:14)	Qur'an, chapter 87, Intro 1 in 720
7. Makes kingdoms tremble (Isa 14:16)	Historical 1 in 5,040
8. Overthrew cities & kill captives (Isa 14:17)	Historical 1 in 40,320
9. Destroyed land & killed people (Isa 14:20)	Historical 1 in 362,880
10. Mouth that spoke boastfully (Da 7:8)	Qur'an 43:81, 33:21-22 1 in 3.6×10^6
11. Subdued three kings (Da 7:24)	Historical 1 in 4×10^7
12. Spoke against the Father & Son (Da 7:25)	Countless, 43:81 1 in 5×10^8
13. Oppress Christians & Jews (Da 7:25)	Historical, Qur'an 5:51 1 in 6×10^9
14. Try to change A.D. to A.H. (Da 7:25)	Historical, Qur'an 1:85 1 in 9×10^{10}

15. Try to change the Laws (Da 7:25)	Historical, Qur'an 33:40, 40a 1 in 10^{12}
16. Strengthened by foreign god (Da 8:24)	Historical, 3:81-83, 81a-83a 1 in 2×10^{13}
17. Causes astounding devastation (Da 8:24)	Historical, Qur'an 5:33 1 in 3.5×10^{14}
18. Destroy mighty & holy people (Da 8:24)	Historical, Qur'an 8:39, 5:33 1 in 7.5×10^{15}
19. Cause deceit to fool billions (Da 8:25)	Historical, Qur'an 1:1-7, a-7a 1 in 1.4×10^{17}
20. Considers himself superior (Da 8:25)	Countless, Qur'an 33:21 1 in 3×10^{18}
21. By 'peace' destroy many (Da 8:25 KJV)	Qur'an 61:9, 5:33, 2:279a 1 in 6×10^{19}
22. Stand against Jesus (Da 8:25)	Countless, Qur'an 4:171, 43:81 1 in 1.3×10^{21}
23. Distribute plunder (Da 10:24 & Eze 38:10-13)	Historical, Qur'an 8:1, 1a 1 in 3×10^{22}
24. King who exalted himself (Da 11:36)	Qur'an 43:81 1 in 7×10^{23}
25. Blaspheme the God of gods (Da 11:36)	Qur'an: Too much to list 1 in 2×10^{25}
26. Been successful for 1,400 years (Da 11:36)	Historical 1 in 5×10^{26}
27. No regard for gods of fathers (Da 11:37)	Qur'an 2:170 1 in 1.5×10^{28}
28. Exalt himself above all other gods (Da 11:37)	Qur'an 24:35, 35a 1 in 4×10^{29}

The Prophet

29.	Honors god of fortresses (Da 11:38)	Qur'an 85:3, 3a, p. 1197 1 in 10^{31}
30.	Introduced god unknown to fathers (Da 11:38)	Qur'an 2:170 1 in 3.5×10^{32}
31.	Honors his god with GOLD (Da 11:38)	Qur'an, chapter 43 1 in 10^{34}
32.	Honors his god with silver (Da 11:38)	AMoH, 29:8, note 6, p. 302 1 in 3.5×10^{35}
33.	Honors with precious stones (Da 11:38)	Qur'an, 2:149, 149a, p. 67 1 in 10^{37}
34.	Honors with costly gifts (Da 11:38)	Qur'an, chapter 8 1 in 4×10^{38}
35.	Attack the mightiest of fortresses (Da 11:39)	History, Qur'an 4:78 1 in 1.4×10^{40}
36.	Helped by a foreign god (Da 11:39)	Qur'an 1:4 1 in 5×10^{41}
37.	Makes rulers over the land (Da 11:39)	Qur'an 4:58-59 1 in 2×10^{43}
38.	Distribute the land at a price (Da 11:39)	Qur'an 8:69, 2:191, 191a-d 1 in 7×10^{44}
39.	[His army] has invaded Jerusalem (Da 11:41)	Historical 1 in 3×10^{46}
40.	He has extended power over Egypt (Da 11:42)	Historical 1 in 10^{48}
41.	Libyans & Sudanese in submission (Da 11:43)	Historical 1 in 4.5×10^{49}
42.	He [his army] destroyed many (Da 11:44)	Historical 1 in 2×10^{51}

43. Abomination on Temple Mount (Da 11:45)   Historical
    1 in 8×10^{52}

44. Man who introduced new covenant (Da 9:27)   Multiple, Qur'an 2:27, 27a
    1 in 3.5×10^{54}

45. End of [gift of God], middle of seven (Da 9:27)   Qur'an 1:4
    1 in 1.6×10^{56}

46. Temple – abomination of desolation (Da 9:27)   Historical
    1 in 7×10^{57}

47. Introduced book of seven thunders (Rev 10:2)   Qur'an 1:1-7
    1 in 3.5×10^{59}

48. Compares his words to "honey" (Rev 10:9-10)   Qur'an 16:68-69
    1 in 1.7×10^{61}

49. Man of lawlessness (2The 2:3)   Qur'an 33:40, 40a
    1 in 8×10^{62}

50. Opposes Father & Son (2The 2:4)   Qur'an 43:81
    1 in 4×10^{64}

51. Exalts himself over all that is God (2The 2:4)   Qur'an 87, Introduction
    1 in 2×10^{66}

52. Is a liar (1 John 2:22)   Countless, Qur'an 24:35, 43:81
    1 in 8×10^{67}

53. Denies that Jesus is the Christ (1 John 2:22)   Qur'an 43:81
    1 in 4×10^{69}

54. Denies the Father & the Son (1 John 2:22)   Qur'an 43:81
    1 in 2×10^{71}

    Was flesh and blood like the Lamb…   Historical
    Too vague…

55. …but spoke like [for the] dragon (Rev 13:11)   Countless, Qur'an 33:45-46
    1 in 1 in 10^{73}

The Prophet

56.	Exercised authority of dragon (Rev 13:12)	Qur'an 4:69, 33:40 (a) 1 in 7 X 10^{74}
57.	Made people worship his god (Rev 13:12)	Qur'an 61:9, 8:39 1 in 4 X 10^{76}
58.	Performed the miracles [ayahs] – (Rev 13:13)	Qur'an 13:38-39 1 in 2 X 10^{78}
	Causes fire to fall upon men (Rev 13:13)	Partially fulfilled, Qur'an 13:35 Incomplete
59.	Deceives men, worships false god (Rev 13:14)	Qur'an 33:40 1 in 10^{80}
60.	Set up the little book (Rev 13:14)	Multiple, Qur'an 6:19 1 in 8 X 10^{81}
61.	Gave breath [spoke] the little book (Rev 13:15)	Multiple, Qur'an 75:17 (a) 1 in 5 X 10^{83}
62.	Directs his own to kill opponents (Rev 13:15)	Historical, Qur'an 47:4 1 in 3 X 10^{85}
63.	Force [ayahs] by belief & deeds (Rev 13:16)	Historical, Qur'an 66:6 1 in 2 X 10^{87}
64.	Buys & Sells on a Faith Scale (Rev 13:17)	AMoH, Ch 22, rule 5, p. 240 1 in 10^{89}
65.	Calligraphic, (3) Greek Numerals (Rev 13:18)	Historical, Current Symbol 1 in 8 X 10^{90}

Then there are the prophecies about Gog, Magog, the Valley of Hamon Gog, and Hamonah that have been fulfilled by The Prophet and his Prophetiers. The Valley of the crowded place of The Prophet matches the name they have given it. Hamonah, the city that is the crowded place and mother of all towns adopts the name. There is no doubt that he is the most influential man in the territories between lower Meshech and Tubal. Being the metaphorical son of the dragon, he would qualify as the prince – awaiting the ultimate throne. He leads an army of billions, most of which live in the territories of Persia, Cush, Put, and Gomer – with Beth Togarmah being their northern allies. He is the man, and his fortresses are the people who demonstrate their hatred against Israel and the Israelis. The

Israelis (Jews) were initially attacked by The Prophet while they resided in Sheba and Dedan after fleeing the Roman intrusions in 70 A.D. The Prophet is the man who plundered these unguarded people and admittedly robbed the caravans that carried the wares of the merchants of Tarshish. He's the "one" that God spoke about through His prophets. He is the lone, antichrist prophet to reject and oppose the testimony that had been held sacred in the writings of prophets who lived 600 to 1,900 years before him. The incredible accuracies of Scripture even include the name of The Prophets home, *Hamonah*, as it reflects his assertion that it is the crowded place (hordes)[583] and mother of all towns. That argument is validated by the meaning of *the Valley of Hamon Gog* (the Valley of Bakkah) as being that of an earthly hell – affectionately said to be a nurturing place, with The Prophet comparing the fires of hell to a mother nursing her baby. It is the Valley of Hamon Gog that stops the noses of those who travel east. They travel east because it is obligatory that every able-bodied Prophetier make the journey at least once in their lifetime. In the end, John tells us that Satan, Gog (The Prophet), and Magog (the Prophetiers) "will go out to deceive the nations in the four corners of the earth… to gather them for battle… surrounding the camp of God's people." The Prophet and his Prophetiers have done those very things!

There will still be many who reject the truth of God because it is simply too dreadful to accept. Rebellion has claimed its toll. Billions have been led astray. Over the centuries, tens of billions have been led astray. But, for those who still cannot wrap their heads around the enormity of the odds, there are a few simple truths that seal the argument. The Prophet is antichrist by the very definition of the term. He is lawless by his own admission. He readily states that he changed God's 'outdated' Laws. He has attempted to change the set times. He subdued Sheba, Dedan, and the Tarshish. He boasts of being a thief. His own testimony has him oppressing his neighbors – primarily Christians and Jews. He has given himself the title of God as *the Morning Star* while exalting himself above everything that is worshiped as God. The Prophet is the man who shook the earth and made kingdoms tremble. He is the very image of the murderous god he introduced – even instructing his loyalists to murder anyone and everyone who opposes them. And the calligraphic illustration of his name incorporates the three Greek numerals penned by John as the beast out of the earth. The evidence is in. The Prophet has played his biblical role.

The Prophet

Chapter 22

The Whole World Waits

We Have Arrived

The whole world waits. We wait to see if there is a God and if His biblical Word did, indeed, give us the accurate end of this generation of man from his meager beginning. Written upon the earth is the story of man as it is told by the Word, the Son of God, He who was with God in the beginning. Mankind has been given a prophetic compilation of over 60 books and letters, written by more than 40 authors who lived and died some 1,400 years apart. They are all in agreement about God, the story of man, and the diabolical plagues that now cover the world in Satanic lies. But the Word is the foundation of truth – formed by God's faithful when they wrote about future events, which then become reality. Can there be any explanation, other than the driving force in the Spirit of God, to explain how so many men, over such a long period of time, could all be so accurate in their prophetic writing? Who or what, other than God, could have guided their pens in such a perfect manner?

Now come the questions of rebellion. What fog of delusion is so thick that it has kept men from seeing that which has been so obvious for so long? How is it that so many people can accurately recite God's Word and warnings about His nemesis, yet these same people choose to make the conscious decision to shut their eyes and cover their ears when confronted by the truths of God and His prophetic perfection?

Those who know Jesus acknowledge that another man, a villainous thief, would appear sometime after Jesus' departure from this earth. This is absolute. God's prophets delivered the many names that the villain would adopt and hide behind, accepting royal titles that he would present as his own. The biblical Word describes many things The Prophet would say, and it even offers the details about specific mannerisms he would demonstrate while he delivered the original beast's covenant. Prophet upon prophet wrote about Lucifer's predetermined accomplishments of dread and his stunning ability to deceive. Author after author warned us about the man who would oppose God's chosen people as 'those upon whom wrath is brought down'[241] and oppose Jesus' followers as 'those who go astray.'[241] Yet, men, even some of the elect, refuse to accept the prophecies which have already been fulfilled. They consciously choose to reject the evidence. Why? The answer is that some traditions of men include a pre-determined set of events, a pathway, that seemingly satisfy the prophecies. The result of such traditional thinking is now obvious. It lends itself to cause blurry vision and diminished hearing. These are the adopted weaknesses of mankind that helped achieve the purpose of God. He made it clear that He would reveal the man of lawlessness only when He knew it was the proper time.

Since John penned the warning about the prophet who would deny the Father and His Son, the world has become accustomed to watching for the antichrist. They have invented false scenarios and distracting images of such a beast. But the scenarios must now yield to a man who speaks as the devil spoke – with deceit in his heart. He is the mouthpiece of the liar who convinced many that God has no Son - appearing after Jesus' selfless act of sacrifice. It seems reasonable to assume that any supposed prophet of God who would appear after Christ's earthly presence and boastfully proclaim that "God has no Son!" would immediately be recognized as the antichrist or, at least, be categorized within that large category. But that did not happen. When such a man appeared in the deserts south of Jerusalem and boastfully erupted with his mission statement that "The Beneficent [God] has no son..." the world made exceptions and allowances. Many in the West now bow to the East. They travel to the East. They worship the East. They cannot see the antichrist nature of the cause. But those who travel to the East are about to have their noses stopped. By the very definition of *antichrist*, The Prophet can be nothing less than a leading member of that lawless club!

Still, the world awaits another

The Word of God clearly teaches that those who kill in the name of God do not know God. They do not know the Father and His Son. Does the world understand this simple fact? In these days of mourning over many mass killings, it is worth repeating: **Those who kill, thinking they are doing a service to God, do not know God!** But history has served up a unique character, an undeniable antichrist, who sees it differently. His teaching is wholly opposed to God's Word. According to The Prophet, anyone who makes mischief in the land by breaking his newly formed laws must be murdered – not simply killed but specifically *murdered!* This sounds like the beverage of many hues that are a healing to mankind... This nourishing directive has landed upon billions of ears over hundreds of years. The Prophet urges his people to kill anyone who is at war with him or his god. And who's at war with them? The answer is simple. Anyone who disobeys their new laws is at war with The Prophet and his god. As though his coercion was not convincing and did not go far enough, he utilizes the threat of cancellation upon his people and dangles paradise just out of reach for those who refuse to use their own (right) hands to institute the punishment of death upon the supposed wrong-doer. Ultimately, The Prophet uses the false pretense of 'defending the faith' to justify killing in the name of God.

Still, the world awaits another

Isaiah writes a revealing tale of mockery toward the man who thinks he can unseat the Christ. Isaiah taunts The Prophet and lets him know that the grave awaits him. In his Spirit-driven glee, we can almost see Isaiah grinning as he tells the liar that his ruse has not gone unnoticed. With maggots spread beneath him and a blanket of worms spread above, The Prophet is taunted by the voices of the dead who mock him for being powerless in his death. Once a supposed *star of piercing brightness that appears at the end of the night*, The Prophet is now revealed to be lower than dirt - literally. A bright shining star he is no longer! Knowing that the Father would not mock His own Son, He who pleases the Father, the reader can easily determine that *the morning star* mocked by Isaiah is a satanic character. Jesus' place is at the right hand of God – not immersed in the grave amongst maggots and worms. The evident mockery of this 'morning star,' Lucifer, is directed exclusively at the man who made kingdoms tremble. As he would tell it, he is the speaking image of the god he calls *The Dawn*. The speaking image of the liar, commonly known as Lucifer (Latin for *morning star*), boasts of being the foremost to serve and the closest thing to ever be considered the son of the Dawn. But, because he denies the Father and the Son, he reduces the reference and significance of the term 'son' to hold meaning that is little more than a metaphor. Lucifer denies Jesus Christ as the Son of God and then assumes the role of the son as a metaphorical reference to himself. He attempted to claim the throne that belongs to Jesus. The Prophet certainly cannot replace the Son as the bright Morning Star, but he did his best to steal the title! "How you have fallen from heaven, O morning star, son of the dawn!" Your eternal home amongst maggots and worms is well deserved! Eternity will welcome you as nothing more than a man who has earned never-ending torment. "You are covered with the slain, with those pierced by the sword, those who descend to the stones of the pit. Like a corpse trampled underfoot, you will not join them in burial, for you have destroyed your land and killed your people." This is the story of Lucifer, The Prophet.

Still, the world awaits another

Daniel writes about the same man, but with very different imagery. He describes a man with eyes and a boastful mouth who will call himself *the Most High*. Daniel further describes this man as a horn of another beast. Hence, his imagery of a horned goat is a favorite among those who wish to create satanic images with their hands. In appropriate fashion, goats perish in the fire prepared for and originating from Satan. Sitting on His throne in heavenly glory, Jesus separates the goats from the sheep. He is the good Shepherd. He has earned the highest position at the Right Hand of God – unlike The Prophet. Yet, it is The Prophet who declared that "… I am the foremost to serve God." It is a bit difficult to imagine any man boastfully lifting himself above the likes of Abraham, Jacob, Moses, David, and the rest of God's prophets. But to place oneself above the Son of God… is simply Luciferian!

Still, the world awaits another

One does not need to be Christian to know that the Word warns about a false prophet who is to appear in the days following Jesus' departure. Written into the earth is the knowledge that The Prophet will oppose Jesus' teaching and attempt to change the Laws of the Father. But God's Laws never change. They do not change in the way that the harlot tells it. They do not change in the way that The Prophet tells it. And they do not change in the way that newfound religions tell it. These Laws have been in place and practiced for over 3,300 years. They were written 1,300 years before the appearance of the Son. And the Son is adamant and steadfast in His adherence to the Laws of His Father. He is specific in telling the world that did *not* come to change the Law but to fulfill it! However, Jesus' opposition had better ideas. He admittedly changed the Laws – calling his changes 'improvements' over Laws that were long-since outdated. The law that forbade murder held little value in The Prophet's kingdom. Such a law neither served The Prophet nor would it advance his endeavors of intrigue. Deluded minds who admire The Prophet and his ways agree with him. Many of his like-minded scholars, those who study and accept The Prophet's teaching, have gone so far as to say "… the law of The Prophet is decidedly superior to and more comprehensive than the previous laws…" This well-documented opinion is shared by billions of people who think stealing, killing, and destroying are the righteous acts of God's new people - those who bend their knees and submit to a tender and delicate god. Can anyone successfully steal, kill, and destroy in any manner that can be described as tender and delicate? Something is amiss!

Still, the world awaits another

How could a murderous beast serve the needs of a god whose identity teeters on the wonderful attributes of being tender and delicate? This is a contradiction of terms. The beast, awaited worldwide, is mistakenly known by the number 666. John wrote a compelling mystery about this beast over two-thousand years ago. Most people, particularly the elect, are certain that they will know him when they see him. They are mistaken. The man, The Prophet, the beast - has been around for 1,400 years; as has been his calligraphic name. When the Word was written into the earth, the intent was to translate it into every language so that every man and every nation could know the Word of God. But translation erased the intent of the three numeric symbols written by John. The number has no known meaning. Mankind will certainly never see the number 666 in the name of The Prophet. For the numeric system responsible for the current translation was developed a thousand years after John laid down his prophetic pen. The meaning of the symbols is nonsense apart from one another. But, put them together in their existing Greek form and they become what we know to be The Prophet's name. Independently, they are three puzzle pieces that any toddler can stack together in perfect fashion. Yet, these three symbols have stymied people for two millennia. They will stymie men no longer. The three symbols give us the name of The Prophet. It is that simple. As a collective body, Jesus' bride has been stumped over this ridiculously simple mystery for one reason and one reason alone… It is God and God alone who chooses the appropriate time for this to be seen. Seeing The Prophet's name in this form now serves as a certainty that the man who called himself *the Most High*, he who denied the Father and the Son, is the same man whose numeric name has baffled men for centuries.

Still, the world awaits another

The world waits upon a very bad actor. He will appear upon this earth in a bid to oppose God's chosen people and oppress Jesus' bride. Because he did not know the Word of God, The Prophet gained much of his understanding about Christianity from the actions of the harlot. Since that body insists upon worshiping Mary as *the mother of God* (found nowhere in biblical teaching) it seems reasonable that an illiterate man would assume she was the third deity alongside the Father and Son. This is how falsehood creates falsehood - an easy mistake for men who hear what their itching ears want to hear.

Initially, The Prophet's opposition and oppression of God's elect was instituted by his own hand and actions. After his death, his intrigue was advanced by hordes of Prophetiers (Hamon Gog). Since the days of his flight from the king of the south, the Prophetiers have attempted to change the set times to something more honorary to The Prophet as *the most high*. By his direction, the Prophetiers restarted time and set up a new calendar. This new calendar honors The Prophet and his cowardly flight from his pursuers. The Prophet's hordes utilize the world standard, Anno Domini, or A.D. (the year of the Lord), as a secondary measure of time.

Still, the world awaits another

Jesus came into the world to lay down His life. He made this sacrifice and offering so that men may have life and have it in full. For this selfless act, He is hated and mercilessly mocked by most. The gift of God has become a running joke for today's academics. Though most acknowledge that Jesus did, indeed, lay down his life, they reject the notion that He was raised to life again. Many see this as nothing more than the suicidal act of a religious zealot. Man's reaction to such a gift is something of biblical prophecy. He told the world that He would be hated for who He is and what He does. He told the world that Christians would be hated for Him as well. He is hated for who He is. Christians are hated for who they are. At the time that Jesus spoke of such things, those around Him called Him demon possessed. Does a man who is possessed by demons teach men to love their neighbor as their own self? Does a man who is possessed by demons pray for those who persecute Him to death? It seems better suited that the demon possessed man would teach men to kill their neighbors and pray for their demise. Such a man would certainly make kingdoms tremble. One can see how such a man might overthrow cities and make the world a desert. The world knows such a man. The cities he overthrew are now too many to be counted. He did not lay down his life for mankind. Instead, he is quoted as saying that he is to fight mankind until everyone submits to his teaching. His thirst for blood was so engrained in him that he prayed he might be killed during battle only to be brought back to life so that he might kill again. This is what demon-possessed looks like. His hordes of people see this as 'perfection.' They do as he did. None of them know Jesus' lesson about sinners and the stones they throw. The thief's repeated lessons about stealing, killing, and destroying in the name of God makes reasonable people cringe – until they hear that the teaching emanates from the cultural origins of an illiterate desert-dweller. Then, the teaching is somehow accepted as a form of culture and worship – thereby benefitting from the world's exemptions for diplomatic immunity and cultural appropriation. There is no accusation of statutory rape when a 58-year-old man consummates his marriage to a 9-year-old girl, assuming the marriage is formed and consummated under a cultural moniker. These are the behaviors of The Prophet. They cannot be factually denied or dismissed as erroneous. His actions and deeds have been passed onto his people in written form. To deny their existence is futile and a mere act of intentional ignorance. But do not make the mistake that pointing these things out to others will convince them otherwise. The world has determined that pointing out these cultural exemptions (murder that isn't murder, rape that isn't rape, theft that isn't theft, and destruction that isn't destruction) is hateful and worthy of public scorn. The new-worldly demand is that such statements, factual as they may be, are not to be made about any one man or membership. Of this, the Word is unwavering and clear – Satan and his demons lead the whole world astray. The Prophet and his Prophetiers have found a great defense in this politically correct world with its fearful allies. The last best hope for man on earth has been crushed by the gathering of many cultures that now encourage and approve of the things that God detests and forbids.

Mocked in his death for being no more than a man, The Prophet has lived and died – exactly as it has been written. The dead know about his pathetic ruse. Unfortunately, his deceit carries far beyond the grave. Though he has long-since been dead, his power and influence have never been stronger than they are today. His elected officials have been seated in the highest government capacities, infiltrating most nations around the world. As the number of Prophetiers increase globally, so increases the implementation of his changed laws. Third-world countries yield to his lethal force while the free world submits to his diabolical political grooming which demands acceptance of his coercive form of peace. Few have any interest and fewer still have taken the time to read and understand how and what 'peace' means to The Prophet. The world would rather not know that peace comes about when all religions and all men bow only to his god. With two billion Prophetiers in the world and a global political system that protects their advancements, John asks the right question: "Who can make war against the beast?"

Still, the world awaits another.

Isaiah warned us about Lucifer, the man who would attempt to assume the role and honorary titles of the Messiah. Isaiah was specific about the things that Lucifer would say and do to pursue his evil endeavor to unseat Jesus as God's speaking image. According to Isaiah, Lucifer, the speaking image of the dragon, would tell the world that:

- I will ascend to heaven
- I will raise my throne above the stars of God
- I will sit enthroned on the mount of assembly
- I will ascend above the tops of the clouds
- I will make myself like the most high

What a boastful and well-known mouth this man has! The stunning thing about these five statements *(the Five I's)* is that the world has already heard him speak these things. The world knows him. He has been described as a prophet of God who rejects the biblical teaching that God is a Father. He is the prophet who rejects the Son. That qualifies him as an antichrist prophet. He's The Prophet who declared that he ascended to heaven in the early days of his prophethood. Lucifer is the man who placed himself above all his predecessors and said he is the foremost to serve God. He is the man who said he was to be raised to perfection and proclaimed that he was to become like The Most High. He has said all these things and his people recite them as fact.

Still, the world awaits another.

For nearly 2,000 years, mankind has awaited the arrival of an intriguing character who will appear upon the face of the earth and execute his illicit plans. He will do as God warns and 'come against the prophets of Israel.' The warning is specific in that this liar, Gog, will oppose the light that is Jesus. He is described as becoming quite powerful and very stern. This man will cause astounding devastation and succeed in whatever he does. Men have been warned that he will destroy the mighty men and the holy people. But what prophet of God is sent to destroy God's holy people? The promise is that he will cause deceit to prosper and that he will consider himself superior to 'all' other men. The Prophet has accomplished these things. As far as his being superior to all other men, keep in mind the biblical lesson about Jesus' disciples who were corrected for arguing over which one was closest to and most loved by Jesus. Though the drunken harlot will vehemently protest, those who know the Son understand that no such position exists. Jesus does not love one prophet over another. This is particularly important in the moment that Jesus gives the care of His mother over to her second eldest son – *James*. Like the rest of His disciples, James was among the disciples whom Jesus loved. With four living sons, it would have been highly inappropriate for Jesus to give Mary's care away to a man outside of the family. Again, the harlot will be inflamed by such remarks. But this highlights the fact that no prophet under the Messiah holds the first position. Sitting at the right hand of the Mighty One is *I AM*, the Christ. He and He alone has been granted that position. But The Prophet disagrees. Coming against the prophets of God, he leapfrogs all of those before him and declares that he is to hold that throne. Yet, he is not descended from David. And only a descendant of David can assume that throne. Such is the Word. Such is the lineage of biblical royalty. The Prophet descends from the other vine – that of the slave. Opposing the Spirit-driven Word of the prophets before him, he is steadfast in declaring that Jesus is not the Son of God, and He did not selflessly sacrifice Himself upon the cross. As he tells it, that which was written before him about truth, evidence, witness, and Old Testament prophecies, was largely mistaken. But he pardoned the prophets responsible for speaking such grievous errors! Remarkable how these mistaken prophets described the Word and the Word's opposition so perfectly!

The world has come to know and accept Jesus' opposer, a ruthless and terrifying man, as The Prophet who teaches how to destroy many by peace. He opposes Truth and instructs others to kill, specifically 'murder,' in the name and good of God. His efforts have resulted in a global nation that acts and supports those who act in such a manner. The world has witnessed this man's examples of 'peace' on February 26, 1993, and again on September 11, 2001. It watched again in horror on September 11, 2012; April 15, 2013, and again on December 2, 2015. Helplessly, the world watched as his 'peace' was demonstrated November 26-29, 2008; January 7, 2015, and November 18, 2015. With a willful blind eye and conscious denial, the world has become acquainted with him and his military tactics. Of this man and his many hordes, mankind has become ostrich-like in that they refuse to accept what their eyes have seen. They refuse to acknowledge what their ears have heard. Over fear of reprisal and public scorn, most refuse to challenge The Prophet's institution of peace. He has become everything we were warned he would be.

Still, the world awaits another.

The world largely understands the warning about The Prophet and how he would raise himself above all others as some sort of king. They have been warned that he would show no regard for the gods of his fathers. Instead, he would introduce a new god - one with new rules and new laws. The Prophet would reinvent everything that is called God and introduce a foreign god who defies nearly 1,400 years of biblical testimony. Daniel tells us that he will honor this new god with gold and silver, with precious stones and costly gifts. The world knows of such a man! He verbally honored his god with a lesson he titled *GOLD*, with the main thrust of this lesson denying the divinity of Jesus.

The golden temple, erected on the Temple Mount, was raised in honor of his god and is unmistakable today as the defining shrine in Jerusalem. The honor is an abomination. Seen standing where it does not belong, that gold dome now occupies the most desolate place on earth as it is void of any prayers to God. Praying to the Holy One of Israel is illegal in that place.

The Prophet honors his god with silver - namely a silver signet ring. He used this ring to seal letters that he was not capable of writing himself. The world should know he was illiterate – incapable of reading or writing anything on his own.

He honors his god with precious stones; three blackened and broken pieces of rock that are currently held together by a ring of silver. They adorn a corner of this man's main house of worship. He calls these gathered pieces of precious stones *the cornerstone*. He claims that these stones are the 'biblical' cornerstone. But the biblical cornerstone is out of Jerusalem. He is the Rock that the builders rejected. Again, The Prophet denies Jesus in this role as the Rock that the founders rejected.

Like the home of the harlot, Jerusalem is not The Prophet's primary residence. One might take particular interest in a rather coincidental biblical application of The Prophet's broken pieces of honorary stone. This account can be found in the biblical testimony of 2 Kings 10:26-27. With The Prophet's precious cornerstone broken and burned, it readily describes a similar stone from the house of Baal that was removed, broken, and burned. Better yet, The Prophet has openly acknowledged that his main house of worship was used as a latrine during the time of his prophethood.

Lastly, this self-exalted king honors his god with the highest priced gifts of all - the lives and souls of men. He justifies his mandated acts of murder as deeds consistent with sacrificing people to the gods with his 'Voluntary Gifts.' In effect, he sacrifices people to and for the god he introduced. How many coincidences does it take before the world finally concedes and recognizes that none of this is coincidence?

Still, the world awaits another.

The Word warned that Jesus' nemesis would appear as a thief; a dishonest merchant who would teach others to steal, kill, and destroy as righteous deeds on behalf of the god he introduced. No longer can men dismiss the boastful words of The Prophet and his braggadocious manner of endorsing theft. In an unrepentant rant, he openly admits his life revolved around being a thief. This is not something he did prior to becoming a prophet of God. This is about who he became after his revelations. The mainstay of his stealing was during the time he taught as a prophet of God. His own testimony endorses the idea that fighting in defense of his teaching was to include looting those they encountered. Six hundred years after Jesus' ascension, this fellow comes about and institutes theft as a worthy endeavor.

Still, the world awaits another!

The world knows of the biblical riddle about a thief that comes in the night. Most will envision the image of a man breaking into a house under the cover of darkness. But the biblical warning is given with specific intent. The Prophet was a boastful thief who convinced billions of people that he was the bright morning star - the light that comes at the end of the night. He taught and continues to teach he was the light that appeared at a time of darkness. As he tells it, that darkness included the prophetic Word of God's two witnesses – the Spirit and the Son. Men no longer need to ponder the curious statement Jesus made about 'coming like a thief in the night.' Jesus, the true *bright Morning Star*, came as a light that shines in the darkness. The Prophet laid claim to being *the star of piercing brightness* who was *the comer by night*. Both men claim to be the light in the darkness and *the bright Morning Star*. One of these men has many of God's prophets describing Him as *the star* and *the light*. Their written testimonials account for the Messiah before, during, and after Jesus' arrival and ascension. The other man made the bright morning star declaration solely on his own account. One of these two men is the Lord *I AM*. The other is *Lucifer*.

STILL, the world awaits another!

John warned the world about a horrible beast, a vile man, who was to appear upon the face of the earth and masquerade as the light. The Lamb was flesh and blood, a man, sent by God to deliver His Word and teaching. Lucifer was flesh and blood, a man, who spoke the deceptive lies of the dragon. Declaring himself to be *the seal of the prophets*, The Prophet contradicted previous prophetic testimony and made claims to correct the wrongs of the prophets who preceded him – all of them. This seal of the prophets, he who appeared 500 years after God's witnesses laid down their pens, changed the teaching that spanned 1,400 years and all the prophets before him.

While negating the Word, The Prophet exercised all the authority of the first beast - Satan. The beast that spoke the lies of the dragon opposed the written testimony of those who came before him. After reading his collection of statements, there can be no arguing that The Prophet made the earth, and its inhabitants worship his foreign god as *The Light*. He further claimed that his revelations were miraculous and that the recorded testimony he verbally delivered bears his literal *marks*. The sum of his marks creates the image of the beast he testifies for. Applied literally, his verbal testimony gave breath to the image of the dragon. All The Prophet had to do was speak. Capable of little else, the unlearned prophet relied on others to write and record his misleading marks. The 'seal of the prophets' was unlike any before him as he was illiterate and could neither read nor write. All he knew of the prophets before him was discovered by either word of mouth or by the whisperings of the menace found within his own mind. The evidence attesting to his tactics of forcing everyone to receive his marks is astounding! He went so far as to institute the rule that buying and selling should be based solely upon a *faith balance*. This rule is found within his recorded testimony. The resulting consequences of The Prophet's rule is obvious, those who have no faith in his marks also have no ability to buy or sell. To test this rule, try buying from or selling to any one of the hordes of Prophetiers as one who has no faith during the hordes' annual pilgrimage. This will not go so well.

STILL, THE world awaits another!

In a letter to the Thessalonians, Paul warned about the world falling prey to the son of perdition, he who would appear in accordance with the previous warnings of Ezekiel and come against the prophets of God. He is the man who opposed everything that the prophets called *God*. He is the man who exalted himself over everything that is worshiped as God. His actions and documented testimony reveal that he set himself up long ago in the temple of God as God Himself. This should be obvious and easily recognizable to all – even for those who do not know God. After all, how many men have set themselves up on the Temple Mount and called themselves God? As history reveals, the answer is not as simple as one might think. For example: Most do not know that *the temple of God* is the Lord God Almighty and the Lamb. It is not a stone building. The Lord God Almighty is the light, and the Lamb is the lamp of that light. Knowing this, how might our nefarious villain, The Prophet, 'set himself up in the temple of God and declare himself to be God?' The answer has now become rather simple. The Prophet and his god need only to assume the titles of *the light* and *the lamp*. Thanks to the recorded testimony of The Prophet, we know he did exactly that. He repeatedly claimed that his god is the light and that he is the lamp of that light. In this manner, he has set himself up in God's temple and masquerades as the lamp of light. Until now, the world has either fed themselves with this man's lies or they have chosen to ignore his prophetic role as the son of perdition.

STILL, THE WORLD awaits another!

Jesus testified that He saw Satan fall like lightning from heaven to earth. John's testimony describes Satan as a blazing star that fell upon the waters – poisoning them. John further testified that a mighty angel, with a face like the sun and fiery pillars for legs, would descend upon the earth and present a little book that opens with his seven thunderous lies. Men know that the sound of lightning is thunder. When Jesus saw Satan fall like lightning from heaven to earth, it is reasonable to assume what sound Satan's fall might have made. Thunder is the voice of lighting. It sounds like God, and it looks like God, but the words of the mighty angel's book are *not* the Word of God. Therefore, when John testifies about a powerful angel who descends from heaven appearing as a blazing star and roaring the sounds of thunder, who might that angel be other than Satan? If this mighty angel is Satan and he holds a little book in one hand and raises his other hand to heaven and roars the seven thunders, are his words to be considered trustworthy and true or are they to be rejected as the lies of the dragon? And if Satan is described as standing with one foot on the sea and one foot on the land, isn't he standing on the shore of the sea? According to John, that is exactly where Satan stands!

What might God's direction have been to John upon hearing Satan's seven thunderous roars? John was instructed specifically 'not' to write them down. So, how might men know what these seven thunders were? Daniel gives us a clue. He tells us that 'the people [the Prophetiers] of the ruler who will come [The Prophet] will destroy the city and the sanctuary.' War will accompany this ruler and his people, and desolations will be brought about. He will introduce the "one 'seven' confirming the covenant that puts an end to sacrifice and offering." The sacrifice and offering that The Prophet puts an end to is Jesus' sacrifice and offering. This 'one seven' corresponds to the abomination that causes desolation, the fallen angel who brings about war, and his mouthpiece – he who makes it all happen.

What could that little book be in the hand of the dragon? If Satan wishes to masquerade as an angel of light, wouldn't his charade be enhanced by creating a book in his own image? This is where The Prophet steps in. He is the ruler who spoke like the dragon – even presenting the image of the beast in seven brief statements. This one seven makes up the entirety of the first chapter - the first seven verses in the mighty angel's little book. Honoring the dragon as *God*, The Prophet's first 'seven' discard the sacrifice and offering of the Father and His Son and direct people to rely upon the dragon for help. Among these 'seven' are statements declaring that God's chosen Jews and Jesus' faithful Christians have chosen the wrong path. It seems consistent that the false prophet would find a way to lead people away from God and away from God's people. What better way to accomplish this enormous task other than to reject the Word of God, reject 1,400 years of prophetic testimony, and reject the people who worship the Father and Son?

The ruse continues with The Prophet's comparison of his words to 'honey' as a nourishment and healing for men. He compares his marks to such honey. John gives testimony to the fact that, when ingested, the little book tasted like honey (the Word of God), but it was certainly not nourishing. The book soured in John's stomach and made him ill. This would be expected of a true prophet of God. A true prophet consumes the Word of God, revealing it to be sweeter than honey and in harmony with God's unchanging laws. God's people are taught that 'man does not live on bread alone, but on every word that comes from the mouth of God.' Moses, Matthew, and Jesus all agree on this. John was instructed not to write down the seven thunders because they did not come from the mouth of God.

STILL, THE WORLD AWAITS another!

Paul's testimony teaches that Jesus will *not* return to us, and His body of believers will *not* be captured up *until* The Prophet's rebellion occurs *and* he is revealed to be the speaking image of Satan. Though man's traditional thinking has created much confusion about the timing of Jesus' return, the Word is direct and clear. God's timing on 'revealing' the man of lawlessness is not to be confused with the physical 'appearance' of the man of lawlessness. They are not one and the same.

Isaiah testifies that the fake morning star is mocked in his death by the spirits of the departed. He is mocked by those he joined in death. This means that the fake morning star must have lived and died to fulfill the prophecies related to him. He did both. Yet, as though he were still alive, those of the living are still fed and directed by his deceptive lessons. His influence among men has reached its peak and is as strong today as it has ever been.

The testimony states Jesus will not return, and we will not be captured up until this man has been identified. This event is commonly referred to as *the rapture*. With this, God's people can finally feel validated! Such a man slipped into history, and he made his mark among men. His opposition to Jesus is well documented. The Prophet's desire to unseat the Christ and assume the throne is now obvious. Jesus is clear about being the bright Morning Star, the Root and the Offspring of David. The Prophet is clear that he claims to be the morning star, a descendant of the slave. Jesus came into the world to give us life and give us life to the full. But the thief does as The Prophet did – he came only to steal and kill and destroy. History tells us which of these two men is the Messiah, descended from David, and which is the lawless thief.

STILL, THE WORLD AWAITS ANOTHER!

The fog of delusion is dense and long-lasting. It is that which causes most of mankind to consciously ignore mountains of evidence against The Prophet and wait on another who will fulfill the role of the man of lawlessness. However, the world has reached a breaking point. The fog is lifting. Babel, the purposeful confusion of differing languages, has all but disappeared. Through reliable translations, men can now trust upon the recorded testimonies and histories of these two men. In so doing, reasonable people can come to a few undeniable conclusions:

The Prophet

1. God is *God*
2. He is Father, Son, and Spirit
3. He has given us His faithful and true Word
4. He has given us His Word via His two witness – His Son and His Spirit
5. Father, Son, and Spirit are all in agreement

This Word, now verified by the historical existence of The Prophet, warned us about the war and deception that would descend upon man by flesh and spirit. The Prophet is not in agreement with the Father, Son, and Spirit. Though many false prophets have appeared since Jesus walked the earth, there has been only one who has succeeded in fulfilling all biblical warnings about his coming. In so doing, he has created a massive body of destructive and lawless people. As for his rebellion, the deceptive 'peace' that has caused so much death, pain, and turmoil in the world, has become most prominent in recent days. The Prophet's rebellion continually expands. But the man of perdition is now made known – revealed by the truth and the sword of the Word that will finally strike down wicked nations and crush the rebellion. God is not a prankster. There is no *'psych'* moment coming. There is only one man who brought about the rebellion described to the Thessalonians by Paul. The Prophet has fulfilled all the prophetic warnings regarding the son of perdition. The Word has played itself out on earth. Men now have the evidence proving the historical existence of the biblical bad-guy. The world's majority will gnash their teeth and scoff at the evidence. This, too, is biblically prophetic.

Jesus warns us not to fall asleep and be blinded by the delusion that the world will accept the historical evidence identifying Lucifer, the man, as The Prophet. This world and this kingdom belong to The Prophet and his god. No amount of historical evidence, written accounts, or realized prophecy will open the eyes and ears of the hopelessly deluded. The Word explains this conscious denial as coming from a people who refuse to love the truth because they delight in wickedness. But that time has come to pass. The moment when all will bend a knee to Jesus is when He overthrows The Prophet with the breath of His mouth and destroys The Prophet's work by the splendor of His imminent return. Keep in mind that the man of lawlessness need only to be 'revealed' for Jesus to return and collect His body. The world does not have to agree or be convinced that The Prophet has fulfilled so many diabolical biblical roles. After all, the world now consists of those who cannot be convinced or agree on simple things - such as what defines a man as male and a woman as female. They certainly cannot ascertain that 'illegal' means 'lawless.' Forget about trying to convince the world that the false prophet has succeeded in setting his disciples among the rulers in the world. There is no need to attempt that which cannot be done. Our Father will convince the world with His judgment. Every tongue will confess to God. He told us the truth in the beginning. He'll establish the truth in the end. In the meantime, men will continue with their personal rebellions against Him. God gave the world 2,000 years to accept His selfless act of sacrifice and offering – the gift of His Son as a ransom for our souls. For this, He is mocked. As predicted, few have accepted His gift of life. Unlike the prostitute who was to be stoned by self-declared righteous men, Jesus will not stand between the denier and His Father's judgment. As for those of the original vine, men should consider the last sentence in the Bible: "The grace of the Lord Jesus be with God's people." The Word speaks for itself. God's people are not found among the body of the harlot and the conglomerate beast of nations and kingdoms she rides. These people have freely chosen to become victims of their own religious traditions and false teachings. As the Word warns, they simply refuse to love the truth.

Matching biblical prophecies about Jesus' nemesis to The Prophet who fulfilled them is not about grand intelligence, obedience, or perfection. Matching these things to a world ruler is about timing – God's timing. Few will want to hear it. Even fewer will want to discuss it. Stating that Jesus is Lord and God is offensive enough to most. But revealing the identity of the man of lawlessness as The Prophet will send people into a frenzy! Nonetheless, God's timing is His own. It is time. It is time for Jesus' church, the faithful and true body of the Son, to be good ministers in Christ and share this with others. Anyone can see that the world has lost its way and become completely lawless. Sodom has been celebrated and revived. The whole world is promoting actions and mannerisms that God detests. This rebellious departure from God is of no surprise. It's prophetic. The world had to become completely wicked before God allowed it to be cleansed. Wicked it has become. The Prophet has done as he was prophesied to do. Again, God is not a prankster. He had His prophets describe the man for good reason. This was to fulfill God's purpose. Like it or not, all men are soon to recognize this atrocious man and his wicked ways.

Gathering evidence about The Prophet was largely accomplished by utilizing three books and historical events. This book was written with the intent to assist the reader in matching many biblical warnings with the written and historical accounts of the man who fulfilled them. Sadly, a Politically Correct world serves The Prophet well. Because of the highly charged political environment we now live - his very recognizable name will not be mentioned here. His political allies are neither mentioned by name nor branch of government. His body of believers and political allies will fight vigorously against evidence given here with accusations of hatred, bigotry, and intolerance. This brings us to what God says about Satan and his accusations. He is the accuser of our brothers. The reader should remember that being a witness does not make one an accuser of his brothers. After all this time and reliable translations, men can no longer change the facts. They cannot change the things The Prophet said or the things he did. Though many will try, The Prophet's history cannot be cancelled.

Consider Isaiah's prophetic warning: "Woe to those who call evil good and good evil, who put darkness for light and light for darkness, who put bitter for sweet and sweet for bitter." Now, consider what the world has offered. From the written Word we know that the Messiah offers his elect a pure white stone. This symbol of purity is the cornerstone of the kingdom of heaven; that cornerstone being the Son of God. But The Prophet, he who opposes the Messiah, offers his followers a broken and burned Black Stone – a rock that he claims is the cornerstone of his kingdom. Woe to those who put darkness for light.

Consider the Word of God as it is compared to the sweetness of honey and related to the truth of God's Laws. Compare it to the Opposer's word as it is compared to *the beverage of many hues that is formed by the bee* and how it relates to his changed laws. There is no wonder why Satan's book turned bitter in the stomach of a true prophet of God. This is the word that appeared to be godly but made John sick. Woe to those who put bitter for sweet and sweet for bitter.

Consider the Word of God that plainly tells us that those who kill in the name of God do not know God. Compare it to the Opposer's word that teaches men to murder in the name of God. The Prophet teaches that murder is a deed that leads to paradise. Woe to those who call evil 'good' and good 'evil.'

The truth has been delivered through the breath of Jesus' mouth and the Spirit-driven pens of the prophets. This is Jesus' sword. Truth speaks for itself. Thanks to the truth, historical accounts, and recorded testimony, the man of lawlessness now has an historical identity. Ironically, the historical truths about The Prophet have proven the existence of God the Father and His Son. Such truth was never found within the heart or the mouth of the son of perdition. Jesus gave us His Word about this man. Now, the splendor of Jesus' coming will finally overthrow the rebellion of The Prophet and all who side with him. Some of those who side with The Prophet will surprise many. For they include a harlotous lot who call Jesus *Lord* but refuse to obey His commands. This is a political and spiritual alliance that results in mixing truth with lies - Satan's favored form of deception.

As for the god that The Prophet introduced, he who masquerades as *the Light*, his fate is sealed. He was thrown from heaven to earth - never to escape. His war and deceptive reign are quickly coming to an end. A righteous and eternal earthly torment is now imminently upon the liar and his speaking image.

Prophet

Chapter 23

The Number of His Name is…

Amen!

Ronald B. Stetton

Appendix 1

NIV Hebrew-Greek Key Word Study Bible, AMG International, 1996, Note 9:24-27, p. 1038

This is one of the most important prophecies in Scripture. Daniel had been praying about the rebuilding of Jerusalem and the return of his people [Jews]. God gave Daniel a time frame for all His dealings with Israel. The prophecy pertains to Daniel's people and the holy city (v. 24), and the beginning of the prophecy's fulfillment was marked by the decree to rebuild Jerusalem (v. 25). The seventy 'sevens' (v. 24) can only refer to years, since Daniel specifies "three weeks" in Daniel 10:2 when he refers to seven-day periods. Some biblical scholars suggest that the sixty-nine 'sevens' until the Messiah would come (v. 25) began with the decree that was issued to Nehemiah in 445 B.C. and ended 483 years later on Palm Sunday (based on 360-day years; see Rev 11:3; 12:6; 13:5). The phrase "the Anointed One will be cut off" (v. 26) is a reference to the crucifixion of Christ…

The timeline appears to be accurate up to this point. The note continues:

"…There is likely a gap, a feature which is characteristic of some prophecies, between the sixty-ninth and seventieth 'sevens.' If this is the case, then "the ruler who will come"

(v. 26) refers to the Antichrist, who will make a treaty with the Jews and then break it

(v. 27). Jesus stated that the "abomination that causes desolation" (referring to Daniel 9:27) would take place at the end of the age (mt 24:5)."

There was a gap in the 'sevens' between the sixty-ninth and seventieth 'sevens.' That gap was between Jesus' crucifixion on Palm Sunday to the day that the Antichrist uttered the 'seven' thunders and was ultimately responsible for the abomination that causes desolation that stands on the Temple Mount today.

The man-made tradition about the Antichrist's **treaty with the Jews** that was formed and adopted to fit the prophecy has been rendered incorrect.

Ronald B. Stetton

End Notes

1. Al-Bukhari, Volume 5, Book 58, Number 227
2. AMoH, chapter 1, verse 2, p. 5
3. AMoH, 1:2, p. 7
4. AMoH, chapter 1, verse 2, pp., 3-5
5. AMoH, chapter 5, verse 31, p. 70
6. AMoH, chapter 16, verse 17, pp. 177-178
7. AMoH, chapter 19, verse 11, p. 212
8. AMoH, chapter 19, verse 12, p. 213
9. AMoH, chapter 19, verse 17, pp. 215-216
10. AMoH, chapter 22, rule 5, p. 240
11. AMoH, chapter 29, verse 8, p. 302
12. AMoH, chapter 30, verse 40, note 18, pp. 325-326
13. AMoH, chapter 31, verse 3, p. 329-330
14. Answering-Islam.org, Al-Mi'raj: The Alleged Ascent to Heaven, 1. The Story of the Mi-raj, paragraphs 6 & 7
15. Jay Bennett, Popular Mechanics, Oct 10, 2016
16. The Book of Faith, Chapter 81, Book 1, Number 0352
17. Bostonherald.com, U.S. Rep. Ilhan Omar, Some People Did Something
18. Britannica.com, Medina
19. Catechism of the Catholic Church (CCC), paragraph 841
20. Catechism of the Catholic Church (CCC), paragraph 966
21. The Christian Post, Paul Stanley, May 30, 2012; Edward Klein on 'The Amateur'
22. 1 Corinthians 6:9
23. 1 Corinthians 10:21
24. 1 Corinthians 15:51-52
25. 2 Corinthians 5:21
26. 2 Corinthians 11:1
27. 2018 Counter Extremism Project
28. Daniel 2:34-35, 45
29. Daniel 2:38
30. Daniel 7:8
31. Daniel 7:15
32. Daniel 7:24-25
33. Daniel 7:25; Qur'an 33:40, 40a, pp. 836-7
34. Daniel 8:16; 9:21
35. Daniel 8:23
36. Daniel 8:23, KJV
37. Daniel 8:23-25

38. Daniel 8:24 KJV
39. Daniel 8:24 NIV
40. Daniel 8:25, KJV
41. Daniel 9:24-27, Note 9;24-27, NIV Hebrew-Greek Key Word Study Bible, p. 1038
42. Daniel 9:25
43. Daniel 9:26
44. Daniel 9:27
45. Daniel 9:27 NIV; Daniel 9:27 KJV
46. Daniel 9:27; Qur'an 2:27, 9:75
47. Daniel 10:1 – 11:1
48. Daniel 10:13
49. Daniel 10:13, 20
50. Daniel 10:21
51. Daniel 11:22
52. Daniel 11:23
53. Daniel 11:26
54. Daniel 11:36-39
55. Daniel 11:37
56. Daniel 11:38 KJV
57. Daniel 11:38-39
58. Daniel 11:39
59. Daniel 11:39; Revelation 13:11-12
60. Daniel 11:45
61. Daniel 12:1
62. Daniel 12:3
63. Daniel 12:13
64. Daniel 12:37-39
65. James Dao, The New York Times, Man claims terror ties, 01/21/2010
66. Deuteronomy 9:10
67. Ecclesiastes 12:6-7
68. Ecclesiastes 12:13-14
69. Exodus 8:7
70. Exodus 20:1-17
71. Exodus 20, note 20:1-17, p. 92, NIV Hebrew-Greek Key Word Study Bible
72. Exodus 20:3
73. Exodus 20:13
74. Exodus 20:15
75. Exodus 20:17
76. Exodus 24:12; Daniel 2:34, 45
77. Ezekiel 27:13 NIV, KJV
78. Ezekiel 27:16

79. Ezekiel 27:21
80. Ezekiel 28:15-18
81. Ezekiel 28:17-18
82. Ezekiel 28:18
83. Ezekiel 32:24
84. Ezekiel 32:26-27
85. Ezekiel 32:30
86. Ezekiel 38:2; Revelation 19:8
87. Ezekiel 38:3-6
88. Ezekiel 38:11
89. Ezekiel 38:13
90. Ezekiel 38:17
91. Ezekiel 38:18-19, 21
92. Ezekiel 38:22
93. Ezekiel 39:1-8
94. The Farewell Sermon, lastprophet.info
95. The frozen calm of normalcy bias, Esther Inglis-Arkell, Gizmodo 5/2/13
96. Genesis 2:7
97. Genesis 3:5
98. Genesis 9:13
99. Genesis 9:13-17
100. Genesis 10:2
101. Genesis 10:3
102. Genesis 10:4
103. Genesis 10:5
104. Genesis 10:6
105. Genesis 10:7
106. Genesis 10:19
107. Genesis 10:22
108. Genesis 10:23
109. Genesis 10:30
110. Genesis 10:32
111. Genesis 15:18
112. Genesis 17:2-21
113. Genesis 17:15-16
114. Genesis 17:19
115. Genesis 17:19, 21
116. Genesis 19:4-5
117. Genesis 21:14
118. Genesis 25:1-6
119. Genesis 25:18

120. Hebrews 2:14
121. Hebrews 7:18-22; Luke 22:20
122. Hebrews 12:22; Revelation 14:1
123. Hijaz, www.britannica.com
124. Hebrew-Greek Key Word Study Bible, NIV, AMG Int, 1996, p. 1038
125. Isaiah, Introduction, p. 795, NIV
126. Isaiah 5:20
127. Isaiah 9:6
128. Isaiah 13
129. Isaiah 14:4
130. Isaiah 14:5
131. Isaiah 14:6
132. Isaiah 14:9
133. Isaiah 14:9-12, 15-17
134. Isaiah 14:9-20
135. Isaiah 14:11
136. Isaiah 14:12
137. Isaiah 14:12 KJV
138. Isaiah 14:12 NIV
139. Isaiah 14:13
140. Isaiah 14:14
141. Isaiah 14:16
142. Isaiah 14:17
143. Isaiah 21:13
144. Isaiah 21:13-17
145. Isaiah 28:16, 18
146. Isaiah 29:5-6
147. Isaiah 30:25
148. Isaiah 45:17
149. Isaiah 46:8-11
150. Isaiah 46:12-13
151. Isaiah 47:1
152. Isaiah 47:7
153. Isaiah 47:8
154. Isaiah 47:9-10
155. Isaiah 47:11
156. Isaiah 47:11-14
157. Isaiah 47:11; 48:8-11
158. Isaiah 47:12
159. Isaiah 47:12; Qur'an 8:12
160. Isaiah 47:13

The Prophet

161. Isaiah 48:11
162. Isaiah 56:7; Matthew 21:13
163. Isaiah 66:19 NIV and KJV, the Comparison of...
164. Ibn Ishaq, according to Peters, Muhammad and the Origins of Islam, p. 222-224; The History of al-Tabari, Vol 8, pp. 35-39 (ghayb.com)
165. Islamic-awareness.org, The Arabic Islamic Inscriptions on the Dome of the Rock
166. Islamweb.net, Significance of the Islamic Hijri Calendar, paragraph 3
167. Jeremiah Chapters 7 & 44
168. Jeremiah 7:18, 44:17-25
169. Jeremiah 7:18, 44:17, 25
170. Jeremiah 7:18, 30; 44:17, 25; Acts 17:29-30
171. Jeremiah 25:23-24
172. Jeremiah 44:15-17; Isaiah 47:1-15
173. Jeremiah 44:16
174. Jeremiah 44:16-17
175. Jeremiah 44:17
176. Jeremiah 46:9; Isaiah 66:19
177. Comparison of Jeremiah 46:9 and Ezekiel 38:5 in the NIV and KJV
178. Jeremiah 47:6
179. Jeremiah 51:7
180. Joel 3:2
181. John 2:19
182. John 2:19-21
183. John 3:16
184. John 7:37-39
185. John 8:1-11
186. John 8:3-11
187. John 8:6
188. John 8:11
189. John 8:12
190. John 8:42-47
191. John 8:44
192. John 8:44; Qur'an 5:33
193. John 10:10
194. John 10:16
195. John 10:22-23
196. John 14:6-7
197. John 14:25-26, 16:12-15
198. John 15:1
199. John 15:17-18, 23, 25
200. John 15:18-19, 23, 25

201. John 16:2
202. John 16:2-3
203. John 16:12-15, 14:26
204. 1 John 2:20-21
205. 1 John 2:22
206. 1 John 2:24-27
207. 1 John 3:11-16
208. Jonah 4:11
209. Jude 9
210. Khan Academy, The Dome of the Rock, Dr. Elizabeth Macauley-Lewis
211. 2 Kings 3:4
212. 2 Kings 10:25-27 NIV
213. 2 Kings 10:27
214. 2 Kings 19:30-31
215. Luke 4:5-7
216. Luke 6:45
217. Luke 10:18
218. Luke 18:15-17
219. Luke 20:23-25
220. MMA, AMoH, chapter 19, Introduction, Paragraph 1, p. 205
221. MMA, AMoH, chapter 19, verse 2, p. 207
222. MMA, AMoH, chapter 19, verse 11, note 9, p. 212
223. MMA, AMoH, chapter 19, verse 11, note 9, p. 212; al-Bukhari, Book 56, Hadith 34
224. MMA, AMoH, chapter 29, verse 8, p. 302, note 6; Bukhari 77:52
225. MMA, AMoH, chapter 31, verse 3, note 3, pp. 329-330
226. MMA, Qur'an, Introduction, paragraph 1, p. I-26
227. MMA, Qur'an, Introduction, p. I-26
228. MMA, Qur'an, Introduction, Bosworth Smith, p. I-33, 5th paragraph
229. MMA, Qur'an, Introduction, p. I 37-38
230. MMA, Qur'an, Introduction, p. I-38
231. MMA, Qur'an, Introduction, p. I-38, paragraph 1
232. MMA, Qur'an, Introduction, p. I-60, paragraph 1
233. MMA, Qur'an, chapter 1, narration, p.1; Qur'an 15:87
234. MMA, Qur'an, chapter 1, Introduction, 3rd paragraph, p. 1
235. MMA, Qur'an, chapter 1, Introduction, paragraphs 3-4, pp. 3-4
236. MMA, Qur'an, chapter 1, narration, paragraph 5-6, pp. 1-2
237. MMA, Qur'an, chapter 1, narration, paragraph 6, p.2
238. MMA, Qur'an 1, a and c, p. 3
239. MMA, Qur'an 1:1, 1b
240. MMA, Qur'an, chapter 1, note b, p. 3
241. MMA, Qur'an 1:7, 7a, p. 5

242. MMA, Qur'an 2:27, 27a, 83a; 3:77, 81, 187; 6:152; 13:20, 25; 16:91, 95; 33:15, 23; 48:10
243. MMA, Qur'an 2:39, 39a, p. 23; Introduction, p. I-26
244. MMA, Qur'an 2:65, 65a, p. 34
245. MMA, Qur'an 2:106, 2:106a, p. 50
246. MMA, Qur'an 2:106, 106a, p. 50, paragraphs 3 & 4
247. MMA, Qur'an, chapter 2, note 124a, pp. 56-57
248. MMA, Qur'an 2:149, 149a, paragraph 2, p. 67
249. MMA, Qur'an 2:150, 150a, paragraph 2, p. 68
250. MMA, Qur'an 2:196, 196d, p. 88
251. MMA, Qur'an 2:206, 206a, p. 91; 101:9-11, 9a., p. 1239
252. MMA, Qur'an 2:251, 251b, p. 114
253. MMA, Qur'an 2:279, 279a, p.127
254. MMA, Qur'an 3:13, 13a, p. 138
255. MMA, Qur'an 3:28, 28a, p. 142
256. MMA, Qur'an 3:55, 55a, 55b, 55c, 55d, 55e, pp. 153 -154; 4:156, 156a, p. 237
257. MMA, Qur'an 3:103, 103a, pp. 165-166
258. MMA, Qur'an 3:124, 124a, p. 171
259. MMA, Qur'an 3:144, 144a, p. 175
260. MMA, Qur'an 3:152, 152d; 155, 155a; 3:159, 159a
261. MMA, Qur'an 4:24, 4:24a, p. 202
262. MMA, Qur'an 4:59, 59a, p. 213
263. MMA, Qur'an 5:15, 15a, p. 252
264. MMA, Qur'an 5:15, 15a; 33:46, 33:46a
265. MMA, Qur'an 5:33a, p. 33
266. MMA, Qur'an 5:116, 116a, pp. 282-283
267. MMA, Qur'an 6:101, 101a, pp. 308-309
268. MMA, Qur'an 7:157, 157a, p. 362
269. MMA, Qur'an 7:157, 157a; 29:48, 48a; 96:1, 1a
270. MMA, Qur'an 7:158; 158a, pp. 363-64
271. MMA, Qur'an, chapter 8, narration, paragraph 2, p. 374
272. MMA, Qur'an, 8:5, 5a, p. 377, paragraph 2
273. MMA, Qur'an 8:1, 1a; 8:5, 5a, 8:41, 41a; 8:67-69, 67a; 59:7, 7a
274. MMA, Qur'an 8:44, 44a, p. 387
275. MMA, Qur'an 9:4, 4a, p. 398
276. MMA, Qur'an 9:17, 17a, p. 401
277. MMA, Qur'an 9:73, 73a, p. 416
278. MMA, Qur'an 11:107, 107a, p. 473
279. MMA, Qur'an 14:14, 14a, p. 515
280. MMA, Qur'an 14:37, 37a, p. 519
281. MMA, Qur'an 15:79, 79a, p. 532

282. MMA, Qur'an 15:79, 79a, p. 532; 8:30, 30a, p. 383; 106:1-2, 1a, 2a, p. 1247; 8:7, 7a, p. 377-78
283. MMA, Qur'an 16, narration, opening statements, p. 535
284. MMA, Qur'an 17:1, 1a, p. 563
285. MMA, Qur'an 17:1, 1a, p. 563; 17:60, 60b, p. 574-575
286. MMA, Qur'an 19:92, 92a, p. 627
287. MMA, Qur'an 24:31, 31a-c, pp. 704-705
288. MMA, Qur'an 24:35, 35a, pp. 707-708
289. MMA, Qur'an 24:35; 24:35, 35a, P. 707-708; Qur'an 33:46; MMA, 33:46, 46a, p. 838
290. MMA, Qur'an 24:35, 35a, p. 708; 2:116, 116a, p. 54; 2:120, 120a, p. 55; Chapter 87, narrative, p. 1203; 86:1-3, 3a, pp. 1200-01; 43:81, 81a, p. 965
291. MMA, Qur'an 25:52, 52a, p. 725
292. MMA, Qur'an 25:54, 54a, p. 726
293. MMA, Qur'an 33:21, 21a, p. 829
294. MMA, Qur'an 33:26, 26a, pp. 830-831
295. MMA, Qur'an 33:40, 40a, pp. 836-837
296. MMA, Qur'an 33:49-50, 49a, 50a, pp. 838-840
297. MMA, Qur'an 33:50, 50a, pp. 838-839
298. MMA, Qur'an 39:4, 4a, p. 906
299. MMA, Qur'an 43:81, 81a, p. 965
300. MMA, Qur'an 46:27, 27a, p. 984
301. MMA, Qur'an, chapter 47, Narration, p. 986
302. MMA, Qur'an 48:1, 1a, p. 995
303. MMA, Qur'an 59:7, 7a, p. 1076
304. MMA, Qur'an 61:6, 6a, p. 1087
305. MMA, Qur'an 61:9, 9a, p. 1089 – 33:40, 40a, p. 836
306. MMA, Qur'an 84:18, 18a, pp. 1195-96; Chapter 85, Introduction, p. 1197
307. MMA, Qur'an 85:3, 3a, p. 1197
308. MMA, Qur'an 85, Introduction; 85:3, 3a, p. 1197
309. MMA, Qur'an chapter 86, Introduction, note 3a, p. 1200
310. MMA, Morning Star, Qur'an 86:1-3, note 3a, p. 1201
311. MMA, Qur'an 86:1-3; 86:3, 3a, p. 1200-1201
312. MMA, Qur'an 86:3, 3a, p. 1201
313. MMA, Qur'an, chapter 87, paragraph 1, p. 1203
314. MMA, Qur'an, chapter 87, narration, opening paragraph, p. 1203
315. MMA, Qur'an 87:7, 7a, p. 1204
316. MMA, Qur'an 93:6, 6a, p. 1221
317. MMA, Qur'an 113, Introduction, p. 1258
318. MMA, Qur'an Index, Muslim Wars, p. 1307
319. Malachi 3:6
320. Matthew 1:1-17

321. Matthew 1:2-7, 16-17
322. Matthew 1:16
323. Matthew 1:25
324. Matthew 4:4
325. Matthew 5:17-18
326. Matthew 5:17-20
327. Matthew 10:2-4; Romans 11:13
328. Matthew 10:5-6
329. Matthew 10:28
330. Matthew 13:55-56
331. Matthew 21:42; Acts 4:10-11
332. Matthew 22:19-21
333. Matthew 22:37-40
334. Matthew 24:7
335. Matthew 24:24
336. Matthew 24:27
337. Matthew 24:27, 29-30
338. Matthew 24:30
339. Matthew 24:31
340. Matthew 24:37-40
341. Matthew 25:31-36
342. Minaret
343. More Than A Carpenter, Josh McDowell, pp. 94-95
344. W. Muir, The Life of Muhammad, (Edinburg 1923, Pages 307-8)
345. Nahum 3:9
346. Nakba Day – May 15th of every year since its declaration in 1998
347. Nehemiah 2:1-9
348. NIV 9:27; KJV 9:27
349. 2 Peter 1:19
350. 2 Peter 1:20-21
351. 2 Peter 3:10
352. Peters, *Muhammad and the Origin of Islam*, p. 222-224; MMA 33:26a., pp. 830-831
353. Pew Research Center, Religion & Public Life, January 27, 2011
354. Psalm 83:1-6
355. Psalm 83:1-8
356. Psalm 83:4
357. Psalm 87:1-3
358. Psalm 96:5
359. Psalm 120:5-7
360. Philip Pullella, Reuters, 11/30/14, Pope says it is wrong to equate Islam with violence; Julian

361. Philippians 2:9-10
362. Qur'an 1:6
363. Qur'an 1:7
364. Qur'an 2:124-125
365. Qur'an 2:127; 14:37, 37a, p. 519
366. Qur'an 2:129; 2:260
367. Qur'an 2:158; 3:92
368. Qur'an 2:163; 5:73
369. Qur'an 2:170
370. Qur'an 2:216
371. Qur'an 2:216, 8:39
372. Qur'an 2:216; 8:39; 9:123
373. Qur'an 2:255; 3:2
374. Qur'an 2:255, 3:2, 4:87, 47:19, 64:13
375. Qur'an 2:279
376. Qur'an 3:19
377. Qur'an 3:26
378. Qur'an 3:28
379. Qur'an 3:28; 5:51; 60:1
380. Qur'an 3:102
381. Qur'an 3:151
382. Qur'an 3:152; Qur'an 3:121-22, 121a; Qur'an, Asad Translation, 3:121, note 90
383. Qur'an 3:156
384. Qur'an 3:156; Romans 6:23
385. Qur'an 3:156, 7:158
386. Qur'an 3:167
387. Qur'an 4:3
388. Qur'an 4:24
389. Qur'an 4:59
390. Qur'an 4:78
391. Qur'an 4:157, 157a, pp. 237-238; 5:117, 117a, p. 283
392. Qur'an 5:15
393. Qur'an 5:33
394. Qur'an 5:33; 2:279
395. Qur'an 5:51
396. Qur'an 5:51, 3:28
397. Qur'an 5:116
398. Qur'an 7:4
399. Qur'an 8:12
400. Qur'an 8:12; 3:151
401. Qur'an 8:12; 47:4

The Prophet

402. Qur'an 8:39
403. Qur'an 8:41
404. Qur'an 8:41, 69
405. Qur'an 8:69
406. Qur'an 9:5
407. Qur'an 9:73
408. Qur'an 15:79
409. Qur'an 18:29
410. Qur'an 19:88-92
411. Qur'an 24:2-3; 4:25
412. Qur'an 24:35
413. Qur'an 25:52
414. Qur'an 30:2
415. Qur'an 33:40
416. Qur'an 33:50
417. Qur'an 33:50-52
418. Qur'an 43:81
419. Qur'an 45:36
420. Qur'an 47:4
421. Qur'an 55:27
422. Qur'an 57:3
423. Qur'an 59:7
424. Qur'an 61:6
425. Qur'an 61:9
426. Qur'an 86:1-3
427. Qur'an 108:1
428. Qur'an 113
429. Revelation 2:16; 2 Thessalonians 2:8
430. Revelation 6:12-15
431. Revelation 7:1-8, 20:4-6
432. Revelation 9:11
433. Revelation 10:1-2
434. Revelation 10:2 & 13:1 NIV
435. Revelation 10:7
436. Revelation 10:8
437. Revelation 11:9
438. Revelation 11:18
439. Revelation 12:7
440. Revelation 12:9
441. Revelation 12:9, Isaiah 14:12
442. Revelation 12:9; Luke 10:18

443.	Revelation 12:10
444.	Revelation 12:12
445.	Revelation 13:3
446.	Revelation 13:4
447.	Revelation 13:10
448.	Revelation 13:11
449.	Revelation 13:12-13
450.	Revelation 13:13
451.	Revelation 13:15
452.	Revelation 13:15; Qur'an 5:33
453.	Revelation 16:12
454.	Revelation 16:14
455.	Revelation 16:15
456.	Revelation 16:16
457.	Revelation 17:3
458.	Revelation 17:3-18
459.	Revelation 17:4
460.	Revelation 17:11
461.	Revelation 17:15-16
462.	Revelation 19:4-6
463.	Revelation 19:20; 20:10; 21:8
464.	Revelation 20:4
465.	Revelation 20:4-5
466.	Revelation 20:10
467.	Revelation 20:10; MMA, Qur'an Introduction summary, I-38
468.	Revelation 20:10, 21:8
469.	Revelation 21:2
470.	Revelation 21:8
471.	Revelation 21:8; Romans 1:29-31
472.	Revelation 21:16-18
473.	Revelation 21:22-23
474.	Revelation 21:23
475.	Revelation 21:27
476.	Revelation 22:1-6
477.	Revelation 22:16
478.	Robinson, DailyMail.co.uk, 5/4/18
479.	Romans 1:18-32
480.	Romans 1:24-32
481.	Romans 1:26-27
482.	Romans 1:26-32
483.	Romans 1:29-32

484. Romans 1:32
485. Romans 6:23
486. Romans 11:13
487. Romans 11:13; Galatians 2:7
488. Romans 11:23-26
489. 2 Samuel 5:7
490. 2 Samuel 6:12
491. Saylordotorg.github.io, The Prophet, paragraph 2
492. Simon Henderson, The Washington Institute, Money for Missiles?, Jan 29, 2019
493. Smithsonianmag.com, "What is Beneath the Temple Mount?," Joshua Hammer, April 2011
494. Peter W. Stoner, and Robert Newman, Science Speaks (Moody Press, 1976) p. 106-112
495. The Strongest Strong's Exhaustive Concordance of the Bible, p. 1586; Ezra 4:9-10 (KJV); Acts 2:9
496. The Strongest Strong's Exhaustive Concordance of the Bible, p. 1637
497. The Strongest Strong's Exhaustive Concordance of the Bible, p. 1641
498. The Strongest Strong's Exhaustive Concordance of the Bible, p. 1677
499. 1 Thessalonians 5:2
500. 1 Thessalonians 5:3
501. 1 Thessalonians 5:4
502. 2 Thessalonians 2:1-3
503. 2 Thessalonians 2
504. 2 Thessalonians 2:2
505. 2 Thessalonians 2:3-4
506. 2 Thessalonians 2:3, 8
507. 2 Thessalonians 2:4
508. 2 Thessalonians 2:4; Matthew 22:37-40
509. 2 Thessalonians 2:9-10
510. 2 Thessalonians 2:10
511. 2 Thessalonians 2:10, 12
512. 2 Thessalonians 2:10-12
513. 2 Thessalonians 2:11
514. 2 Thessalonians 2:11-12
515. 2 Thessalonians 2:12
516. 2 Thessalonians 2:13-17
517. 1 Timothy 4:1
518. 1 Timothy 4:1-3
519. 2 Timothy 1:7
520. United Against Nuclear Iran
521. A. Wainscott, www.usip.org, 2019

522. www.al-islam.org/ENCYCLOPEDIA/chapter5b/2.html
523. Zechariah 12:1-9
524. Zechariah 12:2
525. Zechariah 12:3
526. Zechariah 12:9-14
527. Zechariah 13:8-9
528. Zechariah 14:12-15
529. Zechariah 14:16
530. 2 Corinthians 11:14
531. 1 Kings 10:1-2, Note 10:1,2 p. 405 Key Word Study Bible
532. Popular Mechanics, Jay Bennett, Oct 10, 2016
533. Luke 6:45, Qur'an 95:3, 3a, pp. 1225-1226
534. MMA, Qur'an 95:1-3, 3a, pp. 1225-1226
535. 1 Timothy 4:1-5
536. Qur'an 2:256
537. Qur'an 8:39 & 61:9
538. 2 Corinthians 11:14
539. Revelation 9:11 & Qur'an 3:156
540. Luke 3:21-22
541. Genesis 3:4-5
542. Ezekiel 28:17
543. John 16:2-4
544. Ecclesiastes 3:1,3,7,8
545. Revelation 12:17, 20:4
546. 2018 Counter Extremism Project
547. Matthew 3:16-17
548. Genesis 16:6-7
549. Matthew 6:15
550. Revelation 17:16
551. Revelation 18:5
552. Barack Hussein O'Bama – Audacity of Hope
553. Revelation 13:4
554. Isaiah 9:6; Matthew 16:15-16; Luke 2:11; Acts 5:42
555. Matthew 1:25, 13:55-57
556. 2 Thessalonians 2:1-12
557. Sahih al-Bukhari 5:58:148
558. MMA, Qur'an 33:46, 46a, p. 838
559. Isaiah 48:9-11
560. Revelation 21:5
561. Hebrews 2:14; Qur'an 3:156, 7:158
562. MMA, Qur'an 2:215, 125c, p. 59

The Prophet

563. Revelation 18:2
564. AMoH, Chapter 1, verse 3, note 14, p. 8
565. Qur'an 2:275
566. Ecclesiastes 3:1, 3, 4, 7, 8
567. Daniel 12:11
568. Daniel 12:12
569. Mark 12:16-17
570. Qur'an 6:92; 42:7
571. MMA, Qur'an 6:92, note 92a., p. 306; 42:7, note 7a., p. 943
572. Qur'an 3:96
573. MMA, Qur'an 3:96, note 96a., 96b., p. 164
574. Qur'an 101:9
575. MMA, Qur'an 101:9, note 101:9a., p. 1239
576. Galatians 4:26
577. Galatians 4:30
578. Revelation 20:7-10
579. Daniel 7:19-22
580. Al-Bukhari 6982
581. Matthew 18:6
582. Revelation 22:1
583. NIV Key Word Study Bible, Ezekiel 38:11, 16, notes: s11, t16, p. 1009

Ronald B. Stetton

For more information contact the publisher at info@advbooks.com

To purchase additional copies of these books, visit our bookstore at:
www.advbookstore.com

Orlando, Florida, USA
"we bring dreams to life"™
www.advbookstore.com

www.ingramcontent.com/pod-product-compliance
Lightning Source LLC
Chambersburg PA
CBHW070837160426
43192CB00012B/2218